FOUNDING PRINCIPLES OF AMERICAN GOVERNMENT

Two Hundred Years of Democracy on Trial

REVISED EDITION

Edited by George J. Graham, Jr.

and Scarlett G. Graham

CHATHAM HOUSE PUBLISHERS, INC.

CHATHAM, NEW JERSEY

To Carmen's grandparents
Jack, Mary, Lola, Douglas,
and Winnie

FOUNDING PRINCIPLES OF AMERICAN GOVERNMENT
Two Hundred Years of Democracy on Trial
Revised Edition

Chatham House Publishers, Inc.
Post Office Box One
Chatham, New Jersey 07928

Library of Congress Cataloging in Publication Data
Main entry under title:
Founding principles of American government.
Bibliography
Includes index.
1. United States——Politics and government——
Addresses, essays, lectures. I. Graham, George J.
II. Graham, Scarlett G.
JK21.F68 1984 321.8'042 83-21085
ISBN 0-934540-25-X

Manufactured in the United States of America
10 9 8 7 6 5 4 3 2 1

CONTRIBUTORS

JOSEPH M. BESSETTE

The University of Chicago

GEORGE W. CAREY

Georgetown University

MURRAY DRY

Middlebury College

VALERIE A. EARLE

Georgetown University

GEORGE J. GRAHAM, JR.

Vanderbilt University

SCARLETT G. GRAHAM

Vanderbilt University

CHARLES S. HYNEMAN

Indiana University

ROSS M. LENCE

The University of Houston

DONALD S. LUTZ

The University of Houston

CHARLES H. MCCALL

California State College at Bakersfield

RONALD M. PETERS, JR.

The University of Oklahoma

CONTENTS

PREFACE

The Bicentennial is, more than anything else, a celebration of American political life. Territorially and socially, America is substantially older than two hundred years; but, in the period between the *Declaration of Independence* in 1776 and the drafting of the *Constitution of the United States* in 1787, America's political character was formed and incorporated into the institutions of government which serve us today.

A serious assessment of the political principles upon which the American nation was founded seems a particularly appropriate recognition of the Bicentennial. The basic purpose of this volume is to contribute to such an assessment by providing a systematic investigation of American founding principles and how they have endured through two hundred years of national experience. By examining the Founders' conceptions of political principles, and the consequent institutions and practices, the essays presented here help to clarify the foundations of many of the prevailing political values in contemporary American society and thus provide a point of departure for evaluating the two-centuries-long trial of American political life.

The stimulation for this book, both as far as the earlier scholarly inspiration of many of the contributors is concerned, and, later, the specific prescription of the importance of such an enterprise, came from Charles S. Hyneman and his informed concern over the status of American democracy. During his seventy-five years he has seriously studied the documents of the founding period and developed an insight, not only into their relevance for understanding how America came to be what it is but also into the more immediate need to think through our present problems in order to devise a better future. The editors owe him a debt of gratitude for his early organizational efforts which facilitated the final organization of this volume.

Many other individuals have had a hand in the preparation of the book. Of special note is Herbert J. Storing, who was helpful in recommending and evaluating potential contributors, and also during the reviewing stage. The final preparation of the manuscripts was made easier by the good offices and good spirits of Mildred White Tyler and Elizabeth R. McKee, of the Vanderbilt University Department of Political Science. Since the volume represents, in many of its essays, Charles S. Hyneman's "Indiana School" on early American thought (over half of us crossed paths with him there or elsewhere), it was an especial pleasure to have worked with Indiana University Press on the first edition. We also acknowledge our debt to the late William Baroody, Sr., then President of the American Enterprise Institute for Public Policy Research, for his initial interest and continuing support of the studies which resulted in this volume. We owe a special debt of gratitude for the good counsel and hard work of Edward Artinian, our publisher.

GJG
SGG

INTRODUCTION: *The Founding Act*

George J. Graham, Jr., and
Scarlett G. Graham

The founding of a particular form of government has long been recognized in political philosophy as the most demanding of citizenship roles. Theorists as diverse as Aristotle, Machiavelli, and Rousseau have spoken of the enormous obligations of the great lawgivers as well as the difficulties which they faced; the Legislator, in Rousseau's conception, was confronted with the task of discovering the people's common interest in order to set forth the general will as the constitutional law that would embody public consent. Experience, shared customs and traditions, and the rest of the environment, with its economic and cultural potentials and limitations, were acknowledged by the great philosophers as being essential to the successful forging of a frame of government both derived from and consented to by the public. For all three philosophers, the strength of a constitution lay in a necessary linkage between expressed statements regarding an arrangement of offices, on the one hand, and the beliefs, commitments, and internalization of the constitution in the minds of the citizens, on the other. Although discussion and recognition of the lawgiver are replete in the literature of political philosophy, actual examples of a founding act are rare. Even less frequently have a people's own representatives put the theory of the Legislator into effect.

The fifty-five Americans who, during the hot Philadelphia summer of 1787, forged the Constitution of the United States of America were together discharging the role of Legislator. Together they created a new form of government that combined the abstract ideals of a democratic society with the sober realities of self-government. In their political knowledge there were combined abstract political theory, an understanding of history, and the results of diverse but compatible colonial and early statehood experiences. The political principles which they brought to their task, and the institutions and procedures which they set in motion, are the subject of the chapters of this book. In a sense the political principles were not created, but were discovered by these men during their exploration of the problems of government. While articulating and debating these principles, the Founders created a constitution for the longest-lived popularly controlled republic in modern history. The government and the people, in turn, have adapted the founding principles to their perceptions of changing public needs, in what has been a two-hundred-year trial for these principles of American democracy.

Perhaps the central question in evaluating this trial has to do with the ability of those who have acted within the governmental institutions established at the time of founding to maintain popular consent; that is, have popular control and consent been successfully preserved as those who led the country attempted to respond to specific public needs and wants? The answer to this question is inherently complex. Because of immediacies, leaders sometimes have merely adjusted their policy decisions in response to the loudest voices—all leaders in a representative system recognize full well that there are votes behind the voices. In terms of a very simple majority-rule model, such adjustment is not only to be expected but prescribed; yet the principles of a Legislator must have greater depth than that of a simple formula, because he will be confronted with constitutional consent which reaches beyond a mere acceptance of *these* leaders' decision on *this* policy. The notions of popular control and consent embodied in the very idea of a constitution were in themselves fundamental principles of agreement that could produce a framework within which a government could respond to public differences. The trial, then, has been of political principles and constitutional institutions and regulations—not of men and specific policies. The strength of these constitutional principles is reflected in the Founders' ability to overcome the exigencies of specific men, times, and policies—or so Madison well argues in *Federalist* 10.

If one is to make clear the events in Philadelphia, a discussion of the principles of American government must focus on the experiences, practices, and debates previous to the establishment of the United States government; however, some of the clarification also came *after* the Constitution had been ratified and the new government was under way. Each of the colonies had been transformed into a state, and the Articles of Confederation had provided a *national* structure. It is misleading to attribute Legislator status to the fifty-five gentlemen Founders only, since some of the most significant figures in articulating the American principles—such as Patrick

Henry and Thomas Jefferson—were not there. Each of the major principles, institutions, and practices that emerged is explored in this book, with the objective of articulating their meaning at the beginning of the republic, and of seeing how these meanings have withstood the test of extensive practice. Such a test would have been appreciated fully by the American Legislator. What is more: failure under the pressure of practice would be reason enough for a most serious consideration of a need to alter those constitutional principles, a consideration similar to that given to the inadequacies of the Articles of Confederation.

Underlying each principle, institution, and practice explored by the Founders was one basic presupposition that was unchallenged by any theory or experience brought to their deliberations: the government to be founded must be a government of law rather than of men. This principle was so much a part of their thinking—and indeed of our own today—that it may not seem necessary to emphasize it; yet the advice of John Locke against the delegation of constitutional authority, which was so much a part of the Founders' thinking, has been strained by the very complexity of modern societies. Locke felt so strongly about the transfer of constitutional authority that he claimed any such act broke the contract of government; indeed, it transformed the government into a revolutionary institution. Implicit in the articulation of principles by the Founders is the assumption that fundamental laws are binding upon the lawmakers as well as upon the public. Although debate did occur over who should say what the limits of the Constitution meant, the belief that limits and operable restraints upon government were necessary was omnipresent. Without this essential assumption, the very idea of a constitution becomes nonsense. In keeping with this assumption, many basic principles must be established in order to develop a government with the most desirable constitutional arrangements.

Charles S. Hyneman's essay on the meaning and development of the republican form of government (chap. 1) draws together the most general problems pressing on the Founders' minds. He stands back from the immediate issues which the Founders confronted and assesses their classic attempt to merge responsibility to the public with a workable solution for democratic institutions. Political responsibility was provided by achieving a framework based upon government by the people, dispersed among various levels and safeguarded by checks and balances. In assessing these dimensions, Hyneman explores the problems central to the Founders' thinking and the sources they relied upon. An unquestioned commitment to popular sovereignty as a founding principle is demonstrated, its meaning in the founding period becoming definite through an attempt to understand how and why certain practices we now view as undemocratic were not then considered to be impediments to the realization of the principle.

In the next two chapters more specific attention is given to the development of the notions of majority rights and political consent. The Declaration of Independence is sometimes viewed as *the* document expressing the ideals of American democracy; yet, its use as a symbol in politics is not always in line with an analysis of what the Declaration actually says. The principles embedded in it are assessed by Ross M. Lence (chap. 2), with the purpose of analyzing the meanings and the internal, theoretical tensions of the document when articulating the political rights and powers of a people. Clearly, the notion of a people's rights leads analysis to the crux of the founding and its social commitment. Discourse about a majority entails the assumption of a community; it presupposes a general interest and common obligations. Americans accepted the principle of their collective right to independence.

Closely related to the issue of the rights of a people is Donald S. Lutz's analysis of the meanings and mechanisms of popular consent to and control of government (chap. 3). The emerging meanings attached to republican government and to representation and consent are limned in their theoretical backgrounds. The competing theories of consent as reflected in the growth and decline in the use of this term in state constitutions are explored. The meaning of consent reflects compromises between democratic principles necessitated by the realities of democratic practices at the time of founding.

The relation of the principle of a separation of powers to the character of constitutional government is explored in depth by George W. Carey (chap. 4). The difficulty in articulating the meanings of the phrase *separation of powers* is overcome by considering these powers as different functions—legislative, executive, and judicial—each of which is more or less important than the others. The powers are balanced and kept in equilibrium, with checks instituted to moderate the actions of the more powerful branches. After indicating the meaning of this separation, both in the history of political philosophy and among the Founders, Carey illustrates the greater weight of the legislative branch in the solution that emerged at the time of founding. Problems of relating "one-man, one-vote" to this principle are among those discussed in the context of his argument that the original principle remains essentially intact.

The principles entailed in federalism also bear on the problems of establishing institutional checks on the concentration of political power. The framework of a national government for what had been independently related English colonies is traced by Valerie A. Earle (chap. 5) from the First Continental Congress (1774) through the difficult alliance of the states under the Articles of Confederation (1781) to the drafting of the Constitution (1787). Historical developments and the resulting controversies among the states at Philadelphia reflect a trend toward national government. The developments under the Constitution are then traced, leading Earle to the conclusion that its history since drafting reflects the intentions of the Founders.

Ronald M. Peters, Jr. (chap. 6) articulates early notions and assumptions about the character and purposes of written constitutions. Because of the lack of a tradition of natural law, early constitutions tended to reflect a presumption of popular sovereignty and of legislative supremacy, with seemingly few limitations to be put on the people's government. The history of constitutions is considered, in order to isolate the growth of the notion of constitutional rule as limited government, with safeguards on the legislative power. A careful and extensive analysis of the later history of state constitutions is then presented.

The next three chapters explore the Founders' expectations and projections for the three main branches of government, as well as the impact of post-Philadelphia developments. Each chapter discusses the compromises necessary for the transformation of constitutional principles into political reality. It is not incorrect to say that political reality inevitably will have serious impact upon institutional functions as men and times change.

A detailed picture of how the institutionalization of the separation of powers has progressed under the pressures of an expanding republic and the extension of politics within our society is presented by separate chapters focusing on each of the three branches of government. Joseph M. Bessette's assessment of the presidency (chap. 7) demonstrates that the office was intended, in Bessette's view, to create an energetic executive as a check on the legislature and also to permit action on urgent matters with a dispatch not characteristic of the more deliberative legislative body. Bessette carefully outlines the growth of the office and how it has fitted into the original conceptions.

Murray Dry (chap. 8) contrasts the Founders' intentions with the realities of the First and Ninety-Third Congresses. The key to understanding the purpose and function of the legislative branch is its special relation to the President. This office originally was instituted as a check on the power of the legislature; but its involvement in creating public policy has changed greatly during the nation's long and continuous growth. A Congress that counts the introduction of proposals for legislative action in the tens of thousands most surely will be of an order different from that which the Founders imagined. The contrast in Congresses separated by nearly two hundred years provides a valuable test of the original agreement worked out by the Founders.

The weakest of the three branches of government, the Supreme Court, provided an answer to the search for a way to settle contested actions under the Constitution. Evidence for or against an assumption of judicial review as the proper power of the Court is weighed by George J. Graham, Jr. (chap. 9), with the Delphic conclusion that evidence exists for claiming either that the power was built into the system or that it was not. Rather than attempt to attribute agreement among the Founders on the basis of this assumption in the convention or to deny such a settlement, the author considers the role of the Court as a final arbiter of constitutional review to be a solution posed in the *Federalist Papers* and established ex post facto by public consent.

Even less a part of the Founders' convictions of appropriate political solutions to their problems were political parties; yet, as is true of judicial review, parties are now so strongly accepted in the American republic that their comparatively early establishment in our history make them a part—albeit a late part—of the founding act. Charles H. McCall (chap. 10) points to the early tendencies of legislatures to drift into partisan alignments even before the Philadelphia Convention; indeed, even as theoretical fears of the divisive character of parties were discussed by the Founders, specific policies were emerging which were to become the substance around which parties actually formed. In fact, their role was, in part, a consequence of the institutions developed by those who most feared their growth. The intricate relations between political parties and the institutionalization of democracy are carefully surveyed.

Basic to many debates over the intentions of the Founders have been questions of the role of economic forces in shaping the Constitution and the economic consequences intended to result from its design. These issues are addressed by Scarlett G. Graham (chap. 11). The important relationship between the government and the economy is investigated both in terms of the intentions of the Founders with reference to future economic policies of national scope and in terms also of evaluating the Beard thesis that the economic self-interest of the Founders predetermined their political decisions. Beard is judged to have overlooked the Founders' commitment to placing polity before economy in their considerations because of its being, in their view, a prerequisite to economic matters. The relations between the government and the economy are traced.

The final two chapters explore the possible verdicts generated by the two-hundred-year trial of the principles that guided the American founding. Hyneman emphasizes the ways in which we approach fundamental problems today without giving serious consideration to the theories on which the earlier settlements were based. The last chapter explores further the possibilities of "refounding" the nation and the evidence for and against a need for "refounding." For the moment, however, attention must center on the original principles themselves. It is the success of these principles that the nation celebrates.

In presenting the principles and the basic institutions of government as articulated by the American Legislator, it is essential that one stand back from his own preconceptions far enough to see into the minds of these serious men committed to certain principles of government and fully cognizant of the necessity to discover workable solutions for their problems. Unlike the day-to-day articulation of beliefs, or ordinary political discourse, a study of the founding process forces one to seek a deeper understanding of the problems of government, given also the fact that individuals have different and conflicting interests. If human nature leads even some men willfully to seek their own interest, then the Founder knows that institutions must withstand such possibilities. If, as Aristotle observed, neither the rich nor the poor will accept a regime that threatens their interests too much, then institutions safeguarding revolution from either group are needed. The founding of the political institutions of a community requires the blending of principles with a healthy political realism. Unlike the philosopher bent on isolating the "best" society independent of its context, the Legislator is not involved in the construction of Utopia.

Founding Principles of American Government

[I]

REPUBLICAN GOVERNMENT IN AMERICA

The Idea and Its Realization

—CHARLES S. HYNEMAN

It is not an easy task to describe the political system that came into existence in North America approximately two hundred years ago. The difficulty stems in large measure—but by no means altogether—from the circumstances of the founding experience, conceived here to have occurred during, roughly, the quarter century, 1775 to 1800. Among the obstacles to confident description and explanation are the uncertainties in the minds of the Founders and the tentative character of statements given by them as to what distinguishes a just government from an unjust one; regarding differences in their judgments as to what was feasible at the time, and the best means to achieve a result agreed upon; as well as what, in fact, had been accomplished when a constitution was adopted. The misunderstandings due to such slippery evidence, however, are augmented in equal amount, perhaps, by the misapprehensions, biases, and premature convictions which each person who tries to reconstruct the dominant mood and principal events of that agitated and creative period brings to his analysis and interpretation.

As the writer unavoidably introduces misconceptions and questionable interpretations into an account which he lays before the reader, so does each reader warp and mottle the picture which he records in his mind. As every writer has an obligation to be careful not to deceive the reader, so the reader must be on guard against

This chapter and chapter 12 are in substance the Edward Douglass White lectures delivered at Louisiana State University in April 1974.

deluding himself. In this chapter the author from time to time will warn against misapprehensions that lurk in the evidence waiting for a chance to "trip up" the reader's thinking. One precaution, however, must be planted in the reader's mind before our scrutiny of the founding experience gets under way. The words *republic* and *democracy* have been carriers of so much misunderstanding that the variance in their usage must be appreciated as evidences of conviction, intention, and accomplishment come up for inspection.

I

The words *republic* and *democracy* had come into common use in the American colonies well in advance of the founding period, but they did not have precise applications. On some occasions these words were employed to differentiate forms of government; on other occasions they were used interchangeably to identify political systems marked by a considerable amount of popular control. This was a time when governments were being classified, and several different classifications were offered—monarchy, aristocracy, and democracy was a familiar grouping. Most European countries had a monarch, either provided by a royal family or acquired in some other fashion. Polities which had no monarch generally were known as republics. As a consequence, republics varied immensely in the location of power. There might be a ruling prince with authority and marks of status insufficient to merit the title of king; or there might be a ruling oligarchy; or a coming together for decision making of great numbers of people, in which case the polity might be called a democratic republic. On the whole, republics had an unsavory reputation. Intrigue, internecine warfare, and tyrannous rule dominated their public image.

It must have been the case that, as talk about possible separation from England loomed in North America, people increasingly asked "If no longer under England's king and Parliament, what will we do for government?" For some the answer may well have been, "A king and queen of our own, of course." Creation of an American kingdom was not, prima facie, an entirely fanciful notion; for, it had often happened in Europe that a member of a foreign royal house was imported to institute a new royal line. The establishment of royalty and monarchy, however, must have been objectionable to many Americans of that day; and to many others it must have seemed quite impossible to bring about. Consequently there was much talk about the inevitability of instituting some kind of "republic."

How the conversation shaped itself we do not know; but the state of mind of the Founders that eventuated is unmistakably reported in the records of their thought. Whatever be the form of government that was to be established, it would not be forced on the American colonists. It would come into existence as the choice of the white inhabitants of the colonies; and the act of choosing would be a giving of consent by an inclusive, not a narrowly restricted, portion of that population. By way of one chain of connections or another, government rooted in the consent of the governed acquired the convenient title republican government. To argue as late as 1775 that "we must found a republic" would have been an endorsement of government by popular consent; but the knowledge that a person favored republican government was not proof that he wanted active popular participation in the conduct of government. The speaker may have idealized a regime of rule by the wise and the good and thought that debate ought to focus on the question of how to arrange for the people to indicate their willingness to be governed by the wise and the good.

Looking back to quandaries that taxed minds at the time of Independence, one can hardly avoid concluding that the word *republic* had to be used in order to get ahead with talk about what kind of government to set up. And as *republic* and *republican government* rose to prominence in the conversation of the day the words *democracy* and *democratic* (or *democratical*) would intrude also, this because a democratic character suffused so many European republics then existing or long gone. Indeed, democratic tendencies had to be contemplated every time republican experience was seriously discussed because excessive democracy accounted for much of the adverse reputation of European republics.

Recommendations of republican government could get favorable hearing only if associations of the term with malpractice, cruelty, and social disaster could be erased. The "cleaning up" of the word did not take long. Republican government quickly became a synonym for good government among the architects and craftsmen who created the new political structures from New England to Georgia.

Apparently it took a bit more time to "clean up" the word *democracy*. It started out as a bad word in North America because the democratic republics of Europe had a reputation of featuring mob rule, which resulted in monstrous instability. But the word was needed when the discussion turned to the question: How much influence shall the people (the little men who so greatly outnumber the men of recognized influence) have in fixing the form of our republican governments, and what part shall they play in the exercise of control over those to whom the business of governing has been delegated? If one wanted to maximize the influence of, or participation by, the common man he might well say, "I favor a democratic government." If he thought a new state constitution went too far in providing that the citizenry give instructions to the persons they had chosen to sit in the legislature, he was sure to be understood if he asserted that the constitution was too democratic on that point.

If the word *democracy* was useful to identify or to describe one tendency in a government, there was need for a word to describe the opposite tendency. *Elitism* might be chosen today, but it appears not to have been called into service for this purpose two hundred years ago. Popular assemblies and collegial bodies of elected officers were discussed as alternative instruments for policy making; the first was referred to as "democratic government" and the second as "representative government." "Representative government" presented in this context, however, was not usually, and perhaps rarely indeed, thought of as rule by a social class. Rather, it was believed by those who recommended it to provide a more certain way of arriving at policies which the common man would approve in his sober moments. "Republican government" was seized upon and made a synonym for "representative government." Government by popular assembly was democratic; government by elected officials was republican.

From today's point of view this application of the word *republican* was unfortunate, not because tendencies or features of governments ought not be so contrasted but because *republic* and *republican* also had well-established meanings which embraced governments that had both democratic and nondemocratic attributes. Confusion has resulted. One can find instances where an expression of a preference for republican government was meant to announce that the writer (or speaker) wanted public officials to close their ears against noisy demands coming up from the populace, "washed" as well as "unwashed;" it is doubtful that even one instance can be found where the text or a comprehensive context indicates the writer preferred that none of the lawmakers be chosen by an inclusive electorate. A difference of opinion there certainly was in 1775-1800, as there is two hundred years later, regarding how much of the population ought to exert a specified amount of influence on questions of importance; but an examination of the Founding Fathers' use of the words *republic* and *democracy* will prove to be a very poor basis on which to arrange the Founding Fathers along a continuum from populist to elitist. In any event it must never be assumed before reading a given text that a simple declaration of a preference for republican government or a determination to create a republic implies a dislike for effective popular control of government.

II

The year of Independence and the years immediately following were a time for creating new governments; but the creative impulse reached out beyond the design of new forms to stimulate a clarification and a reassociation of ideas and ideals. Looking back upon that experience we are able to say that when the quarter century of creation came to a close the world had a new vision of how government pledged to deal justly with all of its subjects might be brought into existence and a working model that offered genuine promise of effecting the safety and happiness of a new nation could be contemplated. If one inspects that model closely it becomes apparent that the political structure which the founders erected rests firmly on four foundation stones; that is, government in the United States exhibited four distinctive features. We had government by the people. We had government that was established by law and required to act in accordance with law. The business of governing was dispersed, being vested in many governments rather than in only one or even a few. Within the many governments authority to decide and to act was divided, and wielders of power were put in a position to observe and to check other wielders of power. Short labels are convenient. We shall speak of 1. popular government, or government by the people; 2. government by law; 3. distributed self-government; and 4. a separation of powers, and checks and balances.

Such is republican government, American style; it is The American Republic conceived by the Founding Fathers and fashioned in as close an approach to a common ideal as they were able to accomplish. This design was not fully developed in the mind of any one person and traced out in his writings—not clearly seen or foreseen by John Adams, Thomas Jefferson, Benjamin Franklin, the authors of *The Federalist,* or even by all of them when their writings are put together. There was, nonetheless, a remarkable similarity in the political structures erected for the new states that had previously been British colonies; and the likenesses could be accounted for by a common heritage of observation and reading.

For the source materials of the American contribution, republican government dominated by the four elements enumerated above, one must look to reasoned thought in the writings of Europeans, to the prior political experience of the Americans, to the force of circumstances, and to chance. Well may we marvel today that so many of the men who came to the front two hundred years ago could display so great a familiarity with printed descriptions of governments, histories of political experiences, and speculations about the ideal political regime and how to achieve and to preserve it. Personal experience—which is to say remembrance of events labeled alternatively as successes and failures—weighed heavily in shaping the developing thought as to what is most to be desired, what men with different preferences can be got to agree upon, what will work out in practice if given a fair trial. Personal experience and knowledge acquired out of reading would have produced some convictions deep-seated enough to withstand temptations to compromise—commitment to some elementary demands of justice, for instance, or a determination that each individual be allowed to mark out his own route to "safety and happiness" with no more interference from government than might be necessary to keep him from obstructing the progress of other persons engaged in the same quest; but, in respect to some matters on which one felt strongly, circumstances—e.g., the undependability of communications, the inadequacies of resources, the incompatibilities revealed when a number of persons disclose their interests to one another—could induce him to relax his determination to press for his own ideals, lead him to accept compromises which he might regret later on, and even result in the adoption of an instrumentality or device which no one could endorse with confidence. Chance or accident offers the best explanation of why many decisions went the way they did. Considering the short time given over to the making of every one of the constitutions in the period under scrutiny, one cannot avoid a belief that the Founding Fathers merely stumbled into many of the decisions that linked disagreement to compromise to solution.

We do not know enough about how minds are made up to justify estimates of the relative influence of previously formulated political theory and familiarity with prior political experience upon the statescraft that produced the constitutions of 1776 and those of the years immediately following. That the Founding Fathers went to both springs for options, recommendations for action, and cautions against pitfalls cannot be doubted. If their thought had not been enriched in this way they would not so frequently have cited not only the great masters of political thought—Grotius, Pufendorf, and Vattel; Hobbes, Locke, and Montesquieu—but also writers of less renown both then and now (Bolingbroke, Burgh, de Lolme, Gordon, and Trenchard). Even the most stubborn disbeliever in the fact that practical men learn anything from theoretic writings must acknowledge that a common library for literate men and women in all of the colonies contributed to a common focus of attention on certain problems, encouraged like formulations and thus facilitated communication, and fixed limits within which the debate tended to be contained. Doubtless also, the clear formulations and cogent arguments presented to them in books relieved many people of the deliberation which would have been painful and gave to their thought a finish that would not have been attained but for the prepackaged doctrine which they were able to read. One may be wholly confident that the Virginia Declaration of Rights could not have been phrased as it was and fairly certain that it would not have embraced all the threats to free choice and personal comfort which it touches upon if George Mason, Thomas Jefferson, and some other prominent Virginians had not been students of classical literature.

Nevertheless, it is necessary to maintain a constant guard against temptations to exaggerate the influence of prior systematic thought about government and politics. The effusive promise of a separation of powers in the Virginia constitution of 1776 may have come right out of Montesquieu, but the Baron must have been regarded as a master of the forked tongue if he was thought also to have endorsed the mixture of legislative and executive functions incorporated into

Virginia's new state government. One cannot contend that the persuasiveness of an European literature impelled Virginia's political leaders to include a Declaration of Rights in the Virginia Constitution unless he can reconcile that action with the contrary action in four other states that gave meagre attention to personal rights or announced no personal guarantees at all. He might reconcile the two acts by showing that the writings which enjoyed so much respect in Virginia were unknown or found not to be persuasive to leaders in the other four states, or by pointing out some differences in political condition among the five states that made superfluous for four of them the precautions which the theoreticians recommended and Virginia's leaders thought essential for their commonwealth.

It requires colossal audacity to set bounds to the range of history which instructed any group of thoughtful men. In the case of the American Founders virtually all the political experience reported in the Bible must have been in their minds, for in all of the colonies they had been endlessly sermonized on the sad fate of regimes that paid insufficient tribute to God and on the benign relationship of holy worship to economic prosperity apparent in the ups and downs of the Hebrew people, and of late thoroughly rehearsed in the political events which had taught the Apostle Paul that virtuous citizens obey civil magistrates until tyrannous behavior divests them of authority (at which point virtuous citizens are overtaken by an equally binding obligation to resist or to depose their oppressors).

The most widely read of the Founders—a category by no means confined to John Adams, Thomas Jefferson, and James Madison—had an easy familiarity with the political history of all the leading European countries, if not with the more obscure ones as well. English-speaking Americans who had at least a moderate amount of schooling knew a great deal about the organization and the conduct of government in Britain for a long time back, and even those with the least inclination to read had been lectured about the evasions and infractions of the British constitution which precipitated the erosion of rights and liberties in America.

The best understood of all political experience was that of the American colonists themselves—especially that of one's own colony, of course. Everywhere these were events to be surveyed with pride. In all the colonies an elective legislative assembly was now preeminent in political power. In none of them could a determined governor indefinitely thwart a determined legislature; he could balk, irritate, impose delay, but nowhere could a governor by-pass the legislature or make it accept a policy which a firm majority of the members would not accept. In today's vocabulary, home rule had come to be the juridical order in America, and recognition and respect for that order is exactly what Americans had in mind when talk about Independence shed its air of fantasy and took on a mantle of potential reality. It is inconceivable that American political leaders could have entered upon a course of constitution making—of fashioning governments for separate statehood—without taking into that enterprise models of government and associated political relationships which were drawn immediately from the colonial achievements. Proof that this is exactly what they did is manifest in the decisions of Connecticut and Rhode Island to acquire a state constitution by simply retitling the colonial charter. Nothing more was thought required by Rhode Island; but Connecticut added three paragraphs to take some of the harshness out of law enforcement and to guarantee equal treatment in legislation and the administration of justice.

Republican government, as conceived and fashioned by the Founding Fathers, combined into a system four basic beliefs about government that were both energetic and just; but the four components were not thought to be of equal importance. Back of the architecture and construction of the system lay a central objective, a primary goal which organized attention and directed creative effort: government at all times should be constrained to protect and further the well-being of all the population, not the special interests of a social class or of one sector of the population that embraced more than a single class but less than all the people. For achievement of this grand objective the geographic distribution of authority, a separation of powers within government, and the subjection of all governments to a rule of law were necessary, but not of the first order of priorities. Entitled to the Founders' highest confidence and the first to be attended to, was the fourth instrumentality: popular control of government. If, by way of expressions of preference and authoritative actions an inclusive electorate did in fact exert effective control over the offices of government, one could be sure that the ultimate goal had all but securely been attained. The dispersal of the authority to govern, a separation of powers (with arrangements for checks upon them), and the recognition of an obligation to act in accordance with rules fixed in advance; a sufficient provision for these considerations made popular control of government more certain and improved the prospect that elected officials could make the common good their continuing concern.

Limited as we are to a parsimonious account of the founding experience, we are justified in fixing attention from this point forward on that feature of republican government which the Founding Fathers regarded as preeminent: popular control. Before turning to what the Founders said and did on that point, however, it may be useful to supply some summary observations on the connections which tie the other three foundation principles to the one accorded first priority.

The idea that government should be established by law and conduct itself in accordance with law reflected a principle elaborately developed in England and also a conviction which found its fulfillment more than a century later in North America. The notion that there is a due process of law which must regulate the imposition of authority upon a citizen was an elemental feature of the English common law, presented to the Americans as a part of their heritage. They extended the gift of England by adding to the list of immunities from governmental interference in certain aspects of life and by firming up the guarantees that authority be exercised humanely where government was permitted to act. This extension and firming up of the English practice was accomplished by writing the new immunities and guarantees into a constitution which created a government, regulated its procedures, and limited its authority. The thought that a document could fix the structure of a government and regulate its proceedings was not original with the Americans; there were European precedents. The distinctive American contributions were those of broadening the constitutional provisions and packing a substantial amount of reality into two notions that were more fancy than promise in the European prototypes. The Americans found a way of assuring that the written constitution issue from the people; and their constitutions did, in fact, exert constraints on their governments. Neither of these two results can be said to have been achieved in the constitutions that were written in the year 1776. A decade later, it was clear that constitutions are indeed an instrument of popular will; in two decades more, it had been proven that they have the force and effect of law. Reference will be made later to the triumph of the doctrine that a constitution is an act of the people and a principal evidence that republican government is government of and by the people.

Speculation about the separation of powers probably hindered more than helped the development of thought about how to provide for popular control of government. The political histories of England which John Adams and his contemporaries read made much of the provision in the British political system for championship of at least three sectors of the society, each with a main body of interests clearly distinguishable from those of the other two sectors. The great houses of England, sitting together as a House of Lords, were counterposed to the landed gentry and the merchants who dominated the House of Commons; and the king (or queen), specially charged to look out for the propertyless employed and the nonemployed, was viewed as posed between the Lords and Commons to manage the concessions granted by each which made stable political life possible. To the English in America prior to 1776, and generally for the duration of the Revolutionary War, the British constitution envisaged the most benevolent government in the world, and only contemporary corruption kept the government of the day from being the most benevolent anywhere. For many of America's political leaders, at the beginning of their thrust for Independence, it seemed imperative to identify three concentrations of distinguishable interests and set them up as three arms of government that would, by their protective stances and defensive maneuvers, assure a stable order and approximate a regime of justice for all. A configuration of dominant interests which would fit this image could not be detected on the North American continent, of course, but the bent for wishful thinking—or nostalgia, if that is what it was—contributed to the longevity of notions that special provisions ought to be made for balancing personal interests against property interests in the composition of a legislature. It also deflected attention from a challenge to invention which strikes us as obvious today. It is not too much to say that the arrangements which we now know as separation of powers and checks and balances did not come to their full flower until the exigencies of inducing the small states to join in a more compact union with the large states precipitated the extraordinary feats of statescraft exhibited at Philadelphia in 1787.

The state of concern about a geographic dispersal of governing authority in the founding period is a curious matter. Well before Independence was declared political leaders were alert to the fact that separation from England would create a need for a central or a national seat of authority. As sentiment in favor of separation developed and anticipation of Independence increased, colonial legislatures called upon the Continental Congress (no governing authority then) to tell them whether it was appropriate to proceed with plans for statehood and even to issue instructions as to what should be included in a state constitution. A plan for state government was more than the Congress was prepared to supply; but it did, first in recommendations to individual colonies and later (May 10, 1776) in a resolution addressed to all, advise that every colony "adopt such government as shall, in the opinion of the representatives of the people, best conduce to the happiness and safety of their constituents in particular, and America in general." During some sixteen months of 1776 and 1777 a committee of the Continental Congress debated and drew up a constitution for the United States of America (The Articles of Confederation, effective in 1781). Surely it can be argued with thoroughly good reason that this was an act comparable in importance to the writing of a second constitution for the nation at Philadelphia in 1787. One would never guess it from any record of inquiry and contention *in camera* or among the citizens at large. The American people acquired heroes at Philadelphia in 1787. *The Federalist*, written to elucidate, justify, and win approval of the document of 1787, is the nation's number-one exhibit of extended political analysis. If there were comparable masters of constitutional statescraft at Philadelphia ten years earlier, they went unsung.

Equally difficult to account for is the fact that throughout the quarter century of the founding of our national government, insofar as records tell us what was discussed, there was almost no talk about a need for local government or how to secure local self-government. Perhaps there was no need for a new look at local political arrangements in New England. No doubt New Englanders generally believed that their town meetings offered the world its finest model of a local autonomy expressing itself in a widely-diffused popular participation. Of local autonomy there was a considerable measure in places farther south, but of popular participation there was little indeed in the vast stretches of territory below New York, New Jersey and Pennsylvania. Certainly southerners knew about New England's experience, since many of their political leaders had spent time at Harvard and other New England colleges. Perhaps the leaders in constitution making south of the Potomac thought it imprudent to add to the unhappiness seething about local government at a time when the first need was to create a state government and get it going. Whatever the reasons for the rejection of change, the new constitutions of the North, the South, and the states in between let local government remain just what it had been during the final years of colonial status.

III

"That the sovereignty resides in the people," wrote Samuel Adams to his cousin John in 1790, "is a political doctrine which I have never heard an American politician deny." Allowing that Samuel's memory may have failed to record an occasional discordant note, one cannot doubt that he correctly reported the prevailing state of mind. Documents which proclaim the central doctrines of the founding period are explicit and unequivocal in their declaration that government in America is inaugurated by the people and belongs to the people.

Let us marshal the evidence:

Exhibit 1, the Declaration of Independence: "Governments [derive] their just powers from the consent of the governed." And, whenever any form of government becomes destructive of the ends of just government, "it is the Right of the People to alter or to abolish it, and to institute new Government, laying its foundations on such principles and organizing its powers in such forms as to them shall seem most likely to effect their Safety and Happiness." *Exhibit 2*, the Constitution of the United States: "We, the People of the United States . . . do ordain and establish this CONSTITUTION for the United States of America." *Exhibit 3*, the constitution of Virginia (adopted by a convention of elected delegates and proclaimed June 29, 1776) and seven other state constitutions in varying language repeated or elaborated the following assertions:

> That all power is vested in, and consequently derived from, the people; that magistrates are their trustees and servants, and at all times

> amenable to them. That government is, or ought to be, instituted for the common benefit, protection, and security of the people, nation, or community; . . . and that, when any government shall be found [incapable of producing the greatest degree of happiness and safety] a majority of the community hath an indubitable, inalienable, and indefeasible right to reform, alter, or abolish it, in such manner as shall be judged most conducive to the public weal.

For the fuller ease of mind of those who regard *The Federalist* as transcending all other evidences of the intent and determination of the Founding Fathers the following avowal of a fundamental tenet may be added to the foregoing three: "the people are the only legitimate fountain of power, and it is from them that the constitutional charter, under which the several branches of government hold their power, is derived. . . ." [*Federalist* 49, ascribed to Madison.]

Thus was established, indisputably, the principle that popular sovereignty is the quintessential element of government as it was constituted, ordained, and established at the birth of the new nation. Established beyond any reasonable ground for doubt? Only two of the eight constitutions just referred to were, by any means of expression, formally approved by the people, and those two (Massachusetts and New Hampshire) were not proclaimed until 1780 and 1784. Failure to submit drafts of the earlier constitutions to the people cannot be excused on the ground that it did not occur to anyone that a popular referendum was appropriate. In early 1776 there was at least a murmuring to the effect that constitutions ought to be drawn up only by conventions chosen by the people especially for that job. Never should it be done by legislatures whose members were chosen with other public business in mind. It was also commonly held that a document agreed to by a convention ought to be subjected to public scrutiny and debate and finally go to an inclusive electorate for approval, rejection, or recommendations for revision. Still, one must not conclude that failure to consult the general public was a denial that, in principle, constitutions ought to issue from the people. Political leaders had strong reasons for thinking it was impracticable to take that business to the people in 1776 or 1777. The first round of state constitution making was seen as action to meet an emergency. Acts of tyranny in London, said the Pennsylvania constitution, had dissolved and brought to an end all allegiance and fealty to the king and his successors "and all power and authority derived from him [had] ceased in the colonies." Legitimized authority having expired, there was reason for announcing a fresh legitimization in a hurry. But how big a hurry? Pennsylvania put up with an interregnum until late September 1776; and Massachusetts had one until its second proposed constitution received a specified amount of popular support in the spring of 1780. Reject this ground for by-passing popular approval and another reason for doing so remains. Who ought to be invited into the debate and listened to when minds are agitated about whether to declare independence and adopt a constitution, or to negotiate a settlement with the parent government, or to knuckle under to the king and his current advisers? If "the people" includes individuals of bitterly opposed opinions on these questions, who ought to be asked whether the proposed constitution is well adapted to public needs in a new state? Or, for that matter, consulted as to whether a controlling document of any content is needed? Or even asked for a judgment as to whether allegiance and fealty to the king have been dissolved and commands emanating from any source in London are stripped bare of authority when they reach the borders of a colony which some of its citizens now propose to transform into a state? The patriots who led the drive for separation, statehood, and a new constitution were principals in an insurgency, if not in a revolutionary movement. Each proposed state constitution was an instrument of that rebellion or revolution. It could hardly be expected that patriots who were in control of the constitution-drafting process would voluntarily turn their product over for public burial by a population that had not yet made up its mind to support the cause to which the proposed document was an essential instrument. Not yet seeing how they could define an electorate that promised allegiance to the new state that was in the process of being "spanked" into existence, they surely could act arbitrarily at the moment without repudiating an avowal that when a citizenry can be identified it ought always to write its own constitution.

Regardless of the reading given to the pre-1780 methods of constitution making it is an inescapable conclusion that, well before the quarter century of founding had run its course, popular sovereignty was the essential element in mind when America's political leaders announced an attachment to republican government. The prevailing conception is succinctly stated by Madison in *Federalist* 39:

> If we resort for a criterion to the different principles on which forms of government are established, we may define a republic to be, or at least may bestow that name on, a government which derives all its powers, directly or indirectly from the great body of the people, and is administered by persons holding their offices during pleasure, for a limited period, or during good behavior. It is *essential* to such a government that it be derived from the great body of the society, not from any inconsiderable proportion, or a favored class of it; . . . It is *sufficient* for such a government that the persons administering it be appointed, either directly or indirectly, by the people; and that they hold their appointments by either of the tenures just specified. . . ."

Popular sovereignty, strictly delimited or defined, is not surrendered if the business of governing is turned over to a nonelective officialdom, provided that the people retain a capability of altering or abolishing that form if and when they conclude they have made a mistake. In stipulating that those who administer government must be chosen directly or indirectly by the people, Madison added the elective principle to popular sovereignty as a requisite of republican government. By further stipulating that those who are placed in office must be subject to replacement either at the expiration of a fixed term or because they are recalled, Madison infuses republican government with still another requisite: that the business of governing should be carried on with steady attention to, and a due amount of conformity with, the expectations and preferences of the electorate.

Regarding the first requisite of republican government, namely, popular sovereignty, there appears to have been no important difference of opinion among the Founding Fathers, no denial that it was a fundamental condition of republican government, and no illuminating discussion of what the term implied. Regarding the other two requisites—who shall share in the selection of officials, and what degree of response is a due compliance with public demands—there were considerable differences in the positions of men who vigorously avowed their attachment to republican government.

We have no evidence that anyone presented a serious argument in favor of government by popular assembly for a jurisdiction larger than a New England town, but there must have been a brooding apprehension that just possibly a means could be found for taking the vote of a sizable and scattered population on some questions. What else could have accounted for the repeated cautioning that direct democracy was not possible for large populations? Fisher Ames thought that notion had not been buried deeply enough as late as 1788. Speaking in the Massachusetts convention, called for approval or rejection of the proposed new United States Constitution, Ames rejected direct democracy on grounds of desirability, as well as feasiblity:

> Much has been said about the people's divesting themselves of power when they delegate it to representatives, and that all representation is to their disadvantage because it is but an image, a copy fainter and more imperfect than the original, the people. . . . The people must be governed by a majority, with whom all power resides. But how is the sense of this majority to be obtained? It has been said that a pure democracy is the best government for a small people, who may assemble in person. It is of small consequence to discuss it, as it would be inapplicable to the great country we inhabit. It may be of some use in this argument, however, to consider that it would be very burdensome, subject to factions and violence; decisions would often be made by surprise, in the precipitancy of passion, by men who either understand nothing or care nothing about the subject, or by interested men, or those who vote for their own indemnity. It would be a government not by laws but by men. [Punctuation modernized.]

There can have been no doubt—a fact mentioned earlier—that everywhere the popular election of members of the state legislature was taken for granted. One could cavil about the arrangement for selecting the Senate in Maryland, where the electorate that chose members of the House of Delegates also named a number of persons who became an electoral college to choose fifteen men to serve as senators. In seven states the original constitution provided for popular election of the chief executive (ordinarily titled *Governor*); and where the people did not choose him, the legislature did. What difference it made whether the freemen or the legislators did the choosing may elude historians forever. If it becomes fashionable, as it must some day, for students of this formative period to estimate the amount or degree of popular influence in the choice of state executives, the predispositions of the student will be difficult to exclude from the calculations. Individual judgments may turn less on the inferences made when inspecting hard evidence than on personal like or dislike for the presidential form of government (incipient in the Massachusetts constitution) as against the parliamentary form (just as clearly invited by the Virginia document.)

Historians have been exceedingly busy in recent years trying to measure the democratic component of the electoral process during early statehood. The prospect for a long period of full employment with this problem is encouraging. On one count their task is simplified. Authority was concentrated in the legislature to a degree which justifies inattention to other statewide offices even in those cases where the governor was chosen in popular election. From that point on, however, resemblances of simplicity are not coincidental; they are nonexistent. In some states the qualifications for voting varied—the electorate for one legislative chamber excluding a considerable number of persons who could participate in elections for the other chamber. Constitutional and statutory provisions, especially those which specify some tenure of land as a qualification for voting, are difficult to interpret with confidence today and probably were given a variety of interpretations then. In many places, involving at least a few if not every one of the states, it was not unusual and may have been customary to admit to the polls significant numbers of persons who did not meet all legislative requirements for voting; and, even if the historian presumes that administration matched legal requirements, he has small chance of finding out how much of the male population had dwelt for the required period of time in the community, held the required amount of land by appropriate tenure, owned sufficient household goods or other chattels, had paid his taxes, or discharged the military service which would qualify him to vote; and so on.

If, happily, the obstacles raised by the uncertain meanings of laws and the inadequacies of other evidence can be overcome, there is no escape from the traps inherent in tests of democratic character. Possibly the root meaning of the word *democracy* is that only a head count of individuals can fix the democratic character of a political institution or practice. If so, then it may be agreed that democracy recedes as large landholders (or manufacturers, or shipowners) who determine where other people will live or be employed are given extra seats in the legislature, and that therefore, if one approves of this policy, he ought not to contend that giving a bonus is democratic but rather admit that he is willing to settle for a reduced amount of democracy. By such reasoning it may be concluded that an assembly which consists of one member from each incorporated community (a recommendation occasionally heard in the 1770s) is not sufficiently democratic or not democratic at all; irrelevant for that judgment is argument and evidence that a population scattered among many communities might find the output of a community-based legislature more to its liking than the output of an assembly chosen by districts of equal population.

A contention much more frequently encountered, namely, that individuals without title to land should be excluded from the polls, affords a final illustration of how evidence, lexicology, and personal disposition are bound to complicate the evaluation of thought and practice related to voting. There was widespread support for a rule that individuals without land should be denied the right to vote. Inspection of the surviving evidence, a task still not complete, may justify any of several findings regarding the intent back of the recommendation—that the needs and interests of the nonpropertied poor ought to be ignored; or that title to land is the only sure proof of attachment to a community; or that people without land are dependent on someone who has a lot of it and therefore a vote cast by the plantation worker is a vote dictated by the plantation owner. Given the first reading of the evidence, disfranchisement of the nonpropertied stands condemned as undemocratic. Given the second interpretation one is forced to review all of his attitudes toward residence requirements and the functions of community. Given the third reading of the evidence—that disfranchising the economically subservient is a price paid to keep the tycoons of economic power from annexing the political realm—one is challenged to consider whether one-man, one-vote is a dictum of democracy.

These instances are a sparse sample of the questions involving a mixture of fact and theory that confound the student who seeks to establish the democratic character of the electoral process in the first decades after Independence. It may be that they are no more baffling than many other questions that confront us today when we face up to what has heretofore been taken for granted. How faithful are we to a rule of equal numbers when money from the East and movie stars from the West invade a short-grass congressional district to carry the election for a candidate who would not have had a chance if the people with no right to vote had refrained from influencing those who did? How warmly attached are we to the one-man, one-vote rule if Mamma and Papa and their eight minor children are allowed exactly the same number of votes as the childless couple next door?

If one has little hope of tracing out the distribution of influence expressed through the elective process, he must despair of anyone ever making a confident estimate of who exerted how much influence on the acts of public officials in the intervals between elections. Three of the eleven constitutions adopted between 1776 and 1778 (including that of Vermont) and the Massachusetts and New Hampshire constitutions of 1780 and 1784 acknowledged a right of citizens to assemble, petition the legislature, and instruct their representatives. Pennsylvania spoke first: "The people have a right to assemble together, to consult for their common good, to instruct their representatives, and to apply to the legislature for redress of grievances, by address, petition, or remonstrance" (Article XVII of the Declaration of Rights). Citizens met, and petitions went to the legislature even in states where no constitutional right to do so had been announced. Instructions were also issued to locally-elected members of the state legislature and of Congress; but how frequently instructions were issued, by whom and on what subjects, how long the practice lasted, and whether many legislators departed from positions fixed in their minds prior to receipt of an instruction—historians have not yet made a diligent search into any of these questions.

Probably most of the formal instructions that were addressed to state legislators and members of Congress emanated from New England, where regular sessions of the town meetings provided an opportunity to talk about grievances without going to much trouble. Instructions issuing from town meetings may also have carried unusual weight with the legislators, since the instructing group was representative of a community and the instructions would have been adopted by majority vote. It may be assumed that efforts to instruct coming from ad hoc groups which the legislator viewed as representative of his opposition were generally ignored; and there is a possibility, of course, that occasionally a member of a state legislature or Congress generated an "instruction" which could be cited in support of a position he had already decided to take. Whatever be the fact on these matters, constitutional recognition of the right to instruct was withdrawn very early in some states (Pennsylvania in 1790) but continued to be written into the original constitutions as new states were admitted into the Union, Idaho copying the discarded Pennsylvania provision as late as 1889.

In speaking about the issuance of instructions we are dealing with a formal provision for citizen intervention in the decision-making processes of government. Virtually unlimited are the opportunities for citizens to express their satisfactions and dissatisfactions and expose the intensity of their feelings, opportunities for expression that stand a chance of being noticed by someone who might respond favorably if convinced he is being apprised of a just claim or supplied with a cue to a public demand. We know with certainty very little indeed about the impact of individuals and groups on public policy today. Naiveté has to be mixed with optimism to allow a hope that the influence of citizen demand on public policies in the early days of the republic can some day be measured.

IV

The past several paragraphs, setting forth my doubt that historians will ever agree on the democratic character of American governments in the formative period, invite a hostile reception for any personal conclusions I may offer. This chapter, throughout, has reported my reading of evidence selected according to my tests of significance. Readers who found persuasive the argument and analysis provided so far may find something useful in the concluding summary observations.

1. The Founders meant what they said when they wrote into the early state constitutions that "all political power is vested in and derived from the people only" (North Carolina); that "the people of this State have the sole, exclusive and inherent right of governing and regulating the internal police of the same" (Vermont); that "all officers of government, whether legislative or executive, are their trustees and servants, and at all times accountable to them [the people]" (Pennsylvania); and that "every freeman having sufficient evidence of a permanent common interest with and attachment to the community, hath a right of suffrage" (Delaware). Each of these statements is susceptible of a wide range of interpretations, but I do not believe that any of them was meant to be a cliché. Each statement was intended to announce a principle which would guide thought when the time came to formulate a precise rule. Each of them bore the relation to thought and action that "due process of law" and

"equal protection of the laws" bear to individual expectations and public policy today.

2. The right to vote, viewed as a matter of who was actually admitted to the polling place, varied from state to state. Estimates of how free Negroes fared over a series of elections are guesswork for any state that did not categorically exclude all of them from suffrage. If practice conformed to constitutional promises, the polls in several states were open to very nearly all adult white males who had established a limited residence in the community. This would be the case in Georgia, New Hampshire, and Vermont, at least, and in all those Pennsylvania communities where no one was able to evade the tax collector. In striking contrast was the degree of election-day democracy apparent in Virginia and the two Carolinas. There, restriction on the right to vote combined with disproportionate representation of the population in the legislature to make a mockery of any expectation that control of government would be in the hands of all adult free males whose residence and behavior testified to a firm attachment to the community and an immersion in its common interests. It is possible that some of the disfranchisement in those states rested on (or was rationalized as) a conviction that identification with the community is not enough, that the vote should be confined to those persons who make a showing of independence from others, personal autonomy, and a self-sufficiency for forming political judgments. Making a generous allowance for an attachment to principle in fixing the boundaries of the voting right, I think it must be concluded that in these three southern states there was a conscious tilting of the electoral-representative arrangement to the advantage of the more plushly endowed part of the population. In the states that fall between these two extremes, or in at least half of the new nation's population, election-day practice appears to have been reasonably faithful to the promise that the choice of public officials would rest in the hands of the male citizenry believed to have attached itself to a community and to have accepted the obligations entailed by membership in it. Studies of town meeting records support this estimate of election-day behavior in Massachusetts; but I am obliged to say that the conclusion of some historians that 100 percent participation by males aged 21 or more was a frequent occurrence throughout Massachusetts in the early years of statehood, strikes me as more heavily impressed by optimism than by proof.

3. Discounting all reports of voter-participation levels that would be judged remarkable if compared with the electoral experience of our own day, and also allowing that we do not have precise accounts of the advance toward democracy in Switzerland and other small places, it may be said with considerable confidence that, as of 1783, when the Treaty of Paris formally terminated the struggle for Independence, every one of the American states had democratized its electorate far beyond anything that could be pointed to in Europe.

4. The contention, which has been spread prominently in the recent writings of American political scientists, that the men at Philadelphia in 1787 repudiated such promises of popular control of government as had been made in the precedent state constitutions, is not supported by the evidence. The argument pressed by some members of the convention to the effect that the more forceful central government which circumstances clearly called for must be an agency of the member states of the Union, and therefore that the members of its legislative assembly ought to be named by the several state legislatures, neither entails a rejection nor implies a perversion of the principle that an inclusive electorate ought to control the government. Roger Sherman clearly identified the dilemma:

> If it were in view to abolish the State Govts. the elections ought to be by the people. If the State Govts. are to be continued, it is necessary in order to preserve harmony between the national & State Govts. that the elections to the former shd. be made by the latter. The right of participating in the National Govt. would be sufficiently secured to the people by their election of the State Legislatures. [Farrand, *Records of the Federal Convention of 1787*, vol. 1, p. 133.]

The final resolution of the clashes of interest and of differences in the conceptions of need, namely, that the people would elect the members of one branch of the new Congress and the state legislatures would appoint the members of the other branch; that the President and Vice-President would be chosen by electors appointed solely for that purpose; and that the President and Senate together would appoint the judges to compose a new judiciary; the resolution of interests and judgments which produced this new exhibit of federalism affords no support whatever for a supposition that, if the Constitution's framers had decided to dissolve the states and create a consolidated national government, they would have insulated it from effective popular control by defining a more restricted electorate than the state constitutions had assured, or by devising some method of indirect elections. My own reading of the notes taken down by Madison and other members convinces me that an overwhelming majority of the delegates whose sentiments were reported took into and carried out of the Convention a firm conviction that government can be counted on steadily to advance the safety and happiness of the people only if the legislative power is in the hands of an assembly chosen by an inclusive electorate.

Bibliographical Note

An essay as assertive of personal judgments as this one calls for a citation of writings which support, question, or refute the analysis and argument. The summary character of this chapter, however, dictates that the list be brief. Journal articles, even though they provide some of the most critical analysis, are purposefully omitted. In selecting a book for mention I have taken into account the reach and the quality of its contents and also the likelihood that it will capture and hold the interest of anyone who needs the guidance of a bibliography.

We are better informed about the thought and the bargaining that brought the Constitution of the United States into being than we are about the conception and creation of the precedent state constitutions. The debates in the Philadelphia convention are best presented in Max Farrand, *The Records of the Federal Convention of 1787*, rev. ed., 4 vols. (New Haven: Yale University Press, 1937). The debates in the state ratifying conventions are reported in Jonathan Elliot, ed., *The Debates in the Several State Conventions on the Adoption of the Federal Constitution* (Philadelphia: J. B. Lippincott, 1836-1845). The notable explication and justification of the proposed Constitution, *The Federalist,* can be found in several editions offered by as many publishers. Argument opposing adoption of the document is collected in Cecilia M. Kenyon, ed., *The Antifederalists* (Indianapolis: Bobbs-Merrill Co., 1966). Opposition to the proposed Constitution is thoroughly examined by Kenyon in an essay opening her collection and in Jackson T. Main, *The Antifederalists: Critics of the Constitution, 1781-1788* (Chicago: Quadrangle Books, 1961).

The earliest state constitutions can be found in college and other sizable public libraries but are not assembled in any printing designed for sale to the general public. Most informative, perhaps, of the expositions of republican government contemporaneous with the writing of the first constitutions is

Thoughts on Government, by John Adams. It must be read (some fifteen pages) in an edition of Adams's collected papers.

Of the historical accounts of the founding experience, I have found these most useful: Gordon S. Wood, *The Creation of the American Republic, 1776-1787* (Chapel Hill: University of North Carolina, 1969); Elisha P. Douglass, *Rebels and Democrats: The Struggle for Equal Political Rights and Majority Rule During the American Revolution* (Chapel Hill: University of North Carolina Press, 1955); Allan Nevins, *The American States During and After the Revolution* (New York: Augustus M. Kelley, 1969); and Marchette Chute, *The First Liberty: A History of the Right to Vote in America, 1619-1850* (New York: E. P. Dutton, 1971).

Thoughtful examinations of particular facets of the idea of republican government are: J. R. Pole, *Political Representation in England and the Origins of the American Republic* (New York: St. Martin, 1966); Paul K. Conkin, *Self-Evident Truths* (Bloomington: Indiana University Press, 1974); M. J. C. Vile, *Constitutionalism and the Separation of Powers* (Oxford: Oxford University Press, 1967); and Bernard Bailyn, *The Ideological Origins of the American Revolution* (Cambridge: Harvard University Press, 1967).

In *The Basic Symbols of the American Political Tradition* (Baton Rouge: Louisiana State Press, 1970), Willmoore Kendall and George W. Carey trace out a course of thought from the Mayflower Compact to the Gettysburg address. I am impressed by the imaginative and ingenious character of their analysis and argument but unable to share some of their conclusions. In Oscar Handlin and Mary Handlin, eds., *The Popular Sources of Political Authority: Documents on the Massachusetts Constitution of 1780* (Cambridge: Harvard University Press, 1966), there are collected the responses of the people of Massachusetts to two constitutions proposed for that state — one in 1778 (rejected) and one in 1780 (adopted). These reports of opinions and decisions provide a remarkable insight into the states of mind prevailing among persons who won little or no acclaim as leaders.

R. R. Palmer, in volume 1 of his *The Age of the Democratic Revolution* (Princeton: Princeton University Press, 1959), gives an impressive account of the thought and action related to democratic or republican government in Europe contemporaneous with the founding of republican government in North America. For inquiry into who was permitted to vote and estimates of the numbers who actually participated in the choice of public officials see Chilton Williamson, *American Suffrage: From Property to Democracy, 1776-1860* (Princeton: Princeton University Press, 1960); and Robert E. Brown, *Middle Class Democracy and the Revolution in Massachusetts* (New York: Russell, 1968).

Finally, on the emergence and persistence of a notion that the framers of the federal Constitution wanted to, tried to, and actually did scuttle such measure of popular control of government as had been invited and nurtured thereto, see Charles A. Beard, *An Economic Interpretation of the Constitution* (New York: Macmillan, 1913); and Richard Hofstadter, *American Polit-*

ical Tradition (New York: A. A. Knopf, 1973). This thesis was emphatically and effectively refuted, however, in Robert E. Brown, *Charles Beard and the Constitution* (Princeton: Princeton University Press, 1956); and Forrest McDonald, *We the People: The Economic Origins of the Constitution* (Chicago: University of Chicago Press, 1958).

[2]

THE AMERICAN DECLARATION OF INDEPENDENCE

The Majority and the Right of Political Power

—ROSS M. LENCE

Few people would dispute the assertion that the relationship of the Declaration of Independence to subsequent political experience in the United States has not been carefully explored; the Declaration's impact on the content of national and state constitutions, nullification, and secession, for example, has for the most part gone unexamined. There may, however, be much less readiness to accept the conclusion that there is need to scrutinize further the thought expressed in the Declaration itself. If any period in American history has been written and rewritten, interpreted and reinterpreted, surely it must be that of the American Revolution and its "midwife," the American Declaration of Independence. Furthermore, the phraseology of no American document can rival the Declaration of Independence in being familiar to the public at large: consent of the governed; the equality of all men; and the rights to life, liberty, and the pursuit of happiness — these phrases have echoed throughout American history.

A cursory examination of the interpretive literature on the Declaration, however, reveals that further analysis of that famous document may well be in order. On the one hand, the Declaration of Independence is "that immortal emblem of Humanity,"[1] and, on the other, a false doctrine founded upon "glittering and sounding generalities;"[2] it is both "one of the most revolutionary political papers ever written"[3] and one of the most conservative legal documents ever composed;[4] its central themes are the "doctrine of free statehood as a universal right,"[5] "the absolute independence of the individual,"[6] the pursuit of happiness,[7] and equality for all men;[8] at one and the same time it announces the birth of one nation, one people,[9] and thirteen separate and independent states.[10]

There are literally hundreds of books, pamphlets, and articles by scholars, polemicists, apologists, etc., who in one manner or another consider the Declaration and its historical and political manifestations. It is not the purpose of this chapter, however, to review this secondary literature; rather, our purpose here is threefold: 1. To offer a preliminary analysis of the text of the Declaration of Independence; 2. To enumerate some of the inherent tensions and unresolved questions posed by the Declaration itself; and 3. To suggest a means by which to resolve these tensions and thereby identify the rightful heirs of the Spirit of '76.

The Call for Independence

The War of Independence had begun long before the Second Continental Congress issued its declaration justifying separation from Britain. After the "Boston Tea Party" on December 16, 1773, and Parliament's passage of the "Intolerable Acts" in January of the following year, the colonies moved steadily toward independence. Open hostility erupted at Lexington and Concord on April 19, 1775; and, in his proclamation from the Throne in August of that same year, George III declared that open and avowed rebellion existed in the colonies. Radical leaders throughout the colonies — but especially in Massachusetts — were convinced that the only alternative to independence was tyranny. Inspired by Thomas Paine's *Common Sense,* which first appeared in Boston in January of 1776 and circulated rapidly throughout the colonies, many colonists began to echo the claim that reconciliation and ruin were synonymous.

Although the Continental Congress urged on May 15, 1776, that the people in the several colonies seize control of the colonial governments and suppress the authority of the Crown, there was still considerable opposition, especially in the middle colonies, to an official declaration of separation. The Virginia Convention assembled at Williamsburg, unwilling to tolerate further delay, instructed its delegates to the Continental Congress to propose independence — an instruction fulfilled with Richard Henry Lee's

Resolution for Independence on June 7, 1776. This resolution was referred to a Committee of Five, consisting of Thomas Jefferson, John Adams, Benjamin Franklin, Roger Sherman, and Robert Livingston, with instructions to draft a declaration should one be required. The Committee submitted its draft of the Declaration on June 28, and the Congress declared the independence of the American colonies on July 2, 1776. Two days later the Congress officially adopted the document which we today call the Declaration of Independence.

The Declaration: Its Major Objective and General Format

The Declaration of Independence as we know it, then, was a statement approved and publicly distributed by the Continental Congress which both announced a course of action and justified the decision to undertake that action. Its main objective was not to declare American independence per se (for that action had been taken two days earlier), but to promulgate that decision and to clarify the causes which had impelled separation from Britain. In other words, the Declaration of Independence is not really a declaration of independence at all: it is rather an announcement and formal justification of that decision.

The general format of the Declaration consists of four easily identified parts: 1. A brief introductory statement of purpose (Part I, including the title and the opening paragraph); 2. A concise summary of the general political principles of democratic governments (Part II, consisting of the second paragraph); 3. An enumeration of the specific grievances against George III (Part III, including charges [i]-[xxvii]); and 4. Three concluding paragraphs, one dealing with George III, one with the British people, and the last with the formal proclamation of separation (Part IV, including paragraphs [1], [2], and [3], respectively).[11] Let us examine each of these parts in turn.

The Introductory Statement of Purpose

The Declaration opens with these words: "In CONGRESS, July 4, 1776. A DECLARATION By the REPRESENTATIVES of the UNITED STATES OF AMERICA, In GENERAL CONGRESS Assembled." Obviously the document which is to follow is intended to be a formal announcement of some kind by the members of the Continental Congress. We are not told at this point, however, the purpose of this proclamation, to whom it is addressed, or for whom its message is intended. Interestingly enough, there is also no mention of unanimity. In fact, we know that it was not until some time later that the Declaration was unanimously agreed to (July 19, 1776, to be precise), and that it was at that time the Congress ordered the now unanimous Declaration engrossed on parchment with a new title to reflect its unanimity, a title much more familiar to our ears: "In CONGRESS, July 4, 1776. The unanimous Declaration of the thirteen united States of America." The members of Congress affixed their names to this parchment copy of the Declaration on August 2nd; and in January of the following year Congress ordered the reprinting and distribution of the Declaration, bearing both its new title and the names of the original signers.

Evidently the issue of unanimity was of considerable importance to the members of the Continental Congress — important enough, at least, to warrant a change in the title of the Declaration itself, the only change made after its adoption on July 4, 1776. The reasons this unanimity was so important, of course, are open to speculation. Of one thing, however, we may be certain: Congress did not want this evidence of a common mind to go unnoticed. Furthermore, the fact that the resolution of independence was not unanimously adopted by the Committee of the Whole (Pennsylvania and South Carolina voted in the negative, Delaware was divided, and New York abstained because of their previous instructions) suggests that the Declaration — especially the grievances against George III — may be less rhetorical than many of its later interpreters would have us believe. When all is said and done, these good subjects of the king may well have an inalienable right to resist tyranny, but the exercise of that right is not an altogether pleasant task.

Immediately following the title is the introductory paragraph so familiar to Americans:

> When in the Course of human Events, it becomes necessary for one People to dissolve the Political Bands which have connected them with another, and to assume among the Powers of the Earth, the separate and equal Station to which the Laws of Nature and Nature's God entitle them, a decent Respect to the Opinions of Mankind requires that they should declare the causes which impel them to the Separation.

This single-sentence paragraph confirms our earlier expectation about the immediate purpose of the Declaration—that is, to enumerate the causes which necessitated the separation from Britain. Moreover, we are advised that there is more than one cause for the separation and that these causes leave the colonists no alternative, but impel them to the decision which they have made. What kind of separation is involved? At this point we are not specifically told, but we do know: 1. That there are two peoples involved, the British and the American colonists; 2. That there has been a severing of the *political* bands between them; 3. That this separation does not require the concurrence of both parties but represents, instead, unilateral action on the part of the colonies; 4. That the colonies will now assume an equal status with the other nations of the world, because of the laws of nature and nature's God; and 5. That decency requires the colonists to promulgate the sources of contention between themselves and Britain.

In general we have in the opening paragraph a sort of table of contents of what is to follow. It not only establishes clearly the overall purpose of the Declaration but also anticipates the democratic philosophy of the second paragraph, the list of grievances against the king, and the positing of, and commitment to, some general canons of decency.

The Underlying Principles and Beliefs

This brings us to the second paragraph, the most famous passage of the entire Declaration, and an affirmation of democratic principles and beliefs. It can be divided into four discrete parts for the purpose of analysis: 1. The enumeration of certain self-evident truths about the nature of man; 2. The enumeration of two additional self-evident truths, and some general observations about the nature of government; 3. The application of these general philosophical precepts to the specific case of the colonies; and 4. The introduction of the list of grievances against George III. Let us take each of these parts in turn.

In the second paragraph the Declaration first posits three self-evident truths about the natural rights of man: 1. That all men are created equal; 2. That the Creator has endowed all men with certain unalienable rights; and 3. That among these rights are the rights to life, liberty, and the pursuit of happiness. We note that these propositions are not qualified: they are self-evident and universal. The

Declaration, of course, makes the "self-evident" aspect of these propositions explicit, but they are universal as well, for the truths and rights therein proclaimed do not refer to the rights of Englishmen or Americans, but the rights of Man. We are led to assume that these rights, like the condition of equality, are bestowed upon man through the gift of none other than God Himself.

The Declaration does not elaborate this point, however, but continues its enumeration of self-evident truths, bringing the total to five. These two additional truths are: 4. That governments are instituted among men to secure the rights previously cited; and finally 5. That whenever any form of government becomes destructive of the ends for which it was instituted, it is the right of the people to alter or to abolish it. We immediately note that the focal point of concern has now shifted from individual man to men in civil society. Furthermore, unlike the self-evident truths relating to all men, those concerning government have clarifying or qualifying conditions attached.

In the case of the fourth truth, in addition to claiming that governments are instituted for the purpose of securing certain rights, the Declaration adds that governments derive their just powers from the consent of the governed. We are not told, however, why just powers depend upon the consent of the governed, for this claim — like the truth to which it is attached — is apodictic; that is, it is incontestable because demonstrated or demonstrable. Since this observation is not elevated to the level of an independent, self-evident truth, we are led to believe that consent and just powers are correlative with the very purpose of government, and that to elevate them to the level of a self-evident truth would be redundant. Nonetheless, the Declaration still finds it expedient to include these concepts. Consent would seem to be an integral factor in the institution of government.

In the case of the last self-evident truth, or the right of the people to alter or abolish their government, the Declaration offers more than a mere clarifying statement. For the first time the Declaration seems to qualify one of its self-evident truths: the right of the people to alter or abolish their government requires that they institute a new government in its place and that, in doing so, they change the existing conditions in such a manner as seems to them most likely to secure their safety and happiness. This second requirement is enigmatic — to say the least — in that it seems obvious that no people would knowingly and willingly change their condition from bad to worse.

Strangely enough the reflections on the nature of government do not end with these self-evident truths, but continue with additional conclusions seemingly based upon experience and historical evidence. We are told that prudent people will not change their government for light and transient reasons; that people are by nature conservative and resistant to change, being more willing to suffer while the evils are bearable than to attempt to rectify their grievances through forcible change; and that when a long train of abuses and usurpations evinces a design to bring people under absolute despotism, it becomes not only their right, but their duty, to throw off such government and provide new safeguards for their future security. Again we note that the destruction of government is invariably tied to the provision for a new and better system of rule. In general these additional reflections on government seem designed to show that the earlier enumeration of self-evident truths is not utopian or radical, but wholly consistent with prudence and deliberative thought.

What does all this, however, have to do with the conflict between Britain and the colonies? As if to dispel any doubts, the Declaration explicitly asserts that all the issues raised in the first and second paragraphs are pertinent to the case at hand. The colonies have suffered just such a long train of abuses, all of which they have borne with due patience and respect. Furthermore, these offensive acts not only continue to plague the colonists at this very moment, but they all have one direct object — the establishment of an absolute tyranny over the colonies. In at least one sense despotism and tyranny are interchangeable: both are destructive of the ends for which government is established.

In one succinct sentence, the Declaration links all these earlier remarks about democratic government and democratic principles to the list of grievances against the king. The closing sentence of the second paragraph makes it evident that: 1. The history of the present king is, has been, and will continue to be a history of repeated injuries *and* usurpations; and 2. The object of all these repeated injuries and usurpations is the establishment of an absolute tyranny. The king has done more than simply wrong the colonists: he has attempted to set up a system of perpetual tyranny over them. An enumeration of his acts will confirm this to any candid observer.

The implicit premise is that tyranny justifies resistance to those in power. The list of grievances, then, is designed to show that such a state of tyranny exists, not that any or all of the grievances per se would be sufficient to justify resistance to government.

THE GRIEVANCES AGAINST GEORGE III

On the basis of the internal evidence of the Declaration, then, we ought to have arrived at the heart of the document itself — the enumeration of the pernicious acts of George III and his attempt to establish an absolute tyranny over the American colonies. These grievances are the very reason for which the Declaration was written and promulgated: to justify the decision to dissolve the political bands with Britain. Critics of the Declaration, however, have time and again pronounced these grievances rhetorical, mundane, time-bound, and even invalid. For one reason or another, the focal point of the framers' argument has slipped into historical obscurity.

In spite of these critics we must not be dissuaded from the task of providing a preliminary analysis of the Declaration as a whole. Fortunately, the text of the Declaration offers an initial clue as to how to proceed. The charges are divided into three general categories: 1. Those grievances associated with the "injuries," or abuses of constitutional power; 2. Those grievances associated with the "usurpations," or the exercise of power that others have a right to; and 3. Those capricious and barbarous acts of George III which shock all contemporary canons of decency and are the very markings of a tyrant. Under such a scheme, sections [i]-[xiii] constitute the "injuries," sections [xiv]-[xxii] the "usurpations," and sections [xxiii]-[xxvii], the proofs that the king is not only a tyrant, but a barbarian as well (see the copy of the Declaration at the end of this chapter).

There also is a second possible division of the accusations: 1. Interference with colonial representative institutions; 2. Violation of the principle of a separation of powers, at least as the colonists understood that concept; 3. Instances of "pretended acts of legislation," a not-too-subtle assault upon Parliament; and 4. Instances of tyrannical, pernicious acts of the king. Under this division, the first category includes charges [i]-[vii], the second includes [viii]-[xii], the third, [xiii]-[xxii], and the fourth, [xxiii]-[xxvii].

It is interesting to note that the first thirteen grievances assume a capacity on the part of the colonists for self-government, and that the first seven deal specifically with the question of representative institutions and legislative power. Of the remaining grievances, the fourteenth through the twenty-second form a concise history of the conflict between Parliament and the colonies, while the twenty-third through the twenty-seventh prove that the king has sided with Parliament in the controversy. It is also interesting to note that the grievance parent to the slogan, "No taxation without representation"—at one time the focal point of the conflict between Britain and the colonies—has now been relegated to only seventeenth place in the colonial list of grievances. In a real sense the issue of taxation shrinks into insignificance before the more critical issues of usurpation and tyrannical government.

The Closing Paragraphs

The twenty-eighth charge against George III pronounces him a tyrant, not only summarizing the other charges, but returning us to the point of departure in the second paragraph. In the colonists' minds at least, the case against George III had been clearly established. In this paragraph we are again told that the acts of oppression have been repeated, and that the suffering of the colonists has been of long duration. All attempts at redress have been answered only by new injury. The king not only is a tyrant: he is unfit to be the ruler of a free people.

All that remains is to declare the independence of the colonies; but, once again the colonists hesitate. The following paragraph reiterates the theme which has appeared throughout the Declaration; yet, again we are told that the colonists have not been rash in their actions, but have tried repeatedly to secure redress for their grievances through channels other than separation. The colonists have not only pleaded vainly with the king, but also appealed fruitlessly to the British people themselves. The colonists have warned the British people of Parliament's attempts to extend unwarranted jurisdiction over the colonies; they have cited the circumstances of the colonizing of America; they have called out for justice, a right common to all English-speaking peoples. All this has been for nought, since the British people also have been unattentive to their cries. Again we hear the charge of usurpation; and again it is evident that usurpation per se is not the cause of severance but usurpation uncontrolled and uncontrollable. In the closing sentence of the fourth paragraph we also find a hearkening back to the beginnings of the Declaration and its emphasis on necessity and compulsion as responsible for the decision to separate from Britain.

At last, the closing paragraph announces the dissolution of the political connection between Britain and the colonies. This act, moreover, is founded upon the authority and good intentions of a good people—a people, we are led to believe, with more honorable intentions than those of either Parliament or the king; and, as proof of the sincerity of their intentions, they call upon the judgment of God Himself.

The Inherent Questions

At several points in this overview of the Declaration, we have encountered a number of concepts or principles which are hardly self-explanatory; for example, we have discovered that the precise nature of the separation from Britain was not clear. At times this imprecision, coupled with the lack of any elaboration of the point at issue, has led to mysterious affirmations, for example, that people change their condition only for the better. Although we passed over these ambiguities and impressions in our brief recapitulation, our preliminary investigation of the Declaration could hardly be complete without at least some mention of the questions inherent in the Declaration.

THE CRITICAL QUESTION

One of the principal problems left unresolved by the Declaration centers around the issue of who may alter or abolish government and under what conditions and what circumstances. The Declaration speaks only of the "Right of the People" to alter or to abolish their government. There appear to be three alternatives: 1. The Declaration concerns itself only with the right of a people sufficient in numbers, strength, and position to survive as an independent power; 2. The Declaration allows every individual the right to resist government when that government is, in his opinion, acting in a tyrannical manner; and 3. The Declaration envisages some intermediary condition which would affirm the right of certain communities to function as enclaves within the whole state. What precisely does the Declaration mean when it speaks of *a people*? If it means a number greater than any one individual, then an obvious tension arises between the people's right to change their government, on the one hand, and the individual's right to resist tyranny, on the other.

The question of what constitutes *a people* is the critical question; for, unless this question can be resolved, the American Declaration of Independence loses its position of pre-eminence among the symbols of the American Revolution. One cannot talk meaningfully about either the unalienable rights of man—especially the right to resist a tyrannical government—or the just powers of government, if one does not know who has the authority to alter or to abolish the government which fails in its objectives. Nor can one believe that the grievances against the king are more than rhetorical nonsense if the people he has injured and whose power he has usurped cannot be identified.

The Secondary Questions

In addition to this critical question there are, of course, many other questions posed by the Declaration; for example, a moment's reflection on the self-evident truths will raise serious doubts as to their apodictic character. Perhaps such is most obvious in the case of the very first truth enumerated, namely, that all men are created equal. The manner and extent to which men are equal is indeed an enduring problem; and this problem is compounded in the Declaration itself by the use of the past tense of the verb "create." Furthermore, if men are endowed with *certain* unalienable rights, among which are the three enumerated, there must be some unenumerated ones as well—not to mention those which are alienable. Then, too, there must be some process or institution for resolving conflicts which are certain to emerge between and among these various natural rights.

That governments are instituted to secure the rights of man is obvious from the Declaration, but in it the purpose of government is not limited to this function alone. The qualification that all just powers come from the consent of the governed does nothing to clarify matters, but merely compounds the confusion. Like just powers or the purposes of government, the components of consent—how and when it will be expressed, and on what kinds of issues—go unexplained; and, in addition to all these limitations, the Declaration implies the right of resistance may only be used against a government which has become destructive of the rights of the people, not against one which has merely shown poor judgment about how to advance those ends.

Nor are these perplexing questions restricted to the self-evident truths of the Declaration. When we have established what the Declaration means by *the people*, it is still necessary to ascertain what is meant by *throwing off government*, and also what is the relationship between the power to destroy and the power to create and institute anew. Legitimate government is safe, for the Declaration clearly differentiates light and transient causes from those which justify resistance. Again, however, two questions get no consideration: Who shall be the judge? When is it legitimate to assume the designs of the rulers on the rights of the people have as their object absolute despotism? Instead of answers, one encounters more and more undefined terms and phrases; for example, duty, obligations, usurpations, injuries.

The Question of the Legitimate Heirs of the "Spirit of '76"

Because these inadequacies and other defects pervade the entire Declaration, the list of secondary questions would appear to be infinite. There is, however, yet another set of questions to be resolved—those associated with the legitimate heirs of the "Spirit of '76." The partisan use of the Declaration has been widespread. Abolitionists, suffragists, populists, secessionists—to cite just a few—have claimed to draw inspiration from the Declaration. Interestingly enough, nearly all have based their claims on paragraph two and its affirmation of democratic principles and beliefs. These same principles and beliefs have thus been used to justify a wide range of resistance to government: the secession of the southern states from the Union during the Civil War; the refusal of state authorities to enforce federal law (i.e., nullification); the refusal of private citizens to obey judicial orders involving such matters as desegregation of public schools; the attempt to overthrow the government by force (or, at a minimum, to assassinate its leaders) if the persons who engage in such activities solemnly swear that they believe the present government is trying to establish an absolute tyranny over the American people.

The uncertainty and the confusion regarding the legitimate heirs of the Declaration and how far they may go in pressing their claims against others are, in large part, a result of the failure to answer the critical question of what the Declaration means when it speaks of *the people.* To offer an answer to that query one would not only have to construct the parameters within which to resolve the second-order questions, but also suggest an initial means for identifying those who are justified in citing the Declaration in support of their cause. Let us turn briefly, then, to the question of what constitutes *the people* in the Declaration of Independence.

The Critical Question: Who Are THE PEOPLE?

The task of determining what the Declaration means when it refers to the people is complicated, of course, by the fact that the Declaration nowhere makes its meaning explicit. Nevertheless, if the single reference in paragraph two to the natural rights of man is excluded for the moment, it becomes obvious that all references to either the people or the colonists are in collective terms; thus, in the text:

> 1. "One people" dissolves the political bands connecting the colonies and Britain and decency requires that "*they* should declare the causes which *impel* them to the separation."
> 2. It is "the Right of the People" to alter or abolish government and to institute another in its place which "to *them* shall seem most likely to effect *their* Safety and Happiness."
> 3. It is "the good People of these Colonies" who "solemnly publish and declare" their independence, dissolving "all political connections" between the American States and the British Crown.

If the decision to dissolve the political bands which connect two peoples is a collective one, and if the people who are to exercise this right of altering or abolishing the government must do so in their collective capacity, then there must be a decision-making rule for determining what course of action is, in fact, to be undertaken. In the final analysis, there is but one of three alternative rules available: unanimous consent, minority rule, or majority rule.

That the colonists did not believe that unanimous consent was necessary to justify resistance to governmental authority is obvious, for some colonists remained loyal to George III and the British Parliament throughout the War of Independence; but, this historical evidence aside, the Declaration itself confirms the fact. It will be recalled that the Declaration as adopted by the Continental Congress opened with the title: "In CONGRESS, July 4, 1776. A DECLARATION By the REPRESENTATIVES of the UNITED STATES OF AMERICA, In GENERAL CONGRESS Assembled." As was noted earlier, the document as adopted on July 4, 1776, did not become "the unanimous Declaration of the thirteen united States of America" until some two weeks after the decision to separate from Britain. The fact that the colonists issued their proclamation prior to obtaining unanimity confirms the supposition that they did not think unanimous consent was necessary for *the people* to alter or abolish their government.

Only two alternatives remain: either the majority alone has the right to alter or dissolve government, or some number less than a majority may legitimately exercise this right. The wording of the second paragraph of the Declaration concerning the unalienable rights of all mankind has led many critics to claim that a minority (and even a single individual, for that matter) has the right to attempt to alter or to throw off any government which violates or is destructive of man's natural rights. Such an interpretation, however, is not without its own difficulties and can be claimed only if one is willing to ignore other passages in the same paragraph. Paragraph 2 explicitly refers to five self-evident truths, committing itself not only to the unalienable rights of man, but the broader principles of democratic governments, as well; thus, while it is true that governments are established to secure the natural rights of all men, it is also true that they derive their just powers from the consent of the governed. Common sense tells us, and all the antecedent writings of the Declaration confirm the assumption, that unanimity is no more possible in the operation of government than in its dissolution. Once civil society has come into being, consent of the governed means nothing other than the consent of the majority or a majority of their representatives. This problem had been anticipated by Locke who, while arguing that the property of no man could be taken without his consent, readily admitted that a man's own consent was, in fact, "the consent of the majority, giving it either by themselves or their representatives chosen by them." Any exercise of political power which has the support of a majority, therefore, must be by definition just, and any attempt to resist the exercise of such a power cannot be justified.

It might be argued, of course, that while unanimity may not be required for the operation and/or dissolution of government, it is certainly a requisite for the creation of the body politic. The manner and extent to which the framers of the Declaration entertained this notion shall be examined shortly. It must not be forgotten, however, that this document purports to offer an enumeration and clarification of the causes which have necessitated the severing of the political bands with Britain, and that the colonists' immediate concern is not the rise of government, nor its maintenance, but its dissolution for good cause. The implication is obvious: the majority alone has the right to alter or abolish government, for the consent of the majority is what determines whether the powers of the government are just.

The conclusion that for the purposes of the dissolution of government the framers of the Declaration understood *the people* to mean a majority of the community is also consistent with the antecedent thought of the colonists to be found in the political pamphlets which circulated in the colonies in the years immediately preceding the proclamation of independence. Time and again the colonial pamphleteers argued that while each man has a right to decide for himself whether his own preservation is called into question, only the people collectively can decide for the society as a whole. To this effect Richard Wells argues:

> It hath always been allowed that the happiness of the people was the true end of government, therefore whenever a state has diverged from that point, it becomes the business, nay duty, of every individual, to bring about a restoration; and whenever *they* discover a tendency in the ruling power, to deviate from the general good, *they* ought with resolute firmness to remonstrate against it. . . .*The people can do no wrong*, I mean *the whole people collectively*; for it is to be presumed, from that great first principle self-preservation, they will primarily consider their own happiness; therefore when *a whole people* complain, we may be certain it is not without just foundation.[12] [Emphasis added.]

Wells does not explicitly tell us what constitutes *the whole people*, but he does acknowledge much later in his essay: "That mankind can never be brought to one way of thinking, and the minority must *always* give way to the majority, are obvious and necessary truths."[13] Samuel West's response, on the other hand, is more emphatic. He claimed that, for the purposes of political decision-making, the people is nothing other than the majority. It is necessary and right that the minority should submit to the majority. As he wrote:

> When legislators have enacted a set of laws, which are highly approved by a large majority of the community, as tending to promote the publick good, in this case, if a small number of persons are so unhappy as to view the matter in a very different point of light from the publick, tho' they have an undoubted right to shew the reasons of their dissent from the judgment of the publick, and may lawfully use all proper arguments to convince the publick of what they judge to be an error, yet if they fail in their attempt, and the majority still continue to approve of the laws that are enacted, it is the duty of those few that dissent, peaceably and for conscience sake to submit to the publick judgement. . . *It is the major part of the community that have the sole right of establishing a constitution, and authorizing the magistrates; and consequently it is the major part of a community that can claim the right of altering the constitutuion, and displacing the magistrates.*[14] [Emphasis added.]

When the issue is to alter or abolish the government, the minority is absolutely bound by the wishes of the majority. The right to throw off government and to provide for the safety and happiness of the people is a right which belongs "not [to] a few disaffected individuals, but [to] the collective body of the state."[15]

The conclusion that the right to alter or abolish government is a right of the community as a whole is consistent not only with this antecedent thought of the Declaration, however, but also with the various state constitutions and bills of rights written during this same period. Time and again it is announced that governments are instituted to secure the rights of the community, and that the community alone has the authority to remove their rulers or abolish their government. The 1776 constitution of Maryland, for example, opens with a declaration of rights in which the first truth enumerated is: "That all government of right originates from the people, is founded in compact only, and *instituted solely for the good of the whole.*" As a consequence, "whenever the ends of government are perverted, and *public liberty* manifestly endangered . . . *the people* may, and of right ought, to reform the old or establish a new government."[16] The Pennsylvania constitution, also written immediately after the colonists proclaimed their independence, is even more explicit than the Maryland constitution:

> That government is, or ought to be, *instituted for the common benefit, protection and security of the people, nation or community; and not for* the particular emolument or advantage of *any single man, family, or sett of men, who are a part only of that community;* And that *the community hath an indubitable, unalienable and indefeasible right* to reform, alter or abolish government in such manner as *shall be by that community judged* most conducive to the public weal.[17]

Or, in the words of the Massachusetts constitution adopted during the War of Independence:

> Government is *instituted for the common good;* for the protection, safety, prosperity, and happiness *of the people; and not for* the profit, honor, or private interest of *any one man, family, or class of men:* Therefore *the people alone have an incontestible, unalienable and indefeasible right to institute government; and to reform, alter or totally change the same,* when their protection, safety, prosperity, and happiness require it.[18]

Much of the confusion regarding what constitutes a people could well have been avoided had those who drafted and signed the American Declaration of Independence used the wording found in the Virginia Declaration of Rights adopted by the Virginia Convention on June 12, 1776. Even if Thomas Jefferson had not seen the Virginia Declaration—a possibility which seems highly unlikely, given the fact that the Virginia document had been in circulation among the members of Congress from the very earliest days of June—it is significant that no member of Congress who had seen that document insisted upon a clarification of what constitutes the people. The Virginia Declaration of Rights reads in part:

> That government is, or ought to be, *instituted for the common benefit, protection, and security of the people, nation, or community*; of all the various modes and forms of government, that is best which is capable of producing the greatest degree of happiness and safety, and is most effectually secured against the danger of maladministration: and that, when any government shall be found inadequate or contrary to these purposes, *a majority of the community hath an indubitable, inalienable, and indefeasible right to reform, alter or abolish it,* in such a manner as shall be judged most conducive to the public weal.[19]

On the matter of the dissolution of government, in other words, the Virginia Declaration of Rights, unlike the Declaration of Independence, is most explicit: *a majority* alone has the right to alter or abolish government. We shall never know, of course, why Jefferson and the other signers of the Declaration of Independence did not adopt the wording of the Virginia document. Perhaps the point regarding what constitutes a people for the purposes of resistance to governmental authority was so well established that it was thought unnecessary, if not redundant, to repeat it. Perhaps it was thought that, in a document designed to expose the long train of abuses of George III, a cruel and absolute tyrant, it would be unwise to employ words which might convey to some the idea that the colonists were simply disloyal subjects, radical republicans who could never be happy even under the most benevolent of monarchs. Perhaps it was thought that to signify only a majority was necessary to dissolve the political bands connecting Britain and the colonies would distract from the image of *one* people united against another.

These speculations aside, however, certain theoretical difficulties emerge once the term *the people* is clarified to mean a majority of the whole community. The first, and undoubtedly the most obvious, difficulty is to decide what constitutes a community; that is, who is to be counted and who is not to be counted as a member so that we will be able to tell when we have reached the requisite majority to justify resistance? The implication, of course, is that everyone counts. The Declaration of Independence makes no distinctions: "All men are created equal;" yet in actual fact whole classes of people were excluded from consideration: children, women, Negro slaves—each was for one reason or another excluded from the analysis.

Even if it is assumed that everyone with the franchise was to be included and all others excluded, the question must still be answered: How far do the political boundaries of *one people* extend? The British pamphleteers argued that Britain and the colonies were not *two peoples* at all, but merely *one people* separated by the Atlantic. Henry Goodricke said in his assault upon Richard Price's pamphlet on the nature of civil liberty: "We [who support the Crown] deem not the Colonies by any means *another people*, under distinct supreme free *governments of their own*, but a people *within the state*, just as the people of Yorkshire are."[20] Once one makes the further admission "that Great Britain is the *majority* of the British empire," argued John Fletcher, the Americans lose the argument on their own grounds. "According to your own concession [that the minority must always submit to the majority for the good of the whole], the *determinations* of Great Britain are to be *always considered as the determinations* of the whole British empire."[21]

Even if one grants the further concession that the colonists were in fact one distinct people and the British another, there is still the question of evidence whether those colonists favoring independence were, in fact, in the majority. The loyalists argued until the very end of the Revolutionary War that a majority of colonists favored reconciliation with the Crown. In a letter to George III on March 9, 1782, a group of American loyalists called upon the king to appeal to foreign powers for assistance, so as to "save and deliver us, his majesty's American loyalists, who we maintain, in every one of the colonies, compose a great majority of the inhabitants, and those too the first in point of opulence and consequence."[22] Even those contemporary historians sympathetic to the American cause noted the difficulty:

> But could the truth be ascertained, it would probably be discovered, that in most of the town and other meetings, even in New England, far more than half the parties having a right to attend, from various causes were absent; and that there were a great many among the absentees, who were such, because they knew that matters would be carried at such meetings contrary to their own sentiments.[23]

Discrepancies such as these convinced the supporters of George III that the colonists did not in fact have a genuine theory of revolution. On the contrary, they thought the colonial arguments nothing other than a clever manipulation of words designed to conceal dishonorable intentions; that the colonists believed justice is nothing other than the advantage of the stronger; and that they were consequently determined to settle the controversy with Britain through brute force, rather than according to principles of justice and right. As one embittered loyalist pamphleteer said in the closing paragraph of his essay:

> Rouse, therefore, my friends! Support the Congress, and assert your native right of doing as you please. Your only danger will arise from your failing to attain the end you aim at. In that case you will indeed be *rebels*, and may chance to be hanged. But if you *succeed*, it will only be

> a *revolution*, and you will be justified before God and man. Nothing, my friends, was wanting to make Lucifer's rebellion in Heaven *a glorious revolution*, but success.[24]

The rebellious Americans, on the other hand, while noticeably silent about Negro slaves, vehemently denied the validity of these objections. There was no doubt in their minds that they in fact were one people and the British another, for not only did the Americans and the British differ fundamentally on both the methods and the objectives of government—differences evidenced by the injuries and usurpations of George III—but they could no longer be united "together into one coherent living body"[25] through a common legislature. For a people to live together in a state of peace requires the existence of a common forum for resolving the differences which must inevitably arise in any society. Time and circumstances, however, have caused the Americans and the British to grow apart; meaningful representation of the colonial interests can never be secured through the British Parliament, where the political connections "must unavoidably be very loose, the intercourse difficult and tedious, [and] the fellow-feeling and mutual sensibility too faint."[26] It is the legislative power which "*gives form, life and unity* to the commonwealth,"[27] and distinguishes one people from another. Whenever any group of persons of sufficient numbers and strength to survive as an independent power cannot be adequately or fairly represented in a single legislative body with the other members of that community, then they are a separate people and have a right to establish their independence and to place the legislative power in such hands as shall seem to them most likely to secure their safety and happiness.[28]

If the Americans appeared certain that they in fact were one people and the British another, their discussion of when a majority favored altering their government was less definite. The fact that there is no direct confrontation of this issue, however, does not mean that the Americans believed a revolution to be merely a successful rebellion. It is true, of course, that most revolutions in the very early stages are indistinguishable from rebellions, for both are apt to be characterized by a minority resisting a government because of alleged grievances against its personal rights. Even when a government is overthrown, it may still not be clear that those who favor the altering of that government are in the majority; thus, James Burgh argued in his *Political Disquisitions* that even during the Glorious Revolution of 1688 "it was not certain . . . that the *majority* of the people were for the exclusion."[29]

What is certain about the majority and the right to alter or abolish government is included in four things: First, the decisions that the rulers have been guilty of tyranny and oppression, and that resistance to government is therefore justified, have not been hastily made, for the people will bear all the "impudence and mistakes of their rulers" with unwearied patience.[30] Only when the designs against the people's rights have been general, deliberate, persistent, and with evil motive are the people apt to stir. Second, because of this hesitancy to resist government, the people will almost by definition be correct in their actions. It "may be said of the publick, which can't always be said of individuals, viz. that the publick is always willing to be rightly informed, and when it has proper matter of conviction laid before it, its judgment is always right."[31] Third, because of the number of persons involved, there is "good reason to judge that they have sufficient power and strength to maintain their just rights against their oppressors."[32] Francis Hutcheson, whose *A System of Moral Philosophy* first appeared in 1755, had advanced a similar argument which proved very popular among the colonists, namely that "the people of any colony so increased in numbers and strength that they are sufficient by themselves for all the good ends of a political union . . . are not bound to continue in their subjection, when it is grown so much more burdensome than was expected."[33] Finally, the consent of the majority alone vindicates resistance to government, for resistance, "unless it be by a clear majority of the people, is rebellion . . . the true criterion between rebellion and reformation . . . [consisting] not in the atrociousness of the abuses to be reformed, but in the concurrence of the people in desiring reformation."[34]

The Declaration of Independence presumes, then, that a majority of the whole community constitutes *the people*, and that this majority alone has the right to decide when the rulers have violated their trust and government has been dissolved. If the phrase "consent of the governed" is applied to the origins of government, however, rather than to its ordinary operations or dissolution—an application which seems more than justified, in that the reference to the consent of the governed immediately follows the provision for the instituting of governments—the question of unanimity and the individual arises once again. Although a majority may have the right to decide whether to alter or abolish an existing government, each and every man would seem to have an individual right to decide for himself whether to join with others under a new government. In other words, once the majority has dissolved government, each man returns to the state of nature and is at liberty to give or to withhold his consent to any new government. Both John Locke and his colonial disciples argue that just governments have their foundations in the unanimous consent of the governed, and that all other governments are founded on force and fraud. Does *the people* mean one thing for the dissolution of government, and then, another for its origin? It is conceivable that in the case of the dissolution of government *the people* refers to a majority, while in the case of the institution of a new government, it refers to *all* the people.

This is a most serious objection, for, if unanimous consent alone can make a government just and also obligate the individual to the decisions of the majority under penalty of law, then under no pretense of right could those Americans who remained loyal to George III be obliged to follow the directives of the Continental Congress and the other provincial assemblies. Peter Van Schaack, for example, denied any obligation to the provincial convention of New York, and argued "that you cannot justly put me to the alternative of choosing to be a subject of Great Britain or to this State, because should I deny subjection to Great Britain, it would not follow that I must necessarily be a member of the State of New York." The source from which Van Schaack claimed to draw his political principles was the American Declaration of Independence:

> The declaration of independency proceeded upon a supposition, that the constitution under which we before lived was actually dissolved, and the British government, as such, totally annihilated here. Upon this principle, I conceive that we were reduced to a state of nature, in which the powers of government reverted to the people, who had undoubtedly a right to establish any new form of government they thought proper; that portion of his natural liberty which each individual had before surrendered to the government, being now resumed, and to which no one in society could make any claim until he incorporated himself in it.[35]

The signers of the Declaration of Independence, however, were unwilling to grant the legitimacy of the claims of Van Schaack and the other loyalists. In the case of Queens' County of New York, for example, the inhabitants—and a majority at that—refused to send deputies to the convention being held in the colony. This led Congress to claim that the inhabitants of Queens' County had "deserted the American cause," and that "those who refuse to defend their country should be excluded from its protection, and be prevented from doing it injury." The Congress then ordered the publication of the names of all who had voted contrary to its wishes, and also that all persons loyal to the American cause should refuse any and every form of trade or communication with them. Furthermore, the offenders were denied the right to travel outside the County of Queens on punishment of three months' confinement.[36]

Nor did the good people of Massachusetts grant the arguments of the western towns of the county of Berkshire to the effect that the disruption of the political connections with Britain had terminated all legitimate authority within the colony and returned men to the state of nature, where each was at liberty to give or withhold his consent as he saw fit. The provincial assembly of Massachusetts not only proclaimed itself the legitimate heir of political power, but soundly denounced the inhabitants of Berkshire as rebels. Even when the conflict between them had been resolved, the words used by the provincial assembly in announcing the concordat did not yield the point regarding the holder of lawful power: "That all riots, routs, and unlawful assemblies committed . . . within the said county of Berkshire . . . be and hereby are pardoned."[37]

On what grounds did the leaders of the Revolutionary movement reject the claims that men were at liberty to give or to withhold their personal consent to the new governments? In every case it was argued that while the Declaration of Independence dissolved the political bands between Britain and the colonies, it did not terminate the societies of men; that is, while the governments in the thirteen colonies had been dissolved, the social bonds among the colonists remained undisturbed. Men had not returned to the state of nature at all; on the contrary, they now found themselves responsible for the exercise of political power as well, for, in the words of the Declaration, "the Legislative Powers, incapable of Annihilation, have returned to the People at large for their exercise; the State remaining in the meantime exposed to all the dangers of invasions from without, and convulsions from within."

The distinction between the dissolution of government and the dissolution of society was hardly new to the colonists. John Locke in his *Second Treatise*, for example, argued that while the overturning of government by conquest involves the dissolution of both the government and society, the dissolving of government through the alteration of the legislative power or the violation of the public trust involves the dissolution of government alone. Society remains intact. This fact is critical in that if men do not return to the state of nature, they are presumably still *a people*, and a *majority* may once again place the legislative power where it wants. In the words of Locke:

> When the government is dissolved, *the people* are at liberty to *provide for themselves* by erecting a new legistative, differing from the other by the change of persons or form, or both as *they* shall find it most for *their* safety and good; for the society can never by fault of another lose the native and original right it has to preserve itself, which can only be done by a settled legislative, and a fair and impartial execution of the laws made by it.[38]

It was this very reasoning that William Whiting used in his *Address to the Inhabitants of the County of Berkshire Respecting Their Present Opposition to Civil Government.* In his refutation of the Berkshire claims, Whiting argued that, although the Declaration of Independence had destroyed the political connections with Britain, the people of Massachusetts had not returned to the state of nature, but had found it necessary to place the legislative power anew; and, because the majority of the colony had acquiesced in the establishment of the provincial assembly, the inhabitants of Berkshire were obligated to honor the decision of the majority. "No revolution in, or dissolution of, particular constitutions or forms of government, can absolve the members of the society from their allegiance to the major part of the community."[39]

The Latent Premise

There can be no doubt, then, regarding what the American Declaration of Independence means by *the people*. Whether one considers the origin, extent, or end of government, the answer is the same: the majority alone has the right of political power. The latent premise waiting to be examined, of course, is that the central concern of the Declaration is not the individual rights of men, but the rights of the majority and of the political community in general. It is within this context, then, that such issues as the unalienable rights of man and the grievances against George III ought to be examined. Furthermore, this preliminary analysis suggests a critical test for those who claim to be the legitimate heirs of the "Spirit of '76." Those heirs who base their arguments upon a single term or phrase—even one as noble as life, liberty, equiality, or the pursuit of happiness—are suspect. Only those who can make their claims consistent with the majoritarian implications of the Declaration can be legitimate heirs: all others must draw their inspiration from a source other than the American Declaration of Independence.

Notes

1. "Address at Lewistown, Illinois, August 17, 1858," in Roy P. Basler's *The Collected Works of Abraham Lincoln,* 2 vols. (New Brunswick, N.J.: Rutgers University Press, 1953), 2:547.
2. "Rufus Choate to the Main Whig State Central Committee" in Samuel Gilman Brown's *Works of Rufus Choate,* 2 vols. (Boston: Little, Brown, & Co., 1862), 1:212, 215.
3. James A. Van Osdol, *Sketches from our Constitutional History,* rev. ed. (Anderson, Ind.: Herald Publishing Co., 1935), p. 27.
4. Robert Ginsberg, "The Declaration as Rhetoric," *A Casebook on the Declaration of Independence* (New York: Crowell, 1967), p. 234 (hereafter cited as *Casebook*); Otto Vossler, "The American Argument," trans. and ed. Robert Ginsberg, in *Casebook,* p. 154; and Thad W. Tate, "The Social Contract in America, 1774-1787, Revolutionary Theory as a Conservative Instrument, " *William and Mary Quarterly,* 3d ser., 22, no. 3 (July 1965): 386.
5. Alpheus Henry Snow, *The American Philosophy of Government* (New York: G. P. Putnam's Sons, 1921), p. 40.
6. Robert G. Ingersoll, "1776. The Declaration of Independence," *The Ghosts and Other Lectures* (Washington, D.C.: C. P. Farrell, 1882), p. 169.
7. Herbert Aptheker, *The American Revolution, 1763-1783* (New York: International Publishers, 1960), p. 104.
8. Adrienne Koch, *Power, Morals and the Founding Fathers: Essays in the Interpretation of the American Enlightenment* (Ithaca, N.Y.: Great Seal Books, 1961), p. 26.
9. Richard Frothingham, *The Rise of the Republic of the United States* (Boston: Little, Brown, & Co., 1872), p. 554; Sydney George Fisher, *The Struggle for American Independence,* 2 vols. (Philadelphia: J. B. Lippincott Co., 1908), 1:460-465; and George Bancroft, *History of*

the United States, 10 vols. (Boston: Little, Brown, & Co., 1860), 8:474.

10. Edward Dumbauld, *The Declaration of Independence and What it Means Today* (Norman, Okla.: University of Oklahoma Press, 1950), p. 33.
11. I have included in the Appendix a copy of the broadside edition of the Declaration (published in Philadelphia by John Dunlap, July 4, 1776, by order of the Continental Congress). I have taken the liberty of numbering the parts and the paragraphs in the margins for convenience in referring to the text. Throughout this essay all citations to the Declaration are taken from this broadside edition unless specifically stated to the contrary.
12. [Richard Wells], *The Middle Line* (Philadelphia: Printed and Sold by Joseph Crukshank, 1775), pp. 15-16.
13. Ibid., p. 29.
14. Samuel West, *A Sermon* (Boston: Printed by John Gill, 1776), pp. 18-19.
15. Ibid., p. 27.
16. Francis Newton Thorpe, ed., *The Federal and State Constitutions, Colonial Charters, and Other Organic Laws*, 7 vols. (Washington, D.C.: U.S. Government Printing Office, 1909), 3:1686-1687.
17. Ibid., 5:3082-3083.
18. Ibid., 3:1890.
19. Ibid., 7:3813.
20. [Henry Goodricke], *Observations on Dr. Price's Theory* (York, [Eng.]: Printed by A. Ward, 1776), p. 58. Hereafter cited as *Observations*.
21. John Fletcher, *A Vindication* (Dublin: Printed for W. Whitestone, 1776), pp. 24-25.
22. H[ezekiah] Niles, ed., *Principles and Acts of the Revolution in America* (Baltimore: Printed and pub. for the ed. by W. O. Niles, 1822), p. 397.
23. William Gordon, *The History of the Rise, Progress, and Establishment of the Independence of the United States of America*, 4 vols. (London: Printed for the author, 1788), 1:427.
24. *The Triumph of the Whigs* (New-York: Printed by James Rivington, 1775), p. 8.
25. John Locke, *An ESSAY concerning the True Original Extent and End of CIVIL GOVERNMENT* (Boston: Reprinted and Sold by Edes and Gill, 1773), sec. 212 (hereafter referred to as *The Second Treatise*).
26. [Henry Goodricke], *Observations*, p. 19.
27. John Locke, *The Second Treatise*, sec. 212.
28. Francis Hutcheson, *A System of Moral Philosophy*, 2 vols. (London: Sold by A. Millar and T. Longman, 1775), 2:308 (hereafter referred to as *Moral Philosophy*).
29. [James Burgh], *Political Disquisitions*, 3 vols. (London: Printed and

sold by Robert Bell and William Woodhouse, 1774), 3:434.
30. Francis Hutcheson, *Moral Philosophy*, 2:272.
31. Samuel West, *A Sermon*, p. 27.
32. Ibid.
33. Francis Hutcheson, *Moral Philosophy*, 3:308.
34. [James Burgh], *Political Disquisitions*, 3:429-430.
35. Henry C. Van Schaack, *The Life of Peter Van Schaack* (New York: D. Appleton & Co., 1842), pp. 72-73.
36. Worthington Chauncey Ford, ed., *Journals of the Continental Congress, 1774-1789*, 34 vols. (Washington, D.C.: U.S. Government Printing Office, 1904-1937), 4:25.
37. E. Ames and A. Cheney Goodell, eds., *The Acts and Resolves, Public and Private, of the Province of Massachusetts Bay*, 21 vols. (Boston: Wright and Potter, 1869-1922), 5:932.
38. John Locke, *The Second Treatise*, sec. 220.
39. [William Whiting], *Address to the Inhabitants* (Hartford, Conn.: Printed by Watson and Goodwin, 1778), pp. 10-16, 25-26.

Appendix

[I] *In Congress, July 4, 1776.*

A DECLARATION

By the Representatives of the

UNITED STATES OF AMERICA

In General Congress Assembled.

When in the Course of human Events, it becomes necessary for one People to dissolve the Political Bands which have connected them with another, and to assume among the Powers of the Earth, the separate and equal Station to which the Laws of Nature and of Nature's God entitle them, a decent Respect to the Opinions of Mankind requires that they should declare the causes which impel them to the Separation.

[II] We hold these Truths to be self-evident, that all Men are created equal, that they are endowed by their Creator with certain unalienable Rights, that among these are Life, Liberty, and the Pursuit of Happiness—That to secure these Rights, Governments are instituted among Men, deriving their just Powers from the Consent of the Governed, that whenever any Form of Government becomes destructive of these Ends, it is the Right of the People to alter or to abolish it, and to institute new Government, laying its Foundation on such Principles, and organizing its Powers in such Form, as to them shall seem most likely to effect their Safety and Happiness. Prudence, indeed, will dictate that Governments long established should not be changed for light and transient Causes; and accordingly all Experience hath shewn, that Mankind are more disposed to suffer, while Evils are sufferable, than to right themselves by abolishing the Forms to which they are accustomed. But when a long Train of Abuses and Usurpations, pursuing invariably the same Object, evinces a Design to reduce them under absolute Despotism, it is their Right, it is their Duty, to throw off such Government, and to provide new Guards for their future Security. Such has been the patient Sufferance of these Colonies; and such is now the Necessity which constrains them to alter their former Systems of Government. The History of the present King of Great-Britain is a History of repeated Injuries and Usurpations, all having in direct Object the Establishment of an absolute Tyranny over these States. To prove this, let Facts be submitted to a candid World.

[III]

[i] He has refused his Assent to Laws, the most wholesome and necessary for the public Good.

[ii] He has forbidden his Governors to pass Laws of immediate and pressing Importance, unless suspended in their Operation till his Assent should be obtained; and when so suspended, he has utterly neglected to attend to them.

[iii] He has refused to pass other Laws for the Accommodation of large Districts of People, unless those People would relinquish the Right of Representation in the Legislature, a Right inestimable to them, and formidable to Tyrants only.

[iv] He has called together Legislative Bodies at Places unusual, uncomfortable, and distant from the Depository of their public Records, for the sole Purpose of fatiguing them into Compliance with his Measures.

[v] He has dissolved Representative Houses repeatedly, for opposing with manly Firmness his Invasions on the Rights of the People.

[vi] He has refused for a long Time, after such Dissolutions, to cause others to be elected; whereby the Legislative Powers, incapable of Annihilation, have returned to the People at large for their exercise; the State remaining in the mean time exposed to all the Dangers of Invasion from without, and Convulsions within.

[vii] He has endeavoured to prevent the Population of these States; for that Purpose obstructing the Laws for Naturalization of Foreigners; refusing to pass others to encourage their Migrations hither, and raising the Conditions of new Appropriations of Lands.

[viii] He has obstructed the Administration of Justice, by refusing his Assent to Laws for establishing Judiciary Powers.

[ix] He has made Judges dependent on his Will alone, for the Tenure of their Offices, and the Amount and Payment of their Salaries.

[x] He has erected a Multitude of new Offices, and sent hither Swarms of Officers to harass our People, and eat out their Substance.

[xi] He has kept among us, in Times of Peace, Standing Armies, without the consent of our Legislatures.

[xii] He has affected to render the Military independent of and superior to the Civil Power.

[xiii] He has combined with others to subject us to a Jurisdiction foreign to our Constitution, and unacknowledged by our Laws; giving his Assent to their Acts of pretended Legislation:

[xiv] For quartering large Bodies of Armed Troops among us:

[xv] For protecting them, by a mock Trial, from Punishment for any Murders which they should commit on the Inhabitants of these States:

[xvi] For cutting off our Trade with all Parts of the World:

[xvii] For imposing Taxes on us without our Consent:

[xviii] For depriving us, in many Cases, of the Benefits of Trial by Jury:

[xix] For transporting us beyond Seas to be tried for pretended Offenses:

[xx] For abolishing the free System of English Laws in a neighbouring Province, establishing therein an arbitrary Government, and enlarging its Boundaries, so as to render it at once an Example and fit Instrument for introducing the same absolute Rule into these Colonies:

[xxi] For taking away our Charters, abolishing our most valuable Laws, and altering fundamentally the Forms of our Governments:

[xxii] For suspending our own Legislatures, and declaring themselves invested with Power to legislate for us in all Cases whatsoever.

[xxiii] He has abdicated Government here by declaring us out of his Protection and waging War against us.

[xxiv] He has plundered our Seas, ravaged our Coasts, burnt our Towns, and destroyed the Lives of our People.

[xxv] He is, at this Time, transporting large Armies of foreign Mercenaries to compleat the Works of Death, Desolution, and Tyranny, already begun with circumstances of Cruelty and Per-

fidy, scarcely paralleled in the most barbarous Ages, and totally unworthy the Head of a civilized Nation.

[xxvi] He has constrained our fellow Citizens taken Captive on the high Seas to bear Arms against their Country, to become the Executioners of their Friends and Brethren, or to fall themselves by their Hands.

[xxvii] He has excited domestic Insurrections amongst us, and has endeavoured to bring on the Inhabitants of our Frontiers, the merciless Indian Savages, whose known Rule of Warfare, is an undistinguished Destruction of all Ages, Sexes and Conditions.

[IV]

[1] In every stage of these Oppressions we have Petitioned for Redress in the most humble Terms: Our repeated Petitions have been answered only by repeated Injury. A Prince, whose Character is thus marked by every act which may define a Tyrant, is unfit to be the Ruler of a free People.

[2] Nor have we been wanting in Attentions to our British Brethren. We have warned them from Time to Time of Attempts by their Legislature to extend an unwarrantable Jurisdiction over us. We have reminded them of the Circumstances of our Emigration and Settlement here. We have appealed to their native Justice and Magnanimity, and we have conjured them by the Ties of our common Kindred to disavow these Usurpations, which, would inevitably interrupt our Connections and Correspondence. They too have been deaf to the Voice of Justice and of Consanguinity. We must, therefore, acquiesce in the Necessity, which denounces our Separation, and hold them, as we hold the rest of Mankind, Enemies in War, in Peace, Friends.

[3] We, therefore, the Representatives of the UNITED STATES OF AMERICA, in GENERAL CONGRESS, Assembled, appealing to the Supreme Judge of the World for the Rectitude of our Intentions, do, in the Name, and by Authority of the good People of these Colonies, solemnly Publish and Declare, That these United Colonies are, and of Right ought to be, FREE AND INDEPENDENT STATES; that they are absolved from all Allegiance to the British Crown, and that all political Connection between them and the State of Great-Britain, is and ought to be totally dissolved; and that as FREE AND INDEPENDENT STATES, they have full Power to levy War, conclude Peace, contract Alliances, establish Commerce, and to do all other Acts and Things which INDEPENDENT STATES may of right do. And for the support of this Declaration, with a firm Reliance on the Protection of divine Providence, we mutually pledge to each other our Lives, our Fortunes, and our sacred Honor.

Signed by ORDER AND IN BEHALF *of the* CONGRESS,
JOHN HANCOCK, PRESIDENT.
ATTEST.
Charles Thomson, Secretary.

[PHILADELPHIA: PRINTED by JOHN DUNLAP.]

[3]

POPULAR CONSENT AND POPULAR CONTROL
1776–1789

—DONALD S. LUTZ

From the very beginning the people settling on American shores had used and developed institutions based on consent. The letters patent to Sir Humphrey Gilbert from Queen Elizabeth in 1578 declared that all Englishmen emigrating under the terms of the patent "shall and may have, and enjoy all the privileges of free denizens, and within our allegiance: any law custom or usage to the contrary notwithstanding." Sir Walter Raleigh's charter in 1584, as well as the charters in 1606 issued to the Virginia Company of Plymouth and to the Virginia Company of London, contained the same provision. The colonists used these words to justify the establishment of local systems of self-government. In 1619 the Virginia Company summoned the first representative assembly in America, and the burgesses were elected by virtually universal manhood suffrage.

The Puritans, in the Mayflower Compact of 1620, laid the groundwork for an equally liberal political system; and while the rest of New England came under policies more restrictive with respect to suffrage, they too established local self-rule, and the pattern was set. The monarch watched with dismay as these colonial legislatures became more and more independent. The combination of colonial obstinance and English preoccupation with events elsewhere resulted in the colonies setting up sophisticated and effective institutions for self-government that were largely independent of interference from the mother country. When Parliament tried to regain control of the colonies through the mercantilist-inspired Navigation Acts, Stamp Act, etc. of the middle 1700s, the Americans possessed both the will to resist and the means to organize that resistance.

With the Declaration of Independence these colonial institutions were quickly transformed into republican government. This much every high school Civics student knows. What is not widely appreciated is that Americans in 1776 had just transformed *republican government* from a phrase with negative connotations into one with positive implications; that there was no settled meaning for the term but, instead, several competing definitions; and that between 1776 and 1789 the dominant political theory shifted through several of these definitions. In short, the political theory underlying the Declaration of Independence of 1776 is not the same as that underlying the American Constitution of 1787. The theory of consent implicit in the Declaration not only does not naturally evolve into the Constitution but in some important respects is contradictory to it.

As late as the end of 1775 the term *republic* had primarily negative connotations. Worse: to be branded a *republican* in the 1750s was equivalent to being termed a socialist in the 1950s, insofar as it implied a radical, that is, someone outside the dominant political culture and not to be trusted because of his subversive tendencies. John Adams used *republic* in its pejorative sense until January of 1776, when, barely five months before the writing of the Declaration of Independence, he became the first major American thinker to use the term in a favorable sense, as a form of government to be sought after. Even then it is significant to note that not one of the eighteen state constitutions adopted between 1776 and 1787 used the term, and the federal Constitution adopted in 1789 was the first major public document in American history to use *republic,* although it does not appear until Article IV, where the states are guaranteed a republican form of government without there being given any hint as to how that form of government is to be identified.

During the 1700s, the English dictionary definition of *republic* was, "A commonwealth without a king", thus distinguishing between only two forms of government: monarchies and republics. In 1775, though the colonies had local self-government (or home rule), with representative legislative assemblies elected by way of a more or less liberal franchise, second houses which served as Senates, well-established judiciaries, governors (with Connecticut and Rhode Island actually electing theirs), and limitations on these governors (even those who represented the Crown); although the colonies were so provided, only a few individuals would have been willing to label these governments *republican* because to do so meant, by definition, breaking with the monarchy.

Furthermore, there was a strong tendency to identify republican government with democracy. Democracy continued to be defined in the classic Greek sense until the end of the eighteenth century. This entailed the notion of an entire populace gathering in one place to vote as a body on political matters. Aristotle had equated democracy with anarchy on the basis of Greek experience, and American political leaders continued to make the same identification; thus, to favor a republic was in some quarters to imply support for anarchy. In England those opposing the Whigs continually attempted to fasten on them the label *republican*, so as to sully them with unsavory implications. The Tories in America, supporters of a continued allegiance to the English king, attempted to vilify American Whigs in the same fashion. As a result, from the moment American intellectuals adopted the term *republicanism* in 1776 to describe the theory underlying the Revolution, they strove to distinguish a republic from a democracy in an effort to make the former term acceptable to Americans. In no sense was the American Revolution fought to create a democracy, although the Constitution does embody the democratic principle in several key institutions. Rather it was fought to establish a republic, something other than a monarchy.

Generally speaking, then, republican government was something between a monarchy and a democracy. It included popular consent, the rule of law, and representation; but these principles could support a variety of political institutions. Within these general theoretical confines the Americans of the 1780s fought bitter and historically important political battles which set the institutional patterns for the next two centuries. The variety of ideas advanced was astonishing; but these ideas tended to cluster around three competing theories of republican government, each undergirded by a different theory of consent. Perhaps the best way to outline the major positions, as well as to set the scene for the discussion that follows, is to consider three prominent definitions of republican government.

Some Definitions of Republican Government

American political theory in 1776 was dominated by a view of politics partly borrowed from England and partly derived from American practice. It was known as Whig political theory. Central to Whiggism was the notion of a mixed regime, or "mixed" government, in which the democratic, aristocratic, and monarchic principles were blended and balanced in a single government. A popularly elected lower house embodied the first principle, an upper house based upon wealth embodied the second, and the king embodied the third. This traditional Whig perspective automatically resulted in serious ambiguity once the colonies declared independence, since the monarchic principle was removed from the blend. An elected executive made a reasonable substitute; but, as we shall see, the Whigs were reluctant to identify elected governors with the full role of monarch.

John Adams was, and would continue to be, the most successful thinker in the traditional Whig mode. With his usual care in the use of words, he provides a definition for republican government from this point of view:

> Whenever I use the word *republic* with approbation, I mean a government in which the people have collectively, or by representation, an essential share in the sovereignty. [John Adams in a letter to Samuel Adams, 18 October 1790.]

Traditional Whigs were immediately challenged by more radical Whigs who, while accepting most Whig assumptions, agitated for broader popular control of government. There were forces in almost every state pressing to strengthen any institution based on popular consent. These forces arose partly from the century-and-a-half-old American practice whereby town and county government were often in the hand of local majorities. Besides, in the course of fighting the Revolution, principles and symbols were developed to justify the split with England; and this rhetoric was easily applied against those in power in the new states. The debt owed to the common yeomen for providing the backbone of the war effort gave added force to yeomen demands for more self-rule.

Samuel Adams's response to John Adams's definition is instructive because it underlines the central disagreement between radical Whigs like himself and the more traditional Whigs:

> Is not the *whole* sovereignty, my friend, essentially in the people? . . . [I]s it not the uncontrollable, essential right of the people to amend and alter, or annul their constitution and frame a new one . . . [to hold] annual or biennial elections . . . and by empowering their own representatives to impeach the greatest officers of the state before the Senate . . . ? [Samuel Adams in a letter to John Adams, 20 November 1790.]

This is not a mere quibbling over words. If the people at large only share in sovereignty, as John Adams has it, then the actions of government are only partially subject to the consent of the people; whereas, if sovereignty resides entirely in the people, then we have complete popular control where, at least in theory, no governmental action can take place without the consent of the citizens. John Adams is trying to preserve some power for the few who own wealth in the form of property. Thus, he is using the traditional Whig notion of balancing the interests of the few and the many by requiring the explicit consent of both groups. Samuel Adams, a more radical Whig of the sort that temporarily became dominant during the Revolutionary War years, is arguing for a more egalitarian notion of consent, as well as a more direct form whereby governmental action is so tied to popular consent that representatives essentially "mirror" the general will.

A third major definition was advanced by the Federalists. Our example, written by the Federalist generally conceded to have been most influential in putting meaning into the federal Constitution, if not in drawing up the document itself, is by Madison. It was not considered to be controversial by the Federalists:

> . . . A government which derives all its powers directly *or indirectly* from the great body of the people, and is administered by persons holding their offices for a limited period, *or during good behavior* . . . .It is essential to such government that it be derived from the great body of the society, not from an inconsiderable portion, or a favored class of it."[1] [Emphasis added]

Despite its emphasis on the people at large and its apparent similarity to the radical Whig definition attributed to Samuel Adams, there are subtle but important shifts in the Federalist formulation that constitute a backing away from the directness of the radical Whig notion of republican government. The Federalists, while placing sovereignty completely in the people, nevertheless insisted that institutions be so designed that consent would be given very indirectly. Such an approach resulted in representatives being elected by the many, who yet subsequently remained relatively free from direct influence by the people and not very much subject to pressures reflecting popular demands; for example, the popularly elected House was to be checked by several other institutions which, although still resting on popular consent, were progressively less directly tied to that consent. At the same time, the Federalists were not merely moving back to the more conservative consent theory of the traditional Whigs like John Adams; they were not balancing the many with the few. Rather, they were facing squarely the reality that Americans were a diverse, heterogeneous people subject to numerous factions; and they attempted to prevent the rights of any minority from being trampled upon (excluding, of course, Blacks and Indians). Also, Federalist emphasis on individuals and their interests ran contrary to the Whig emphasis on community. The Whigs wished to balance the many with the few, not because they had different interests but because the majority of the people and the major part of the wealth were involved when one uncovered the common interests of an organic community. For the Whigs, consent came from the community; for the Federalists, it came from individuals organized in subgroups within the community.

The issues separating traditional Whigs from radical Whigs, and Whigs from Federalists, were real and important. What permitted our Founding Fathers to get along at all was a common adherence to the popular control of government, that is, government by consent. What divided them were the questions: 1. Who is to give consent? 2. To whom is consent to be given? 3. What constitutes giving consent? and 4. Over what range of issues can consent be given, or, on what issues should consent be permanently withheld? Each definition of *republic* implied a different set of institutions, which in turn implied a different theory of consent with its own answers to these four questions.

The Meaning of Consent

It is fruitful to begin an in-depth analysis of consent with the English theorist, the judicious Richard Hooker, since he first enunciates the essential ambiguity with which we still live. Writing in the

1590s, although his work was not published until after his death in 1662, Hooker identified two forms of consent:

> Whatsoever hath been after in free and voluntary manner condescended unto, whether by express consent, whereof positive laws are witnesses, or else by silent allowance famously notified through custom reaching beyond the memory of man. . . .[2]

The first form, *express consent,* implies a free, conscious, and deliberate decision; the second, *silent allowance,* indicates acquiescence which may not be free, conscious, or deliberate. Hooker recognized that only occasionally, if ever, are human activities the result of express consent, but rather activity generally conforms to the pathways earlier set by ourselves or others—what we term custom or tradition.

It is worth contrasting John Locke and Hooker on this point since Locke's *tacit consent* might at first glance appear similar to Hooker's *silent allowance*. The difference is instructive. Locke recognized that, even if one generation does "sign a contract," giving express consent to the setting up of a society and government, this consent in no way binds future generations. Locke had to contend with the obvious fact that if there had been an historical contract it was so distant in time that it was "beyond the memory of man."

To solve the problem he argued that when a man reaches adulthood he can either stay where he is and thus give tacit consent to the ongoing society and government, or he can migrate to another place, thus expressing dissent. The only other possibility is to rebel; but, as Locke pointed out, the majority is the greater force and will invariably win, so that to rebel is basically futile.[3] On the other hand, if one is in the majority there is by definition no need to rebel since society and government will follow one's will as it follows the will of the majority. The only practicable alternatives, then, are migration or submission; and submission amounts to giving tacit consent. Perhaps migration was easier or less costly in Locke's England of 1669, but the only two avenues of dissent he offers are both quite forbidding. Furthermore, by American standards of the 1780s, tacit consent ends by being no consent at all.

The problem runs deeper than this. Americans in the 1770s and 1780s recognized four levels of consent which we shall call: *societal consent, governmental consent, agency consent,* and *programmatic consent*. Locke considers only the first two, whereas the Americans, while not using these terms, developed institutions for all four. In so doing they made important contributions toward a complete theory of consent.

Societal consent entails approval of a way of life, of an entire social system. When men establish a society they are in effect consenting to a culture, a set of mores, a series of rules for carrying on social intercourse. Locke argued that there were two contracts, the first of which established a society; and he reasoned that this first contract required unanimity, a fact which means that no individual is bound to a society to which he has not explicitly consented as an individual.

The second contract, according to Locke, established a government; and this occurred through the action of a majority. At this level men agreed to a set of procedural rules and institutions for collective decision-making. Such is *governmental consent*. Once having given societal consent, says Locke, they are then bound by the majority when it comes to governmental consent.[4] It is important to realize that at this level Locke did not see consent as resulting from individual action per se. Contrary to the notion that men cannot be bound by decisions of a government to which they have not *personally* consented, Locke argued that governmental consent comes from the majority and not the individual. Consenting to live in the society has bound the individual to the will of the majority in future political action; and that is why migration—withdrawing individual consent from society—is the only real alternative. It must be emphasized that Americans during the period under study generally understood consent as residing in the majority, although there was also another tradition which tried to put certain matters beyond the power of the majority. Even though the rise of the Federalists brought a strong assumption of individualism into American political culture, they, as well as the American tradition before them, emphasized the majority as the source of consent rather than individuals as such.

In a real sense the nature of this second agreement is closely allied with the first, since the type of political system erected will tend to reflect social and cultural presuppositions. It is for this reason, probably, that Locke shied away from openly advocating a particular form of government. The majority could establish any form it wished. While his readers in seventeenth century England naturally tended to imagine some type of monarchy with a powerful Parliament, another people with a different set of suppositions could prefer other institutional arrangements without doing violence to Locke's theory.

Agency consent refers to approval for those who shall be the primary actors in the decision-making institutions established by governmental consent—the elected or appointed agents. Agency consent is important only if collective decisions are going to be made indirectly by a specialized group of people rather than directly by the entire populace. Locke can be read to mean that the second contract simultaneously designates the governing agents, so that when we speak of a government falling it refers to both turning the agents out of office and simultaneously reordering the institutions of government. Such a tortured interpretation creates more problems than it solves; and it is certain that neither the English nor the Americans ever practiced such an interpretation.

Programmatic consent refers to permission for specific policies and laws. Locke is almost completely silent here although a staightforward inference can be drawn to the effect that until government breaks the contract by threatening our lives and/or our property we end up acquiescing to all of its actions. By failing either to emigrate or rebel when a bill is passed we are giving tacit consent to the legislation. Locke creates not so much a theory of consent as he establishes a theory of dissent; that is, he emphasizes the conditions under which dissent is permissible rather than indicating the conditions for giving positive programmatic consent.

At this point it becomes clear that Richard Hooker's notion of consent is both more positive and more complete. He speaks of express consent producing "positive laws." Consent for Hooker requires positive action rather than mere acquiescence; and it implies that every piece of legislation requires specific consent. Even "custom reaching beyond the memory of man" is "condescended unto" only in a free and voluntary manner. Hooker's position might be termed the *direct sense of consent*, whereas Locke's might be termed the *indirect sense*. Generally speaking, the direct sense argues that positive permission constitutes consent, whereas the indirect sense holds that acquiescence is sufficient for expressing consent. The first sense is also direct in that it implies a meeting between the two agents, whereas in Locke's sense consent can be given without the actors ever seeing each other.

There are many definitions of consent but only two need to be considered for the purposes of the discussion to follow. The first we shall call *indirect consent*:

> Indirect consent is evident whenever one acts in such a fashion as he or she knows, or is assumed to know, will not prevent another from acting.

As noted before, this is really a theory of dissent, since simply staying out of the way constitutes consent and the alternatives are to attempt to block another's action or to emigrate and hence prevent the other's action from affecting the migrant.

The second type we shall term *direct consent*:

> Direct consent is evident whenever the right of one person to act in a certain way is conditional upon another's having expressed the wish that he or she act that way.[5]

In this case there is a direct link between the two actors in the form of *explicit permission* given *before* action can take place.

If we were clever enough and had the time, we could probably come up with complicated definitions representing various degrees between these two definitions, but it is probably sufficient to distinguish here between a theory that relies upon institutions of *dissent* producing indirect consent, from a theory which tends to rely upon institutions requiring direct, positive permission before government can act. It should now be apparent that Madison's definition of republican government implies a less direct sense of consent than does that of Samuel Adams.

We turn now to an examination of developments between 1776 and 1789 and later. With reference to each of the four levels of consent—societal consent, governmental consent, agency consent, and programmatic consent—we shall ask: Who gives consent? To whom is consent given? What constitutes the giving of consent? And what is the range of consent?

Because there were thousands of pamphlets, letters, sermons, and similar materials written during the period in question, it is possible to support any perceived trend simply by being selective in the materials chosen. Here the serious and widely held ideas are separated from the peripheral by focusing on the state constitutions that were written during that era. In each constitution there were "frozen" the balance of forces of its specific time and place, only the most important alternatives being represented. There will be no attempt to argue that those writing constitutions between 1776 and 1789 were consciously developing a theory of consent. Any student of the period recognizes the extent to which institutions and theories were responses to experiences and events rather than logical imperatives. Our approach is to abstract trends and connections from the constitutions by using internal evidence as well as the writing surrounding these documents. We will be attempting to uncover the assumptions that underlie thinking during the period and to link these assumptions together.

The men who wrote constitutions in America between 1776 and 1789 made three significant contributions to consent theory. First, they developed institutions for all four levels of consent. Second, they moved from a relatively indirect to a more direct form of consent at each level. Third, they tried to develop coherence by making all four levels approximately equal in directness. As we shall see, they failed with respect to programmatic consent. The Federalists made consent less direct with respect to some institutions than to others, with the result that the American Constitution does not embody a coherent consent doctrine. Instead, it blends two theories; and although historically we have brought agency consent back to its former strength, we have failed to do so with programmatic consent. The Americans of that period worked their way through to a relatively coherent and sophisticated theory of consent, but failed to completely exploit and retain the implications of their elaboration. Even with this failure their contributions still represent a high point in the history of consent theory.

The General Use of CONSENT in Early State Constitutions

Between January 1, 1776 and the adoption of the American Constitution in 1789 the original thirteen states, plus Vermont, wrote and adopted a total of eighteen constitutions. Between the adoption of the American Constitution and 1800, these same states drafted seven more constitutions which were joined by the maiden constitutions of Kentucky (1792) and Tennessee (1796). Altogether, then, Americans during the last quarter of the eighteenth century wrote and adopted twenty-eight constitutions, not including the ones that were drafted, debated extensively, and then rejected.[6] It was an extraordinary period of constitution writing. We will focus on the first eighteen documents, since they contain the essential developments leading from Whig to Federalist political theory, although a brief contrast with those written after 1789 will also prove instructive.

The first eighteen constitutions can be divided into two "waves" of constitution writing. The first wave took place within a year after the writing of the Declaration of Independence. With the war swirling around the writers there was a pressing need for effective government in order to carry on hostilities; and there was also little time to debate the niceties of political theory. Consequently, the first state constitutions were little different from their respective colonial charters to which they, in fact, bore a strong resemblance, except for the universal emasculating of the executive power which represented the Crown under most charters; indeed, Rhode Island and Connecticut simply readopted their colonial charters from the 1660s, and Massachusetts did not bother to go through the formalities, being content, instead, to live under the 1725 charter as if nothing had changed. The only exceptions were Pennsylvania and Vermont.

The first constitution in the second wave was the 1777 constitution of New York. That state was heavily occupied by the British forces early in the war, and one consequence was that those who were writing the state constitution were kept constantly on the move, meeting whenever and wherever they could. Ironically this circumstance seems to have given them more time to think matters through, since their constitution was the first to exemplify a number of trends that were to become common only during the second wave of constitution making. Most notable was the fact that they began the resurrection of the executive branch, putting it "in harness" with the legislature in a manner which we find familiar today. There also was increased concern for popular control over the process of constitution making. The first half dozen state constitutions were written and ratified by the state legislatures, the 1776 constitution of Delaware being the first drafted by a convention elected expressly for that purpose. In New York the state legislature also felt that:

> The right of framing, creating or new modeling civil government, is,

> and ought to be in the people . . . . Doubts have arisen, whether this Congress are invested with sufficient power and authority to frame and institute such new form of internal government and police.

A body elected with such express authority ended by framing the New York constitution; and such practice became standard. It was not until the Massachusetts constitution of 1780, however, that the document was written by a special convention *and* submitted to the people for ratification—a practice which was to become standard as a result of the second wave of constitution making.

It is interesting to observe how the term *consent* was used in the first eighteen constitutions. An initial count shows that it appears 93 times in these documents, or an average of 5.2 times per constitution. The frequency varies by document as also does the context. In general, the term becomes much more common during the second wave of constitution writing, as is evident in Table 1. Consent is used 57 times in the six constitutions of the second wave, or an average of 9.5 mentions per document; whereas, the first twelve constitutions mention the word only 36 times, or an average of 3.0 per document. If frequency of use means anything, then framers during the second wave of constitution drafting were much more concerned with the idea than during the first wave. The use of the word falls off during the third wave in the 1790s, when the Federalists brought some state constitutions more in line with their principles. The seven constitutions written in states which can be compared to the earlier periods use *consent* 34 times, or an average of 4.9 per document. Again it would appear that the Federalists displayed a more moderate attachment to the concept than the radical Whigs of the late 1770s and 1780s.

Frequently, those who wrote constitutions used the words *assent* and *concur* to describe a relationship similar to that described by *consent*. In a few instances, the context implies that they are being used as a stylistic alternative for consent; but in other contexts they imply something a little different. Usually these two alternative words are used to describe the relationship between the two legislative houses or between the executive and the upper house. Almost never are they used to describe the relationship between citizens and government, or in bills of rights. The context of their usage is also typically one in which action has already occurred and some sort of ratification is required. As we shall see, the term consent for a while came more and more to mean a positive form of control as exemplified in the definition of direct consent. Concur and assent often seem to imply something closer to what we defined as indirect consent. Such a distinction in the use of words can never be proved; in fact, it can easily be challenged, since the state constitutions of that era were often as susceptible to multiple interpretations as is our federal Constitution. Nevertheless, an examination of the use of these words reveals an interesting pattern. Assent is used about equally in the early, middle, and late documents, but concur, which is used only once or twice in the early constitutions, becomes prominent in the third wave of constitution making, where it is used 21 times in comparison to 5 times for assent. The tendency for these two words to be used in describing relationships within and between governmental institutions, coupled with the frequency of use implies that such relationships became more important during the second wave of constitution writing than during the first, and almost as important as consent relationships in the third wave. In fact, the Federalists were very much concerned with such things as checks and balances and the relationships between the two houses and between the legislature and the executive. The increase in the use of concur especially reflects this concern. The Federalist Papers express the concern of the authors over unbridled majorities, and their related concern for institutional complexity to impede factions from taking over government. The shift from the radical Whig emphasis on public policy accurately reflecting popular will to the Federalist emphasis on downgrading that relationship through the interposition of balanced and mutually interdependent institutions is clearly summarized in the figures of Table 1. It is worth pointing out that during the second wave the alternative words were used about as often per constitution as in the more Federalist documents of the third wave. The major difference is the substantial decline in the use of consent itself.

The increased frequency of the word consent during the second wave represents not only greater interest in the concept, but also a more diverse usage. In the first twelve constitutions, consent is often mentioned in the context of a people or king establishing the body politic. At best, this represents an appreciation of what was earlier termed *societal consent*, and perhaps *governmental consent* as well. Later constitutions speak of consent being given by and through a variety of actors. Likewise, there is a greater diversity in terms of what constitutes giving consent, to whom it is given, and the range of issues covered. What is important to understand now is the extent to which all four levels of consent defined earlier, including agency consent and programmatic consent, are covered by the state constitutions of the 1780s.

The passages where consent is used make up a major part of the evidence in the following analysis. In addition, certain institutions which were discussed without the word being used are nonetheless relevant to our problem; for example, this term does not appear in any discussion of elections, even though they are generally agreed to be consent-giving situations. Whenever a constitutional provision establishes a relationship where one's ability to act is dependent on another's behavior, it is thus a candidate for consideration as a consent-giving institution.

TABLE 1

The Frequency of the Words CONSENT, and ASSENT *or* CONCUR, *in State Constitutions*

Constitutions	*No. of times* CONSENT *used*	*No. of times* ASSENT *or* CONCUR *used*	*Combined usage*
1. 1725 Mass.	1	3	4
2. 1776 N.H.	1	1	2
3. 1776 S.C.	5	1	6
4. 1776 Va.	5	1	6
5. 1776 N.J.	1	1	2
6. 1776 Md.	6	4	10
7. 1776 Dela.	2	0	2
8. 1776 R.I.	2	0	2
9. 1776 Conn.	0	0	0
10. 1776 Penna.	6	2	8
11. 1776 N.C.	3	0	3
12. 1777 Ga.	4	0	4
Subtotals	36	13	49
AVERAGES	3.0	1.1	4.1
13. 1777 N.Y.	9	5	14
14. 1777 Vt.	6	2	8
15. 1778 S.C.	10	4	14
16. 1780 Mass.	13	3	16
17. 1784 N.H.	12	4	16
18. 1786 Vt.	7	2	9
Subtotals	57	20	77
AVERAGES	9.5	3.3	12.8
19. 1789 Ga.	0	2	2
20. 1790 S.C.	1	3	4
21. 1790 Penna.	5	2	7
22. 1792 Dela.	7	8	15
23. 1792 N.H.	12	3	15
24. 1793 Vt.	4	3	7
25. 1798 Ga.	5	5	10
Subtotals	34	26	60
AVERAGES	4.9	3.7	8.6
Overall Totals	127	59	186
AVERAGES	5.0	2.4	7.4

Societal Consent

Because societal consent is so difficult to separate from governmental consent the distinction is usually overlooked. John Locke made the distinction between the contract-establishing society, which requires unanimity, and the contract-establishing government, which requires only a majority. Regardless of whether such contracts were ever made, Locke put his finger on an important idea.

Beginning with the Mayflower Compact Americans had the habit of turning their major political documents into cultural statements as well, statements which outlined the basic presuppositions of social and cultural activity in that particular society; for example, the Mayflower Compact reveals a religious people devoted to "radical" Protestant theology, dedicated to deliberative social and political processes, and determined to measure human activity in terms of whether and how it contributes to the well-being of the entire community. Because these cultural presuppositions have obvious political consequences, and because students of politics tend to read only the major political documents, it is easy to pass these off as mere political assumptions. In fact, the Mayflower Compact establishes no particular government, nor do the other major documents generally celebrated as political statements, such as the Fundamental Orders of Connecticut, the Massachusetts Body of Liberties, the Virginia Bill of Rights, and the Declaration of Independence. In each case we have an outline of the major socio-cultural norms and not a design for government. Even the colonial documents explicitly designed to establish a form of government, always begin by laying down the basic socio-cultural norms. The Rhode Island Charter of 1663 is quite typical in that it begins with a dedication to "sober, serious and religious intentions" as forming the basis for a "livlie experiment" in the establishment of civil government. In a sense we have people defining themselves culturally, but we also have something else that will require a short discussion of Whig political theory.

As mentioned earlier, until at least 1776 and for a time thereafter, Whig political thinking was dominant in America. Central to their view of the political process was the belief that the executive was the primary source of tyranny, with the legislature standing between the executive (monarch) and the people as protector.[7] Furthermore, since members of the legislature returned to the people-at-large after sitting in session, the legislature was not really distinguished from the people. Lastly, their notion of limited government differed from our own essentially Federalist position. Whereas the Federalist idea was to limit government by withholding large portions of political power from it altogether, the Whigs assumed government potentially had all political power except for those specific powers which were withheld. There were two primary ways to withhold power. One was to state the fundamental socio-cultural presuppositions and thus dramatize for citizen and legislator alike that some things ought not be tampered with. The second was to include a bill of rights. The early bills of rights are interesting precisely because they lack specificity. Rather, they are general statements. The bill of rights to the 1776 Virginia Constitution provides an excellent example for the reader who wishes to pursue this matter further. In effect, both methods place those in government on formal notice that: 1. there is a socio-cultural consensus arising from the general consent of the people; and 2. the results of societal consent are not to be tampered with by a government resulting from governmental consent. Occasionally, the framers would go a little further by explicitly stating at the end of the constitution that certain portions are not subject to amendment; for example, the New Jersey constitution of 1776 requires that everyone elected to office take an oath not to repeal four sections of the constitution—annual elections, trial by jury, and two sections dealing in detail with religion and the exercise of conscience. In short, then, societal consent is represented in the state constitutions negatively through prohibitions on the use of governmental power. In later constitutions the socio-cultural statement tends to appear less frequently at the beginning of the document and wind up in the bill of rights. At the same time the prohibitions become stronger.

The prescriptive nature of the bills of rights is reflected in the first wave of constitution making by the use of the word *ought*; for example, in the 1776 Pennsylvania constitution the bill of rights reads along these lines: "Freedom of the press *ought* not be restrained . . . standing armies *ought* not be kept up . . .," etc. Gradually we see the prescriptive *ought* and *should* replaced by the stronger and legally binding *shall*, *will*, and *do*.[8] In all 25 state constitutions the word shall is used when describing the formal instruments of government in the body of the document, but not until the twelfth constitution written during the era, or the 1777 Georgia constitution, do we find a bill of rights using only shall to the exclusion of the weaker ought. At the same time that bills of rights become stronger in language they become longer and more detailed. The effect is to move closer and closer to the Federalist position by withholding larger and larger portions of power.

Whereas the states continued to rely heavily on expanding bills of rights to adjust to cultural change, the federal Constitution embodied such confidence in the deliberative process producing legislation commensurate with general socio-cultural presuppositions that it allowed societal consent to be given through normal legislative processes as well as through the amending process; thus, the political system becomes the "digestive tract" for cultural change.

It is interesting to compare the development of state constitutions with that of the federal Constitution. The federal system has been able to adjust to cultural change largely through normal legislation, although the 13th, 14th, 15th, 18th, 19th, 21st, and 26th amendments all reflect cultural shifts. The state constitutions, on the other hand, have often tended to pile amendment upon amendment—some amendments shifting governmental consent to be sure, but many others simply being passed to adjust to what is euphemistically called "changing times." It must be emphasized that in explicitly dealing with cultural change by placing societal consent in their constitutions, Americans of the 1770s, 1780s, and 1790s made a significant contribution to consent theory.

Governmental Consent

As mentioned earlier, not until the Massachusetts constitution of 1780, the fifteenth adopted during the era, was a constitution framed by a convention specifically elected for the purpose and then ratified by a referendum of the people at large. In effect, the early practice amounted to the members of the legislature consenting to their own agency in writing the document, and then giving governmental consent by adopting it themselves. Such a practice was entirely in keeping with the Whig political assumptions of the time. Since the legislature was not looked upon as government per se but as a buffer between the people and the government (Crown), and not distinguishable from the people as such, the majority of the legislature was viewed as automatically representing the interests of the homogeneous community at large. The frequent and often bitter factional disputes within the legislatures during the Revolutionary War soon undercut any such set of assumptions to the extent they were still believed by Americans. Instead, the Americans found themselves increasingly divided on important political matters, only one of which was the mutual animosity and suspicion between the wealthier, more cosmopolitan cities and towns along the coast and the smaller, more locally oriented towns of the interior. The legislatures reflected these splits but with varying accuracy. The outcome of bitter legislative debate was more likely to reflect the balance of forces within the legislature than the pattern of sentiment in the general population, since, for instance, legislatures invariably overrepresented the older, coastal towns. With the absence of the Crown, and the state executives reduced to creatures of the legislature, the legislature *became* government, the potential source of tyranny, instead of a buffer against an arbitrary executive.

The response to the new perceptions was a logical and straightforward one. If the legislature could not be trusted any longer automatically to reflect the interests of the majority of the community, then the community must become more directly involved with important matters of government. Since representatives giving themselves consent to write fundamental documents which establish procedural rules and institutions for collective decision-making seemed improper if not illogical, the move to constitutional conventions and popular ratification was a natural one.

This shift, although logical and dramatic in its implications, did not proceed in a straightforward fashion. Like many developments in America at that time the process was fitful, indirect, and often unconscious. There were so many competing ideas involving so many people that the development could hardly be viewed as being directed by some commonly held architectonic plan. Nevertheless, the end result was theoretically coherent. The people at large gave direct consent to agents chosen specifically to write a constitution, who then submitted the document to the people for direct approval. There is no question that this represents a shift from an indirect sense of consent, where people elected legislators with no idea of what they would subsequently write into a constitution—indeed, with no idea whether they would even write one—to a consistently direct form of consent. The development is a fundamental one for what Americans would come to regard as republican government.

The amendment procedure became equally direct. The constitutions written during 1776 and 1777 are notable for generally having no provisions for amendment; and, of the two constitutions which mention amendment, Maryland's required only that a majority of two consecutive sessions of the legislature consent, while Delaware's specified approximately two-thirds of the legislature. Although the Massachusetts constitution of 1780 was the first to be written by a separate convention *and* ratified by the people, the 1784 constitution of New Hampshire was the first document to *require* such a procedure for amendment.

Massachusetts and New Hampshire also required that amendments, as well as new constitutions, be ratified by two-thirds of the voters. The use of an extraordinary majority, although not always required, has become common in America and was used with the Federal Constitution. To require an extraordinary majority is consistent with requiring a separate convention of constitutional changes in that it implies a clear distinction between constitutional matters and ordinary legislation. This distinction is a fundamental one for American political theory. Ironically, the distinction may also have served to justify a less direct form of consent for ordinary legislation after the 1780s, a matter to which we shall turn after our discussion of agency consent.

Agency Consent

Agency consent is obviously given through elections. Strictly speaking, there is no "indirect" form of election unless you count the "list system" sometimes used in Europe where voters vote for a party list rather than specific candidates. There are, however, ways in which elections may be used to give only indirect consent for governmental agents. The electoral college, for example, is an instance in which direct consent is given to electors to choose an executive and indirect consent is given to whomever they choose. When we vote for a President we give indirect consent to the cabinet members he appoints.

There is another sense in which agency consent may be indirect. This is seen in cases in which someone else votes for us under the assumption that another person will speak for us. In such a circumstance the other person's vote is his direct consent and our indirect consent at the same time.

The matter of agency consent is thus reduced to two important considerations: 1. What proportion of decision-makers are directly elected as opposed to appointed or indirectly elected? and 2. How broadly is suffrage defined?

With respect to the first consideration, the lower house was in all cases elected, as was the upper house, although in the first wave of constitutions Georgia and Pennsylvania had no upper house and Maryland, the only exception, used an electoral college for the Senate; thus, there is little basis for discerning anything but a constant, direct form of agency consent.

A more interesting case is the election of the executive. During the first wave of constitution making only Massachusetts and New Hampshire elected their executives directly. The rest gave indirect agency consent by having the legislature elect them. As mentioned earlier, the executive was reduced in the early state documents to a rather inconsequential figure, so that his not being elected directly was perhaps no great problem. With the beginning of the second wave of constitutions (New York, 1777), however, which resurrected the executive and once again gave him an important role in government, the governor was with only two exceptions now popularly elected. Georgia and South Carolina continued to be the most conservative states in this respect, as in others, by continuing to have the executive elected by the legislature. In all other states the people gave direct agency consent, thus linking increased popular control with increased power in a logical and consistent manner.

Of course the legislature was still extremely powerful in the 1780s, especially the lower house. Consistent with the executive pattern, the most powerful organ of government, that is, the legislature, was subjected to the most direct popular control. Popular control of the legislature will be traced in detail in considering programmatic consent below.

The federal Constitution utilized indirect consent for both the executive and upper house in contrast with the clear, consistent trend evolved in the state documents. In this respect more than any other the Federalists are open to the charge of attempting to remove government from popular control. As we shall see in our concluding discussion, this charge is in some respects misplaced, although there is an element of truth in it.

The matter of suffrage is complex and, in some respects, controversial. It was once fashionable to argue that suffrage restrictions in the 1700s excluded most people from the polls and resulted in government by the few. If this were true, all our discussion of direct agency consent would be essentially meaningless. As it turns out, the preponderance of evidence does not support this elitist interpretation.[9]

Most of the colonies, especially those founded by Protestant dissenters, had a very broad suffrage in their early years. During the last half of the seventeenth century restrictions were placed on the suffrage which tended to confine the vote to free, white, at least twenty-one year old, native-born Protestant males, with property. Ironically, the New England colonies which were settled by religious dissenters and the first to use virtually universal manhood suffrage, introduced both religious tests and property qualifications in order to retain control of their communities now increasingly inhabited by landless immigrants of other faiths. If the religious oligarchs wished to preserve the purity of their communities, the Stuart monarchs, restored in 1660, wished to enhance efficiency, honesty, and harmony in colonial government for commercial as well as political reasons. Most charters were rewritten to suit the Crown, and suffrage restrictions designed to enhance stability became typical.

The restrictions were not ended with the demise of the Stuarts in the Glorious Revolution of 1688. William and Mary had no reason to extend suffrage. The mercantile interests dominating Parliament had a stake in prosperous, well-run colonies; and property requirements were commensurate with the Whig notion that persons giving consent through elections should demonstrate a stake in the community as well as display virtues of self-sufficiency through ownership of land. It was also congruent with the Whig attachment to virtual representation whereby those not owning property were assumed to be spoken for by those who did. This in turn was supported by the assumption of a homogeneous society, with a community of interests. In such a community it made little difference who voted or ran for office since everyone's interests were indistinguishable from those of the entire community.

Although there was considerable variety in detail, by 1776 the typical requirement was a freehold with a value of about 50 pounds.

This was not an inconsiderable sum, since the best estimates indicate 50 pounds could support a family of seven for a year at the subsistence level, 100 pounds would support a family in decency, and 150 pounds provide real comfort. A new house of average size on an average lot cost around 100 pounds. At the same time, considerable research indicates that a little over 40 percent of all adult males owned farms large enough to qualify for the polls; another 10 percent were artisans with the equivalent in real property; 10 percent were large landowners; and another 5 to 10 percent were upper middle class professionals, businessmen, merchants, etc., with possessions totalling between 500 and 1,000 pounds each. Altogether upwards of 70 percent of all males could qualify for the polls, the percentage being lower in the South but approaching 90 percent in some northern areas. Furthermore, there is considerable evidence that the property requirement was frequently ignored, so that any man of good character was allowed to vote in the community where he was known.

Between 1776 and 1789 there was a general easing of property requirements for suffrage. While no state completely separated property from voting, there was a trend to replace the freeholding requirement with the much less stringent taxpaying qualification. While it is difficult to assess the overall impact of such changes, in Pennsylvania, which was one of the six states to drop the freehold test, 90 percent of all males qualified. Vermont went further and, in effect, instituted universal adult, male suffrage. In New Hampshire, Delaware, Georgia, and North Carolina taxpaying suffrage virtually equaled universal manhood suffrage. New Jersey left a loophole which even permitted women to vote.

At the same time, religious oaths were almost completely eliminated; viva voce voting was gradually replaced by the secret ballot; and polling places were moved and increased in number to reduce sharply the average distance a voter had to travel—an important consideration in those days. It is impossible to sort out the relative impact of these various developments on voting. There was the additional factor of the war experience and democratic rhetoric tending to break down the pre-war "politics of deference" and replace it with an ethic of citizen equality. Certainly the Whig doctrine of virtual representation was seriously undermined. Whereas a 40 percent turnout was typical before the Revolution, 65 percent was more typical in the post-war years, and in some regions 80 percent and above was common.

These figures pertain to state-wide elections. With minor exceptions the suffrage requirements for the many town, county, and local elections were considerably less. As one might expect, the turnout for these elections was even higher.

The easing of property requirements reflected not only the demise of virtual representation but also the strong demands for voting equality. The second and third waves of state constitutions contain increasingly stringent apportionment sections to equalize voting district populations. Often the word *equal* is explicitly used when discussing districts for the lower house. The revolution clearly had brought in many average citizens jealous of their right to give agency consent.

Although there was some desire at the Constitutional Convention to reinstate more rigid property qualifications, the Federalists wisely decided to leave suffrage requirements to the states. Although several theoretical justifications were advanced in support of this move, the arguments of political expediency and practicality were apparently decisive. There was no hope of reversing the trend to broader suffrage without setting the wrath of the many against the proposed federal Constitution. The United States Constitution thus confirmed and underwrote the lessening of suffrage requirements by leaving the matter to the states. In at least this respect the Federalists did not impede the development toward more direct agency consent and greater popular control of government.

Programmatic Consent

To what extent, if any, is it possible for the people at large to give direct consent for specific pieces of legislation? Strictly speaking, this is possible only if the people gather in a stadium or similar place and pass the legislation themselves. Direct democracy (as this would be) is ruled out by definition when a political system uses elected representatives for collective decision-making; thus, giving agency consent rules out the possibility of direct programmatic consent in a strict sense.

At the same time there are degrees of indirectness. A basic trend between 1776 and 1789 was the attempt to make representatives "mirror" the wishes of the people. An excellent statement describing the mirror theory of representation can be found in The Essex Result written by citizens in Essex County to criticize the proposed Massachusetts Constitution of 1778:

> Representatives should have the same views, and interests with the people at large. They should think, feel, and act like them, and in fine, should be an exact miniature of their constituents. They should be (if we may use the expression) the whole body politic, with all its property, rights, and priviledges, reduced to a smaller scale, every part being diminished in just proportion. [10]

Impossible as it sounds, there was a serious and reasonably successful effort to create legislatures which would produce legislation indistinguishable from that passed by the people at large gathered in one room. There were three mechanisms available for furthering this end: frequent elections, reduced requirements for office-holding, and petitions and instructions to the legislature.

Whig doctrine, presupposing common community interests, urged the election of men possessing demonstrated ability and virtue. The first wave of constitutions often stated baldly that "persons most noted for wisdom and virtue" were to be chosen. Once in office these representatives were on their own to protect the best interests of the community and were essentially left alone until the next election. The more frequent the elections, therefore, the more control citizens would have over legislation. The idea was that dissatisfaction with specific items of legislation would be displayed by voting the "scoundrels" out of office. Thus, in theory, representatives would remain tuned to popular sentiment to ensure reelection. Empirical research on modern legislatures casts doubt on the efficacy of this theory, although conditions in the 1770s and 1780s may have made it a more effective tactic then.

However well it worked, only one of the first twenty-five state constitutions gave more than a one-year term of office to members of the lower house. The branch of the legislature designed to embody the democratic principle was kept close to the people. The upper house, which was not supposed to reflect the democratic principle, tended to have one-year terms as well. At the same time the Federalists were writing a six-year term for senators into the federal Constitution, only Delaware (a three-year term), Maryland (a five-year term), and Virginia (a four-year term) diverged from the one-year norm. Shortly after the United States Constitution was adopted Georgia, Pennsylvania, and South Carolina created either three- or four-year terms in each case, but in 1798 Georgia went back to a one-year term. Once again the Federalist document broke with the general constitutional practice. While it is true that there was a constitutional precedent for the Federalist design of an indirectly elected Senate with staggered terms of more than one year (Maryland), just as there was a precedent for electing the executive indirectly, in each of these instances the precedent was the exception to general constitutional practice. Even in the Federalist era of the 1790s, an indirectly elected Senate with a term longer than one year did not become predominant. The important trend in the first twenty-five state constitutions in this regard was that there was no serious departure from the early Whig practice of keeping both houses of the legislature close to the people through frequent elections.

Virtually all states had property requirements for holding office. Some, like Massachusetts, New Hampshire, Virginia, and Delaware, had property requirements similar to those for voting and which thus were quite minimal. Rhode Island and Pennsylvania had no property requirement at all. New Jersey and Maryland had the stiffest requirement: 500 pounds of taxable property to run for the lower house, 1,000 pounds to run for the upper house, and 5,000 pounds to run for governor. Even the stiffest requirement still left at least 30 percent of the adult male population eligible for the lower house.

The common practice of requiring more property of candidates for the upper house was consistent with the Whig notion of balancing numbers in the lower house with wealth and property in the upper house, of balancing the democratic principle with the aristocratic principle. There were no major trends away from a property requirement or toward higher sums during the years in question. In fact, few states materially altered the sums, although those that did do so reduced the requirement a little. Georgia required a 250 pound freehold for the lower house in 1777 and the same sum in 1789 and 1798. Keeping it the same actually amounted to a reduction, given currency changes and increased per capita income over the twenty-one years.

Reducing property requirements for officeholding would have aided programmatic consent by permitting a broader cross-section of the population to run for office. If legislatures were more representative of all classes presumably they would produce legislation closer to what was desired by the people, since then the legislature would be a truer microcosm. There was also the important fact that the towns in the interior were poorer and, in general, had few wealthy people, if any. The property requirement thus also had geographical implications.

That property requirements were only slightly reduced and not eliminated does not reflect a negative attitude toward popular programmatic consent (although there was quite a bit of this) as much as it reflects the fact that such a reduction was probably not necessary to produce the desired change in legislative personnel. Recent historical research, especially that of Jackson Turner Main, has revealed a considerable shift in the kind of men elected to state legislatures during the period.[11] The shift was away from an elite toward very representative bodies. In several states the percentage of farmers in the legislature is almost identical with their percentage in the general population—and here we are speaking not of large landowners but of owners of moderately-sized farms close to what Jefferson held as the ideal size.

The same social revolution was being felt in the upper houses as well. There the wealthy from "established families" provided only about a fourth of the membership. Fewer than one in five senators was an educated man. As a result, and contrary to Whig theory, senators did not tend to defend particular economic interests, but became almost indistinguishable from the members of the lower houses, except that they were somewhat more conservative. This reality forced a reevaluation of the bicameral system and the reasons for having one. The Federalists at the Constitutional Convention made the Senate represent the states as units and the House represent numbers of people. This shift in justification was one of the great compromises at the Convention; and it represented an imaginative solution to one of the most serious political problems facing it. The need for a new justification for bicameralism and the nature of the problem solved by the compromise go far toward explaining the break with earlier constitutional practices. The difference in scale required solutions that transcended the old framework of discussion over the roles of the upper houses and the executive.

In sum, the social upheaval engendered by the Revolution made a reduction in property requirements for officeholding a moot point in some respects. The voters had ceased to confine themselves to electing an elite and were instead selecting men like themselves.

Americans during the Revolutionary era had frequent elections and legislatures that were reasonably representative of the general population despite property requirements for officeholding; but they did not let the matter rest there. In addition, we find numerous passages proclaiming the right of citizens to petition or instruct their representatives; for example, consider the following:

> The people have a right, in an orderly and peaceable manner, to assemble and consult upon the common good; *give instructions to their representatives*, and to request of the legislative body, by the way of addresses, petitions, or remonstrances, redress of the wrongs done them, and of the grievances they suffer.[12] [Emphasis added.]

Maryland, in 1776, was the first state to break with the Whig practice of electing virtuous men and leaving them on their own. A series of four sections in its Declaration of Rights at the beginning of the constitution left no doubt that in the future the legislature would be expected to perform in a manner similar to that later outlined in the Essex Result. Pennsylvania and North Carolina followed suit in the same year and couched the right to instruct in almost the same words as cited above from the Massachusetts document. This formulation would be found in a majority of the documents in the second and third waves of constitutional drafting.

These were not mere paper promises. The people did press their demands vigorously and often, whether their state constitution urged them to do so or not. Feverish lobbying on the part of citizens, coupled with the fact that legislators elected after 1776 came more from the middle class, resulted in very responsive legislatures; indeed, they were at times too responsive for some persons. The Federalists professed horror at the legislative "flip-flops" in response to rapidly shifting popular demands.

In addition to policy instability, overresponsiveness coupled with legislative supremacy pushed the legislature into judicial and executive matters where it did not belong. Records show state legislatures as late as 1792 freely vacating judicial proceedings, suspending judicial actions, annulling or modifying judgments, cancelling executions, reopening controversies, authorizing appeals, granting exemptions from standing legislation, and expounding the law for pending cases. Add to these facts the shifting legislation regarding paper money, dissolved marriages, and the release of particular individuals from debt or taxes, and it is at least understandable how and why the Federalists discovered "majority tyranny" and elevated it to a problem of major theoretical importance. The Americans had succeeded in developing institutions for making programmatic consent as direct as it has ever been. Ironically, the attempt to make programmatic consent direct at the state level gave the Federalists reason to oppose such directness in the federal Constitution.

Framers of state constitutions were themselves apprehensive. Constitutions in the 1780s began to insist upon a separation of powers as a means of reducing legislative incursions into executive and judicial areas. Furthermore, in their bills of rights they specifically prohibited some of the more extreme behavior; for example, section XVII of the 1786 Vermont constitution reflects earlier abuse when it states, "No person ought, in any case, or in any time, be declared guilty of treason or felony by the Legislature;" yet, this same constitution retains the provision that guarantees the right of the people to instruct the legislature, as also do most of the others that came after it. There were constitutional attempts to minimize the more unsavory results, but no attempt at the state level to reject the general principle of direct popular consent.

The Federalist Response

Did the Federalists attempt to remove the national government from popular control? The evidence indicates that the answer to this question is: "No." The federal Constitution limits the power of the national government and thereby keeps as much power as possible at the state and local level where there *is* considerable popular control. Delegates to the Constitutional Convention often spoke in terms of keeping government close to the people when they opposed making government too centralized. In reading Madison's notes to the Convention, we are looking back over a history that includes a bitter struggle over states' rights, and we are often induced to read that struggle into Convention proceedings. It is more likely that the delegates were speaking the plain truth. Most government in the 1780s took place at the state and local level and there many delegates wished it to remain. To the extent that this demand was met, government remained in the hands of the people, regardless of what institutions were adopted at the national level.

Even at the national level the powers expressly delegated were centered in the House of Representatives. This fact is often overlooked. Discussion at the Convention, as well as political discourse in other forums, clearly indicate that three powers were considered most important for national government: the taxing power, the power of the purse, and the power to declare war. All three were given to the House of Representatives, the one branch which was popularly elected and embodied popular control in the most direct sense. Furthermore, there was no attempt to restrict the suffrage in any way. On the contrary, the first paragraph of section 2, Article I of the United States Constitution specifies that when it comes to electing members to the House "electors in each state shall have the qualifications requisite for electors of the most numerous branch of the state legislature." As shown earlier, these qualifications were for the most part quite minimal. This provision is also interesting because delegates to the Continental Congress had consistently been elected by the state legislatures. There was, then, no constitutional precedent for having national representatives elected directly by the people. If the Federalists had followed the constitutional practice of the day they would have had the House of Representatives elected by the state legislatures instead of directly by the people. In this context, having the United States Senate elected by the state legislatures was not unusual, whereas electing the House directly was unusual. This departure from constitutional practice thus ends by being a move toward greater directness. In the *Federalist Papers* James Madison repeated a view commonly held at the Convention, namely, that the new national government must "be erected on the great body of the people." Having the most powerful branch in the national government elected directly by an electorate defined by the very liberal state suffrage requirements for the lower house, does not indicate a desire on the part of the Federalists to remove the national government from popular control.

A better question—and one that gets to the heart of the matter—is the following: Did the Federalists attempt to make popular control less direct than had come to be the case at the state level? The answer to this question is probably:"Yes." The trends embodied in the state constitutions written between 1776 and 1789 reflect a shift in the definition of republican government from one in which the people collectively *share* in sovereignty (John Adams's definition) to one where the *whole* sovereignty rests essentially in the people (Samuel Adams's definition). Furthermore, there was a serious attempt to make all four levels of consent so direct as to approach "a government by its citizens in mass, acting directly, according to rules established by the majority." Madison's definition of republican government, on the other hand, explicitly permits indirect as well as direct consent. His definition is disarmingly honest in describing the institutions designed by the Federalists.

Article VII of the federal Constitution required that the document be ratified by conventions elected for that purpose in at least nine states. The states, on the other hand, had developed the practice of submitting proposed constitutions directly to the people in a constitutional referendum. Specifications for amending the national document are even less direct, which means that societal and governmental consent cannot be given directly by the people in a referendum as had become common in the states. Furthermore, Congress can specify whether the proposed amendment shall be sent to the legislatures or to conventions. If it goes to the legislatures, popular control is less direct than if it goes to conventions, because it is then subject to all the vagaries inherent in programmatic consent discussed earlier. Only once has the first method come close to being used when the school prayer issue fell two legislatures short of the two-thirds required to call a national convention. Congress has, with only one exception, sent amendments it proposed to the state legislatures rather than state conventions, with the result that the first two levels of consent have been consistently less direct at the national level than at the state level.

With respect to agency consent, as discussed earlier, the Federalist document is distinguished by providing that the upper house and the executive be elected indirectly, contrary to the practice evolved in the state constitutions. The broad suffrage defined by the state documents is retained for the House, but made irrelevant for the other institutions at the national level. Both the House and the Senate have longer terms of office than was universally the case at the state level. The net effect, regardless of intent, is also to place programmatic consent on a different footing; indeed, there is no mention in the United States Constitution of that frequently repeated right of the people to instruct their representatives. There is a revival at the Constitutional Convention of the Whig doctrine of electing more virtuous men to office, but this was not the decisive reason for removing the Senate from direct agency consent. The Federalists had the Senate represent the interests of the states rather than those of the wealthy; but, regardless of the justification, the effect was still to make agency and programmatic consent less direct.

The problem here is to distinguish what the Federalists ended up actually doing from what they intended to do. Did the Federalists *intend* to enshrine a form of republican government which would embody less direct consent than that found in state constitutions? The question perhaps can never be answered with certainty. There is no doubt that the Federalists had to solve crucial political problems not encountered at the state level. The need to create a government that would act directly on individual citizens and at the same time protect the political reality of existing states created a novel situation not faced squarely before. The need for an effective national government was also paramount, given the experiences under the Articles of Confederation. At the same time senators and the President could have been popularly elected as they are today without interfering with either of these goals.

There is evidence that Federalists and non-Federalists alike were very concerned with the dangers of unbridled majorities acting directly on legislatures. The policy instability and legislative encroachment on the other branches discussed earlier were not uncommon in the early state legislatures and were well-known to the Federalists. Furthermore, there were many examples of civil unrest to which Madison and others often referred. North Carolina and Massachusetts had both experienced serious insurrection. There were similar threats in other states. Madison and Hamilton considered the control of factional violence as their main theoretical goal in the *Federalist Papers*. (See, for example, the opening sentence in *Federalist* 10). The tyranny of a majority was the specific form of factional control which most interested them. It is tempting to draw the obvious conclusion that these preoccupations reflect an intent on their part to remove decision making from direct involvement by the majority.

Regardless of intent, it is probably accurate to characterize their institutions in the following manner. The Federalists did not remove government from popular control but based it ultimately on the consent of the majority. The involvement of the majority in decision making was made less direct, not to prevent majority rule but to slow it down. The President and Supreme Court were very weak in the early years. There was doubt that they could survive in the face of the very powerful Congress. At best, they could delay congressional will and force the decision making process to be more deliberate. The mixing of direct with indirect consent can be viewed as a series of stumbling blocks in the path of the majority, forcing it to be more careful, less capricious, and thereby hopefully eliminating most of the problems experienced with the state legislatures operating under conditions of direct consent. Government would still be by majority rule; but the combination of an extended, diverse republic which would impede the formation of majorities, and the institutions of delay which were placed in the path of Congress would screen out majorities based on emotion or short-term interests. The result, it was hoped, would be a more stable and effective government.

Critics of the American political system have often contended that it moves too slowly, is responsive to interest groups rather than to the majority, and is often not responsive at all. It is possible that the Federalist framers, if they were around today, would agree with this assessment. After all, they did not foresee the President and the Supreme Court becoming so powerful vis-à-vis Congress. They had no concept of mass-based political parties and the myriad of highly organized interest groups. They had no experience with legislatures having highly organized committee systems tightly controlled through a seniority system. As can be expected, the institutions they designed have evolved, expanded and also been undercut in ways independent of their predictions and intentions.

The Federalists chose a version of republican government different from that which had developed during the 1780s. Their version may or may not be explained and justified by the conditions and problems they faced. What is clear is that the Federalists broke with the definition of republican government embodied in state constitutions. The political forces behind these documents eventually forced changes in the federal Constitution in the direction of more direct agency consent with respect to the President and the Senate; but part of the Federalist legacy is a doctrine of consent with contradictions and ambiguities. Americans continue today to debate how direct majority consent should be, and the Constitution embodies different answers for different institutions. It is not unfair to say that American contributions to consent theory through the design of consent-giving institutions reached a peak in the 1780s but were deflected by the United States Constitution and consequently never brought to fruition. At the same time, leaving theoretical niceties aside, recognition must be given for the ability of the Federalists effectively to link theory with practice. The alternative may not have been a coherent consent theory but political chaos.

Some Implications for Today

The year 1789 found two different theories of consent integral to American politics. At the state level Whig political theory, with its emphasis on direct control by local majorities and the primacy of the community over the individual, was dominant. At the national level Federalism, with its emphasis on indirect control by a broader majority of individuals attached to interests rather than to communities, was dominant. We have lived with the bifurcation in consent theory ever since, with those defending the Whig perspective finding themselves an ever-declining minority.

Political movements with strong Whig overtones have recurred in American history. William Jennings Bryan is one prominent example of a leader who challenged the dominant political theory in the name of localism, community, and political virtue. Although periodically resurgent, Whig political theory has continued to diminish as an effective political force. The great increase in the power of national government which began with Lincoln's presidency has relegated state and local government more and more to a subordinate role. Urbanization, increased levels of education, the advent of mass media, the drastic decline in the rural population, a high level of mobility, and increased involvement in world affairs have all tended to reinforce individualism over community, rationalism over religiosity and traditional virtue, and cosmopolitanism over localism. Although still a sizeable minority, the numbers supporting this dissenting political culture have diminished to the point where neither major party really needs to speak for it, or so they feel. When the Republicans speak of local control they mean reactivation of state politics and local interests, but not state government controlled from below. There is no real commitment to majority rule at the local level, and the Republican propensity for supporting business interests is not a Whig trait. The Democracts support legislation that often aids members of this minority, but their strong preference for big national government and the prominence of cosmopolitan intellectuals among its leaders are not Whig traits. Also, Democrats are definitely not localist in their orientation but nationalist and internationalist.

Does it make any difference? Apparently so; for, while the coherent doctrine of Whiggism has relatively few adherents, the idea of rule by direct consent of majorities in local communities has increasingly been expressed in recent years by a very diverse set of groups. George Wallace has found fertile ground for his appeals against distant government and "big business." His arguments on behalf of "the little people" echo earlier populist leaders, even though there is no strong evidence of a commitment to majority rule. Many of the so-called new Left during the 1960s had the same symbolic enemies in the form of "big business" and distant government. Except for the more violent extremist elements, these dissidents made themselves most obnoxious by insisting on the application of direct consent to every aspect of life. Their efforts at "retribalization," considered frivolous by many, expressed a longing for community that many Whigs of the 1780s would have found congenial, although the "feathers" and "beads" might have led our forefathers to view them "with rifles in hand."

The youth movement seems to have run its course, but polls show continued disaffection among both young and old, allegiance to both major parties continues to decline, many whites continue to press for local control of schools, and many blacks find themselves arguing for the same local control. In the light of the history of American political thought, all of these trends may be viewed as conservative in nature, perhaps even reactionary. The legacy of our bifurcated doctrine of consent is still with us. The unresolved question of how strongly we are committed to direct popular control of government continues to agitate our politics. The battle between Congress and the President over control of foreign policy is just one facet of this agitation. The matter of campaign finances is another.

After three hundred and fifty years of living with political institutions based upon popular consent, Americans are still struggling to adapt these institutions to the changes history thrusts upon them. If historical circumstances have changed, the basic, recurring American impulse to retain institutions based upon popular consent remains. Most Americans appear to support the relatively indirect form of consent taught us by the Federalists. Many, on the other hand, still press for a political system based upon consent that is as popular and as direct as possible. Some Americans view the latter with suspicion; but the more extreme version of the commitment to government by consent does not flow from any foreign ideology. Instead, it is indigenous to our shores. Indeed, the best expression of commitment to popular consent and popular control of government is not to be found overseas, but in the theory and institutions evolved in America during the 1780s.

Notes

1. Jacob E. Cooke, ed., *The Federalist* (Cleveland: The World Publishing Company, 1967), p. 251.
2. "The Laws of Ecclesiastical Polity" in *The Works of Mr. Richard Hooker in Eight Books*, 3 vols. (London, 1821), vol. 3, bk. 8, p. 242.
3. Cf. John Locke, *The Second Treatise on Government* (Indianapolis: Bobbs-Merrill Company, 1952), p. 55.
4. Locke, p. 55.
5. John P. Plamenatz, *Consent, Freedom, and Political Obligation* (2d. ed.; London: Oxford University Press, 1968), p. 4.
6. All colonial charters and early state constitutions can be found printed in Francis N. Thorpe, ed., *The Federal and State Constitutions, Colonial Charters, and other Organic Laws of the United States of America*, 7 vols. (Washington, D.C., 1907). All information regarding the early state constitutions is based on Thorpe.
7. All discussion of Whig political theory is based upon three excellent books: Bernard Bailyn, *The Ideological Origins of the American Revolution* (Cambridge: Harvard University Press, 1967); H. Trevor Colbourn, *The Lamp of Experience* (Chapel Hill: University of North Carolina Press, 1965); and Gordon S. Wood, *The Creation of the American Republic, 1776–1787* (Chapel Hill: University of North Carolina Press, 1969).
8. For this idea I am indebted to Professor Charles S. Hyneman through private correspondence.
9. There are a number of useful books detailing suffrage during the era. The most readable and in some ways the most informative is Marchette Chute, *The First Liberty: A History of the Right to Vote in America, 1619–1850* (New York: E. P. Dutton and Co., Inc., 1971). Another excellent treatment is that by Chilton Williamson, *American Suffrage from*

Property to Democracy, 1760–1860 (Princeton: Princeton University Press, 1968).

10. Reproduced in Oscar Handlin and Mary Handlin, eds., *The Popular Sources of Political Authority* (Cambridge: Harvard University Press, 1966), p. 341.
11. Three books by Jackson Turner Main are relevant. See his *The Social Structure of Revolutionary America* (Madison: University of Wisconsin Press, 1965); *The Upper House in Revolutionary America* (Madison: University of Wisconsin Press, 1967); and *Political Parties Before the Constitution* (Chapel Hill: University of North Carolina Press, 1973).
12. Thorpe, p. 1892.

[4]

THE SEPARATION OF POWERS

—GEORGE W. CAREY

Considerable controversy surrounds the matter of precisely what political principles underlie our Constitution. We can say without fear of contradiction, however, that its framers were convinced beyond any doubt that a separation of powers was absolutely necessary for a just and stable political order; indeed, a separation of powers ranks as the most fundamental of our constitutional principles. We need only to look at the Constitution to see this. Article I begins, "All legislative powers herein granted shall be vested in a Congress of the United States. . . ." The very first sentence of Article II reads, "The executive power shall be vested in a President of the United States of America." Likewise, Article III starts with these words, "The judicial power of the United States shall be vested in one Supreme Court, and in such inferior courts as the Congress may from time to time ordain and establish." Although at no point does the Constitution expressly declare a separation of powers to be a fundamental and inviolable principle upon which the Constitution was constructed, organization of the Constitution, principally the first three articles, and also its phraseology, leave no doubt that such was indeed the case.

Any uncertainty regarding the doctrine of a separation of powers being absolutely essential will be dispelled by looking at the "external" evidence; that is, evidence other than the federal Constitution itself. In every state constitution at the time of its adoption, there was a provision for a separation of powers in one form or another. The Massachusetts constitution of 1780, while reflecting a sentiment general to the states, is probably the most emphatic in this respect. Article XXX of the first part of this constitution, entitled "A Declaration of the Rights of the Inhabitants of the Commonwealth of Massachusetts," declares:

> In the government of this Commonwealth, the legislative department shall never exercise the executive and judicial powers, or either of them: The executive shall never exercise the legislative and judicial powers, or either of them: The judicial shall never exercise the legislative and executive powers, or either of them: to the end it may be a government of laws and of men.[1]

Interesting also is Jefferson's Draft Constitution for Virginia in which he stipulated, "The Legislative, Executive, and Judiciary offices shall be kept forever separate and no person exercising the one shall be capable of appointment to the others, or to either of them;"[2] and in his *Notes on Virginia* he listed among the defects of the existing Virginia constitution the fact that "all the powers of government, legislative, executive, and judiciary, result to the legislative body. The concentrating of these in the same hands is precisely the definition of despotic government." Immediately following this comes his oft-quoted statement, "It will be no alleviation that these powers will be exercised by a plurality of hands and not by a single one. One hundred and seventy-three despots would surely be as oppressive as one."[3] In the same vein, John Adams said, "A despotism is a government in which the three divisions of power, the legislative, executive and judicial, are all vested in one man;"[4] and in *Federalist* 47 Publius writes:

> No political truth is certainly of greater intrinsic value, or is stamped with the authority of more enlightened patrons of liberty, than that . . . the accumulation of all powers, legislative, executive, and judiciary, in the same hands, whether of one, a few, or many, and whether hereditary, self-appointed, or elective, may justly be pronounced the very definition of tyranny.[5]

To the foregoing we can add that three of the last four of the original thirteen states to ratify the Constitution (Virginia, North Carolina, and Rhode Island), despite the built-in provision for a separation of powers, submitted amendments to the Constitution which read in part, "The legislative, executive, and judiciary powers of Government should be separate and distinct. . . ."[6] This provision, despite its endorsement by these states, never received serious consideration in the first Congress, which winnowed through similar proposals in formulating what today is known as the Bill of Rights. We may reasonably surmise that the members of the first Congress felt such a stipulation to be redundant. Though beyond any question it is redundant, we should not overlook the fact that this recommendation is a manifestation of a deep and abiding concern to insure a separation of powers at the national level.

Bearing in mind the indisputable fact that a separation of powers was most certainly regarded as an indispensable principle at the time of the founding of our national government, we will examine its historical development and the practical and theoretical problems surrounding its implementation during the formative period.

Development of the Doctrine: Aristotle to Montesquieu

The contributions of ancient political theory to the doctrine of a separation of powers are indirect. Their nature and their tangential relation to the doctrine is probably best seen in the works of Aristotle. His notion of a mixed government contains the first traces of the more modern conception of a separation of powers, and it was carried over in refined form into the Middle Ages. One of the central themes of Aristotelian thought is moderation, or, stated in other words, an emphasis on the mean to the exclusion of the extremes. This is reflected in his *Politics*, wherein he speaks of the various constitutional orders founded on the principle of rule by one, the few, or the many. In this connection, he writes:

> The words constitution and government have the same meaning, and the government, which is the supreme authority of states, must be in the hands of one, or of a few, or of the many. The true forms of government, therefore, are those in which the one, or the few, or the many, govern with a view to the common interest; but governments which rule with a view to the private interest, whether of the one, or of the few, or of the many, are perversions.[7]

He continues to identify the pure forms as monarchy (rule by one);

aristocracy (rule by the few); and constitutional government (rule by the many). The perverted forms are, respectively, tyranny, oligarchy, and democracy.

It is precisely when the rulers—whether one, a few, or the many—begin to rule in their own interest that we may say the form is perverted; and, when perverted, there can be no justice. The ruler or rulers will promote their own interests at the expense of others and, what is more, they will also be the judges of their own causes and actions. More specifically, when speaking of the weaknesses and other reasons for the instability of democracies and oligarchies, Aristotle lays great stress on the fact that these regimes tend to develop excesses. In democracies, the people will be motivated by an insatiable desire for equality, which can only come about through a common leveling. The people will consider this strict notion of equality to represent justice; but, Aristotle contends, justice also involves the conception of proportionality or ratio, of treating unlike things differently, so that strict equality, in the democratic sense, lacks much of embodying the whole of justice. By the same token an oligarchy will be motivated by a conception of justice which holds that only inequality should be the guiding principle; hence, it will operate to treat equal things unequally, a principle which also is a perversion of justice. The many are bound to suffer as much in this system as the few will in a democracy.

We can readily see from these considerations that a perverted form of government embodies all that later doctrines of a separation of powers were intended to eliminate, and that one of the root causes of the perversion is the concentration of the powers of government in the hands of individuals who—as, by definition, is the case in oligarchies and democracies—have similar or identical interests. One of the questions, therefore, that Aristotle had to face was this: How is it possible to have rule by the many without a perverted government? In other words, how is it possible to have *constitutional* government? How can such a government resist the impulses that lead to its corrupted form: democracy? In answer, Aristotle hit upon a "solution" that was later to form the essence of a conception of mixed government. He wrote:

> It is manifest that the best political community is formed by citizens of the middle class, and that those states are likely to be well-

> administered, in which the middle class is large, and stronger if possible than both the other classes, or at any rate than either singly; for the addition of the middle class turns the scale, and prevents either of the extremes from being dominant. Great then is the good fortune of a state in which the citizens have a moderate and sufficient property; for where some possess much, and the others nothing, there may arise an extreme democracy, or a pure oligarchy; or a tyranny may grow out of either extreme — either out of the most rampant democracy, or out of an oligarchy; but it is not so likely to arise out of the middle constitutions and those akin to them.[8]

The middle class should "moderate" the claims of both the rich and the poor, a result quite in keeping with Aristotle's more general philosophy of moderation, or the mean. What if a state lacked a large enough middle class to perform this moderating role? In such a case, Aristotle advised that the ruling authorities govern as if there were a large middle class, in order to insure the necessary moderation in their policies for the entire society.

From Aristotle's formulation of the problem and the conditions necessary for its solution, it is not difficult to see what course the development of the doctrine would take. The simplest way to insure adherence to the mean would be to devise a system with three bodies or assemblies, each representing a different class: the royal, the aristocratic, and the democratic. By vesting each of these bodies with the total powers (that is, functions) of government, and specifying that the concurrence of each is necessary for any governmental decision, one could be assured that any decision or output from such a system would, indeed, be moderate. It remained for Polybius, in the second century B.C., to present with greater precision a theory which related economic and social class to governmental institutions.

The contributions of the ancients were twofold. They dwelt on the need for moderation and the avoidance of extremes. They exalted the notion of justice which embodied so many of the ideals associated with the later development of this doctrine. Their theory of mixed government also envisaged a structure of government institutions which would best conform to a separation of powers based upon a tripartite division of functions. We must take care, however, to note in what important ways the doctrine of a mixed government did not contribute to, or differed markedly from, the pure doctrine we have set forth. In the first place, and perhaps most importantly, the idea of a separation of functions was almost totally absent. Each branch of the government, representing a distinct social class, was to participate in all governmental functions. In the second place, and in large part because of this fact, there was no provision to preclude the overlap of personnel in the exercise of functions, once the different branches had come to some agreement concerning specific policies. Finally, because these branches reflected a threefold class distinction, with elements of royalty, aristocracy, and democracy, a mixed government in the form of a king, an aristocratic assembly, and a popular assembly (such as that in England in the seventeenth century) could be obtained with relative ease; but such a division could not very well be accommodated to an independent judicial branch. Moreover, as we shall see, this fact became one of the major theoretical difficulties in the development of the modern doctrine.

Although the theory of a mixed government was known to the Middle Ages, at which time it formed the basis for theories designed to limit the power of a monarch, little theoretical advance was made toward the development of our modern doctrine. One of the major reasons for this failure, we may surmise, was the early medieval conception of law which prevailed well into the fourteenth century. Commenting on this conception of the law and of its relation to the doctrine of a separation of powers, Professor Vile writes:

> The connection between modern theories of law and sovereignty and the emergence of the concepts of the legislative, executive and judicial function of government is very close. The idea of an autonomous 'legislative power' is dependent upon the emergence of the idea that law could be *made* by human agency, that there was a real power to make law, to legislate. In the early medieval period this idea of making law by human agency was subordinated to the view that law was a fixed unchanging pattern of divinely-inspired custom, which could be applied and interpreted by man, but not *changed* by him. In so far as men were concerned with 'legislation' they were in fact declaring the law, clarifying what the law really was, not creating it. Legislation was in fact part of the judicial procedure.[9]

Although there is some dispute about precisely what time this conception of law began to wane, the writings of Marsilius of Padua in the fourteenth century certainly introduced new conceptions which help us understand the emergence of the doctrine of a separation of powers. The character of law changed from that of either a received or a given, wherein the details for its application remained to be worked out through political agencies, to that of positive commands made independent of a background of "higher" law. In this new context, Marsilius saw that a distinction must be made between commanding, or *enacting*, a positive law — the function of a sovereign — and *executing* it, an act which depends upon the specific circumstances surrounding its enforcement. More simply put: he perceived that, in executing a law, circumstances and conditions might require certain modifications, make the law subject to varied interpretations, or even force some deletions in the law. Here we find a fairly clear statement regarding a two-fold division of functions.

Of equal significance is the fact that Marsilius placed the lawmaking authority with the people. At the time this was something of a "revolutionary" idea; however, it does lead to one of the central controversies that was to emerge in later periods regarding who ought to possess the power to promulgate positive law. Claims could be made — and they were advanced — for the one, the few, and the many; but, in any event, the resolution of this matter was of the utmost importance, since positive law assumed the same function that the "higher law" had assumed previously.

Although differentiation of function can be attributed to Marsilius, there are two aspects of his theory which are important because of their being at variance with the pure doctrine. He did suggest a separation of function in order to guard against tyranny, uphold the rule of law, or further any of the other ends normally attributed to the doctrine. He rested his case principally on efficiency or practicality, grounds which can hardly be invoked in defense of the doctrine today. Moreover, even though he deviated from the mixed-government model in shifting to a division of functions, he did not make provision for an independent judiciary. Presumably he felt, as did many who came later, that this function was subsumed under the executive one.

The most important period in the development of the doctrine of a separation of powers was the middle 1600s, a time marked by the English Civil War and the *Interregnum*. It was in this era of English history that the concept of a mixed government collided with the still inchoate theory of a separation of powers. The background for this collision may be stated briefly. During this era it was clearly apparent to most observers that England did not enjoy the benefits of a mixed government, because few effective restraints existed to check the king. The theories designed to bring about control of the monarchy naturally turned to bestowing greater powers on Parliament and divesting the king of certain powers. These theories, concerned as they were with the distribution of functions, form, in certain of their particulars, the basis of the doctrine of a separation of powers very much as we know it today.

These theories were numerous and complex; and they differed in certain important respects. There were two fundamental points, however, upon which there seemed to be general agreement. First, the monarchical element in the constitutional fabric was to be retained, together with certain substantive powers, enough at any rate so that the monarchy would not become simply a titular position — all form and no substance. It was agreed that there should be a reduction of royal powers or functions but not to the point of total elimination. Consonant with this supposition, these theories, utilizing the conceptual framework of the doctrine of a separation of powers, urged severe limitations on the legislative prerogatives of the king; however, along with this demand, there was to be a recognition of the king's responsibility to rule. Second, as a corollary of these considerations, the Parliament was to possess the legislative power. In this connection, provisions were usually stipulated to give Parliament a life of its own, independent of the king. Among these provisions was one which fixed the frequency and the terms of parliamentary sessions. During this period, then, the division of functions between two authorities, the Parliament and the king, had come to be accepted as a general maxim.

Such was the state of theory at the time of the execution of Charles I, whose Royalist forces had been defeated by the armies of Parliament. With the subsequent establishment of the Cromwellian Protectorate, events took an extreme turn when both the monarchy and the House of Lords were abolished, so that, for a certain period, all vestiges of a mixed government disappeared. In 1653, the *Instrument of Government*, the first written constitution in English history, was promulgated by Cromwell. This document is notable because, *in theory* — most certainly this was not the case in practice — it not only provided for parliamentary supremacy with respect to the legislative function, but also incorporated the theories of a twofold separation of functions which had gained currency. The Protector, or executive, possessed only a suspensive veto of twenty days over an act of Parliament; he could wield only limited powers of dissolution; and he was bound strictly to execute the laws of Parliament, with the assistance of the Council of State. On the other hand, as defenders of the *Instrument* were to write, the Parliament should strictly confine itself to making laws, and not interfere with their execution and adjudication.

There were obvious differences between the *Instrument* and the pure doctrine. For one thing, the Council of State, the chief administrative arm of the Protector, was not entirely independent of the Parliament, since its members not only could, but did, serve on it; and, for another, although there seemed now to be a greater awareness of the distinct character of the judicial function, no provision was made for an independent judiciary — something it would have been relatively easy to arrange, given the fact that the government was deprived of a mixed character. Generally speaking, however, the theories of this period were deficient in that there had been insufficient exploration of the functions and, particularly, of the manner in which they could be related to each other. It remained for later theorists, most notably Locke, to point out some of the complexities involved in an attempt to separate functions. Nevertheless, within this brief period of English history, the doctrine of a separation of functions became a powerful theoretical force, so powerful that it hastened the end of a mixed government and produced the doctrine of a *balanced* government.

With the ascension of William and Mary to the throne in 1688, the structures of a mixed government were reestablished on a firm but modified basis, for there could be no question about the sovereignty of Parliament. In this setting, John Locke, in his *Second Treatise,* was to explore in greater detail legislative and executive relationships and functions. That he clearly held to the twofold separation of functions is beyond question:

> Therefore in well order'd Commonwealths, where the good of the whole is so considered, as it ought, the *Legislative* Power is put into the hands of diverse persons who duly Assembled, have by themselves, or jointly with others, a Power to make Laws, which then they have done, being separated again, they are themselves subject to the Laws, they have made; which is a new and near tie upon them, to take care, that they make them for the public good.

> But because the Laws, that are at once, and in a short time made, have a constant and lasting force, and need a *perpetual Execution*, or an attendance thereunto; Therefore 'tis necessary there should be a *Power* always in being, which should see to the *Execution* of the Laws that are made, and remain in force. And thus the *Legislative* and *Executive* Power come often to be separated.[10]

Three remarks are in order. First, Locke's system called for the participation of the executive in the legislative function. The executive was to be a part of the legislative body, and only if he consented could a measure have the full force of law. In this sense, then, there was to be a partial mixture of functions, the key characteristic of a *balanced* government. Once a law was passed, however, the executive alone assumed the function of executing or administering it.

Second, Locke, like Marsilius, clearly saw the need of an executive prerogative:

> This Power to act according to discretion, for the publick good, without the prescription of the Law, and sometimes even against it, *is* that which is called *Prerogative*. For since in some Governments that Lawmaking Power is not always in being, and is usually too numerous, and so too slow, for the dispatch requisite to Execution; and because also it is impossible to foresee, and so by laws to provide for, all Accidents and Necessities that may concern the publick; or to make such Laws, as will do no harm, if they are Executed with an inflexible rigour, on all occasions, and upon all Persons, that may come their way, therefore there is a latitude left to the Executive power, to do many things of choice, which the Laws do not prescribe.[11]

Third, expanding upon the suggestions of previous theorists who held that the power to wage war was inherent in the executive, Locke spoke of the *federative* powers of the executive. To quote:

> There is another *Power* in every Commonwealth, which one may call natural, because it is that which answers to the Power every Man naturally had before he entered into Society. For though in a Commonwealth the members of it are distinct Persons still in reference to one another, and as such are governed by the Laws of the Society; yet in reference to the rest of Mankind, they make one Body, which is, as every Member of it before was, still in the State of Nature with the rest of Mankind. Hence it is that the Controversies that happen between any Man of the Society with those that are out of it, are managed by the Publick; and an injury done to a Member of their Body, engages the whole in the reparation of it. So that under this Consideration the

> whole Community is one Body in the State of Nature, in respect of all other States or Persons out of its Community.
>
> This therefore contains the Power of War and Peace, Leagues and Alliances, and all the Transactions, with all Persons and Communities without the Commonwealth, and may be called Federative, if any one pleases. So the thing be understood, I am indifferent as to the Name.[12]

As we can readily see, all of these aspects of Locke's theory have a direct bearing upon past and present controversies in American constitutional history. This is particularly true with respect to the nature and extent of the President's prerogative and federative powers; yet, Locke seems still to hold the idea that executive power subsumes the judicial power or function. At least, he did not expand his conception of the separation of powers to include an independent judicial branch.

Though there seems to be a direct relationship between Locke's teachings and certain of our constitutional provisions, Montesquieu's theory of a separation of powers, beyond any reasonable doubt, exercised a far greater influence over the framers of our Constitution. As Publius wrote:

> The oracle who is always consulted and cited on this subject [separation of powers] is the celebrated Montesquieu. If he be not the author of this invaluable precept in the science of politics, he has the merit at least of displaying and recommending it most effectually to the attention of mankind.[13]

Montesquieu's writings on a separation of powers are quite ambiguous. Nevertheless, the general thrust of his theory is clear enough: There can be no liberty, if the functions of government are together in the hands of the one, the few, or the many. For Montesquieu liberty was the "right of doing whatever the law permit"; and it could not be preserved if the functions of government were not separated:

> When the legislative and executive powers are united in the same person, or in the same body of magistrates, there can be no liberty; because apprehensions may arise, lest the same monarch or senate should enact tyrannical laws, to execute them in a tyrannical manner.
>
> Again, there is no liberty, if the judiciary power be not separated from the legislative and executive. Were it joined with the legislative, the life and liberty of the subject would be exposed to arbitrary con-

> trol; for the judge would be then the legislator. Were it joined to the executive power, the judge might behave with violence and oppression.[14]

While adamant about the need for a separation of functions, Montesquieu was equally concerned to insure a moderate government, one not prone to extremes in its policies and operations. In this regard, he was very much an Aristotelian. To insure a moderate government Montesquieu advocated a form of mixed government. The legislative power he committed "to the body of the nobles, and to that which represents the people, each having their assemblies and deliberations apart, each their separate views and interests." The executive power he consigned to the monarch; and he wrote: "The judiciary power ought not to be given to a standing senate; it should be exercised by persons taken from the body of the people at certain times of the year, and consistently with a form and manner prescribed by law, in order to erect a tribunal that should last only so long as necessity required."[15]

To a separation of functions and a mixed government, Montesquieu added an elaborate system of checks and balances. The result of this was a balanced government far more intricate than the one proposed by Locke. First, Montesquieu subsumed the prerogative and the federative powers under the executive power; but from the executive, as the quotations above intimate, he withdrew the judicial power and elevated it to a status coordinate with those of the legislative and the executive. The aim of the judicial branch was to insure, as far as possible, the impartial settlement of disputes under fixed and known law. As such, it was "next to nothing." Montesquieu certainly did not envision an active or powerful judicial branch of the kind that has developed in the United States; and, because, in his system, the judiciary would lack the enormous and important discretionary powers of the legislative and executive branches, there was little need to check or to balance it.[16] Second, Montesquieu, like Locke, provided the executive with a veto over legislative acts; however, Montesquieu's executive was to be independent of the legislature. As he wrote: "If the prince were to have a part in the legislature by the power of resolving, liberty would be lost. But as it is necessary he should have a share in the legislature for the support of his own prerogative, this share must consist in the power of rejecting."[17] In addition, the executive possessed the power to convene and adjourn legislative meetings. Third, Montesquieu pictured the two legislative bodies as checking each other, so that the moderate government he envisioned could be a reality. Finally, the legislature could check the executive by exercising its power over appropriations and also by holding the executive's ministers to account for the faithful execution of the laws. This latter power extended to impeachment of the executive's ministers (not the executive himself) by the lower house, and to removal by the upper.

The essence of the system in Montesquieu's words is this: "The legislative body being composed of two parts, they check one another by the mutual privilege of rejecting. They are both restrained by the executive power, as the executive is by the legislative."[18] In this respect, we should note that Montesquieu, unlike those who preceded him, did not rely upon a separation of powers alone to prevent tyranny or extremism. He saw a need for each branch to possess a positive check on the operations of the other, in order to produce that result. Though he was aware that his intricate system might well seem to be an invitation to deadlock wherein nothing could be accomplished, he could answer: "These three powers should naturally form a state of repose or inaction. But as there is a necessity for movement in the course of human affairs, they are forced to move, but still in concert."[19]

Implementation in America: The Constitutional Convention

Given this background, the American experience can be viewed as unique, since it was a deliberate effort to draft a constitution which would implement theoretical constitutional principles, the need for a separation of powers being the foremost among them. Locke and Montesquieu, for example, could, and did, draw quite heavily upon the English experience for the major elements of their theory. They could, and did, add a little bit here and there; but they clearly were dealing with a given situation, and one, moreover, that worked. At least Montesquieu was reasonably sure he had discovered those principles of the English system which had contributed so much to the development and maintenance of a moderated form of liberty; yet, to state this in the vernacular, Montesquieu did not have to "put his money where his mouth was." The framers of the Constitution did.

Whether Montesquieu was right in his assessment of the English system is, in large measure, beside the point when considering our constitutional experience. As we have noted, his doctrine did have wide-scale support, and, in one form or another, it seemed quite suitable to the temper of the people at the time of founding. True enough: the Articles of Confederation, that constitution under which there was only a modicum of national government, did not by any stretch of the imagination embody the principle of a separation of powers. The reason for this lack is not hard to find: save for certain functions, principally of an executive character, the Congress under the Articles was powerless; hence, there was no need for concern about the abusive exercise of governmental power from this quarter. As a matter of fact, it was this very lack of power and the inability to take effective action that had spurred the demand for a *revision* of the Articles. Looking back at the situation, however, we can see clearly that something more than *revision*, as that word normally is understood, would be necessary if a stronger national government were to be formed; for, with every new power given to the national government, the need for some kind of control to prevent the abuse of power would become more clear. What we also see is that the participants came to look to a separation of powers to provide the needed control. In so doing, they could not help but go beyond a revision of the Articles of Confederation to the drafting of a completely new constitution.[20]

Two major difficulties confronted the framers of our Constitution. The first of these emerged out of the fact that European theories relative to a separation of powers were not entirely applicable to the American situation. Montesquieu's theory, for example, was based on the existence of monarchy and aristocracy. The United States, however, lacked a nobility. This fact was well noted during the debates at the Constitutional Convention; for example, as Pinckney observed:

> Much has been said of the constitution of Great Britain. I will confess that I believe it to be the best constitution in existence; but, at the same time, I am confident it is one that will not or cannot be introduced into this country for many centuries. If it were proper to go here into an historical dissertation on the British constitution, it might easily be shown that the peculiar excellence, the distinguishing feature, of that government cannot possibly be introduced into our system; that is

> balance between the crown and the people cannot be made a part of our Constitution; that we neither have nor can have the members to compose it, nor the rights, privileges, and properties, of so distinct a class of citizens to guard; that the materials for forming this balance or check do not exist.[21]

For this reason, significant modifications in implementing the doctrine were called for, and certain questions naturally arose; for instance, since the former colonies lacked the social and economic classes to be found in European systems, what interests should be checked against each other? How would the representation of these interests be provided for? To these and related concerns we must add other complicating factors like the desire to establish a republican form of government, wherein sovereignty resided in the people; along with the conviction on the part of some that the federal or confederate principle, in accordance with which each state would retain a share of sovereignty, ought to be incorporated into the new constitution.

The second difficulty lay in the fact that, while a separation of powers was an almost universally accepted objective at the time of founding, for the most part this acceptance was merely verbal. As the late and noted constitutional authority, Edward Corwin, wrote:

> That the majority of the Revolutionary constitutions recorded recognition of the principle of the separation of powers is, of course, well known. What is not so generally understood is that the recognition was verbal merely, for the reason that the material terms in which it was couched still remained undefined; and that this was true in particular of "legislative power" in relation to "judicial power."[22]

The task of the framers, then, certainly was not a simple one, for, as the proceedings will indicate, various notions were entertained concerning what the doctrine entailed in practice.

The debates in the Constitutional Convention provide us with the clearest evidence of how these and other difficulties were resolved. It is to these proceedings that we now turn.

Two major and relatively detailed plans for a new government were set before the Philadelphia Convention: the Virginia ("the large state" or Randolph) plan, and the New Jersey ("the small state" or Paterson) plan. The most important was the Virginia plan. It formed the basis for most of the discussion and debate. While it provided for a separation of powers by suggesting three branches of government, it is more notable for its wide departure in fundamental respects from the pure or model doctrine. Article 7 provided that the national executive "be chosen by the national legislature." Article 4, which dealt with the lower house of the legislature, stipulated that its "members ought to be elected by the people of the several states;" but Article 5, which dealt with the upper house, provided that "the members of the second branch ought to be elected, by those of the first, out of a proper number of persons nominated by the individual legislatures."

Perhaps the most interesting provision was Article 8, which called for a *council of revision*. It read in its entirety:

> Resolved, that the executive, and a convenient number of the national judiciary, ought to compose a council of revision, with authority to examine every act of the national legislature, before it shall operate, and every act of a particular legislature before a negative thereon shall be final; and that the dissent of the said council shall amount to a rejection, unless the act of the national legislature be again passed, or that of a particular legislature be again negatived by [the number to be agreed upon] of the members of each branch.[23]

This *council of revision* should not be confused with the judiciary. While it is true that members of the latter would compose the bulk of its membership, the judiciary and its functions were elaborated in section 9, which called for independent tribunals whose members were to be selected by the national legislature, and would serve during "good behavior."

The New Jersey plan was more in keeping with the Articles of Confederation, both in terms of its structure and the powers granted to the national government. Under its provisions, the Congress of the Articles was to be retained, with certain added powers, principally that of requisitioning funds needed for the operation of the government. This meant, of course, that the legislature would be unicameral, with each state possessing one vote in all decisions.

Other features of the plan are noteworthy from the viewpoint of a separation of powers. With respect to the executive, the plan provided: "That the United States in Congress be authorized to elect a federal executive, to consist of——persons. . . ." This article apparently was written with the supposition that executive powers could be exercised more effectively and safely by a few rather than by just one. Article 5, the judiciary article, read in part: "That a federal judiciary be established, to consist of a supreme tribunal, the judges of which to be appointed by the executive, and to hold their offices during good behavior. . . ."[24]

Each of the two plans, while adhering to the doctrine of a separation of powers in creating three branches of government, provided a degree of *interdependency* between the branches which was lacking in previous formulations of the doctrine. In the Virginia plan, for instance, the composition of the upper house was entirely dependent on that of the lower. Likewise, in each plan the national executive was to be elected by the legislative branch. Moreover, both plans, because of this interdependency, can be viewed as legislative-supremacy documents, for, in both, the legislature (only the lower house in the Virginia plan) was to be the "mainspring" upon which, in one degree or another, all other branches were dependent.

While it can be said that the New Jersey plan corresponded rather closely to the pure doctrine, the Virginia plan deviated rather markedly in its provision calling for a *council of revision*. Not only did the composition of this council represent a blending of personnel (the executive with selected members of the judiciary), it also involved a sharing of powers (legislative and executive). In effect, by suggesting that the judiciary and the executive be united, a "fourth" branch, unparalleled in the history of the doctrine, had been proposed.

In these two plans various ideas were expressed concerning the proper relationship, the powers, and the structure of the branches. The resultant compromises are to be found in our present Constitution. What is vitally important to remember when viewing the final product is the fact that the members of the Philadelphia Convention were, so to speak, "juggling three balls": *federalism*, or state participation in the constitutional order; *republicanism*, or popular participation in and control over the national government, which would be direct in the sense that the states would not act as intermediaries between the people and the national government; and a *separation of powers*, which required a division of functions between the independent branches, without which no viable and nontyrannical government was thought to be possible.

As far as a separation of powers is concerned, the proposed

plans—as we have just seen—did call for a high degree of interdependence, with the legislative body acting as a "kingpin" or "centerstone." A good deal of the deliberations, therefore, centered on securing the independence of the other branches from the legislature. In the debates, Madison put the matter in these terms:

> If it be essential to the preservation of liberty that the legislative, executive, and judiciary powers be separate, it is essential to a maintenance of the separation, that they should be independent of each other. The executive could not be independent of the legislature, if dependent on the pleasure of that branch for a reappointment. Why was it determined that judges should not hold their places by such a tenure? Because they might be tempted to cultivate the legislature by an undue compliance, and thus render the legislature the virtual expositor, as well as the maker, of the laws. In like manner, a dependence of the executive on the legislature would render it the executor as well as the maker of laws; and then, according to the observation of Montesquieu, tyrannical laws may be made that they may be executed in a tyrannical manner.[25]

Why, we can ask, was there this fear of the legislative branch? The answer is to be found in the fact that the framers of the Constitution almost to a man had reservations about unlimited popular control which, because of the republican character of the legislature, was bound to come from that quarter. In other words, the legislature—particularly the lower house—was most likely to respond to the passions of the multitude, thereby doing harm to the society. Some were quite outspoken in their fear of, and contempt for, popular rule. Elbridge Gerry's comments are of this order:

> The evils we experience flow from the excess of democracy. The people do not want virtue, but are the dupes of the pretended patriots. In Massachusetts, it had been fully confirmed by experience, that they are daily misled into the most baneful measures and opinions, by the false reports circulated by designing men, and which no one on the spot can refute.[26]

Others, speaking to the need for a second legislative chamber and for restraints on the legislative branch in general, expressed more moderate views; but they still saw a need for restraint because of the nature of the people. Gouverneur Morris, inquiring into the purpose of a second branch, put the matter in these terms:

> To check the precipitation, changeableness, and excesses, of the

> first branch. Every man of observation had seen in the democratic branches of the state legislatures, precipitation—in Congress, changeableness—in every department, excesses against personal liberty, private property, and personal safety.[27]

Madison enumerated in greater detail why and how a second chamber could serve to restrain the people from both errors and excesses. "A people deliberating in a temperate moment, and with the experience of other nations before them," he declared, would realize:

> That they themselves were liable to temporary errors, through want of information as to their true interest; and that men chosen for a short term, and employed but a small portion of that in public affairs might err from the same cause. This reflection would naturally suggest, that the government be so constituted as that one of its branches might have an opportunity of acquiring a competent knowledge of the public interests. Another reflection equally becoming a people on such an occasion, would be, that they themselves, as well as a numerous body of representatives, were liable to err, also, from fickleness and passion. A necessary fence against this danger would be to select a portion of enlightened citizens, whose limited number, and firmness, might seasonably interpose against impetuous counsels.[28]

The greatest single controversy in the Convention took place over the composition and mode of selection of the second chamber. Should the upper chamber be selected by the lower? Should the people participate directly in the selection or election of senators? What role should the state legislature play? As we know, these matters, after long and heated debate, were resolved by the Connecticut (or "Great") compromise, which provided for election by the state legislatures and equality of representation in the upper chamber. While the doctrine of a separation of powers in no way dictated any such compromise or solution, we cannot help but note that its historical development had provided for, albeit for totally different reasons, a second chamber. This in itself is important, for, we can say that the doctrine as it was understood at that time also provided an institution which gave room for the issues involved in the Connecticut compromise to be worked out and resolved. Specifically, a second chamber allowed room for the incorporation of the confederate principle of equal representation of the states. One is left to wonder what kind of a compromise could have been achieved if the doctrine had been mute in the matter of a second chamber.

Of more importance from the standpoint of guaranteeing the independence of the other branches, a bicameral legislature, with different modes of selection, was an important step toward insuring that the legislature not act in a hasty and ill-considered fashion to gather all governmental functions into its own hands. The compliance of both houses would be necessary to execute any such scheme.

In this connection, we must note another matter often overlooked today but which, at the time of founding, was felt to be important, namely, that no member of the legislative branch hold any other office under the United States. Section 6 of Article I fixes this principle in our Constitution with the following provisions:

> No senator or representative shall, during the time for which he was elected, be appointed to any civil office under the authority of the United States, which shall have been created, or the emoluments whereof shall have been increased, during such time; and no person, holding any office under the United States, shall be a member of either House during his continuance in office.[29]

Not only does this provide for a separation of personnel in keeping with the general tenor of the doctrine, it also reduces the chances that the executive might be able to hold out lucrative positions, in order to sway the deliberations of legislators.

Quite obviously, independence of the branches also required that the executive be isolated as far as possible from the legislature. Both plans before the convention called for the legislature to select the executive; but, not unexpectedly, strong objections of varying character were presented against any such means of selection. One objection rested naturally on the grounds that election by the legislature would make the executive unduly dependent on it. Gouverneur Morris struck this theme in urging that the people directly elect the chief executive:

> He will be the mere creature of the legislature, if appointed and impeachable by that body. . . . If the legislature elect, it will be the work of intrigue, of cabal, and of faction; it will be like the election of a people by a conclave of cardinals; real merit will rarely be the title to the appointment.[30]

James Madison, in supporting election by the people, reiterated his strongly held belief in the separation and independence of the branches:

> If it be a fundamental principle of free government, that the legislative, executive, and judiciary powers should be *separately* exercised, it is equally so that they be *independently* exercised. There is the same, and perhaps greater, reason why the executive should be independent of the legislature, than why the judiciary should. A coalition of the two former powers would be more immediately and certainly dangerous to public liberty. It is essential, then, that the appointment of the executive should either be drawn from some source, or held by some tenure, that will give him a free agency with regard to the legislature. This could not be, if he was to be appointable from time to time, by the legislature.[31]

We have seen that fear of the legislature impelled a majority of the framers of the Constitution to divide that branch into two distinct and relatively independent bodies. By the same reasoning, a majority felt that unity in the executive branch, as represented in a single executive, was called for. Only with unity could the executive act firmly and with resolution to the demands of the office and the possible threats posed by the legislature.

While today we take a single executive for granted, the issue of whether the office should be filled with one man or more than one (the usual figure suggested: three) was far from settled at the beginning of the Convention. The New Jersey plan, as we have noted, appeared to call for a plural executive; and a number of the framers urged such upon the Convention. Even Randolph, who had introduced the Virginia plan, was a staunch opponent of a single executive. As has been pointed out:

> He felt an opposition to it which he believed he should continue to feel as long as he lived. He urged, first, that the permanent temper of the people was adverse to the very semblance of monarchy; secondly, that a unity was unnecessary, a plurality being equally competent to all the objects of the department; thirdly, that the necessary confidence would never be reposed in a single magistrate; fourthly, that the appointments would generally be in favor of some inhabitant near the centre of the community, and consequently the remote parts would not be on an equal footing. He was in favor of three members of the executive, to be drawn from different portions of the country.[32]

These arguments were countered by James Wilson:

> He observed, that the objections of Mr. Randolph were levelled not so much against the measure itself as against its unpopularity. If he could suppose that it would occasion a rejection of the plan of which it should form a part, though the part were an important one, yet he would give it up rather than lose the whole. On examination, he could see no evidence of the alleged antipathy of the people. On the contrary, he was persuaded that it does not exist. All know that a single magistrate is not a king. One fact has great weight with him. All the thirteen states, though agreeing in scarce any other instance, agree in placing a single magistrate at the head of the government. The idea of three heads has taken place in none. The degree of power is, indeed, different; but there are no coordinate heads. In addition to his former reasons for preferring a unity, he would mention another. The *tranquillity*, for not less than the vigor, of government, he thought, would be favored by it. Among three equal members, he foresaw nothing but uncontrolled, continued, and violent animosities; which would not interrupt the public administration, but diffuse their poison through the other branches of government, through the states, and at length through the people at large. If the members were to be unequal in power, the principle of opposition to the unity was given up; if equal, the making them an odd number would not be a remedy. In courts of justice, there are two sides only to a question. In the legislative and executive departments, questions have commonly many sides. Each member, therefore, might espouse a separate one, and no two agree.[33]

Elbridge Gerry introduced still another consideration which seemed to carry great weight in the Convention. He "was at a loss," he stated, "to discover the policy of three members for the executive. It would be extremely inconvenient in many instances, particularly in military matters, whether relating to the militia, an army, or a navy. It would be a general with three heads."[34] Principally for these reasons, only three states (each acting as a unit) voted against a single executive.

Not content with the foregoing measures designed to provide for executive independence, the Convention also conferred upon the President the veto power. At an early point in the deliberations, Wilson remarked: "If the legislature, executive, and judiciary, ought to be distinct and independent, the executive ought to have an absolute negative. Without such a self-defence, the legislature can at any moment sink it into nonexistence;"[35] but the final form which the veto power assumed was intimately connected with deliberations concerning the Council of Revision. This segment of the debates, in which the framers differentiated between executive and judicial functions, represents our most unique and significant contribution to the doctrine of the separation of powers. One may appreciate this by recalling that heretofore, with the exception of Montesquieu who did not carry the matter very far, the executive and judicial functions were theoretically blended or subsumed under the executive function. Now, in the United States the judiciary was recognized as a distinct branch, and the task fell to the framers to differentiate its functions from those of the executive.

We have remarked that the Council of Revision as set forth in the Virginia plan involved a blending of both executive and judicial personnel and power. The power which was shared was that of a limited or modified veto as distinct from the absolute veto proposed by Wilson. While the convention, or at least a considerable majority in it, was amenable to a veto on legislative action, certain questions fundamental to the doctrine of a separation of powers arose. Would not the Council of Revision violate the tenets of a separation of powers because of its composition? Would not allowing the judiciary, whose members would dominate the Council, to veto an act of the legislature really amount to giving it—the judiciary—executive powers? Was not the veto solely a power of the executive? The following exchanges illustrate the dimensions of this controversy.

Wilson, Madison, and Mason were the foremost proponents of associating the national judiciary with the exercise of the veto power. Here again the desire to limit and check the legislature seemed to be uppermost in their minds. More than this: it seems that they did not believe a veto power vested in the executive alone would be sufficient for this purpose. Mason thought that such a provision "would give a confidence to the executive which he would not otherwise have, and without which the revisionary power would be of little avail."[36] Wilson thought that a sharing of the "revisionary power" with the judiciary would allow the judges to counteract "by the weight of their opinions, the improper views of the legislature;"[37] and Madison did not see any grounds for apprehension that the executive and judicial branches would possess "too much strength" vis à vis the legislature. In his words:

It was much more to be apprehended, that, notwithstanding this cooperation of the two departments, the legislature would still be an overmatch for them. Experience in all the states had evinced a powerful tendency in the legislature to absorb all power into its vortex. This was the real source of danger to the American constitutions, and suggested the necessity of giving every defensive authority to the other departments that was consistent with republican principles.[38]

The response of the opponents to any such union of executive and judicial powers was entirely predictable. Gerry, who throughout the debates remained a staunch opponent of any such mixture, summed up what seemed to be the feeling of the majority:

The object, he conceived, of the revisionary power was merely to secure the executive department against legislative encroachment. The executive, therefore, who will be known and be ready to defend his rights, ought alone to have the defence of them. The motion was liable to strong objections. It was combining and mixing together the legislative and the other departments. It was making statesmen of the judges, and setting them up as guardians of the rights of the people. He relied, for his part, on the representatives of the people, as the guardians of their rights and interests.[39]

Oddly enough, Madison, who had on other occasions in the proceedings used this very line of argument—that is, the need for a separation of the branches—responded to Gerry and others of like mind in the following fashion:

[He] could not discover in the proposed association of the judges with the executive, in the revisionary check on the legislature, any violation of the maxim which requires the great departments of power to be kept separate and distinct. On the contrary, he thought it an auxiliary precaution in favor of the maxim. If a constitutional discrimination of the departments on paper were a sufficient security to each against encroachments of the others, all further provisions would be indeed superfluous. But experience had taught us a distrust of that security, and that it is necessary to introduce such a balance of powers and interests as will guaranty the provisions on paper. Instead, therefore, of contenting ourselves with laying down the theory, in the Constitution, that each department ought to be separate and distinct, it was proposed to add a defensive power to each, which should maintain the theory in practice. In so doing, we did not blend the departments together. We erected effectual barriers for keeping them separate. . . . If such a union was an improper mixture of powers, if such a judiciary

> check on the laws was inconsistent with the theory of a free constitution, it was equally so to admit the executive to any participation in making of laws; and the revisionary plan ought to be discarded altogether.[40]

As we know, Madison did not win the day, and the veto power was vested exclusively in a single executive. This veto power did not take the form of an absolute negative, as Wilson suggested, principally because the delegates felt this would be too great a grant of power which conceivably might bring the entire government to a standstill. The provision requiring a two-thirds vote of both houses of Congress was decided upon largely as a compromise between those who advocated a simple majority of both houses for this purpose and others who deemed a three-fourths vote necessary to preserve executive independence.

Having provided for executive independence and powers, the framers were keenly aware that some check was needed to guard against executive encroachment on the other branches as well as to insure that the executive perform his functions in accordance with the Constitution. Some were content with merely the electoral process by which an executive could be removed at the expiration of his term. The delegates did divide on whether the Constitution should provide for removal of the chief executive through an impeachment process. Gouverneur Morris set forth the principal arguments of those who were opposed to impeachment and removal of the President. His remarks on this score are worthy of extensive quotation:

> The executive is also to be impeachable. This is a dangerous part of the plan. It will hold him in such dependence, that he will be no check on the legislature, will not be a firm guardian of the people and of the public interest. He will be the tool of a faction, of some leading demagogue in the legislature. . . . As to the danger from an unimpeachable magistrate, he could not regard it as formidable. There must be certain great officers of state, a minister of finance, of war, of foreign affairs, etc. These, he presumes, will exercise their functions in subordination to the executive, and will be amenable, by impeachment, to the public justice. Without these ministers, the executive can do nothing of consequence.[41]

This position, we should note, is a return to the solution provided by Montesquieu, namely, that the chief executive be kept in line through legislative control of his subordinates. The position was not without strong support, particularly on the grounds that the branches, as Morris intimated, would not be separate and distinct as long as the legislature possessed the power to remove the chief executive. Rufus King was adamant on this point: "Under no circumstances ought he to be impeachable by the legislature. This would be destructive of his independence and of the principles of the Constitution. He relied on the vigor of the executive, as a great security for the public liberties."[42]

Madison and others successfully countered these arguments. Madison noted that: "The limitation of the period of his service was not a sufficient security. He might lose his capacity after his appointment. He might pervert his administration into a scheme of peculation or oppression. He might betray his trust to a foreign power."[43] Randolph thought:

> Guilt, wherever found, ought to be punished. The executive will have great opportunities of abusing his power, particularly in time of war, when the military force, and in some respects the public money, will be in his hands. Should no regular punishment be provided, it will be irregularly inflicted by tumults and insurrections.[44]

The impeachment process as specified in our Constitution was again, no doubt, the result of compromise. Most importantly, the impeachment process could not be carried through too easily or the independence of the executive would be threatened; nor could it be made so difficult as to be ineffectual when circumstances required it.

Deliberations in the Convention concerning the structure of the judiciary gave rise to other difficulties with reference to a separation of powers. Appointment or nomination by the President was opposed by some, like Mason, who felt that this would constitute "a dangerous prerogative," because it would give the executive "an influence over the judiciary itself."[45] Others felt that the executive would not be familiar enough with "fit" characters to make suitable appointments to the bench. Ellsworth contended, "As he will be stationary, it was not to be supposed he could have a better knowledge of characters" than the Senate. Moreover, Ellsworth maintained, "He will be more open to caresses and intrigues than the Senate."[46] Those who favored presidential nomination and Senate confirmation, however, were not without answers to these and like contentions. Randolph argued that "appointments by the legislatures have generally resulted from cabal, from personal regard, or some other consideration than a title derived from the proper qualifications."[47] Morris declared:

> It had been said the executive would be uninformed of characters. The reverse was the truth. The Senate will be so. They must take the character of candidates from the flattering pictures drawn by their friends. The executive, in the necessary intercourse with every part of the United States, required by the nature of his administration, will or may have the best possible information.[48]

Although the Convention originally rejected the provision requiring nomination by the President and confirmation by the Senate, it finally came around to this method for filling judicial positions. The process, of course, involved a blending: the executive *and* part of the legislature would select the members of the judiciary.

THE FEDERALIST on Separation of Powers

What has been said to this point indicates the rather intricate compromises which had to be hammered out in the Convention. At almost every stage of the debates on these and equally important features of our Constitution, the doctrine of a separation of powers and the various conceptions of its meaning were of immense significance. When we turn to *The Federalist*, principally essays 47 through 51, we find a defense of the Constitution on grounds that it does not, in any significant way, deviate from the basic principles underlying the doctrine of a separation of powers. To be sure, Publius admits in these essays, a blending of functions has been proposed; but, he is quick to add that the doctrine as properly understood through Montesquieu's teachings does not prohibit a mixing or blending of the degree and kind to be found in the proposed Constitution. On the contrary, the doctrine requires only that the whole power of one department not be exercised by another. As he said:

> From these facts [the British example], by which Montesquieu was guided, it may clearly be inferred that, in saying "There can be no liberty where the legislative and executive powers are united in the same person, or body of magistrates," or, "if the power of judging be not separated from the legislative and executive powers," he did not mean that these departments ought to have no *partial agency* in, or no

> *control* over, the acts of each other. His meaning, as his own words import, and still more conclusively as illustrated by the example in his eye, can amount to no more than this, that where the *whole* power of one department is exercised by the same hands which possess the *whole* power of another department, the fundamental principles of a free constitution are subverted.[49]

In addition, Publius points out, the national Constitution merits "very high marks" in adhering to the doctrine of a separation of powers, properly understood, when contrasted with the then-existing state constitutions. After examining these constitutions in some detail and pointing out major deviations in them from the pure doctrine, he concludes:

> It is but too obvious that in some instances the fundamental principle under consideration has been violated by too great a mixture, and even an actual consolidation, of the different powers; and that in no instance has a competent provision been made for maintaining in practice the separation delineated on paper. What I have wished to evince is, that the charge brought against the proposed Constitution, of violating the sacred maxim of free government, is warranted neither by the real meaning annexed to that maxim by its author, nor by the sense in which it has hitherto been understood in America.[50]

The remaining essays, dealing specifically with a separation of powers (48, 49, 50, and 51), drive home two interrelated points. First, as we have observed throughout the Convention debates, the legislative branch was seen to pose the greatest threat, in a republican system, to a separation of powers. This view is reiterated at various points in *The Federalist*. Whereas, in other systems which have a nobility and hereditary monarchs, the chief threat to liberty probably would come from the executive branch, the situation is markedly different in a representative republic:

> But in a representative republic, where the executive magistrate is carefully limited, both in the extent and the duration of its power; and where the legislative power is exercised by an assembly, which is inspired, by a supposed influence over the people, with an intrepid confidence in its own strength; which is sufficiently numerous to feel all the passions which actuate a multitude, yet not so numerous as to be incapable of pursuing the objects of its passions, by means which reason prescribes; it is against the enterprising ambition of this department that the people ought to indulge all their jealousy and exhaust all their precautions.[51]

Second, it follows from this, that some means had to be devised to keep the legislative branch within its proper constitutional limits. This conclusion may seem strange at first glance. After all, would not the checks provided for in the Constitution suffice to limit the Congress and keep it within its prescribed boundaries? Why should Publius be concerned with this problem in the light of the constitutional barriers to legislative encroachment? The answer comes to this: The proposed Constitution, as well as the existing state constitutions, have provided for a separation of powers—in theory; that is, the written provisions do, in fact, provide for such a separation. In *practice*, however, this separation has broken down, due to the aggressiveness of the legislature, and the other branches have found themselves helpless when faced with these acts of aggression. So the primary question to which Publius addresses himself in the essays is this: How can the necessary partition of powers be maintained in practice?

He first considers the expedient of "paper barricades," or written declarations, which would specify in great detail the respective powers of each branch; but he finds this method, used by a majority of the states, to be inadequate:

> The legislative department derives a superiority in our governments from other circumstances [than those found in systems with a hereditary monarch]. Its constitutional powers being at once more extensive, and less susceptible of precise limits, it can, with the greater facility, mask, under complicated and indirect measures, the encroachments which it makes on the coordinate departments. It is not unfrequently a question of real nicety in legislative bodies, whether the operation of a particular measure will, or will not, extend beyond the legislative sphere. On the other side, the executive power being restrained within a narrower compass, and being more simple in its nature, and the judiciary being described by landmarks still less uncertain, projects of usurpation by either of these departments would immediately betray and defeat themselves.[52]

More than this: the legislature controls the purse strings, and this fact provides it with a means to bend the other branches to its will. Publius concludes: "A mere demarcation on parchment of the constitutional limits of the several departments, is not a sufficient guard against those encroachments which lead to a tyrannical concentration of all the powers of government in the same hands."[53]

The question arises: Will appeals to the people, either periodically or occasionally, help to redress any imbalance that may occur in the power relationships of the three branches? Because "the people are the only legitimate fountain of power, and it is from them that the constitutional charter, under which the several branches of government hold their power," it would seem reasonable, and also to be in accordance with the republican principle, that the people police these departments when controversies arise concerning their respective jurisdictions. Publius rejects these considerations for a variety of reasons. With respect to *occasional* appeals—and these arguments would apply with almost equal force to periodic appeals—they would carry with them an "implication" of a serious defect in the governmental forms, and this fact, in turn, would "deprive the government of that veneration which time bestows on every thing, and without which perhaps the wisest and freest government would not possess the requisite stability."[54]

Recourse to the people would also disturb "the public tranquility by interesting too strongly the public passions."[55] Publius's concern on this score can be explained in the following way. Constitution making, or the political founding of a society, is an extremely delicate and demanding task. Perhaps it is the most important task which any society can undertake, involving as it does the very rules by which its component parts are to act on one another. The practical difficulties and the differences of opinion at the Philadelphia convention alone indicate the magnitude of such an undertaking, even among a people whose customs, traditions and values were basically similar. Appeals to the people, then, over such a fundamental constitutional question as the proper distribution between the branches of government could not help but stir the most basic and intense passions of the people. In this climate narrow partisanship and selfish interest would have every opportunity to emerge, along with the distinct possibility of eventual political and social disunion.

Publius felt, however, that "the greatest objection of all is, that the decisions which would probably result from such appeals would not answer the purpose of maintaining the constitutional equilibrium of the government",[56] because Congress, the most likely branch to commit unconstitutional encroachments, would enjoy a popularity among the people, who would be inclined to "ratify" these encroachments. The members of Congress would be numerous, well known, and intimately linked to members of the more general society; and, for these reasons, they would possess a distinct advantage over the executive and judicial branches in any popular showdown. As Publius put it:

> The nature of their public trust implies a personal influence among the people, and that they are more immediately the confidential guardians of the rights and liberties of the people. With these advantages, it can hardly be supposed that the adverse party would have an equal chance for a favorable issue.[57]

With reference to periodical appeals, Publius notes still another difficulty:

> If the periods be separated by short intervals, the measures to be reviewed and rectified will have been of recent date, and will be connected with all the circumstance [such as those noted above] which tend to vitiate and pervert the result of occasional revisions. If the periods be distant from each other, the same remark will be applicable to all recent measures; and in proportion as the remoteness of the others may favor a dispassionate review of them, this advantage is inseparable from inconveniences which seem to counterbalance it. In the first place, a distant prospect of public censure would be a very feeble restraint on power from those excesses to which it might be urged by the force of present motives. Is it to be imagined that a legislative assembly . . . would be arrested in their career, by considerations drawn from a censorial revision of their conduct at the future distance of ten, fifteen, or twenty years? In the next place, the abuses would often have completed their mischievous effects before the remedial provision would be applied. And in the last place, where this might not be the case, they would be of long standing, would have taken deep root, and would not easily be extirpated.[58]

In *Federalist* 51, certainly one of the most famous of these essays, Publius addresses himself to the question of how the departments, in practice, are to be kept within their constitutionally-specified bounds; and he replies:

> The only answer that can be given is, that as all these exterior provisions are found to be inadequate, the defect must be supplied, by so contriving the interior structure of the government as that its several constituent parts may, by their mutual relations, be the means of keeping each other in their proper places.[59]

In this connection Publius suggests that each department have a "will of its own." The members of each branch "should have as little agency as possible in the appointment of the members of the others." He notes that the appointment of a judiciary involves a necessary deviation from this principle; but he writes:

> In the constitution of the judiciary department in particular, it might be expedient to insist rigorously on the principle: first, because peculiar qualification being essential in the members, the primary consideration ought to be to select that mode of choice which best secures these qualifications; secondly, because the permanent tenure by which the appointments are held in that department, must soon destroy all sense of dependence on the authority conferring them.[60]

The picture presented by Publius at this point is that the proposed constitution does outwardly, on paper at least, provide a structure in which the branches can maintain their separation; but, as we have seen, his chief preoccupation is to go beyond this arrangement because "parchment barricades" alone are insufficient for this purpose. His answer to the question which he has set for himself is as follows:

> But the great security against a gradual concentration of the several powers in the same department, consists in giving to those who administer each department the necessary constitutional means and personal motives to resist encroachments of the others. The provision for defence must in this, as in all other cases, be made commensurate to the danger of attack. Ambition must be made to counteract ambition. The interest of the man must be connected with the constitutional rights of the place. It may be a reflection of human nature, that such devices should be necessary to control the abuses of government. But what is government itself, but the greatest of all reflection on human nature? If men were angels, no government would be necessary. If angels were to govern men, neither external nor internal controls on government would be necessary.[61]

In this "solution," Publius is going beyond constitutional formalism. He is, in the main, relying on personal and distinctly noninstitutional provisions for the maintenance of a separation of powers. The system, in sum, is designed to give the members of each branch motives to wield the constitutional weapons at their disposal, and thus preserve the necessary separation. The assignment of different functions, different modes of election, different constituencies, and varying lengths of term, tends to produce this effect;

thus, the infusion and cultivation of interest and motive—something which, we might note, was not necessary in mixed regimes, where social and economic interests provided sufficient incentive —represent a central and an essential element in the maintenance of our constitutional order.

Separation of Powers: Its Status and Future

For two substantial reasons any basic or external reform of our constitutional system seems most unlikely. First, one has only to look at the contemporary world to realize that the problems of which the framers of our Constitution were acutely aware are still very much with us. By traditional standards, more than half of the world's population currently lives under tyrannical governments of one form or another. Consequently, to tamper with a constitutional principle which has been specifically designed to prevent any such fate befalling us would—and with good reason—be viewed with alarm. Some persons, no doubt, would argue that we cannot attribute our relatively high degree of freedom to a separation of powers;[62] yet, there is no way of telling with certainty how much, and in what ways, our separate governmental structures have contributed in a positive manner to our present free state. For this reason, any external reform would, understandably enough, be greeted with a high degree of skepticism.

In the second place, the American people over the years have come to venerate their Constitution. The mere thought of holding another constitutional convention seems to strike fear into the hearts of the more articulate, liberals and conservatives alike. On this matter there seems to exist a built-in conservatism nurtured by the realization that 1787 might well have represented a unique moment in the history of the nation for an act of founding. Of this fact our Founding Fathers seemed to be aware. They feared the opportunity once lost might never again appear. So, too, do many contemporary students of the American system, particularly when they contemplate the enormous difficulty the nation would face in undertaking a second act of founding.

Finally, we can fruitfully ask: Would the framers be surprised at the way the separation of powers has developed over the years? How far, in other words, do our present practices vary from those intended? Of course, there can be no definitive answer to this question because the framers themselves were not of like mind concerning all aspects of the doctrine and its operation. This much we have seen in the early congressional debates; however, if we take *The Federalist* as the standard by which to measure practice in comparison to intent, the conclusion that we are operating within tolerable limits of the intended design seems warranted.

Such an assessment may seem startling in the light of what we have said about the expanded role of the presidency and the judiciary in recent decades; yet, in this respect, there can be no doubt that theories of expediency have served to create a "smoke screen" and blurred our perception of certain of the more fundamental constitutional arrangements which have remained unaltered by the passage of time. More specifically: whenever the Court or the President advance the goals most cherished by certain portions of the nation, theories of expediency are also advanced to justify, on constitutional grounds, these decisions and actions. It would thus seem that many have come to regard the American system as possessing three coordinate and equally powerful branches, each with special claim to represent the "real" will of the people. From this theoretical vantage point the American system cannot help but look like "a three-ring circus." Paradoxically, it is the emergence of the theories of expediency which have contributed to the confusion and lack of unity which the theories, themselves, decry.

As the persistent calls for external reform indicate, however, the basic constitutional structure of power remains relatively unaltered. The Congress retains—like it or not,—the major powers of government which, within our broader constitutional morality of deliberation and moderation, it is free to use to curb the excesses of the other branches; and the people, of course, are free to curb the excesses of the legislature. We may say that as long as this condition prevails, the Founders' dream of a nontyrannical republic also will continue to be a reality.

Notes

1. Oscar Handlin and Mary Handlin, eds., *The Popular Sources of Political Authority: Documents on the Massachusetts Constitution of 1780* (Cambridge: Harvard University Press, 1966), pp. 447-448.

2. Thomas Jefferson, *The Political Writings of Thomas Jefferson*, ed. Edward Dumbald (New York: Liberal Arts Press, 1956), p. 12.
3. Ibid., p. 103.
4. John Adams, *The Political Writings of John Adams*, ed. George A. Peck (New York: Liberal Arts Press, 1954), p. 129.
5. *The Federalist*, ed. Edward Mead Earle (New York: Modern Library, 1937), p. 313. All subsequent references to *The Federalist* are to this edition.
6. Charles C. Tansill, ed., *Documents Illustrative of the Union of the American States* (Washington: U.S. Government Printing Office, 1927), pp. 1028-1029, 1045, and 1053.
7. *The Politics of Aristotle*, trans. Benjamin Jowett (New York: Modern Library, 1943), Bk. 3, chap. 11.
8. Ibid., 3, chap. 11.
9. M. J. C. Vile, *Constitutionalism and the Separation of Powers* (Oxford: Oxford University Press, 1967), p. 24.
10. *A Second Treatise of Government*, ed. Peter Laslett (New York: New American Library, 1965), chap. 12, secs. 143-144.
11. Ibid., sec. 160.
12. Ibid., secs. 143-146.
13. *The Federalist*, p. 313.
14. *The Spirit of the Laws*, trans. Thomas Nugent (New York: Hafner Publishing Co., 1949), bk. 11, sec. 6.
15. Ibid.
16. Montesquieu would allow his upper chamber to mitigate unduly severe or harsh penalties imposed by the judicial branch.
17. *The Spirit of the Laws.* By *resolving*, Montesquieu meant "the right of ordaining by [its] own authority, or of amending what has been ordained by others."
18. Ibid.
19. Ibid.
20. John Randolph put this view of the matter before the Convention in the following manner: "We must resort, therefore, *to national legislation over individuals;* for which Congress are unfit. To vest such power in them would be blending the legislative with the executive, contrary to the received maxim on this subject. If the union of these powers, heretofore, in Congress has been safe, it has been owing to the impotency of that body." *Debate on the Adoption of the Federal Constitution*, ed. Jonathan Elliot, 5 vols. (New York: Burt Franklin, 1888), 5:198. Hereafter cited as *Elliot.*
21. Ibid., p. 234.
22. Edward S. Corwin, "The Progress of Constitutional Theory Between the Declaration of Independence and the Meeting of the Philadelphia Convention," *American Historical Review*, 30 (April 1925): 525.
23. Elliot, p. 128.
24. Ibid., p. 192.

25. Ibid., p. 326.
26. Ibid., p. 136.
27. Ibid., p. 270.
28. Ibid., p. 242.
29. In this regard, we should also note the provision in Article II, Section 1, paragraph 2, which also seeks to insure separation:
"Each State shall appoint, in such Manner as the Legislature thereof may direct, a Number of Electors, equal to the whole Number of Senators and Representatives to which the State may be entitled in the Congress: but no Senator or Representative, or Person holding an Office of Trust or Profit under the United States, shall be appointed an Elector."
30. Elliot, p. 322.
31. Ibid., p. 337.
32. Ibid., p. 149.
33. Ibid., p. 160.
34. Ibid., p. 151.
35. Ibid.
36. Ibid., p. 345.
37. Ibid., p. 344.
38. Ibid., p. 345.
39. Ibid.
40. Ibid., p. 347.
41. Ibid., p. 335. Morris was to change his position subsequently to provide for impeachment of the President for "corruption, and some few other offenses." He thought "the cases ought to be enumerated and defined." Ibid., p. 341.
42. Ibid., p. 342.
43. Ibid., p. 341.
44. Ibid., p. 342.
45. Ibid., p. 351.
46. Ibid., p. 350.
47. Ibid.
48. Ibid.
49. *The Federalist*, pp. 314-315.
50. Ibid., p. 320.
51. Ibid., p. 323.
52. Ibid.
53. Ibid., p. 326.
54. Ibid., pp. 330-331.
55. Ibid., p. 331.
56. Ibid., p. 330.
57. Ibid.
58. Ibid., p. 333.
59. Ibid., p. 336.
60. Ibid.

61. Ibid., p. 337.
62. Such is the position, for example, of Robert A. Dahl. See his *A Preface to Democratic Theory* (Chicago: University of Chicago Press, 1956), chap. 1.

[5]

THE FEDERAL STRUCTURE

—VALERIE A. EARLE

On June 7, 1776, Richard Henry Lee of Virginia introduced into the Continental Congress a Resolution Proposing a Declaration of Independence. The third clause of this Resolution reads as follows: "That a plan of confederation be prepared and transmitted to the respective colonies for their consideration and approbation."[1]

The Congress postponed for three weeks action on the proposition of declaring independence, in order that delegates from those colonies which had not already given authority to vote this decisive measure might consult their constituents. During that period a committee of the Congress was at work preparing a draft of the Declaration of Independence, which, as all know, was adopted on July 4, 1776.

A second committee of the Congress, however, composed of a representative of each colony, had begun work, even before July 4, on a plan of confederation "for the future management of the common interests, which had hitherto been left to the discretion of Congress, guided by the exigencies of the contest, and by the known intentions or occasional instruction of the Colonial Legislatures."[2] It is probable that a plan entitled "Articles of Confederation and Perpetual Union of the Colonies," drafted by Benjamin Franklin in July 1775, served as a model for the proposal made by the Committee to the Congress on July 12, 1776. After debate and amendment it was adopted on November 17, 1777, and proposed to the legislatures of the states, with an explanatory letter. At length, in March 1781, the last of the states, Maryland, ratified the plan. The Articles of Confederation then went into effect.

In examining the national government constructed by the Articles, it is useful to bear in mind that the First and Second Continental Congresses were called into being by the colonies because of a clear threat of British action against the large measure of autonomy enjoyed by each colony.[3] In the first of its repressive actions, Parliament sealed the Port of Boston until "satisfaction" might be offered by the Massachusetts colony for the tea thrown overboard and the losses sustained by royal officials in the Boston riots. This prompted a bloodless insurrection in the colony which by the fall of 1774 had made it virtually independent under the government of an illegally elected convention, and had confined the authority of the royal governor to the Boston area. Within Massachusetts committees of correspondence sprang up to organize and maintain resistance.

Other colonies quickly expressed their support by sending food and money for the relief of Boston, by passing resolutions of sympathy, and, in the case of Virginia, by denouncing the military occupation of Boston as a hostile invasion. A resolution passed by the Virginia Assembly caused the royal governor to dissolve the Assembly, but, before returning to their homes, the burgesses met at Raleigh Tavern in Williamsburg and proclaimed that an attack on one colony, to compel payment of arbitrary taxes, constituted an attack on all British America. The Virginia Committee of Correspondence began exchanging views with the Committees of Correspondence of other states on the possibility of summoning a continental congress to effect a resolution of the difficulties with England and restore to the colonies control over matters of significance to them. The First Continental Congress was thus convened on September 5, 1774.

The Congress had as its principal and very difficult task the devising of a means by which to reconcile the colonies' desire for autonomy with what were regarded as the imperatives of continued British rule by Lord North's government. Americans did not at this point wish to make a complete break with England. Rather, they wished to be free of parliamentary control of their affairs but to continue to recognize the authority of the king. They were developing only *very* slowly a limited sense of nationhood, as in the case of the Virginia resolution which expressed solidarity in the face of hostile actions and arbitrary taxes.

The Continental Congress believed that Americans wanted what later came to be recognized as dominion status: the king, together with his Privy Council, would conduct foreign relations, determine matters of war and peace, and regulate imperial trade; the internal affairs of the colonies would be left to them. The Congress debated a plan by which an American parliament parallel to that in England might be established, it and the British Parliament to have a veto on acts of the other relating to America. Clearly, the idea of an American parliament was attractive to the colonists as a means by which to gain independence of English parliamentary control, not as a means of achieving either total independence or a national government.

No proposal made by the Congress was accepted by the government in England; and, indeed, the rush of events in the colonies, including not only the accomplishment of virtual independence in Massachusetts and the spread of Committees of Correspondence, but, also, in April 1775, Lexington and Concord and, in May 1775, the successful expedition led by Ethan Allen from Vermont against the British Forts Ticonderoga and Crown Point in Canada, effectively nullified any negotiations up to the convening of the Second Continental Congress in May 1775.

The point deserving of emphasis is that decisive steps were being taken by the individual colonies. The prevailing sentiment continued through 1775 to be against a final break; but, since the government in England appeared unwilling to offer or to accept a compromise solution, the colonists believed they must have a Congress to manage common concerns and speak for them when they were not speaking for themselves, as they so often did, by deeds which were unmistakable and unambiguous.

The Second Continental Congress converted the militia besieging the British in Boston into the "Army of the United Colonies;" appointed Colonel George Washington to be Commander in Chief; began to raise a navy of the United Colonies; embarked on negotiations to make Canada the fourteenth colony; and declared that the United Colonies were not fighting the king, but rather the Parliament, and specifically the king's ministers in Parliament who were giving him bad advice. In sum, the Congress conducted foreign policy, and managed the war, or, rather, the war-like acts which were still very much left to the initiatives of individuals and individual colonies.

All efforts at reconciliation proved unavailing. Relations grew steadily worse as the feeling for independence grew stronger, even though as late as January 1776, four colonies—New York, New Jersey, Pennsylvania, and Maryland—specifically instructed their delegates to the Continental Congress to hold out against independence. In May 1776, the Virginia burgesses, sitting by themselves, voted to instruct the Virginia delegates in the Congress to proclaim the United Colonies free and independent states; subsequently, the burgesses adopted the Virginia Bill of Rights, and a constitution for an independent state. Shortly thereafter, Georgia, North Carolina, and South Carolina voted in their assemblies for independence. Then, in a rush, the decision was made in all the colonies, and independence was declared. The colonies became states and set about adopting constitutions, in the great majority of which, although reference was made to a separation of powers, the legislature was, in fact, supreme. The Continental Congress remained in place to fight the war and to manage national affairs until a permanent national government could be established.

If a brief account of the events preceding the Declaration is not sufficient to show the extent to which the colonies perceived themselves to be separate and individual colonies, then, certainly, the manner in which the army was raised to fight the Revolutionary War should demonstrate the strength of the tradition of individualism among the states. Congress set quotas for each to fill for the army, but it had no authority to enforce these quotas. General Washington was given authority to make all promotions through the rank of Colonel; but usually he had to consult state officials on any appointment above the rank of Captain. Usually, troops from one state would not fight under the regimental officers from another state. Certainly, General Washington's difficulties in maintaining an army of sufficient size and adequately supplied were not attributable alone to the stubborn preservation of their sovereignty by the states; but this sovereignty was a considerable factor in the long and difficult war for independence, a war which many apparently thought would be won simply by a Declaration of Independence, with little or no further effort required. There was a widespread desire among Americans to attend to business, to shopkeeping, to planting and harvesting crops, with only a limited amount of time out for fighting the war. It was not that Americans did not want independence—they wanted it in order that they be left alone. The Continental Congress and the steps it took to prosecute the war were not regarded as one of the prime concerns for Americans generally.

The Articles of Confederation

Given such a tradition of colony, later state, independence and separateness, save in the face of the most direct emergency such as the sealing of the Port of Boston, any form of government significantly different from that of the Articles of Confederation would have been generally unacceptable.

Although Article I proclaims that the confederacy is to be called "the United States of America," Article II asserts that "each State retains its sovereignty, freedom, and independence, and every Power, Jurisdiction and right, which is not by this Confederation expressly delegated to the United States, in Congress assembled;" and Article III declares that the states enter into "a firm league of friendship with each other, for their common defense, the security of their Liberties, and their mutual and general welfare, binding themselves to assist each other, against all force offered to, or attacks made upon them, or any of them, on account of religion, sovereignty, trade, or any other pretence whatever."[4]

Article IV stipulates that "the better to secure and perpetuate mutual friendship among the people of the different states in this Union," the free inhabitants of each state are to enjoy the privileges and immunities of free citizens in all other states, to have free ingress and egress to and from any other state, and to enjoy the same privileges of trade and commerce. Moreover, full faith and credit is to be given in all states to records, acts, and judicial proceedings of the courts and magistrates of each state.

A Congress of one house, composed of delegates chosen annually by state legislatures, with each state having one vote, was established to manage "the general interests of the United States."[5] Each state was to select at least two, but not more than seven, delegates, who could be recalled at any time during the year's term. No person could sit as a delegate for more than three years in any term of six years. The compensation of the delegates while sitting in Congress, or in the Committee of States (a body chosen by the Congress, composed of one representative of each state, which met between sessions of Congress) was to be provided by each state.

In Article IX the powers of the United States in Congress assembled are listed as follows: 1. The sole and exclusive right and power of determining peace and war, except when a state is actually "invaded by enemies, or shall have received certain advice of a resolution being formed by some nation of Indians to invade such state, and the danger is so imminent as not to admit of a delay till the United States in Congress assembled can be consulted;"[6] 2. The sole and exclusive power to send and receive ambassadors, and to enter into treaties and alliances, providing that no treaty of trade or commerce should restrain the state legislatures from imposing on foreigners the same imposts and duties as are imposed on their own citizens, or from prohibiting the exportation or importation of any species of goods; 3. The sole power to establish rules for deciding which captures on land or water shall be legal and in what manner prizes taken by forces in the service of the United States shall be divided or appropriated; 4. The sole power to grant letters of marque or reprisal in times of peace, to appoint courts for the trial of piracies and other felonies committed on the high seas, and to establish courts for receiving and determining, finally, appeals in all cases of capture; 5. The sole power to serve as the last resort on appeal in all disputes between or among states concerning their boundaries or jurisdiction and in cases concerning private claims to land arising under grants from two or more states; 6. The sole and exclusive power to regulate the alloy and value of coins struck by the Congress and by the states, and to fix the standards of weights and measures; 7. The power to regulate trade with, and manage all affairs of, Indians who were not members of any state, providing that the legislative rights of any state within its own limits be not infringed or violated; 8. The power to establish post offices and exact such postage as might be sufficient to defray the expense of the postal service; 9. The power to appoint all officers in the naval forces, and all officers in the land forces of the United States, excepting regimental officers, and to commission all officers whatever in the service of the United States; 10. The power to make rules and regulations for the government of the land and naval forces and to direct their operation; 11. The power to appoint the committee of states to sit in the recess of Congress; 12. The power to appoint one member of Congress to preside over its sessions, providing that no person be allowed to serve in the office of president for more than one year in any term of three years; 13. The power to appoint such other committees and civil officers as might be needed to manage the general affairs of the United States under the direction of Congress; 14. The power to ascertain the necessary sums of money to be raised for the service of the United States, and to appropriate and apply the same; 15. The power to borrow money or to emit bills of credit, an account of the money so borrowed or emitted to be transmitted semiannually to the states; 16. The power to build and to equip a navy; and 17. The power to agree on the number of land forces and to make requisitions from each state for its quota in proportion to the number of white inhabitants, this quota to be binding, and each state legislature to appoint the regimental officers, to raise the men and to clothe and otherwise equip them in a soldier-like manner, but at the expense of the United States.

To give emphasis to those matters regarded as being of general concern to the United States, Article VI prohibited the states from sending ambassadors to, or entering into treaties or alliances with, foreign countries without the consent of Congress; from entering into treaties or confederations among themselves, also without the consent of Congress; from laying imposts or duties which might interfere with treaties entered into by the United States in Congress assembled; from engaging in war without the consent of Congress, unless the state were in fact invaded or had information about imminent attack by Indians; and from maintaining troops or ships of war in time of peace, except as deemed necessary by the United States in Congress assembled for the defense of the state or its trade.

Article VIII stipulates that all charges of war and all other expenses incurred for the common defense or general welfare shall be defrayed out of a common treasury to be supplied by the several states in proportion to the value of all land within the state. The taxes for paying each portion were to be laid and levied by the authority and at the direction of the state within the time agreed upon by the United States in Congress assembled.

A favorable vote of nine states in Congress was required to declare war, grant letters of marque and reprisal, enter into treaties or alliances, and coin money and regulate its value; also to emit bills of credit, borrow money, ascertain the sums necessary for the defense and welfare of the United States, and to appropriate money; to set the number of land forces and of vessels of war to be built or purchased, and to appoint a commander in chief. Only by a favorable vote of all state legislatures could any amendment proposed by the Congress in the Articles of Confederation be adopted.

The Committee of States which sat between sessions of Congress could not exercise any of the powers requiring a vote of nine states in the Congress.

The defects and failures of government under the Articles of Confederation are well known. They are most notably attributable to: 1. The inability of the Congress to raise revenue by taxing citizens directly, and to raise an army by drafting men directly; 2. The incapacity of a numerous body like the Congress to formulate and implement even the rather simple foreign policy required for the new nation; and 3. A lack of power to implement decisions by enforcing law directly upon states and citizens. The unwillingness of Congress to give more than minimal freedom to operate to those executive officers, offices, or committees which the Congress itself established, even including the Commander in Chief himself, contributed to the widespread perception that the government of the Articles was incompetent to perform the tasks given it. But the fatal defects lay in the attributes mentioned previously.

Even before ratification by the thirteenth state put the Articles into effect in March 1781, a number of leaders believed the Articles to be clearly deficient for the purposes of the new nation.[7] James Madison proposed to the Congress in March 1781 that the states be asked to give authority to the united states to employ the forces of the united states to compel the states to fulfill their federal obligations.[8] George Washington spoke and wrote on a number of occasions of the need for Congress to "dictate, and not merely recommend." He wrote of the impossibility of carrying on the war "without a controlling power in Congress;" and he added, "We shall speedily be thirteen distinct states, each pursuing its local interests, till they are annihilated in a general crash."[9] Washington lamented the fact that the states tended to employ their ablest men at home "while the common interests of America were mouldering and sinking into irretrievable ruin. . . . How useless to put in fine order the smallest parts of a clock, unless the great spring which is to set the whole in motion is well attended to."[10] Washington observed with alarm that in his own State, Virginia, the legislature had expressed alarm in 1779 at what it described as the great assumption of power by Congress; and it also had asserted the right of each state legislature to accept or to reject measures proposed by Congress.

In May 1781, William Barton of Pennsylvania wrote in a pamphlet that the Congress "should not be left with the mere shadow of sovereign authority, without the right of exacting obedience to their ordinances, and destitute of the means of executing their resolves."[11]

Alexander Hamilton prepared a series of papers called "The Continentalist" in July and August of 1781, in which he wrote:

> There is hardly a man who will not acknowledge the confederation unequal to a vigorous prosecution of the war, or to the preservation of the union in peace, the federal government, too weak at first, will continually grow weaker. . . . Already some of the states have evaded or refused the demands of congress; the currency is depreciated; public credit is at the lowest ebb; our army deficient in numbers and unprovided with everything. . . . We ought therefore not only to strain every nerve to render the present campaign as decisive as possible, but we ought without delay to enlarge the powers of Congress. Every plan of which this is not the foundation will be illusory. The separate exertions of the states will never suffice. Nothing but a well proportioned exertion of the resources for the whole, under the direction of a common council with power to give sufficient efficacy to their resolutions can preserve us from being a conquered people now, or can make us a happy one hereafter.[12]

A committee of three members of the Congress, Edmund Randolph of Virginia, Oliver Ellsworth of Connecticut, and James M. Varnum of Rhode Island, was commissioned by the Congress in 1781 to present "supplemental articles" for the Articles of Confederation. Their report, made on August 22, 1781, pointed to the necessity for Congress to have the power to compel compliance with its decisions regarding needed revenues, men for the armed forces of the United States, and other important national concerns; however, the report offered no suggestions regarding how to coerce either states or men: "Coercion of a state by force of arms is civil war, and, from the weakness of the confederacy and the strength of organization of each separate state, would have been disunion."[13]

The years following the acceptance by all the states of the Articles of Confederation amply demonstrated the weaknesses of the Congress. The states did not fulfill their obligations with respect to either money or men requisitioned by the Congress. The requirement of a vote by nine states in support of many actions of the Congress meant very often that no action could be taken on some of the most important business of the country. Nor was significant change possible in the Articles, since that required the unanimous consent of all thirteen states.

The Congress had been unable to agree upon terms for a peace treaty with England and also unable, therefore, to instruct its delegates adequately; among members of Congress, factions of Anglophiles and Francophiles wrangled bitterly and unceasingly.

Congress meddled in administrative matters, both large and small, probably in part because legislation, being unenforceable, appeared a fruitless undertaking. The Secretary of Foreign Affairs, John Jay, eventually complained so bitterly of his being left out of the flow of correspondence with other countries that Congress reluctantly made the concession that such correspondence would pass through his hands on the way to Congress. The Commissary General of the Army, who had by all accounts been remarkably efficient, quit in disgust at congressional interference; eventually the job was filled by a member of Congress who took it only on the terms he dictated. There was peculation, and other forms of corruption as well.

By 1784 it was increasingly difficult to sustain a session of the Congress; many members stayed only briefly or did not come at all. Even the Committee of States functioned intermittently during the absence of Congress, because only rarely were the representatives of nine states present. In November 1784 members of the Congress arrived so slowly that Monsieur Marbois, the representative of France, reported to his government: "There is in America no general government, neither Congress, nor president, nor head of any one administrative department."[14] In reply Marbois was told: "The American confederation has a strong tendency to dissolution; it is well that on this point we have neither obligations to fulfill nor any interest to cherish."[15]

Richard Henry Lee wrote to Madison that many in the Congress were suggesting there be a call to the states to form a convention to revise the Articles "so far as to enable Congress to execute with more energy, effect, and vigor the powers assigned to it than it appears by experience that they can do under the present state of things." Madison replied, in part:

> The union of the states is essential to their safety against foreign danger and internal contention; the perpetuity and efficacy of the present system cannot be confided in; the question, therefore, is in what mode and at what moment the experiment for supplying the defects ought to be made.[16]

Meanwhile, commercial rivalry among the states grew apace, with Congress powerless in fact to do anything about the trade barriers steadily being erected. Within many of the states legislative power was misused to devalue the currency, postpone the payment of debts, set aside contracts, remove pending cases from the courts and decide them, overturn court decisions already made, and nullify marriages.[17] The inland states found themselves taxed severely for the use of ports in coastal states.

Among many persons, apprehension grew that the new nation would not long retain its independence nor be able to provide conditions for peace, prosperity, happiness and stability.

In January 1786 the General Assembly of Virginia called for a meeting of commissioners from the states "to take into consideration the trade of the United States; to examine the relative situations and trade of the said States; to consider how far a uniform system in their commercial regulations may be necessary to their common interest and their permanent harmony; and to report to the several States, such an act relative to this great object, as, when unanimously ratified by them, will enable the United States in Congress effectually to provide for the same."[18]

From the abortive meeting at Annapolis—only five states had sent commissioners, although four others had also chosen them—came a report addressed to the legislatures of the states whose commissioners were present, with copies to be transmitted to the United States in Congress assembled and to the executives of all other states. The men who drew up this report concluded that a second meeting of representatives of the thirteen states should be convened on the second Monday in May 1787 in Philadelphia, to consider subjects in addition to trade. They said:

> The power of regulating trade is of such comprehensive extent, and

> will enter so far into the general System of the federal government that to give it efficacy, and to obviate questions and doubts concerning its precise nature and limits, may require a correspondent adjustment of other parts of the Federal System. That there are important defects in the System of the Federal Government is acknowledged by the Acts of all those States which have concurred in the present Meeting; that the defects, upon a close examination, may be found greater and more numerous, than even those acts imply, is at least so far probable, from the embarrassments which characterize the present State of our national affairs, foreign and domestic, as may reasonably be supposed to merit a deliberate and candid discussion, in some mode, which will unite the Sentiments and Councils of all the States.

Although the commissioners at Annapolis did not enumerate the defects in the Articles, they considered them to be "of a nature so serious as . . . to render the situation of the United States delicate and critical, calling for an exertion of the united virtue and wisdom of all the members of the Confederacy."[19]

The New Constitution

On February 21, 1787, Congress adopted a resolution calling for a convention of delegates of the several states to meet on the second Monday in May "for the sole and express purpose of revising the Articles of Confederation and reporting to Congress and the several legislatures such alterations and provisions therein as shall when agreed to in Congress and confirmed by the states render the federal constitution adequate to the exigencies of Government and the preservation of the Union."[20]

Even before passage of this resolution, seven states—New Hampshire, Virginia, New Jersey, Pennsylvania, North Carolina, Delaware, and Georgia—took legislative action authorizing the Philadelphia Convention. Thereafter, New York, South Carolina, Massachusetts, Connecticut, and Maryland, in the order named, took legislative action to be represented in the Convention. Only Rhode Island took no action and was not represented.

A plan from Virginia was laid before the delegates on May 29 by Edmund Randolph.[21] It proposed the correction and enlargement of the Articles so that the objectives proposed by their institution might be accomplished; that is, the common defense, the guaranteeing of liberty, and the furtherance of the general welfare. The plan proposed to vest in the Congress all "the Legislative Rights vested in

Congress by the Confederation" and, in addition, authority "to legislate in all cases to which the separate States are incompetent or in which the harmony of the United States may be interrupted by the exercise of individual legislation." Moreover, the Congress was to possess the right to veto all laws passed by the several states "controvening, in the opinion of the National Legislature, the articles of union, and to call forth the force of the Union against any member of the Union failing to fulfill its duty under the articles thereof."[22] The legislative, executive, and judiciary powers within the several states were to be bound by oath to support the articles of union.

The Congress was to become bicameral, the lower house being elected by the people of the several states and the upper house by members of the lower out of a proper number of persons nominated by the individual legislatures. Voting in the Congress was to be proportionate to the quotas regarding contributions or to the number of free inhabitants, "as the one or the other rule may seem best in different cases."

There were to be a national executive, chosen by the national legislature and vested with authority to execute the national laws and to enjoy "the Executive rights vested in Congress by the Confederation;" and a national judiciary, composed of one or more supreme and other inferior tribunals, the members of which would also be chosen by the national legislature. In Text C of the plan, the executive was designated as a single person.

The role of the inferior judicial tribunals was to hear and determine in the first instance—and that of the supreme tribunal to hear and determine on appeal—cases involving piracies and other felonies on the high seas and captures from an enemy; cases in which foreigners or citizens of other states might be interested; cases involving the collection of the national revenue, and the impeachment of national officers; and other questions "which may involve the national peace and harmony."

The executive and a convenient number of the national judiciary were to form a Council of Revision to examine every act of the national legislature, and to possess a power of suspensive veto. The Council was also to examine state legislation before a congressional negative thereon became final. Were the Council to reject a congressional negative, Congress would be empowered to reconsider, and to veto once again.

The plan proposed that a republican government ought to be

guaranteed by the United States to each state. There was provision for admittance of new states into the Union, with the consent of some part of the national legislature. Text C provided that amendments to the Articles of the union were to require the consent of the national legislature. Finally, the plan proposed that the work of the Philadelphia Convention be submitted to Congress, and, after its approval, to "an assembly or assemblies of representatives, recommended by the several Legislatures, to be expressly chosen by the people to consider and decide thereon."

The principal counterproposal to the Virginia plan was the Paterson or "small state plan."[23] It was laid before the delegates on June 15 by Samuel Paterson of New Jersey. In its final version, or Text C, it proposed that "an union of the states, merely federal, ought to be the sole object of the exercise of the powers vested in this convention"; and "that the articles of confederation ought to be so revised, corrected, and enlarged as to render the federal constitution adequate to the exigencies of government, and the preservation of the Union." The plan proposed to give to the United States in Congress, in addition to those powers already vested, authority to raise revenues by laying duties on all goods or merchandise imported into the united states, by imposing stamps on paper, parchment, and vellum, and by a postage on all letters and packages passing through the general post office; to make and to amend rules for the collection thereof, and for the regulation of trade and commerce with foreign nations and among the states. Punishments, fines, forfeitures and other penalties incurred for contravening such rules and regulations were to be adjudicated by the common law judiciaries of the state in which the alleged offense occurred, subject to an appeal in the last resort to the judiciary of the united states.

If the revenues from duties, stamps, and postage were insufficient for federal purposes, the Congress would be authorized to make requisitions on the states in proportion to the number of free citizens and inhabitants of every age, sex, and condition, and three-fifths of all other persons, not including Indians who paid no taxes. Congress was to be authorized to direct the collection of its requisition in any noncomplying state, and, for that purpose, to devise and pass acts.

Legislative acts of the union "made under and in pursuance to the articles of union, and all treaties made and ratified under the authority of the united states" were declared to be "the supreme law of the respective states," the judiciaries of the several states being bound thereby, anything in the laws of the states to the contrary notwithstanding. If any state or body of men within a state were to oppose or prevent the execution of legislative acts of the union or the execution of a treaty, the federal executive was authorized to call forth the powers of the confederated states to compel obedience. The legislative, executive, and judiciary officers within the several states were to be bound by oath to support the articles of union.

The Paterson plan proposed no change in the structure or composition of Congress. There was to be a national executive chosen by the united states meeting in Congress, with authority to execute federal acts, appoint all federal officers, and direct all military operations (although not, on any occasion, to conduct personally any military enterprise, nor to take command of any troops).

There was also to be a federal judiciary consisting of a supreme tribunal, the judges to be appointed by the executive and to hold office during good behavior. The supreme tribunal would be empowered to hear, in the first instance, impeachments of federal officers and, on appeal, cases touching the rights and privileges of ambassadors, captures from the enemy, and piracies and other felonies committed on the high seas; as well as cases in which foreigners were interested in drawing up a treaty, or cases arising from any act or ordinance of Congress for the regulation of trade or the collection of federal revenue.

The plan made provision for hearing and deciding all disputes arising between the united states and an individual state respecting territory. It was also proposed that new states be admitted into the union. The plan stipulated that the requirement for naturalization be the same in every state. Citizens of one state, committing an offense in another state, were to be bound by the law of the state in which the offense was committed. Finally, it was recommended that there be a definition of what offenses committed in any state were to be considered treason against the united states.

It is clear from the summary statements of the provisions of the Virginia and the Paterson plans that each contemplated a significantly different form of union, significantly different roles for the national or federal government, and significantly different positions for the states.

The differences between these plans lay in the powers assigned to the national government, in its structure, in the sources from which it drew support, and over whom or what its powers might be exercised.

Both plans sought to remedy the deficiencies in powers assigned to the central government, the Virginia plan through its general wording concerning matters to which the separate states had shown themselves inadequate or in which the peace and harmony of the United States might be involved; the Paterson plan by assigning to the Congress authority to regulate foreign and interstate trade and commerce and to lay duties upon imports, require stamps and make other charges on official documents and on letters and packages passing through the central post office. Through the duties on imports and the sale of stamps the sponsors of the Paterson plan hoped to make Congress less dependent upon requisitions on the states. Clearly, the sponsors of the Virginia plan were prepared to move farther in the matter of powers given to Congress than were the sponsors of the Paterson plan.

Other provisions of the two plans make differences in the thinking of their sponsors more clear. In the Virginia plan, the lower house of the bicameral Congress was to be chosen by the people of the separate states, rather than in whatever manner the state legislatures might choose; and the upper house was to be chosen by the lower house from persons nominated by the state legislatures. Voting in the Congress would be in proportion either to the quota of contributions or the number of free inhabitants in each state, in contrast to the existing scheme, which the Paterson plan proposed to continue in part, of equality of voting power for all states; thus, the Virginia plan moved away from the classical idea of a union of sovereign states, each with the same voting power. This was a source of great alarm for the small states, which feared the loss of their identity.

Both plans proposed an executive branch, to be chosen by the Congress, the final text of the Virginia plan recommending that this be a single person. The sponsors of both plans recognized that the endless involvement in administration of the Congress under the Articles of Confederation, sometimes even to the pettiest of details, had diverted attention from more appropriate matters and sharply reduced its credibility.

History has demonstrated that the national executive has been a source of very great strength for the national government. A *single* executive has undoubtedly been an important aspect of this strength, although other characteristics of the executive—to be found in neither of these plans, but, instead, worked out in the convention—have contributed significantly to the power of the executive.

Both plans proposed a national judiciary, although in the Paterson plan there was to be only a single supreme national tribunal with appellate jurisdiction from the state courts on cases involving, generally, the foreign policy or international relations of the united states, and regulations of trade and acts of revenue passed by the Congress. The original jurisdiction of this court was to be only over the impeachment of national officers. In the Virginia plan, there was provision not only for a supreme tribunal but inferior tribunals as well, the latter to have jurisdiction not only over cases involving foreign affairs and revenue acts passed by Congress but also over cases involving "the national peace and harmony."

Both plans stipulated that the legislative, executive, and judiciary branches of the states were to be bound by the articles of union, the Paterson plan adding that legislative acts and treaties of the union were to be the supreme law of the respective states, the state judiciaries to be bound thereby, the laws of the states to the contrary notwithstanding. Both plans provided for use of the forces of the union against any member state failing to comply with the articles of union, the Virginia plan vesting the power in the Congress, the Paterson plan in the executive.

The Virginia plan further provided that the Congress veto state legislative acts which, in the Congress' opinion, contravened legislation of the union or treaties made under its authority. It also proposed that the United States guarantee to each state a republican form of government. This suggests a somewhat different view of the relationship between the central government and the states. Finally, the Virginia plan provided ultimately for the ratification of the work of the Philadelphia Convention by the people in each state meeting in assemblies called by the legislature for the specific purpose of passing upon that work.

In brief, the sponsors of both plans were conscious of "the defects, the deformities, the diseases, and the ominous prospects" of the Confederation.[24] They knew that some persons in the new country were not unfavorable to a partition of the union into several confederacies, and that a, perhaps, small number of Americans looked with favor upon monarchy. Neither those aligning themselves with the Virginia plan nor those with the Paterson plan wished to have dismemberment or monarchy; but it is clear that supporters of the Virginia plan were more apprehensive about the inefficacy of a mere confederacy, and more nearly prepared, then, to move in the direction of a consolidated government which, in the words of James Madison, would provide a central government "organized into the regular departments, with physical means operating on individuals, to be sanctioned by *the people of the States*, acting in their original and sovereign character."[25]

Early in the Philadelphia Convention, on May 30, the members having gone into a Committee of the Whole, Edmund Randolph moved to postpone consideration of the first section of the Virginia plan; to so correct and enlarge the Articles of Confederation that they would accomplish the objectives proposed at the time of their institution; and, to this effect, that the Convention consider the following propositions:

> 1. That a union of the states merely federal in character will not accomplish the objectives proposed by the Articles of Confederation, namely, a common defense, a guarantee of liberty, and a furtherance of the general welfare.
> 2. That no treaty or treaties signed by all or a part of the states, each as an individual sovereignty, will be sufficient.
> 3. That a *national* government, consisting of a *supreme* legislature, an executive, and a judiciary, ought to be established.[26]

This motion, seconded by Gouverneur Morris of Pennsylvania, was unanimously agreed to. On May 31 to June 1, the Committee of the Whole agreed that there be a bicameral legislature; that the first or lower house be elected by the people in each state; that the powers of the national legislature include all the legislative powers of the Congress of the Articles of Confederation and also the power to pass laws where the separate states had proven to be incompetent or where otherwise necessary to preserve the harmony of the nation; and to invalidate state laws contravening these articles of union. It was also agreed that there would be a national executive with the power to execute national laws and to appoint to office where not otherwise provided for. The delegates did not agree, however, to the proposed selection of members of the second house by the first; and they postponed consideration of the proposal to use force against states not complying with the articles of union. James Madison, who originally was in favor of the possession of such a power by the Congress, now expressed his doubts as to its wisdom, since the use of force would look too much like war. The power to use force did not appear in the draft presented later, on August 6, by the Committee of Detail. There was, then, general agreement to drop this proposal.

From June 1 until June 19, when the delegates ceased to be a Committee of the Whole, by far the greatest amount of time was spent in debating the nature of the commission given to the Convention and the structural aspects of the Virginia plan and that offered by Mr. Paterson on June 15. Mr. Paterson and his supporters argued that the commission that had been given to the delegates was limited to the passage of suitable amendments to the Articles of Confederation. They emphatically held that the delegates were not authorized to change the nature of the union in a way that would abolish the sovereignty of the state in order "to move to a consolidation of the States, and a national government."[27] They viewed the proposition that the Congress be given a veto over state acts as unacceptable; and equally unacceptable was the proposal that representation in the Congress be in proportion to state contributions or population. That the lower house be elected by the people in each state was less objectionable to them than the principle of proportional representation. They believed that all that was authorized—and necessary—was that Congress have more power, but only enough to give it a greater degree of independence from the financial support of the states and also to enable it to move effectively in the areas of foreign policy and the regulation of foreign and interstate trade. Certainly, Mr. Paterson was unprepared to accept such a sweeping delegation of powers to the Congress that it would be able to legislate on all matters in which the states had proved to be incompetent or the harmony of the united states might be involved. In sum, no structural changes in the Congress nor any substantial enlargement of its powers were viewed as compatible with a confederate union of sovereign states.

From June 19 until August 6, when the Committee of Detail reported a draft of a constitution, on only two occasions was there some debate on the powers to be given Congress. On June 27 consideration of the resolution of the Virginia plan which referred to the powers of the Congress was postponed, in order that the body might be able to debate resolutions regarding the bases of representation in the two houses of Congress, or what were considered to be "the most fundamental points."[28] Luther Martin of Maryland argued "with great eagerness, that the General Government was meant merely to preserve the State Governments, not to govern individuals;" and he also maintained:

> That individuals, as such, have little to do but with their own States. . . .That to resort to the citizens at large for their sanction to a new government will be throwing them back into a state of nature; that the dissolution of the State Governments is involved in the nature of the process; that the people have no right to do this, without the consent of those to whom they have delegated their power for State purposes. . . . That an equal vote in each State was essential to the Federal idea, and was founded in justice and freedom, not merely in policy. . . . That the States, being equal, cannot treat or confederate so as to give up an equality of votes, without giving up their liberty. That the [Virginia plan] propositions . . . were a system of slavery for ten States.[29]

Mr. Martin continued to maintain on June 28 that:

> The General Government ought to be formed for the States, not for individuals; that if the States were to have votes in proportion to their numbers of people, it would be the same thing, whether their Representatives were chosen by the Legislatures or the people, the smaller States would be equally enslaved.[30]

On July 17 the Convention returned to a consideration of the proposed assignment of powers to Congress as outlined in the Virginia plan. Roger Sherman of Connecticut moved to delete the passage concerning matters to which the individual states might be incompetent and to substitute the clauses: "to make laws binding on the people of the United States in all cases which may concern the common interests of the Union; but not to interfere with the government of the individual States in any matters of internal police which respect the government of such States only, and wherein the general welfare of the United States is not concerned."[31]

Gouverneur Morris opposed this wording because "the internal police, as it would be called and understood by the States, ought to be infringed in many cases, as in the case of paper-money, and other tricks by which citizens of other States may be affected."[32]

In explaining his idea, Mr. Sherman read a list of powers to be assigned to Congress, including the levying of taxes on trade—but not direct taxation. Mr. Morris, remarking this omission, concluded that it was the intention of Mr. Sherman that "the General Government should recur to quotas and requisitions, which are subversive of the idea of government."[33] Mr. Sherman, conceding that his enumeration did not include direct taxation, said that he understood some provision must be made for supplying funds needed by the general government over and above those obtained from taxing foreign imports, from charges on legal documents and from the sale of stamps, but that he had no suggestions to offer.

Mr. Sherman's motion was defeated, only Connecticut and Maryland voting for it, and Massachusetts, New Jersey, Pennsylvania, Delaware, Virginia, North Carolina, South Carolina, and Georgia voting against.

The convention proceeded then to consider congressional nullification of state laws which contravened national legislation or treaties. Although James Madison spoke in favor of nullification "as essential to the efficacy and security of the General Government" which must be protected from the "propensity of the States to pursue their particular interests in opposition to the general interest," Gouverneur Morris opposed it as unnecessary "if sufficient legislative authority be given to the General Government."[34] Roger Sherman also opposed it as unnecessary, since the courts of the states would not consider as valid any law contravening the authority of the union; and Luther Martin, wondering if all state laws would be required to be reviewed before they were permitted to operate, considered nullification improper and inadmissible. Gouverneur Morris spoke again, asserting his increasing opposition, since he believed that nullification would disgust all the states, and, futhermore, that any law that ought to be nullified would be set aside by the judiciary. Nullification was defeated, only three states —Massachusetts, Virginia, and North Carolina—voting in favor.

Luther Martin then proposed what has become the supremacy clause of Article VI of the Constitution; and this was accepted—really, in place of nullification—by unanimous vote.

On August 6 the Committee of Detail reported a draft of the constitution. The enumeration of the powers of Congress, in Article VII, was clearly similar to that now to be found in Article I, Sec. 8, of the Constitution; it included the power to tax citizens, and, at the end, the "necessary and proper" clause, now the eighteenth clause of Sec. 8. Although, on thirteen of the days of the Convention between August 6 and September 17, the powers of Congress were debated, a much larger portion of the time was spent on the structure of the three branches of government; for example, the draft which came from the Committee of Detail provided that the single executive be chosen by the legislature for a single term of seven years; it gave the executive no part in the making of treaties. The draft also did not specify what should be the jurisdiction of the inferior courts when they might be constituted by the Congress.

Finally, on September 17, the expanded Constitution was read and passed by the Convention. It was then transmitted to Congress with a resolution requesting that the Congress, after considering it, pass it on to a convention of delegates in each state to be chosen by the people thereof, in the manner recommended by the state legislature. Upon the ratification of nine states being transmitted to the Congress of the United States, the Congress should fix the day for presidential elections, following which members of the two houses of the new Congress would be elected in each state. When the President and the new Congress had been elected, they should forthwith proceed to carry out the Constitution.[35]

On September 28 the Congress submitted the proposed constitution to the states to be considered by their conventions of delegates.[36]

Ratifying the Federal Structure

The struggle for ratification was an intense one. Finally, ratification was obtained in all thirteen states, Virginia (June 27, 1788), New York (July 26, 1788), North Carolina (November 21, 1789) and Rhode Island (May 29, 1790) being the last. New Hampshire's ratification on June 21, 1788 brought the Constitution into being. Several of the state conventions proposed amendments, including guarantees which eventually formed the Bill of Rights.[37]

A major issue raised during the ratification debates in all the states was the nature of the union proposed by the Constitutiton. Those in opposition to the document, now described as Anti-Federalists, in fact thought of themselves as Federalists. They spoke *for* preservation of the federal union of sovereign states and against what they described as the *consolidated* union of the Constitution, in which the general government would have power, exceeding that of the states, to deal with matters internal to the states, and to bind the states to accept national action. They vehemently opposed representation in the lower house in proportion to population, and also the provision that population play a role in the votes cast for President in each state by the presidential electors. They argued that the general government be one in which the states were equally represented, a government of narrowly and precisely limited powers, and one capable of acting only on the states, and not on individual citizens.[38]

Opponents of the Constitution believed there could be no middle ground between a federal union, or confederacy, and a consolidated government, or unitary one, *confederacy* and *unitary* being here used in their current sense.

Proponents of the Constitution argued that there could be a middle ground. Believing, as they did, that confederacies had always either failed outright or provided union only in the face of the most clearly recognized threat from outside,[39] and knowing that a unitary government was unacceptable, they argued that the government proposed by the Constitution embodied the essential elements of a federal or confederate union and also of a national government; in other words, that it was a compound.[40]

Alexander Hamilton, in *Federalist* 9, argued that the only essential element of a federal union is the continuing existence of member states. Although many confederacies had been charcterized by 1. an equality of voting power for member states in the general government; 2. a prohibition laid on the general government regarding any concern being given to the internal affairs of member states; and 3. a provision that the general government act on the states rather than on individual citizens, Hamilton insisted that these considerations are not essential to the existence of a federal union. Rather, they have been "the cause of incurable disorder and imbecility in the government." Drawing support from Montesquieu, he asserted that the most successful confederate republic was that of Lycia, in which there was unequal suffrage of member states and also power given to the general government to intervene in highly important internal affairs of these member states.

Close to the end of *Federalist* 9, Hamilton wrote:

> The definition of a *confederate republic* seems simply to be "an assemblage of societies," or an association of two or more states into

> one state. The extent, modifications, and objects of the federal authority are mere matters of discretion. So long as the separate organization of the members be not abolished; so long as it exists, by a constitutional necessity, for local purposes; though it should be in perfect subordination to the general authority of the union, it would still be, in fact and theory, an association of states, or a confederacy.

Thus, Hamilton insisted that attributes thought by opponents of the Constitution to be essential to a federal union were not actually essential but only happened to be characteristic of most federal unions of the past; and he further asserted that an important characteristic of a federal union is that the constitutionally protected member states retain their power to deal with "local purposes," even though in subordination to the general authority of the union. Here is the contemporary understanding of federalism: a union of member states that retain sovereignty within their local spheres but are part of a national body that possesses sovereignty in other spheres.

In *Federalist* 39, James Madison made the case for the Constitution as a compound of federal and national elements:

> In order to ascertain the real character of the government, it may be considered in relation [1] to the foundation on which it is to be established; [2] to the sources from which its ordinary powers are to be drawn; [3] to the operation of those powers; [4] to the extent of them; and [5] to the authority by which future changes in the government are to be introduced.

The foundation Madison described as federal; for, while ratification will be by the people, and not by the states, it will be by the people in their respective states. This is taken to be an action by the states, not through organs of government but through their citizens.

With respect to the sources from which the ordinary powers are to be drawn, Madison characterized the House of Representatives as national because it derives "its powers from the people of America . . . in the same proportion, and on the same principle, as they are in the legislature of a particular State." The Senate is a federal institution because it derives its powers from the states. The presidency is a mixture of federal and national elements.

In the exercise of its powers directly upon individual citizens, Madison believed the government to be national; but with regard to the extent of its powers he argued that "the proposed government cannot be deemed a national one; since its jurisdiction extends to certain enumerated objects only, and leaves to the several States a residuary and inviolable sovereignty over all other objects."[41]

Finally, the authority by which changes in the government might be made Madison described as a compound:

> Were it wholly national, the supreme and ultimate authority would reside in the majority of the people of the Union. . . . Were it wholly federal, on the other hand, the concurrence of each State in the Union would be essential to every alteration that would be binding on all. . . . In requiring more than a majority, and particularly in computing the proportion by *States*, not by *citizens*, it departs from the *national* and advances toward the *federal* character; in rendering the concurrence of less than the whole number of States sufficient, it loses again the federal and partakes of the national character.

It cannot be doubted that *The Federalist* was a powerful and effective force in securing ratification of the Constitution, and also that the arguments made by Hamilton and Madison concerning the preservation of the essential federal element in the proposed union allayed much of the anxiety created by the charge of critics of the Constitution that it, in fact, proposed a consolidated union.

Martin Diamond has argued that both Hamilton and Madison believed that the new national government would prove to have advantages far superior to those of the state governments, and that the affairs of the union would come to be of much greater interest to citizens at large.[42] Both men were aware of the vigor of centrifugal tendencies in the country, and they did not expect that these tendencies would at once diminish when the Constitution went into effect. Because they hoped that the union would be strong, they also hoped, and believed, that the centripetal tendency would ultimately predominate because of the greater interest in national affairs.

They did not attach much value to the federal elements in the new government, since they regarded them as a necessary evil in order to secure ratification of the Constitution. Certainly they did not define "federal union" as now defined, e.g., as "the division of political power between a central government, with authority over the entire territory of a nation, and a series of local governments. . . ."[43] They did not believe they had created a new principle of union, but only a compromise, which could accomplish the necessary purposes of the nation, having first won acceptance from a people largely hostile to central authority.

That the centrifugal tendencies were not diminished upon the adoption of the Constitution is clear from the most cursory reading of our history.

Practices and Growth

The Kentucky and Virginia Resolutions (which grew out of the Alien and Sedition Acts of the late 1790s); the resistance of New England to the national course set before the War of 1812 and to the declaration of that war (a resistance expressed in part by the refusal of the New England governors to accept the state militia being called into national service when the President believed a national emergency to exist); the resistance to and nullification of tariffs found objectionable by various states; these are dramatic examples of the strength of the tradition of state sovereignty.

The members of the First Congress, sensitive to the vitality of centrifugal tendencies, took a number of steps to vitalize the new Constitution and the new national government. One of the most important of these steps was the passage of the Judiciary Act of 1789.[44] Section 25 of the Act gave final jurisdiction to the United States Supreme Court in any case involving a question arising under the United States Constitution, when the highest state court having jurisdiction had made its decision. The Act also created lower national courts, which ensured that the supremacy of the national Constitution and national statutes and treaties would not wholly depend upon the uncertain sympathies of state trial courts.

That the true meaning and effect of Section 25 was quickly recognized by the state judiciaries is shown in *Martin* v. *Hunter's Lessee*.[45] In the first arguing and decision, the Supreme Court itself appeared somewhat uncertain as to the powers given it in Section 25. Mr. Justice Story's opinion for the Court on the second arguing of the case comes through as a clear statement of the meaning of the supreme law of the land clause in Article VI of the Constitution, of the importance of the Judiciary Act of 1789, and, in particular of Section 25, which the state judiciary asserted to be unconstitutional but which was held by the Court to be a proper exercise of Congress's power and a signally important means of implementing the supremacy clause.

The role of the Supreme Court as the explicator of national powers and as an umpire between the national and the state governments in disputes over their respective powers, grew in importance throughout the nineteenth century. The Court made a signal contribution to the development of the modern understanding of federalism as a form of union in which powers are divided between a central government and local governments, because it provided a forum in which disputes over powers could be settled by the orderly process of law. Very probably, the Court in performing this function made it appear that sovereignty could, indeed, be divided, and the division be maintained effectively and amicably. Certainly, the Court gave to federalism an overwhelmingly *legal* cast.

It should, however, be noted that, despite the decisions of the Marshall Court explicating powers assigned to the Congress in Article I, Section 8, in a manner highly favorable to expanded use of national power,[46] the Congress did not, on the whole, until the latter part of the nineteenth century, choose to exercise its powers in a way that would disturb state governments in the use of their powers. This is particularly true of the control over interstate and foreign commerce.

The Civil War, preceded by diverse and acrimonious debates over national and state powers, has seemed to settle the question of whether states are free to secede from the Union when no longer in sympathy with important national policies. Rather contradictorily, Reconstruction settled the issue of whether the Congress can impose upon rebellious states stiff conditions for their readmittance into the Union, notably their giving consent to the thirteenth, fourteenth, and fifteenth Amendments to the Constitution.

These Amendments, intended to protect the freedmen from southern state action, were given rigorously restricted meaning by the Supreme Court in the decades immediately following the Civil War.[47] Not until the mid-1940s, and then at an accelerating pace in the 1950s, 1960s, and 1970s did the Supreme Court use the fourteenth and fifteenth Amendments—but especially the fourteenth—to require that states meet national judicially determined standards with respect to rights, not simply of the Negro but also of many other groups.[48]

These interpretations of the Court, designed to protect rights, have been joined by enactments of Congress, beginning with the Civil Rights Act of 1957, and most notably including the Voting Rights Act of 1965.[49]

In interpreting the Voting Rights Act, the Court has asserted that Congress has an affirmative power to implement the post-Civil War Amendments, and that it has chosen so to implement the fourteenth and fifteenth Amendments.[50] The Court has interpreted the legislation to mean that federal consent to changes in the voting laws in states covered by the formula includes: districting plans alleged to be so drawn as to discriminate against minorities;[51] state or local legislation weighting voting in special elections in favor of those with a particular stake in the outcome;[52] the determination of which offices will be elective;[53] and qualifications for office.[54] In a very recent decision (February 1975), the majority held that national political parties are not bound by constitutional requirements as to "one-man, one-vote," but the decision was written in language strongly intimating that the majority would not rule out the possibility that at a later time it might hold parties subject to constitutional standards.[55]

The Industrial Revolution, which began before the Civil War but came to full flower afterward, eventually prompted Congress significantly to use its power to regulate commerce, in order to deal with economic problems of national, rather than local character. The first instances of such a congressional exercise of power were the passing of the Interstate Commerce Act of 1887 and the Sherman Anti-Trust Act of 1890. The first sought to regulate a number of practices of railroads, the second to prohibit contracts, combinations or conspiracies in restraint of interstate commerce.

For some time the Supreme Court, in cases concerning these Acts, was cautious in its approach to them, or openly hostile, more particularly with reference to the Sherman Act;[56] but, again in the 1930s, the Court reversed itself, accepting the national character of the economy, and sustaining interpretations of congressional enactments which seemed to place little, if anything, beyond the reach of the congressional power over commerce.[57] At almost the same time, the Court announced interpretations of the power to tax and to spend which seemed to leave few impediments to Congress' use of these powers.[58]

In summary, one might say that, after 1937, the Court, by giving a very broad interpretation to the commerce and taxing and spending powers of the national government, largely withdrew from its function as umpire between the national and state governments in disputes over their respective powers. The withdrawal of the Court was an acquiescence to the very substantial scope of power being exercised by Congress.

One other development relevant to the status of national and state powers should be noted. The grant-in-aid, a device begun in the nineteenth century, by which Congress provided money for programs to be implemented by the states, has, in the 1960s, become a means by which Congress sets national goals and provides states and localities with funds to carry them out.[59] After World War II, grant-in-aid programs shifted from dollar-for-dollar matching programs to being up to 90 percent federally funded, 10 percent state or locally funded. It was, of course, always true that the national government set the general purpose for which a grant-in-aid was to be set up. There was, however, in the 1960s, a shift in emphasis, away from program goals largely recognized as desirable at the state and local levels—which, then, pressed for national funds to implement them—to congressional initiatives in determining goals. State and local governments became more clearly administrative units only.

Conclusion

In the light of the very substantial centralization of forces during the last several decades—forces which prompted an assertion of its powers by Congress which has been upheld, even perhaps induced, by decisions of the Supreme Court—it may be appropriate to ask: "What is the state of American federalism today?"

If the thesis concerning the intentions of many of the framers of the Constitution is accepted—that they sought a national government, with the states subordinate to it; that they anticipated the predominance of more interesting national issues; that they envisioned states as administrative units, important administrative units, to be sure, because decentralization in administering programs seemed practical and desirable—if this thesis is accepted, then the answer to our question must be that American federalism has become what it was expected to become.

There is a basis for some degree of concern that the centralization of policy decisions has gone too far, that men and women in Washington—in Congress, in the executive branch, on the Court—cannot know or understand all aspects of the issues, and of the policy decisions being made. Some examples (to be sure, perhaps not acceptable as examples to all) are the national standards for school busing and other affirmative action programs. Certainly some Supreme Court decisions—for example, those on abortion, school prayer, and public aid to private schools—have provoked considerable uneasiness in much of the country.

Those who share the concern that too many decisions have been centralized will look to the political process to effect change. That is the reason for the alarm over national party actions, such as the rules regarding delegate selection in 1972 and 1975 for the Democratic National Conventions, and over Supreme Court decisions such as *Cousins* v. *Wigoda*.

It seems unlikely that there can be any shift in Supreme Court decisions significant enough to effect a notable degree of decentralization in policy decisions.

Notes

1. *Documents Illustrative of the Formation of the Union of the American States* (Washington, D.C.: U.S. Government Printing Office, 1927), p. 21.
2. James Madison, *Journal of the Federal Convention*. Reprinted from the Edition of 1840 which was published under direction of the U.S. Government from the original manuscripts. (Chicago: Albert, Scott and Company, 1893), p. 23.
3. The historical material appearing in the following pages has been derived mainly from Samuel Eliot Morison, *The Oxford History of the American People* (New York: Oxford University Press, 1965).
4. *Documents Illustrative of the Formation*, p. 27.
5. Ibid., p. 28.
6. Ibid., Art. VI, p. 30.
7. Much of the material on the perceived defects of the Articles of Confederation is taken from George Bancroft, *History of the Formation of the Constitution of the United States of America*, 3d ed. (New York: D. Appleton and Company, 1883), vol. 1.
8. Bancroft, p. 23.
9. Ibid., pp. 22-23.
10. Ibid., p. 19.
11. Ibid., p. 24.
12. Ibid., pp. 25-26.
13. Ibid., p. 28.
14. Ibid., p. 166.

15. Ibid., p. 167.
16. Ibid., pp. 166-167.
17. E.S. Corwin, "The Progress of Constitutional Theory Between the Declaration of Independence and the Meeting of the Philadelphia Convention," in A.T. Mason and Gerald Garvey, eds., *American Constitutional History* (New York: Harper and Row, 1964).
18. *Documents Illustrative of the Formation*, p. 38.
19. Ibid., p. 42.
20. Ibid., p. 46.
21. "Variant Texts of the Virginia Plan, Presented by Edmund Randolph to the Federal Convention, May 29, 1787," *Documents Illustrative of the Formation*, pp. 953-966.
22. Ibid., p. 954. This wording with reference to the proposed powers of the Congress appears in Texts A, B, and C of the Virginia Plan (pp. 958, 961), with the single addition in Texts B and C of a power to veto any state act contravening a treaty subsisting under the authority of the union.
23. "Variant Texts of the Plan Presented by William Paterson (N.J.) to the Federal Convention, June 15, 1787," *Documents Illustrative of the Formation*, pp. 967-978. Charles Pinckney of South Carolina presented a plan to the Convention, Ibid., pp. 964-966; and so, too, did Alexander Hamilton, whose plan was revised four times (Texts A-E), Ibid., pp. 979-988. A full text of the Pinckney Plan, which was referred to the Committee of Detail, can be found in James Madison's *Journal of the Federal Convention* (Chicago: Albert, Scott and Company, 1893), pp. 64-72. Of particular interest is the enumeration in Article V of the powers of the Congress of the United States.
24. Ibid., "Introduction," p. 48.
25. Ibid.
26. Ibid., p. 73.
27. Ibid., p. 168.
28. Ibid., p. 250.
29. Ibid., pp. 251-252.
30. Ibid., pp. 252-253.
31. Ibid., p. 361.
32. Ibid., p. 362.
33. Ibid.
34. Ibid., p. 363.
35. *Documents Illustrative of the Formation*, pp. 1005-1006.
36. Ibid., p. 1007.
37. For the texts of the letters of ratification from each state, see *Documents Illustrative of the Formation*, pp. 1009-1059. See also *The Debates in the Several State Conventions on the Adoption of the Federal Constitution*, 5 vols., ed. Jonathan Elliot (New York: Lenox Hill, 1888-96).
38. See Richard Henry Lee, "Letters of the Federalist Framer" in *Pamphlets on the Constitution of the United States, 1787-88*, ed. Paul

Leicester Ford (Brooklyn, New York, 1888).

39. See the remarks of James Madison to the Philadelphia Convention on June 19, 1787, in *Journal of the Federal Convention*, pp. 187-196. See also *Federalist* ed. E. M. Earle (New York: Modern Library edition), 9, 15-20.
40. *Federalist* 9, 39.
41. In *Federalist* 45, Madison wrote concerning the powers of the new national government that the change was much less an addition of powers than an invigoration of the original powers.
42. Martin Diamond, "The Federalist's View of Federalism," in George C. S. Benson, ed., *Essays in Federalism* (Claremont, California: Institute for Studies in Federalism, 1961).
43. Robert K. Carr et al., *Essentials of American Democracy*, 7th. ed. (Hillsdale, Illinois: Dryden Press, 1974), p. 117.
44. 28 U.S.C., Sec. 1257. For an interesting account of other actions taken by the Congresses and the Presidents in the first decade in order to strengthen the national government, see L. D. White, *The Federalists, A Study in Administrative History* (New York: MacMillan Company, 1948). See also Charles S. Hyneman and George W. Carey, eds., *A Second Federalist* (New York: Appleton-Century-Crofts, 1967).
45. In its first appearance before the Supreme Court, the style of the case was *Fairfax's Devisee* v. *Hunter's Lessee*, 7 Cranch 603 (1813). *Martin* v. *Hunter's Lessee* was the style on second appearance, 1 Wheat. 304 (1816).
46. Note, in particular, *McCulloch* v. *Maryland*, 4 Wheat. 316 (1819) and *Gibbons* v. *Ogden*, 9 Wheat. 1 (1824). In the former, the Court upheld the constitutionality of the national bank as a "necessary and proper" means to exercise several of the delegated powers of Congress. In the latter, the Court defined the power to regulate interstate commerce as that of regulating intercourse—not simply, then, goods traveling between States, but citizens, commercial paper and the means of transportation by which they were carried.
47. Note, for example, the decisions in the Slaughter-House Cases, 16 Wall. 36 (1873); *Munn* v. *Illinois*, 94 U.S. 113 (1877); *Davidson* v. *New Orleans*, 96 U.S. 97 (1878); *Mugler* v. *Kansas*, 123 U.S. 623 (1887); *Powell* v. *Pennsylvania*, 127 U.S. 678 (1888).
48. Note, for example, *Smith* v. *Allwright*, 321 U.S. 649 (voting in primaries); *Brown* v. *Board of Education*, 347 U.S. 483 (1954) (segregated schools); *Mayor and City Council of Baltimore* v. *Dawson*, 350 U.S. 877 (1955) (segregated beaches); *Gayle* v. *Browder*, 352 U.S. 903 (1956) (segregated seating in buses); *Holmer* v. *City of Atlanta*, 350 U.S. 879 (1955) (segregated public parks); *United States* v. *Montgomery County Board of Education*, 395 U.S. 225 (1969) (desegregation of public school facilities); *Swann* v. *Charlotte-Mecklenburg Board of Education*, 402 U.S. 1 (1971) (busing to achieve racial balance in schools); *Mapp* v. *Ohio*, 867 U.S. 643 (1961); *Gideon* v. *Wainwright*, 372

U.S. 335 (1963); and a long list of cases concerning the rights of criminal defendants and incorporating guarantees of the Bill of Rights into the 14th Amendment. For a survey of these latter cases, see Gerald Gunther and Noel T. Dowling, *Constitutional Law–Cases and Materials* (Mineola, New York: The Foundation Press, 1970) chap. 12, and the relevant pages of the 1974 *Supplement*. Other examples include: *Baker* v. *Carr*, 369 U.S. 186 (1962) (legislative districts subject to equal protection); *Reynolds* v. *Sims*, 377 U.S. 533 (1964) (legislative districts—one-man, one-vote); *Shapiro* v. *Thompson*, 394 U.S. 618 (1969) (residence requirements for welfare benefits); *Roe* v. *Wade*, 410 U.S. 113 (1973) (right to privacy invalidates anti-abortion statute).

49. 42 U.S.C. (1971). 79 U.S. Stat., L. 437.
50. *South Carolina* v. *Katzenbach*, 383 U.S. 301 (1966).
51. *Georgia* v. *The United States*, 23 L.Ed. 2d, 647 (1973); *White* v. *Regester*, 37 L.Ed. 2d, 314 (1973).
52. *Cipriano* v. *Houma*, 23 L.Ed. 2d, 583 (1969); *Associated Enterprises, Inc.* v. *Toltec Watershed Improvement District*, 42 L.Ed. 2d, 595 (1973).
53. *Allen* v. *State Board of Elections*, 393 U.S. 544 (1969).
54. Ibid.
55. *Cousins* v. *Wigoda*, 42 L.Ed. 2d, 605.
56. See, especially, *The United States* v. *E. C. Knight Co.*, 156 U.S. 1 (1895).
57. See *NLRB* v. *Jones and Laughlin Steel Corp.*, 301 U.S. 1 (1937); *The United States* v. *Darby*, 312 U.S. 100 (1941); *The United States* v. *Sullivan*, 332 U.S. 689 (1948); *Wickard* v. *Filburn*, 317 U.S. 111 (1942); *The United States* v. *Wrightwood Dairy*, 315 U.S. 110 (1942); *Heart of Atlanta Motel* v. *United States*, 379 U.S. 241 (1964); *Katzenbach* v. *McClurg*, 379 U.S. 294 (1964).
58. See *Steward Machine Co.* v. *Davis*, 301 U.S. 548 (1937); and *Helvering* v. *Davis*, 301 U.S. 619 (1937).
59. See James Sundquist, *Making Federalism Work* (Washington, D.C.: Brookings Institution, 1969).

[6]

THE WRITTEN CONSTITUTION

—RONALD M. PETERS, Jr.

The American political system descended from the English political system, but it is very different from it. Among the most significant differences is the fact that the American system is based upon written constitutions while the English system is not. Why did Americans choose to adopt written constitutions, and what have been the effects of that decision? These are the questions which we shall consider here. In order to answer them, we will examine the American constitutional system at its origin, during the period of the American Revolution (Part I of this chapter). We shall argue that the constitutions which were adopted then were perceived to be instruments of popular sovereignty which placed only procedural limitations upon the power of government. These constitutions will then be contrasted with the federal Constitution, and American state and federal constitutional development since the founding period will be discussed (Part II). Here, we will contend that both our federal and state constitutions have departed from the conception which underlay the first state constitutions. The chapter will then conclude by considering the implications of our experience with written constitutions, in the hope of suggesting at this time of the Bicentennial possible improvements in our constitutional system (Part III). It will be suggested that improvements can be made by bringing our constitutions closer in line with the conception of a written constitution which guided our Revolutionary ancestors.

I

The major concept over which the American Revolution was fought was sovereignty—the idea that in every political society there must be an ultimate, all powerful authority from which there is no higher appeal, and from which all subordinate authority derives. Under the English constitution, as it was understood in the eighteenth century, sovereignty resided in the Parliament. William Blackstone, writing in his *Commentaries on the Laws of England* in 1765 described an act of Parliament as

> The exercise of the highest authority that this kingdom acknowledges upon earth. It hath power to bind every subject in the land, and the dominions thereunto belonging; nay, even the King himself, if particularly named therein. And it cannot be altered, amended, dispensed with, suspended, or repealed, but in the same forms, and by the same authority of parliament; for it is a maxim of law, that it requires the same strength to dissolve as to create an obligation.[1]

This concept of parliamentary sovereignty was at odds with the colonists' view of their charters, which was that charters constituted binding agreements between England and her colonies and insured the Americans' rights as Englishmen. Among those rights was that of internal self-government. It was one that they could claim only by denying the right of Parliament to regulate their affairs, or, in other words, by denying the sovereignty of Parliament. When the issue was joined on the question of colonial taxation, the die for the Revolution was cast.

In the Declaration of Independence the new "united States of America" proclaimed their right to govern themselves. According to the argument in the second paragraph of the Declaration, a people oppressed have the right to throw off their old forms of government and to establish a "new Government, laying its foundation on such principles and organizing its powers in such form, as to them shall seem most likely to effect their Safety and Happiness." The list of grievances makes it perfectly clear that the oppression felt by the Americans derived from the belief that the English Parliament was usurping their right to run their internal affairs. Almost all of the grievances have to do with some aspect of the right of self-government. The first six deal specifically with the rights of American legislatures and the power to make policy through law. Other grievances deal with the administration of law through the judicial system, and the procedural due-process rights which the Americans claimed under the common law of England.

While the Declaration was clear in its prescription regarding self-government, it was quite vague regarding the means employed to achieve that end. After independence was declared, however, it was recognized by all patriots that government had to be established on a new basis. As a Pennsylvania pamphleteer put it in 1776, "[A]s, by the tyranny of George the Third, the compact of allegiance and protection between him and the good people of this Colony is totally dissolved, and the whole power of government is by that means returned to the people at large; it is become absolutely necessary to have this power collected and again reposed in such hands as may be judged most likely to employ it for the common good."[2] How should this be done? The long tradition of government under the colonial charters must have made it seem logical to most Americans that a new set of agreements was necessary for a new set of governments. This time, however, the agreements would be compacts among the American people, rather than between them and the English Parliament. These compacts would be formed in the process of adopting constitutions.

During the decade from 1776 to 1786 fifteen state constitutions were adopted in America: Delaware, Maryland, New Hampshire, New Jersey, North Carolina, Pennsylvania, South Carolina and Virginia, in 1776; Georgia, New York, and Vermont, in 1777; South Carolina, in 1778; Massachusetts, in 1780; New Hampshire, in 1784; and Vermont, in 1786. Rhode Island and Connecticut chose to reaffirm their colonial charters. About these constitutions we may ask: 1. What do the circumstances of adoption imply about their character? 2. What do the documents themselves tell us about the Revolutionary conception of a written constitution?

The stress which the Declaration of Independence laid on the rights of American legislatures suggests the high esteem in which the colonial legislatures had been held, at least by those sympathetic to the American cause. During the crisis years of the 1760s and early 1770s it had been the colonial assemblies which had carried the fight against the royalist governors. After the colonial charters were suspended in 1775, these assemblies, now designated as provincial assemblies, were the only source of authority in the American colonies. While a degree of continuity of government was maintained by them, it cannot be said that government continued on a business-as-usual basis during this period. At the local level law enforcement was in the hands of revolutionary committees of safety; and in some colonies the courts of law were suspended. It should be remembered that during these early years the Revolution did not command universal support, even among those who were not outright Tories; therefore the authority upon which the provincial assemblies rested was of questionable validity.

Under these circumstances the adoption of new constitutions by the provincial assemblies was both a necessary and a daring step; and it is not surprising that the formalities of calling a special constitutional convention were not generally undertaken. Of the fifteen constitutions drafted between 1776 and 1786, eleven were drawn up and enacted by legislative bodies either in ordinary session or in a special session designated as a constitutional convention. In most of the states, the legislatures had been elected with a special mandate to form a constitution. The South Carolina constitutions of 1776 and 1778 were declared by the supreme court of that state to be mere legislative acts, alterable as ordinary law by the legislature. Even though circumstances probably precluded any attempt to form constitutions by special conventions in 1776 and 1777, it is not clear that such an alternative was widely appreciated at the time. The provincial assemblies assumed it to be proper for them to adopt new constitutions, and they proceeded to do so without evidencing any doubt about the appropriateness of such action. This implies that the distinction between legislative power and popular sovereignty had not yet emerged in the minds of American lawmakers.

Almost immediately, however, the legislative character of the new constitutions came under criticism from some quarters. When the Massachusetts General Assembly resumed the ancient charter of that colony in 1775 they encountered protests from several towns on the grounds that a legislature could not create a constitution by which it would itself be bound. This issue became more significant during the debates over the legislatively proposed constitution of 1778 in Massachusetts; and it was one of the most important reasons why that document was rejected by the towns. Chastened, the legislature called for a specially elected constitutional convention in 1779, and that convention produced the widely admired constitution of 1780. This was the first written constitution to be drafted by a special constitutional convention. It was also the first to be approved by the people over whom it was to operate. The Massachusetts example was emulated by New Hampshire in 1784, and thereafter the practice became common.

The constitutional convention is the institutional embodiment of the concept of popular sovereignty; and the fact that it became accepted after 1780 suggests that the triumph of popular sovereignty over legislative sovereignty also dates from that time. The idea that the people have the right to govern themselves was, of course, stated in the Declaration of Independence, but the full implications of that idea did not appear right away. Even the acceptance of the concept of popular sovereignty did not bring with it the suspicion of legislative bodies which was to characterize later American constitutions. Those of Massachusetts and New Hampshire, which were drafted by constitutional conventions, granted broad powers to the legislative branch of government, as also did those drafted previously by state legislatures, as we shall see; but, in distinguishing between the sovereign authority of the people and the ancillary authority of a legislature, the people of Massachusetts and New Hampshire laid the groundwork for a constitutional system which was to stress the dangers of government, rather than its beneficent functions. It may therefore be said that the seed of limited government was planted in Massachusetts and New Hampshire, even though that seed did not bear fruit until 1787.

We may conclude, then, that the adoption of the first state constitutions reflects a considerable degree of faith among Americans in their governments, and particularly in their legislatures. This faith is reflected in the texts of the constitutions; and it is to them that we now turn.[3]

The three basic parts of written constitutions as we know them today, namely, the preamble, the bill of rights, and the form of government, were all present in the first constitutions. The contents of each of these parts of the written constitution were, however, somewhat different from their counterparts in the more recently drafted constitutions. The preambles, for example, bear little resemblance to those of our federal and state constitutions today. In some of the constitutions, the history of the events leading up to the Revolution was summarized in the preamble. In two of the constitutions, or those of New York and Virginia, the Declaration of Independence was substantially reproduced. In those of Massachusetts, New Hampshire (1784), and Vermont (1777 and 1786), the preambles contained statements of the "social contract" as a basis of political authority. In none of the preambles to these constitutions, however, were the specific ends of government expressed as they are in the Preamble to the federal Constitution. These differences can be explained in part by the political situation within which the Revolutionary constitutions were framed. As part and parcel of the Revolution, they required the same sort of justification and the preambles were perceived to be the appropriate place for such justification to appear; however, the fact that the Preamble to the Constitution mentions specific ends, whereas those of the state constitutions do not, suggests an important difference between them: the Constitution was a limited delegation of power for specific ends, but the purposes of the first state constitutions were the general purposes of all government, and not the limited purposes of a federal government; thus no enumeration of those ends was either possible or desirable.

The declarations of rights which were prefixed to nine of the state constitutions were very different from the more familiar Bill of Rights of the United States Constitution. Ranging in number of articles from sixteen in Pennsylvania and Virginia to forty-two in Maryland, they covered a correspondingly larger number of topics. From the familiar due process rights of trial by jury, a speedy trial, protection against double jeopardy and ex post facto laws, to such interesting items as the right to hunt and fish and to emigrate from a state, the state declarations presented a myriad of concerns. Two prominent groups of rights were those associated, respectively, with the principles of popular sovereignty and due process of law. All of the due process rights stipulated in the Bill of Rights were also stipulated in the state declarations. Those provisions comprise the largest category of rights which clearly applied to individuals and clearly were intended to constrain government in the way it could act. They did not, of course, set any absolute limits on the authority of government, since they were procedural rather than substantive limitations.

Most prominent among the provisions of the declarations of rights were the numerous articles which emphasized the sovereignty of the people. Each declaration contained several articles which declared emphatically the right of the people to establish and to control the governments created in the constitutions; for example, the Virginia Constitution of 1776 declared in section two of its Bill of Rights that "all power is vested in, and consequently derived from the people; that magistrates are their trustees and servants, and at all times amenable to them." The North Carolina Constitution of 1776 echoed these sentiments in different terms: "The people of this State ought to have the sole and exclusive right of regulating the internal government and police thereof." The Massachusetts Constitution of 1780 put it this way:

> [T]he people of this commonwealth have the sole and exclusive right of governing themselves, as a free, sovereign, and independent state; and do, and forever hereafter shall, exercise and enjoy every power, jurisdiction, and right, which is not, or may not hereafter be, by them expressly delegated to the United States of America, in Congress assembled.

Such provisions are to be found in several articles in the constitutions of Vermont, New Hampshire, Maryland, Delaware, and Pennsylvania. They were the most prominent features of these constitutions. The same principle was expressed in more than one article of each, and these statements of popular sovereignty are absent from the Bill of Rights; thus this emphasis on the sovereign rights of the people stands in sharp contrast to the Constitution; and this contrast suggests that the Constitution was not rooted as firmly in the sovereignty of the people as the state constitutions.

Religion was another prominent topic in the declarations of rights. These provisions were peculiar in several respects. Individuals were promised religious freedom, provided they did not bother others; yet, in several states the Congregational Church was supported by public taxation. In Massachusetts, for example, a Baptist who lived in a town where no Baptist Church was incorporated had to pay to support the Congregational Church in that town. At the same time, all ministers were forbidden to hold public office. This package of provisions suggests three objectives: to guarantee the private right of conscience; to maintain the religious bonds of the community and the moral standards necessary for social and political life; and to make secure the separation of organized religion and the state. The separation of church and state during the American Revolution did not mean what it is held to mean today, i.e., it did not forbid state support of religion, nor prayer in public schools. It did mean that the institutional church should play no role in the formation of religious policy by the state. The concern for the maintenance of public morality was also reflected in one of the most interesting passages of the Virginia Bill of Rights: "That no free government, or the blessings of liberty, can be preserved to any people, but by a firm adherence to justice, moderation, temperance, frugality, and virtue, and by frequent recurrence to fundamental principles." All of these qualities were to be reinforced by religious faith and through the support of religious institutions. We may conclude, then, that the provisions of the declarations relating to religion expanded the authority of government as much as they constrained it.

The famous affirmation of unalienable rights in the Declaration of Independence was paralleled in the several declarations of rights. The Vermont constitutions held "[T]hat all men are born equally free and independent, and have certain natural, inherent and unalienable rights, amongst which are the enjoying and defending life and liberty; acquiring, possessing and protecting property, and pursuing and obtaining happiness and safety." This phrasing, which embellishes interestingly that of the Declaration of Independence, was very typical. It may be observed that, while this phrasing is more precise than the unalienable rights clause of the Declaration, it remains ambiguous. All of the constitutions allowed for deprivations of life, liberty and property by due process of law; and it is certainly not clear on the face of it what sort of governmental actions might have been prohibited by these natural rights clauses. This is surprising, since, according to the Declaration of Independence, it is the purpose of government to protect such rights. The natural rights clauses of the first state constitutions and of the Declaration are sometimes explained by what may be termed a theory of general prescription. This holds that the notion of unalienable natural rights was intended to recommend, in general, that individuals be left free to carve out their own happiness by "acquiring, possessing and protecting property." No doubt there was widespread sentiment during the Revolution to the effect that people ought to be left free to fend for themselves. Whether such a belief, reflected in such general statements as those of the Vermont constitutions, was intended to create or entail constitutionally enforceable rights is another question. While the evidence provided by the texts of the constitutions with natural rights provisions does not conclusively answer that question, the fact that no clear relation can be established between the natural rights clauses and other constitutional provisions certainly leaves the question open.

One of the most interesting features of these first declarations of rights is their prescriptive language, as opposed to the imperative language we might expect from a statement of basic rights; for example, the Maryland Constitution held that "the liberty of the press ought to be inviolably preserved," which is somewhat less forceful than the First Amendment's provision that "Congress shall make no law . . . abridging the freedom . . . of the press." The use of the word *ought* was quite common. Delaware applied it to the self-incrimination clause, holding that "no man in the courts of common law ought to be compelled to give evidence against himself." New Hampshire, in 1784, provided that the "ancient" mode of "trial by jury . . . ought to remain sacred and inviolable." It would be wrong to make too much of these prescriptive statements. Clearly they were meant to be strong prescriptions; but it is also necessary to recognize the plain meaning of the word *ought* within the context of these provisions. The first constitutions did not hold that the governments they created had *no* right to deny basic freedoms. Rather, they held that they ought not to do so. This suggests that the Americans were still groping toward the conception of a written constitution as an absolute limitation upon legislatures, but had not yet arrived at that conception.

The provisions of the declaration of rights have been examined in some depth because of their importance in understanding the conception underlying the first written constitution. Written constitutions are today regarded as limitations upon the power of government. We have already had reason to suggest that the first state constitutions do not fit this mold perfectly, since most of them were adopted and ratified by legislative bodies. We now see that the declarations of rights, which presumably were devoted to protecting individuals against the government, did not comprise powerful limitations on it. Even the important natural rights and freedom of religion clauses appear to have set no absolute limitations on the power of the legislatures; and the use of prescriptive language throughout may have weakened the protections which were provided. The procedural due process rights appear to have afforded the most protection for individuals, but these rights must have been balanced against the substantive right of popular sovereignty set forth in other articles; thus the first declarations of rights provide little evidence that the American people had a strong conception of limited government at the time of the Revolution.

The governments created by the state constitutions of the Revolutionary era were dominated by the legislative branch of government. In the Pennsylvania constitution and the New Hampshire constitution of 1776 there was no governor; and under eight other constitutions the governor was chosen by the legislature. Even in the states which had popularly elected governors, his power was shared with a legislatively selected privy council. In all cases the grants of executive authority were quite limited, except for certain emergency powers necessitated by the exigencies of the Revolutionary War. In six states the power of making political appointments was reserved almost entirely to the legislatures, and in the other states the governor shared the power of making nominations with the privy council. In all cases, the legislatures retained the right of final approval of appointments; and the constitution makers were anxious to avoid that great source of tyranny under the English Constitution: executive prerogative. The arbitrary actions of the king and the colonial governors had been the source of many of their grievances, and they were determined to prevent such abuses on the part of their new republican governors. Significantly, whereas the governor was usually given the power to call together the legislature in emergencies under these constitutions, he was denied the power of proroguing them; the Revolutionaries had not forgotten the cause of their grievance.

The grants of power to the legislatures were broad, either implicitly or explicitly. In some constitutions, they were implicitly given all powers not specifically denied to them by provisions of the declarations of rights; in others, a specific statement of the legislature's power was included. The New Hampshire constitution of 1784 held that:

> Full power and authority are hereby given and granted to the . . . general court, from time to time, to make, ordain and establish, all

> manner of wholesome and reasonable orders, laws, statutes, ordinances, directions and instructions, either with penalties or without; so as the same be not repugnant, or contrary to this constitution, as they may judge for the benefit and welfare of this state. . . .

The Constitution of Massachusetts contained a similar clause. These clauses, in spite of their general phrasing, represented the most restricted grants of legislative power, because they made its exercise subject to constitutional restraint. It is not coincidental that the constitutions which contained such clauses also provided for some nonlegislative mode of amendment. In the other states, where the constitutions were alterable by the legislatures, it was hardly necessary to grant power to them, since they could do whatever they wanted to do anyway.[4] It may be said that under most of the Revolutionary state constitutions, the legislatures came closer to exercising the unlimited power of an English Parliament than the American rejection of that sovereign legislature might seem to have required.

The constitution makers were not unaware of the need to prevent the abuse of powers by the legislative branch of government, but they sought to prevent such abuse through procedural rather than substantive restraints. The major procedural control over the legislatures was, of course, annual elections. The Americans had great faith in the elective principle. They trusted their legislatures because they knew that they could get rid of them if they wanted to. They had suffered at the hands of Parliament because they had no electoral influence on it; and this memory was fresh in their minds. Philosophers proclaimed the principle that "where annual elections end, tyranny begins," but this was not merely a philosophic "bromide" for Americans in 1776. It was the lesson of their entire colonial experience.

As important as they were, annual elections were not sufficient to guarantee that legislative power not be abused. Most states also adopted the principles of rotation and exclusion from office, the incompatibility of offices, and a separation of powers. Each of these principles shared the same premise, namely, that power should be controlled by limiting how much of it each individual could exercise. Rotation in office was effected by requiring that legislators and executives serve only a specified number of consecutive terms. After being out of office for a number of years, a person could become eligible again. As has been noted, ministers were ineligible for public office; and it also was provided that no person could hold more than one major office at the same time. These provisions were responses to the practice of plural officeholding which had been common during the colonial period. By separating the personnel of each department, there was accomplished all that was intended by a separation of powers. In spite of the emphatic declarations of the principle of separation of powers which appeared in several constitutions, the ascendency of the legislatures effectively belied in practice what the principle would seem to have demanded. This apparent anomaly invites the conclusion that the principle was intended to require only a complete separation of the personnel in each branch of the government, and not a complete separation in the substantive allocation of powers.

Almost all of the constitutions provided for an independent judiciary, appointed during good behavior or for a fixed term of office, although there was some sentiment throughout the colonies in favor of an elected judiciary. The question was whether an independent judiciary or one subject to popular control would be more attentive to the rights of citizens. The judiciary was not explicitly given the power of judicial review; and it is questionable whether judges could invalidate an act of the legislature. The limited number of precedents for judicial review in the states during this period provides little assurance that it was perceived to be a logically necessary feature of government under written constitutions, as was later to be contended. Here again is more evidence that the first written constitutions were not guided by the conception of limited government which later came to prevail.

The constitutions of the Revolutionary era were generally wordier than the federal Constitution, although terse when compared with many of the state constitutions today. Generally, the original state constitutions avoided dealing in substantive matters, due to the fact that such provisions were unnecessary in legislatively enacted constitutions where the legislatures could do as they wished. Even in those states where the legislature could not alter the constitution at will, however, legislative detail was avoided. This would seem to imply that the constitution makers recognized the need to restrict attention to the basic structure of government and such other matters as were necessarily related to it; in other words, they recognized that a constitution should embody only fundamental law. One important exception to this general rule—other than that of religion—was the substantive matter of education. In seven states provisions were made for the public support of primary schools; and in Massachusetts the constitution provided for the support of Harvard University. The fact that education was deemed sufficiently important to be included reflects the high value which was placed upon it, and implies a causal relationship between education and the maintenance of free political institutions. The citizens of Massachusetts and New Hampshire made this relationship explicit. The New Hampshire constitution of 1784 contended that, "[K]nowledge and learning, generally diffused through a community" are "essential to the preservation of a free government." The people of Massachusetts put it slightly differently, holding that: "[W]isdom and knowledge . . . diffused generally among the body of the people" is "necessary for the preservation of their rights and liberties."

Most of the state constitutions contained property qualifications for suffrage; and all of them excluded women and slaves from the polls. Historians continue to debate how widely the franchise was granted and exercised during the last quarter of the eighteenth century. Here, we must ask: What did the restricted suffrage imply about the attitudes of the Revolutionaries toward popular sovereignty? The constitutions stressed the right of the people to govern themselves, as had the Declaration of Independence; but who were the people? Was their endorsement of the natural equality of all inconsistent with the restrictions they placed on the suffrage? While we may think so, it is apparent that they did not. It appears that voting was viewed during the Revolution as a privilege rather than as a right. The grounds which were commonly advanced for the restricted suffrage were prudential. On the one hand, it was felt that women, slaves, children and the poor were adequately represented by husbands, owners, fathers and landowners; on the other hand, that persons without independence and independent judgment could not exercise the franchise intelligently and hence should not be allowed to corrupt the electoral process. The reasoning, in other words, was the same as we now employ to exclude children from the polls. Whether this reasoning was correctly applied to women and paupers is a separate question. For the Revolutionaries, the will of the people was adequately expressed by the voting population, and therefore restricted suffrage was not seen to be inconsistent with the sovereignty of the people.

These were the principle features of the Revolutionary state constitutions. What implications may we infer from this description? Clearly, the first written constitutions were viewed by the people who adopted them as instruments of popular will. The facts that most of them were drafted and ratified by legislatures and also set up governments which were dominated by legislatures, suggest that the concept of a constitution as a vehicle for limiting the power of government had not clearly emerged at the outset of the Revolution. The fact that two of the states moved in the direction of constitutional conventions in the 1780s is evidence that such a concept was gaining acceptance during this time; but whether the constitutions were adopted by legislatures or by conventions, they were regarded as acts of the people. Here was a classic instance of a people coming to develop and to accept a value over a period of time, and proceeding to institutionalize that value. The Americans were led by their acceptance of the principle of popular sovereignty to the concept of a written constitution as a means of creating and limiting governmental authority. All of the first state constitutions, however, relied upon procedural rather than substantive limitations.

The first written constitutions were adopted for two purposes. One was to erect institutions of government which would serve the will of the people, and the other was to control the way in which those institutions exercised their power so that they would be used only to serve that will. They were not viewed as devices for severely limiting the substantive authority of government; and they were certainly not viewed as vehicles for enforcing specific policies. We may say, then, that the Revolutionary experience implies two overriding principles of constitution making. First, a written constitution should be an expression of the sovereign will of the people. As such, the people should be free to include in their constitutions anything they wish to include. In the second place, however, a constitution should also be restricted to fundamental matters. If the authorship of a constitution by the people lends it legitimacy, the restriction to fundamentals is what makes it a constitution.

Sometimes it is said that constitutions embody principles of natural law, that there exist legal principles which are binding by nature, antecedent to the establishment of political authority. Constitutions are said to make explicit these antecedently binding principles and substantively, to limit the authority of government by way of them. This view of the written constitution is said to be influential among judges; and it is worthwhile to consider the validity of this view as it applies to the first state constitutions.[5] There is little in them to support the view that they were founded on principles of natural law. The strongest evidence is to be found in the natural rights provisions included in several of the constitutions; but, as we have seen, these provisions were not put into effect in any significant way. The procedural due process of law provisions appear to have been intended to secure justice for the individual, but it is not apparent that they were based upon principles of "higher" law. Rather, they were traditional common law practices which the Americans associated with the principle of rule by law; and the principle of rule by law is compatible with the positive notion of law as an expression of will. When the natural rights and due process provisions of the constitutions are compared to the unequivocal popular sovereignty principles, however, we must conclude that the evidence of the documents weighs against the natural law interpretation.

II

The contemporary American view of the written constitution has been shaped primarily by our experience with the Constitution of the United States. The relative prominence of that document in our history has obscured from view the fact that, at its inception, the Constitution was a different kind of document from the state constitutions which preceded it. This was due to the peculiar circumstances of its adoption. The federal convention was divided by the conflict of interests of the large and small states. There were two theoretical issues around which this conflict of interest centered. First, upon what basis of sovereignty was the Constitution to stand? Second, how extensive would be the powers of the national government? The first issue can be reduced to three specific questions: 1. How should the legislature be apportioned? 2. What provisions should be made for amending the Constitution? 3. How should the Constitution be ratified? The second issue is related to the specific grants of legislative power in Article I of the Constitution and the question of whether a bill of rights should be included in it.

In regard to the basis of sovereignty, we may quickly review the facts. The legislature was divided into two houses, one of which was based upon an equal representation of persons, the other upon an equal representation of states. The Constitution was to be amended in one of four ways, with proposals emanating from Congress, or a national convention, to be ratified by the state legislatures or by special conventions called in each state. The Constitution was ratified by the latter method. What, then, was the basis of sovereignty upon which the Constitution was founded? History produced two answers to this question. The advocates of a consolidated government argued that the Constitution was rooted in the sovereignty of the people. In keeping with this view, the people, in exercising their sovereignty, were free to delegate some of their authority to the national government, some to the state governments, and retain the remainder in their own hands. Opposed to this view was that of the advocates of states rights. According to them, the Constitution was ratified by the states, and therefore rested upon the sovereignty of the states. The question came to a decision in the case of *McCulloch* v. *Maryland* in 1819. At issue in this case were the power of the Congress to charter a national bank and the right of the states to tax an agency of the federal government. In his opinion Chief Justice John Marshall argued that the Constitution rested on the sovereignty of the people, since it had been ratified by them in each state, rather than by the state legislatures. Marshall contended—somewhat ambiguously, however—that the states retained a residual sovereignty, since the people had delegated only limited powers to the federal government. Marshall's opinion was controversial at the time, and was not accepted by many persons in the southern states. The question was definitely answered only by the force of arms in the Civil War. In the ensuing discussion we shall speak of the Constitution as based upon the sovereignty of the people, with the states retaining authority over internal affairs.

Although it was a matter of controversy, the scope of national power seems to have been the subject of less disagreement. All agreed that the federal government was to be supreme within its sphere of action (according to the supremacy clause of the Constitution), but it was also agreed that it would be, as Marshall put it in *McCulloch* v. *Maryland*, "limited in its powers." How limited was it to be? Marshall argued for a broad construction of the enumerated powers of the national government, drawing upon the necessary and proper clause of the Constitution and also upon the general observation that a legislative body should have at its disposal means sufficient to accomplish its designated ends. Other prominent statesmen, including Thomas Jefferson, believed that the principle of government under written constitutions required a narrow construction of the Constitution. On these grounds Jefferson had held the chartering of a national bank to be unconstitutional. Marshall's view prevailed, and the broad construction which was thereafter given to the enumerated powers of Congress, taken together with the supremacy clause, provided the basis for the expansion of federal authority over the state governments as time went on. But no matter how broadly the enumerated powers of Congress were construed, and no matter how far the scope of federal power was expanded, both were necessarily limited, and therefore the national government was constitutionally restricted in a way in which the state governments were not.

It was the United States Constitution, then, which first established the principle that a written constitution should limit, in substantive matters, the powers of the government created by it. It is interesting to note that the federal government was not limited by means of a bill of rights under the original Constitution. Moreover, the Founders seem not to have entertained very seriously the idea of including a bill of rights. It is clear that they expected the state governments to bear the burden of governing the day-to-day lives of the American people, and therefore the state constitutions were those which required bills of rights; yet this fact implies that the many concerns covered by the state declarations, including due process of law in criminal cases, religion, and freedom of the press, were not expected to be relevant to the scope of national authority. Clearly, this establishes the fact that the Founders viewed the federal Constitution as a kind of document different from state constitutions. Those who opposed ratification on the grounds that the Constitution contained no bill of rights viewed this provision as a means of limiting the authority of the federal government over citizens and states. They realized that the enumerated powers of the Constitution were sufficiently broad to be subject to abuse, and perhaps they also feared that the federal government would not long remain within the bounds of its enumerated powers. Much would be their surprise to learn that the Bill of Rights has been used by the Supreme Court as an avenue for expanding the authority of the federal government over the states through the power of judicial review.

The principle of limited government under written constitutions was first established in the Constitution, but it was a principle which was untenable from the time of its adoption. By the time of *McCulloch* v. *Maryland* in 1819, the national government was already struggling to shed the shackles of its enumerated powers. The history of the development of the Constitution since then has been marked by the continual expansion of the power of the federal government through a broad construction of its powers. All branches of the federal government have contributed to this expansion. The pressures of social change, political expedience, and public opinion have driven Presidents, Congress and the Supreme Court to ever broader and more tenuous interpretations of the language and intent of the Constitution. Occasionally, the three branches of the federal government have been in conflict regarding its interpretation. The Supreme Court in some instances has blocked a President and a Congress bent on political change; for example, the Court stood in the path of both the federal income tax and child labor laws for many years. In the case of the income tax it required a constitutional amendment to circumvent the Court, while child labor laws had to wait until the membership of the Court changed. On other occasions, however, the three branches of government have worked together to enforce a broadened constitutional mandate upon the states. The recent legislative lowering of the voting age to eighteen prior to the adoption of the Twenty-sixth Amendment, supported by both the President and the Court, is an example of this collaboration.

Of the several ways to change the meaning of the Constitution and expand the power of the federal government, that of judicial review has been by far the most important, in both practical and theoretical terms. The Supreme Court claims, on the basis of the power of judicial review, to be the only final authoritative interpreter of the Constitution. Since, as we shall see, the power of judicial review finds its justification in the conception of the written constitution as an instrument of limited government, it is important to understand the nature and effects of this power if we are fully to understand the significance of the written constitution for the American political system.

Although the power of judicial review is not specified in the Constitution the Supreme Court has, since the famous case of *Marbury* v. *Madison* in 1803, assumed the right of invalidating federal and state laws when, in the view of the Court, they have conflicted with the Constitution. The rationale for the power of judicial review derives from a conception of the written constitution as an instrument of limited government. Since a constitution is a delegation of the power of the people which is supposed to limit the authority of political institutions set up by them, it follows that when those institutions exceed the boundaries of the constitution their exercise of that power is illegitimate. It is the province of the Court to determine when such a violation has taken place and to declare the law invalid as it applies to parties in the case before the Court. This reasoning was stated definitively by Alexander Hamilton in *The Federalist* 78:

> The interpretation of the laws is the proper and peculiar province of the courts. A constitution is, in fact, and must be regarded by the judges as, a fundamental law. It therefore belongs to them to ascertain its meaning as well as the meaning of any particular act proceeding from the legislative body. If there should happen to be an irreconcilable variance between the two, that which has the superior obligation and validity ought, of course, to be preferred; or, in other words, the Constitution ought to be preferred to the statute, the intention of the people to the intention of their agents.

It is apparent that Hamilton's defense of judicial review presupposes relatively clear standards for defining an "irreconcilable variance" and the "intention of the people." In the absence of such standards, the power of judicial review could raise the opposite problem: the substitution of the will of the Court for the will of the people and the will of their agents. Over the years the Court has been accused on many occasions of doing precisely that. From the vested rights cases of the early nineteenth century, through the substantive due process cases of the early twentieth, to the new individual rights cases of the post-World War II era, the Court has been attacked by those who held that it has substituted its own political preferences for the plain meaning of constitutional provisions. These criticisms have come from both the political right and the political left and have been against the constitutional basis for Court decisions.

This chapter is not the proper forum in which to examine the issue of judicial review. Our discussion will deal with the implications of the American institution of judicial review for the concept of the written constitution. Here, it must be noted that the issue is much tidier in theory than in practice. All written constitutions contain principles subject to varying interpretations. Even the most specific provisions of the United States Constitution must be applied to individual cases on the basis of interpretive rules; for example, the first amendment provision that "Congress shall make no law . . . abridging the freedom of speech" seems clear, but, in applying it, the Court has developed, among others, the "clear and present danger" rule which allows for the suppression of speech in some cases. Such interpretive rules theoretically should be no more than an elaboration of the meaning of general constitutional prescriptions as they were intended to apply in specific cases. This ideal is, however, hardly realizable in practice. Principles often harbor implications not apparent to those who formulate them; and, even where the principles are clear, their entailments for particular cases are often obscure.

The necessary ambiguity of written constitutions leads to disagreements over how they shall be interpreted. Such disagreements have occurred in the United States among judges and between judges and other people. Occasionally the Court has been accused of reading natural law concepts into the Constitution through such general principles as the due process clauses of the Fifth and Fourteenth Amendments.[6] It is true that the Court has often had recourse to concepts which bear a closer resemblence to the rhetoric of eighteenth century natural law than to the Bill of Rights. In the 1965 case of *Griswold* v. *Connecticut*, which dealt with the right of privacy in relation to a state law outlawing the use of birth control devices, Justice Black provided a list of Court dicta including such phrases as: "decencies of civilized conduct," "some principle of justice so rooted in the traditions and conscience of our people as to be ranked as fundamental," "fundamental notions of fairness and justice," and "rights . . . basic to our free society." Such dicta have often been applied in cases involving procedural issues of due process of law. In such cases, the position of the Court has been that certain procedural guarantees are implicit in the concept of rule by law. In some cases, however, the general notions of fairness and justice have been applied in other areas of the law; for example, in the right of privacy cases. It is not clear that the right of privacy (which has been held to entail the right to an abortion during the first trimester of pregnancy) is logically implied by the concepts of rule by law or due process of law.

That the Court's interpretations of due process of law actually have been based on a belief in natural law or a conviction that the Constitution embodies natural law precepts, would be difficult to establish. If they have been so based, then it may be argued that the judges have contributed something to our constitutional law which was not a part of the intention of the framers of the Constitution. We have seen that the first state constitutions apparently were not based on natural law concepts. There also is nothing in the record to suggest that the framers thought they were writing natural law into the Constitution. It must not be forgotten that the Bill of Rights was adopted after the Constitution was ratified, and, too, that the Bill of Rights contains no reference to the "unalienable rights" of man. Whether the judges have added natural law concepts to our constitutional law, it may be said without fear of contradiction that the Supreme Court has given a broad interpretation to constitutional prescriptions such as due process of law. In so doing, the Court has used the power of judicial review to establish the meaning of the Constitution through the judicial process.

Constitutional change by way of the process of judicial review is sometimes characterized metaphorically. The Constitution is described as a "living" document which "grows" through judicial interpretation. The implication is that whatever does not grow stagnates and dies. Things which are not living (such as constitutions) cannot grow, of course—they can only change; and change can be either for the better or for the worse. The fact that the primary method of changing the United States Constitution has been through the process of judicial review has created another significant difference between it and the first state constitutions. Whereas the states were concerned to maintain extensive popular control over their governments through their constitutions, the federal Constitution has been placed beyond the easy reach of the people while at the same time undergoing significant changes, which have taken place without the express approval of the people. The power of judicial review thus comes into conflict with the conception of direct popular sovereignty.

Judicial review is not peculiar to the federal courts. State courts also exercise the power, both in relation to the federal Constitution and to their respective state constitutions. Judicial review, however, has not had the same impact on the state constitutions as it has had on the federal Constitution. Generally speaking, judges in state courts have given a much more strict interpretation to their state constitutions than the Supreme Court to the United States Constitution. This is undoubtedly related to the fact that the state constitutions are much easier to change, and, in fact, have been amended, revised, and even completely rewritten with great frequency; indeed, the development of American state constitutions is so very different from that of our federal constitutions that it must be described if we are to have a complete picture of the American experience with written constitutions.

America has had an extraordinarily active history of constitution writing.[7] This is obscured by the fact that we have only redrafted our national constitution once (in 1789), and also by the further fact that we have not changed our state constitutions very often in recent years (only six times since the 1920s, plus the new constitutions adopted by Alaska and Hawaii). Our recent constitutional passivity makes all the more startling the fact that we have adopted 137 constitutions (including the Articles of Confederation and the Constitution) in our two-hundred-year history. These constitutions have come in waves, as new states were added to the union. By far the most fertile constitutional area in the country has been the South, due mostly, but not entirely, to the Civil War. In the decade from 1860 to 1869, thirty constitutions were drafted in the United States, twenty-four of them in the South. The Civil War experience aside, the South still leads the way in constitution making. All of the eight states which have had five or more constitutions are in the South. The eastern seaboard has had the next largest number of constitutions. This is due to the fact that the states in the East are much older than those in the West. Most of the western states have had only one constitution each. Chronologically, there were fifteen state constitutions adopted prior to 1789, forty-seven between 1789 and 1859, thirty during the Civil War decade, thirty-five between 1870 and 1921, and eight since 1921, all after World War II.

These 135 American state constitutions usually have been framed by conventions. Through 1968, or the most recent year for which compiled data is available, there had been 217 constitutional conventions in the fifty states. These conventions usually have been called into being by legislatures, with popular approval of their proposals via referendums. Occasionally they have been called into session through popular initiative and referendum. There have been both limited and unlimited conventions; and they have not always produced proposals which were accepted by the electorate. Submission to the electorate, however, has been a regular practice. Of the 135 constitutions, only forty-eight have been adopted without being submitted to the voters. This has occurred with noticeably diminishing frequency. Of the fifteen constitutions adopted between 1776 and 1786, thirteen were not submitted to the voters; of the forty-seven between 1789 and 1859, eighteen were not; of the thirty between 1860 and 1869, nine were not; of the thirty-five between 1870 and 1921, seven were not; but all eight constitutions adopted since 1921 have been submitted to the voters. Although the basic law in several states makes no provision for popular ratification, it is unlikely that a state would choose that course of action today.

The large number of state constitutions is merely a small part of constitutional change. Much more significant has been the amendment process at the state level. Through 1968, the fifty states had adopted nearly 5,000 amendments to their present constitutions! Again the southern states lead the way. Georgia has adopted 654 amendments to head the list of states, Louisiana is second with 530, South Carolina third with 330, Alabama fourth with 284, and California fifth with 227. As might be expected, the large number of amendments has greatly increased the length of the state constitutions. Compared with the brevity of the federal Constitution and the relatively brief state constitutions of the Revolutionary era, contemporary state constitutions are extremely wordy. The Louisiana constitution with 530 amendments runs to over 250,000 words! Many other states have constitutions which run into the tens of thousands of words.

What explains the vastly greater degree of formal constitutional activity at the state level than at the national level? In part, it is because the state constitutions are easier to amend. In most states an amendment must pass in two successive legislative assemblies, however, and many states require ratification by a referendum. In some states, they can be proposed and ratified by the people through the initiative and referendum. These procedures are much simpler than the amendment procedures of the federal Constitution. Because they are simpler they have been used more often and more successfully. This, in turn, has created a positive expectation absent at the national level. One wonders how many potential amendments to the Constitution have died in embryo because their proponents despaired of any chance of success. Advocates of change in states where the citizenry has already adopted dozens, or even hundreds, of amendments have had grounds for greater optimism.

The procedural advantages enjoyed by the states, however, seem insufficient to explain the very great difference between the state and national experience. Simple amending procedures make change easier, but they do not make it more desirable; and the large number of amendments to state constitutions suggests that the desire for change has existed. It is probable that no general set of causes would accurately characterize the experience of any state in explaining its constitutional development. Adequate explanation would require a knowledge of local history in each case. One may speculate, however, regarding certain causes which may have been widely influential, if not determinative. First among these is social change. Surely all of our states had to adjust their laws to changing conditions brought about by industrialization and urbanization. Over the years state constitutions have been amended to provide for such public functions as taxation, bond issues and other public indebtedness, corporate charters, the regulation of utilities and of transportation, and urban development and redevelopment. It is not clear why the states have included all of these matters in their constitutions. All could more easily have been handled by statute; inclusion into the basic law has burdened it with unnecessary detail. In these and other matters, the inclusion of detail has sometimes been carried to extremes of triviality; for example, the Louisiana constitution provides for the construction and naming of bridges, and the South Carolina constitution forbids a woman to consent to sexual intercourse before her fourteenth birthday.[8]

Excessive detail has not been restricted to substantive matters. Even in those articles dealing with the basic structure of the three branches of government, state constitutions have been made too specific. Modern ones have followed the example of the federal

Constitution in providing for elaborate systems of a separation of powers and checks and balances. They have gone beyond the federal Constitution, however, in the extent to which they have sought to regulate each branch. Elections have been regulated in detail, salaries for public officials fixed, legislative procedures specified, and the judicial branch of the government deluged with constitutional "administrivia." The inclusion of so much detail has necessitated frequent amendment and revision merely to adjust these details to changing conditions and preferences. Why have the states chosen to establish so many substantive and procedural regulations in their constitutions? One possible answer is that the people have not trusted their state governments. The only reason to specify details in a constitution is to limit the power of the legislature or other institutions to determine matters of detail. The only motive for limiting the power of the legislature is a distrust of it. Of course, in most cases the state legislatures have participated in this, putting into the constitutions by way of amendment restrictions upon their own powers. This has occurred when the controlling legislative party wished to use its temporary majority to effect enduring changes. The attitudes of both lawmakers and citizens, then, have revealed a suspicion and a distrust of flexible institutions of self-government.

If this be true, then it reflects a considerable change from the attitude of the American people at the time of the Revolution. Then, they trusted their legislatures; and, in setting them up under constitutions, they wished to control only the abuses of power, not the details of government. There is, of course, nothing inconsistent between their view of a constitution as an instrument of popular will and the most extreme kind of legislative detail, but the inclusion of this detail is inconsistent with their belief that a constitution should be restricted to only fundamental concerns. It is not clear when the American people turned against their state legislatures. Some have held that a transition occurred very early in our history, perhaps prior to the adoption of the federal Constitution.[9] If we can measure the distrust and the detail by the length of the constitutions, then we may place the turnabout somewhat later. Among constitutions operative today, the thirty which were adopted prior to 1800 average thirty-two pages in length; the eight adopted between 1820 and 1859, thirty-one pages; the twenty-six between 1860 and 1899, fifty pages; the six between 1900 and 1921, 143 pages; and the seven between 1954 and

1965, thirty-five pages.[10] Although these figures include the numerous amendments added over the years, they still give evidence of a movement toward constitutional prolixity during the half century following the Civil War.

III

"A frequent recurrence to the fundamental principles of the Constitution," held the New Hampshire constitution of 1784, "[is] indispensibly necessary to preserve the blessings of liberty and good government." The two fundamental principles of the state constitutions of the Revolutionary era were popular sovereignty, or the idea that a constitution should be an expression of the popular will, and fundamental law, or the idea that a constitution should be restricted to the basic structure and procedures of government. The first state constitutions placed procedural rather than substantive limitations upon the power of governments which they created. Over the years the states have emphasized the first of these principles at the expense of the second. The people have vigorously exercised their sovereignty; but, in the process, they have destroyed the foundation of their basic law. They have placed many substantive restrictions on their state governments by specifying the details of government in their constitutions.

There is today a widespread recognition of this fact. The relative brevity of the most recently drafted state constitutions reflects the current of reform which has developed over the last two decades.The Connecticut constitution of 1965, for example, is only thirteen pages in length! The principal objective of the reformers has been to simplify a constitution by removing matters which could as well be handled by statute. Under these reforms, much of the regulation of the executive agencies and the judicial branch of a state government would be handled by legislation, within broad constitutional guidelines. Alternatively, some favor giving much greater authority to governors and the chief judicial officers in organizing the executive and the judicial branches, respectively. In either case,the objective is clear:to get the details of administration out of the constitutions. The movement toward simplification even reaches the legislative branch, with some sentiment now in favor of that American heresy, the unicameral legislature. In general, we may say that such reforms would be useful, and fully consonant with the intentions which motivated the Revolutionaries in initiating our state constitutional system.

The United States Constitution was based upon the sovereignty of the people, but it differed from the state constitutions which preceded it in that it contained substantive limitations upon the government created by it. These substantive limitations were the result of the peculiar historical circumstances in which the Constitution was adopted, rather than of the considered judgment that all political power should be substantively limited. This departure from the principles of the first state constitutions has had specific consequences. Many of the conceptual and political difficulties which have marked our constitutional history could have been avoided if the national government had been given a more generally-defined grant of power in the Constitution. In struggling to establish a truly national government through the broad construction of the enumerated powers of the Constitution and the expansive use of judicial review, we have accomplished with difficulty and divisiveness what could perhaps have been accomplished more simply and less controversially. The difficult process of amending the Constitution, which also derives from the circumstances of its adoption rather than general constitutional theory, has made it difficult for the people to initiate changes in their basic law. The primary instrument for popular constitutional initiatives, the national constitutional convention, has never been used because many people who have favored changes in the Constitution have feared that a convention might precipitate uncontrolled and wholesale revisions; thus, we have been left to rely upon judicial review as the primary means of bringing about constitutional change, with all its attendant theoretical and political problems.

These considerations suggest that we might improve our Constitution by amending it in the directions indicated. The grant of power to the Congress could be redefined in suitably general terms, the amendment process could be simplified and made subject to more popular control, and the power of judicial review could be more explicitly defined. A conclusion to this effect must, however, be tempered by other considerations. It must not be forgotten that the constitutional limitations upon the power of the national government are related to the maintenance of the federal system. America is a diverse society, and the federal system allows that diversity to be expressed through multiple layers of authority. Many believe that the vitality of our state and local governments depends upon their autonomy in relation to the federal government; and they trace the atrophy of state and local administrations to the growing federal presence in areas of public life previously reserved to the states and localities. While it is true that many advantages accrue to our federal system, it is equally true that many of them could be maintained within the context of the constitutional changes suggested above. Those who rely upon constitutional limitations as a last line of defense against the growth of a federal "leviathan" must operate on the assumption that the value of strong state and local governments would not be recognized under a more flexible constitutional system.

To inject more flexibility and more popular control into our federal Constitution would prove to be a great error, however, if it became subject to the same abuses that have characterized our state constitutions. Our state experience has proven that a flexible constitution can lead to an inflexible government. If our federal constitutional experience has reflected a distrust of democracy through constitutional restrictions on the power of the people to form their basic law, that of our states has indicated that we have had little faith in our ability to govern ourselves through representative institutions. In both respects the American constitutional system has developed in ways contrary to the principles for which our Revolutionary forebearers fought.

Notes

1. William Blackstone, *Commentary on the Laws of England* (London, 1765), bk. 1, chap. 2, pp. 185-186.
2. Demophilus, *Genuine Principles of the Ancient Saxon, or English Constitution* (Philadelphia, 1776).
3. The Revolutionary state constitutions can be found in Francis Newton Thorpe, ed., *The Federal and State Constitutions* (Washington, D. C.: U.S. Government Printing Office, 1909). This collection contains all American constitutions adopted through 1908. An updated compilation is being edited by William F. Swindler, entitled, *Sources and Documents of United States Constitutions* (Dobbs Ferry, New York: Oceana, 1973). This collection is not yet complete. Persons interested in a more thorough examination of the political debates of the Revolutionary era are directed to Gordon Wood's *The Creation of the American Republic, 1776-1789* (New York: Norton, 1969).

4. In Massachusetts and New Hampshire (1784) the constitutions required the calling of a constitutional convention in a specified year. In New York (1777) and Vermont (1786), amendments were to be proposed by a special body called the council of censors. In the other constitutions there were either no provisions for amendment or the provisions were for amendment by the legislature.
5. See Edward S. Corwin, "The 'Higher Law' Background of American Constitutional Law," 42 *Harvard Law Review* 149 (1928); and Charles G. Haines, "The Law of Nature in State and Federal Judicial Decisions," 25 *Yale Law Journal* 617 (1916).
6. Ibid. See also *Twining* v. *New Jersey* 211 U.S. 78; *Adamson* v. *California* 332 U.S. 46; *Palko* v. *Connecticut* 302 U.S. 319; *Griswold* v. *Connecticut* 381 U.S. 479; and *Roe* v. *Wade* 410 U.S. 113. Justice Black's dissenting opinions in the Adamson and Griswold cases should be particularly noted. *See also* Charles G. Haines, *The Revival of Natural Law Concepts* (Cambridge, Mass.: Harvard University Press, 1930), pt. 5.
7. All current American constitutions can be found in *Constitutions of the United States: National and State,* Legislative Drafting and Research Fund, Columbia University (Dobbs Ferry, New York: Oceana, 1962). The National Municipal League leads the way in scholarly examination of our state constitutional experience. I have drawn freely upon their numerous publications, especially the following three: Robert B. Dishman, *State Constitutions: The Shape of the Document* (New York: National Municipal League, 1968); John P. Wheeler, ed., *Salient Issues of Constitutional Revision* (New York: National Municipal League, 1961); Albert L. Sturm, *Thirty Years of State Constitution-Making: 1938-1968* (New York: National Municipal League, 1970).
8. Ibid., Dishman, p. 31.
9. Cf. Wood, pt. 3, especially pp. 363-390.
10. Dishman, pp. 2-3. Even if the Louisiana constitution adopted in 1921 (413 pages) is excluded, the remaining five constitutions adopted between 1900 and 1921 still average over eighty pages; and they include the second and third longest constitutions: Alabama, 192 pages, and Oklahoma, 104 pages.

I would like to thank Richard Wells, George J. Graham, Jr., and Scarlett G. Graham for their comments on an early version of this chapter.

[7]

THE PRESIDENCY

—JOSEPH M. BESSETTE

When this nation celebrated its centennial during the administration of President Grant, the executive office in little more than a decade had fallen from a position of high political leadership under Abraham Lincoln to its historical nadir in power and prestige. Spurred by its success in wrenching control of reconstruction policy away from Andrew Johnson, Congress dominated major policy matters in the post–Civil War period. Now, a century later, the role of the President in American government is again a major political issue. We have not in the past decade seen a decline in presidential power comparable to that of the 1860s and 1870s; but we *are* witnessing major rethinking about the position the presidency has come to occupy in the American political system. The Vietnam War and the Watergate scandal have led many formerly warm proponents of presidential power to reconsider earlier views. On the other hand, some of those who not long ago feared the presidency as the engine of an ever-expanding and oppressive governmental machine have come to see it as the major source of steady leadership and moderation. It must be admitted that much of the praise and the criticism of the office reflects little more than partisan political preferences. An intelligent assessment of what is good or bad about the contemporary American presidency, whether it is too powerful or not powerful enough, and whether legal or constitutional reforms are called for, should rest on a firmer foundation, namely, a clear understanding of the way the constitutional office of the presidency contributes to the maintenance of just and competent republican government. We must turn first to the founding era; for to understand the character of the presidential office we must fathom the principles that guided the framers in its construction.

"The history of the present King of Great Britain," reads the Declaration of Independence of 1776, "is a history of repeated injuries and usurpations, all having in direct object the establishment of an absolute Tyranny over these States." There follows a long indictment, listing the abuses practiced by George III which justify revolutionary resistance to his once lawful authority. Disputes between the Americans and the British king had a long history, manifested particularly in the perennial struggle between the locally elected colonial assemblies and the king's royal governors. Given their immediate political experience, it is hardly surprising that at the nation's birth the American people felt a deep distrust of executive power and looked to legislatures to secure and protect their liberty.

This distrust of executive power is reflected in the state governments established during the revolutionary period.[1] With the conspicuous exception of that of New York, the early state constitutions placed the executive in a position decidedly subordinate to the legislature. Constitutional arrangements were expressly designed to thwart the development of a vigorous and independent executive branch. Executive terms of office were short, being in most states only one year; strict limitations were placed on reeligibility; and election was by the legislature. Unity in the executive branch was undermined by executive councils, chosen in most states by the legislature, the concurrence of which was required for the exercise of certain executive powers. Finally, and perhaps most importantly, the executive usually received his powers from the legislative body. In sum, these early experiments at self-government were largely grounded on legislative supremacy, with the executive little more than the agent of the legislative will.

Political experience under these constitutions soon revealed the defects of legislative supremacy. Although the state constitutions had established a formal separation of powers, the legislatures frequently undercut executive and judicial independence. Paper barriers proved insufficient to prevent legislative encroachments. Thomas Jefferson gives the following description of the situation in Virginia where he served as Governor from 1779 to 1781:

> All the powers of government, legislative, executive, and judiciary, result to the legislative body. The concentrating of these in the same hands is precisely the definition of despotic government. . . . For this reason that convention which passed the ordinance of government, laid its foundation on this basis, that the legislative, executive, and judiciary departments should be separate and distinct, so that no person should exercise the powers of more than one of them at the same time. But no barrier was provided between these several powers. The judiciary and executive members were left dependent on the legislative, for their subsistence in office, and some of them for their continuance in it. If, therefore, the legislative assumes executive and judiciary powers, no opposition is likely to be made; nor, if made, can it be effectual. . . .[2]

In Pennsylvania the Council of Censors, meeting in 1783 and 1784, reported similar legislative encroachments:

> When the Constitution of this State placed the Legislative power in a single branch, with certain checks upon rash and hasty determination, it was never supposed that any House of Assembly would by special laws made for the purpose, assume the Executive powers, and by blending Legislative and Executive, unite what the Constitution had wisely and decisively separated. . . . It has been one of the greatest objections made to this Constitution, that it has left too little power in the Executive branch; and yet we see daily attempts to make that little less.[3]

The problem of legislative domination was not limited to Virginia and Pennsylvania, as James Madison's observations in the Constitutional Convention demonstrate: "Experience had proved a tendency in our governments to throw all power into the Legislative vortex. The Executives of the States are in general little more than Cyphers; the legislatures omnipotent."[4] In representative republics, Madison later argued in the *Federalist Papers*,[5] the legislative branch is necessarily predominant and, left unchecked, is as likely to become tyrannical as an omnipotent executive. Herein lay the principal failure of the framers of the state constitutions. Believing that liberty was threatened only by executive usurpations, they failed to guard against the equivalent danger of legislative tyranny.

In one state, however, the constitution did establish an executive branch able to hold its own against the legislature. The constitution of New York combined provisions that singly could be found in other state constitutions but together provided the basis for a uniquely independent and energetic executive. The New York governor was elected by the state's freeholders for a three-year term, with no restriction on reeligibility; his powers were not to be parceled out by the legislature but granted directly in the constitution; and with only two exceptions—an appointment power shared with a senatorial council and a veto shared with a special council of revision—the executive power was vested in the governor alone. From this solid constitutional foundation there emerged a chief executive of independence and vigor unparalleled in the newly formed state governments. George Clinton, the first occupant of the office, was, during his eighteen-year tenure, the dominant political force in New York, employing his executive powers to maintain public order, to guide legislative action, and to extend his influence throughout state government. Under Clinton's firm leadership New York enjoyed a more stable and competent administration than was experienced in the other states. The effectiveness of the New York state government helped to teach the framers of our federal Constitution the virtues of executive vigor.

While the state experience was demonstrating the political advantages of an independent and energetic executive branch, the national experience under the Articles of Confederation was teaching a similar lesson.[6] Under the Articles of Confederation there was no national executive authority. All the powers of the government were possessed by a Congress of delegates from the several states. The government did, however, like every other government, require agencies for administering the national business. During the Revolution money had to be raised, an army organized and supplied, and diplomatic negotiations conducted with supportive foreign nations. These administrative tasks were, at first, distributed on an ad hoc basis to committees, councils, or even individuals. As the volume and complexity of governmental business increased, a somewhat more orderly distribution of functions among permanent congressional committees evolved. Congress refused, however, to divest itself of the administrative power. Although the system matured with the passage of time, it did not free Congress from a preoccupation with administrative details, nor did it free the administrative agencies from the deleterious effects of irregular congressional intrusions. The results were bad for Congress and bad for the administration. By 1787 it had thus come to be widely recognized that the central government needed a strong and to some degree an independent executive, and that a formal separation of the legislative and executive branches would both improve the deliberative process within Congress and provide for a more effective and steady administration of congressional policy. An independent executive branch, energized and supervised by a single head, whether individual or committee, would be the most efficient agent of the congressional will.

Political experience during this nation's first decade, then, gave rise to two distinct understandings of the nature and purpose of executive power. Where the national experience taught that a strong and independent executive branch would be the most effective administrator of congressional policy, the state experience taught that the executive should counteract and balance the legislative power, and that the qualities of strength and independence should foster something like executive equality in the political system. These two views—that the executive was essentially to serve the legislative branch, and that he was in good part to counteract and balance the legislature—were brought to the Constitutional Convention; they are reflected in the provisions of Article II of the United States Constitution; and they are the poles between which the debate over presidential power has been fought since the issue was first joined during the hot Philadelphia summer of 1787. On the one side stand the legislative supremacists: Roger Sherman, in the Convention—"he considered the Executive magistracy as nothing more than an institution for carrying the will of the Legislature into effect";[7] James Madison, in the debate over President George Washington's Proclamation of Neutrality in 1793—"[t]o see the laws faithfully executed constitutes the essence of the executive authority";[8] the Radical Republicans, in 1864—"the authority of Congress is paramount";[9] and Senator Sam Ervin, during the recent congressional investigation of executive agreements—"[t]he powers conferred individually upon the President are instrumental only. . . .

[H]e should be merely the executor of a power of decision that rests elsewhere."[10] On the other side stand those who deny the principle of executive subordination: Gouverneur Morris, in the Convention—"One great object of the Executive is to controul the Legislature";[11] Alexander Hamilton, in the *Federalist*—"we can with no propriety contend for [an unbounded complaisance in the executive] . . . to the humors of the legislature. . . . It is one thing to be subordinate to the laws, and another to be dependent on the legislative body";[12] President James Polk, refuting Whig theories—"if the doctrines now maintained be correct, the executive must become practically subordinate to the legislative. . . . Whenever, if ever, this shall occur, our glorious system of well-regulated self-government will crumble into ruins";[13] and Theodore Roosevelt, rejecting the "narrowly legalistic view that the President is the servant of Congress rather than of the people."[14]

The case for legislative supremacy is simple, straightforward, and logical. The essential function of the executive, it is argued, is to carry out the law. Lawmaking is the business of the legislative branch. It is thus the purpose of the executive to carry out the will of the legislature; he is its servant or minister, emphatically not its political equal. Under the United States Constitution, the argument continues, this essentially ministerial role of the chief executive is qualified only to the extent that certain nonministerial powers are granted for purposes of self-defense (the veto power) or political expedience (the pardoning power, appointive power, etc.). Although it is certainly true that part of the intended function of the presidency was to serve Congress by executing its laws, nonetheless few lessons can be as confidently drawn from the records of the Constitutional Convention as that the men who deliberated there resolutely and affirmatively rejected the principle of executive subordination to a supreme legislature.

When one turns to the framers' deliberations regarding the executive what is most striking is their preoccupation with the details of election, the term of office, reeligibility, and removability. Never quite satisfied with previous decisions, they returned again and again to try new combinations of provisions. What would seem to be the more important issue, namely, that the actual powers be vested in the office, received far less attention and was shunted off to committees or squeezed into the late stages of the Convention's business. On closer examination, however, the preoccupation with the specifics of presidential election and tenure reveals the framers' deeper concern with the purpose and functioning of the executive office. In particular, their efforts were directed to two great ends: to make the presidency an independent and coequal branch of the national government, and to make it in the President's interest to carry out his duties.

Early in the debates Roger Sherman argued the case for legislative supremacy. The legislature, he maintained, "was the depository of the supreme will of the Society," the executive "nothing more than an institution for carrying the will of the Legislature into effect. . . ."[15] The legislature should thus be left free to appoint any number of executive magistrates it sees fit and "should have power to remove the Executive[s] at pleasure."[16] Sherman's opinions fell on deaf ears. No one came to his support. No one even suggested that the issue be debated. The delegates had learned the lessons of the state experience, and their words and actions in the Convention demonstrate a thoroughgoing rejection of the principle of legislative supremacy for the new national government. On this there was near unanimity; but how to construct an independent and coequal executive office was another matter.

After the important issue of a single versus plural executive was provisionally settled on the side of unity (more on this below), the delegates turned to the method of presidential selection. Initially they favored appointment by the national legislature, since it seemed the fittest body for the purpose. Popular election, proposed by James Wilson, met with little support. The people are "too little informed" and "liable to deceptions," retorted Elbridge Gerry.[17] They will, he later elaborated, generally vote for a candidate put forward by some elite body like the Society of Cincinnati, leading this seemingly democratic procedure to have oligarchic results.[18] A third alternative, proposed early in the debates, was election by a special group of men who would themselves be popularly elected for this sole purpose.[19] Eventually a modified version of this plan prevailed.

Election by the national legislature immediately raised the problem of executive dependence. If the executive was to be reeligible, the reelection incentive would foster complaisance to the legislative will. It would make the executive "the mere creature of the

Legislature."[20] The provisional solution was ineligibility and a substantial term of office, originally seven years—a proposal, it is interesting to note, that has recently been revived. Later Gouverneur Morris prodded the delegates to think through the effects of ineligibility. It would, he said, "destroy the great motive to good behavior, the hope of being rewarded by a re-appointment. It was saying to him, make hay while the sun shines."[21] Most delegates came to agree with Morris on the benefits of reeligibility; but they then confronted a dilemma: if the executive were chosen by the legislature, then reeligibility, beneficial in itself, would undermine his independence; on the other hand, there seemed to be no suitable alternative to legislative election.

The Convention wrestled with this problem again and again, Wilson declaring it to be "in truth the most difficult of all on which we have to decide."[22] Finally, late in the session a plan was adopted that would provide the benefits of both independence and reeligibility. The President would be elected by a body of men, selected as the state legislatures saw fit, who would meet in their states on the same day throughout the nation to vote for the chief executive. If no one received a majority of the votes the election would be decided in the House of Representatives, each state's delegation counting as one vote. This electoral device would provide for a more informed choice than popular election, and, by removing the election of the President from the hands of the national legislature, would also allow for reeligibility.

What is abundantly clear from the debates on presidential election and tenure is the overriding importance of executive independence. It was a fundamental and essential element of the framers' scheme of the separation of powers. In furtherance of that independence the President's salary was to be free from legislative control while he served. More important, the President's powers, like those of the governor of New York, were vested by an explicit constitutional grant, and thus not subject to legislative determination. They included such substantial powers as the veto, the office of commander in chief, and the pardon (which were vested only in the President), while the making of treaties and appointments were shared with the Senate.

The central constitutional features of the presidency—unity, a nonlegislative mode of election, reeligibility, and a constitutional grant of powers—provided for a firm and energetic chief executive both to execute efficiently the national laws and to counterbalance the predominance that the legislative branch naturally enjoyed in a representative democracy. Creating a sturdy institution and vesting it with substantial powers does not, however, insure that it will fulfill its intended functions. This fact the framers fully appreciated; thus, they designed their constitutional scheme to go one step farther, to provide the institutional incentives that would lead the occupant of the presidential office to exercise his powers as they were *meant* to be exercised. The key, as Hamilton and Madison brilliantly argue in the *Federalist,* is to attach the man to the office, to give him an interest in preserving its energy and integrity. It must, therefore, be an office worth defending. It must have the substantial powers and duration that will foster personal attachment. The prospect of re-election, of a continued enjoyment of the rewards and honors of the presidency, will help make it in the President's interest to preserve the prerogatives of his office. And, more generally, the opportunity to win the respect and honor of his countrymen will foster resistance to legislative measures that are contrary to the public good. The overall scheme is best described in the following famous passage from *Federalist* 51:

> But the great security against a gradual concentration of the several powers in the same department [legislature] consists in giving to those who administer each department the necessary constitutional means and personal motives to resist encroachments of the others. The provision for defense must in this, as in all other cases, be made commensurate to the danger of attack. Ambition must be made to counteract ambition. The interest of the man must be connected with the constitutional rights of the place.[23]

The historical record demonstrates that the framers' scheme has worked remarkably well in stimulating Presidents to defend the constitutional prerogatives of their office. There have been "weak" Presidents, those who conceded congressional supremacy in national policy making, but there have been few Presidents who have not resisted encroachments on the executive domain. This is strikingly evidenced by the example of the Whig Presidents who served between the Jacksonian period and the Civil War. Although committed by party philosophy to legislative supremacy, upon taking office they showed signs of independence and assertiveness that dismayed, in some cases outraged, their party colleagues in Congress. William Henry Harrison, the first of the Whig Presidents, showed during his one month in office "unorthodox signs of independence. He put Henry Clay in his place when Clay tried to push him, and resisted party leaders clamoring for patronage."[24] The Vice-President who succeeded Harrison was John Tyler, formerly a dissenting Democrat who had long opposed Andrew Jackson's vigorous exercise of presidential power. Whig leaders believed they had a President who would willingly submit to congressional control. They were soon disappointed. Tyler twice vetoed bank bills that were central to the program of the congressional Whigs. "The ensuing outburst of fury against the President at this second veto has probably been equalled only by the merciless attack on Andrew Johnson and his supporters by the Radical Unionists after the Civil War. The savage enginery of social terror was let loose by the Whigs on John Tyler."[25] Later in Tyler's term a veto of a tariff measure led to the initiation of the first formal impeachment proceeding against a President in our history.[26] The two succeeding Whig Presidents, Zachary Taylor and Millard Fillmore, proved no less resolute in opposing congressional control.[27] What is most instructive in the example of the Whig Presidents is the degree to which their actions contradicted their party's philosophy of executive dependence and, in several cases, their own previously enunciated views.

Subsequent Presidents, not otherwise known for executive assertiveness, also resisted congressional encroachments. James Buchanan, who would soon declare himself powerless to resist the Southern secession, adamantly opposed an investigation by the House of Representatives in 1860 into the conduct of the executive branch. "Except in [cases of impeachment]," he protested to the House,

> the Constitution has invested the House of Representatives with no power, no jurisdiction, no supremacy whatever over the President. In all other respects he is quite as independent of them as they are of him. As a coordinate branch of the Government he is their equal. . . . He will defend [the people]. . . to the last extremity against any unconstitutional attempt, come from what quarter it may, to abridge the constitutional rights of the Executive and render him subservient to any human power except themselves.[28]

Two decades later, in the midst of the period known as "congressional government," Rutherford B. Hayes acted similarly to defend the prerogatives of his office. Although his "*theory* of the presidency was Whig in its origin, his *practice* was almost the opposite. He defied the Senate leadership in his Cabinet appointments and . . . he stoutly defended the executive office against aggression by both the House and the Senate."[29] (Emphasis in the original.)

In establishing an executive branch that would resist the natural tendency of the legislature to dominate the national government, the framers institutionalized within their system conflict between Congress and the presidency. The history of American government is in large part a working out of this institutional conflict, an unceasing competition between Congress and the presidency for control of national policy. By design, the constitutional scheme would provide for a kind of balance or equilibrium between these two competing political branches; but events during the first forty years under the Constitution led many to believe that the framers' institutional checks were insufficient to prevent an evolution to legislative supremacy.

Under George Washington the executive branch was vigorously independent of Congress. Keenly aware of the precedental impact of his actions, Washington was not reluctant in the face of congressional opposition to exercise his independent executive powers. The principal cases are his Proclamation of Neutrality in 1793, which was challenged by members of Congress as an encroachment on the Senate's power in foreign affairs, and his refusal to fulfill a request from the House of Representatives for papers relating to the negotiation of the Jay Treaty. In the domestic sphere also, the presidency was hardly the mere servant of Congress; for the nation's early economic and commercial policies were the product of Washington's able Secretary of the Treasury, Alexander Hamilton. With the rise, however, in the 1790s of the Jeffersonian-Republican party committed to opposing the "monarchical" tendencies of the national government, and with the succession to the presidency of a less effective, and certainly a less beloved, chief executive in the person of John Adams, Congress came increasingly to resist executive guidance and direction.

In the election of 1800 the Republicans captured both houses of Congress, and their leader, Thomas Jefferson, became the nation's third President. Though a fervent opponent of the "monarchists," Jefferson did not devote his administration to serving the congressional will. On the contrary, he exercised considerable influence on Congress—not mainly, to be sure, by the vigorous and independent exercise of presidential power, although there are cases of this, but more generally by guiding the legislative process through political lieutenants in well-placed positions in Congress. Presidential influence was facilitated by the centralization of legislative decision making in the caucus, the speakership, and the floor leader. Under Jefferson's three Republican successors—James Madison, James Monroe, and John Quincy Adams—this same machinery was employed by congressional leaders to give effect to Republican theories of legislative supremacy.

Madison lacked the leadership qualities of his friend and predecessor. Moreover, he faced strong men in Congress who intended to have their say in determining national policy. They were for the most part successful; in the process the presidency dropped to a subordinate position in the government. Contributing to this subordination was the de facto election of the President by the congressional nominating caucus. As one historian has observed, "Jefferson had made the Republican party, and as maker he ruled it. The party in its turn made Madison president, and what need was there to bow before the idol it created?"[30] In effect, until 1824 congressional election of the President, a method rejected by the framers as subversive of presidential independence, remained in operation. In 1818, with the presidency occupied by James Monroe, Judge Joseph Story of the Supreme Court observed in a letter to a friend, "The Executive has no longer a commanding influence. The House of Representatives has absorbed all the popular feeling and all the effective power of the country. Even the Senate cowers under its lofty pretensions to be the guardians of the people and its rights."[31]

The tendency in a republic for power to be concentrated in the most democratic branch would not have surprised the framers; indeed, it was one reason for the division of the legislature into two branches, one of which would not be directly elected by the people. The attachment the people would have for the branch that most clearly voiced their desires would be the source of great political weight in a struggle with the less democratic branches. Andrew Jackson was to show that the constitutional independence and powers of the presidency were still there to be used when regenerated by the force of his own democratic appeal.

Jackson owed his election in 1828 to his widespread popularity. With the extension of universal white manhood suffrage and the popular election of presidential electors, the electoral college mechanism simply ratified the popular choice (as earlier it had ratified the congressional choice). The first President to be elected by the people, he was also the first to claim to be its direct representative. He was, according to one legal scholar, "the first President in our history to appeal to the people over the heads of their legislative representatives." On the basis of that appeal, "the office itself was thrust forward as one of three *equal* departments of government, and to each and every of its powers was imparted new scope, new vitality."[32] The roots of Jackson's presidency were sunk deep into the people by his leadership of a mass-based party organization and the institution of the national presidential nominating convention in time for his 1832 reelection. Elected directly by the people and serving as their instrument in the national government, Jackson cut the cord of dependence of the legislature, reestablishing the independence and coequal status of the executive branch. He showed in the process that the democratization of the presidency could be the source of great strength in a conflict with Congress.

The central issue of national scope around the time of Jackson's attempt at reelection was the rechartering of the Second Bank of the United States. Amidst a storm of congressional protest over his veto of a rechartering bill in 1832, Jackson took the issue directly to the people. He interpreted his overwhelming electoral victory as an unambiguous statement of the people's will and as a mandate for further action against the Bank before its expiration in 1836. In justifying to the Cabinet in 1833 his decision to remove the federal deposits from the Bank, Jackson maintained that

> the case was argued to the people; and . . . the people have sustained the President. . . . Whatever may be the opinions of others, the President considers his reelection a decision of the people against the bank. . . . He was sustained by a just people, and he desires to evince his gratitude by carrying into effect their decision so far as it depends upon him.[33]

Jackson's rejection of the Bank Bill in 1832 was one of twelve vetoes during his eight-year tenure, a paltry amount by modern standards but enough to revolutionize the then widely accepted view of the scope and purpose of the President's veto power. Previous Presidents had vetoed a total of only nine bills, most of these for constitutional reasons. It had come to be accepted that the veto was intended only for extraordinary circumstances, especially to guard against legislative encroachments, and not to give the President a regular check on the policy-making process. Legislation was the proper business of Congress, and the President was normally to have no part in it. Rejecting this understanding of separation of powers, Jackson legitimized the use of the veto on policy grounds. In so doing he resurrected a use clearly intended by the framers, if long since forgotten: "It not only serves as a shield to the executive," Hamilton affirmed in the *Federalist*, "but it furnishes an additional security against the enaction of improper laws. It establishes a salutary check upon the legislative body. . . ."[34] Indeed, it must be said more generally that Jackson's administration restored much of the framers' original plan for, and understanding of, the executive office. In raising the presidency to its rightful constitutional place as one of three coordinate departments of government, and in maintaining that above all the President served not Congress but the public interest under and through the Constitution, Jackson was allying himself with the institution's architects. The democratization of the executive office, which provided the energy to make this correct constitutional understanding politically effective, was not, however, a restoration of the original design; for, as will be discussed below, the framers expressly rejected a popular, democratic presidency for the new national government.

Jackson's rehabilitation of the framers' view of the independence and coordinate status of the executive branch was not lost on later Presidents. James K. Polk reasserted it in his fourth annual message to Congress (1848):

> The executive, legislative, and judicial each constitutes a separate coordinate department of the Government, and each is independent of the others. In the performance of their respective duties under the Constitution neither can in its legitimate action control the others.[35]

Buchanan made the same argument in defending his office against a congressional investigation (see above); and Lincoln's vigorous exercise of power during the Civil War rested on a similar constitutional understanding. Following Lincoln's assassination, however, the competing view of congressional supremacy, never quite extinguished, was given new force by the Radical Republicans in Congress who were determined to control reconstruction policy. "Congress is the sovereign power," declared Thaddeus Stevens, "because the people speak through them; and Andrew Johnson must learn that he is your servant and that as Congress shall order he must obey. There is no escape from it."[36] With apparent popular support, Congress was able to override presidential vetoes and neutralize the President's influence over reconstruction, going so far as to contravene Johnson's authority over his Cabinet and the army. In the end Congress came but one vote short of actually removing the President from office.

These few years of virtual congressional control of government cast a long shadow, Congress remaining to a greater or less degree the dominant branch of government through the rest of the nineteenth century. Not until the consecutive presidencies of William McKinley (1897-1901) and Theodore Roosevelt (1901-1909) did the office attain a position of influence and importance in American government commensurate with that enjoyed earlier by Washington, Jefferson, Jackson, Polk, and Lincoln. And, following Roosevelt's presidency, forces were at work that led to a sustained, if uneven, movement toward presidential leadership of the American political system in the twentieth century. Since its culmination in the New Deal administration of Franklin Roosevelt, our modern presidency has become responsible for overseeing a vast national bureaucracy, for setting the direction of domestic and foreign policy, and for articulating national ideals and the national purpose. Ours is a government energized by the presidential impulse.

Although the President's energizing and guiding function in the governmental system seems to be the peculiar development of the twentieth century, the essential elements were present in the constitutional scheme from the very beginning. Most commentators agree, for example, that the rise of the United States as a world power and the expansion in the domestic role of the national government have contributed substantially to presidential leadership, yet, in both the foreign and domestic spheres, the President's increasingly important policy-making role is rooted in the framers' original institutional design, especially in their decision for a single executive and a numerous legislature.

When James Wilson proposed a single executive on the first day of the Convention's debate on the presidency, he argued that it would give "most energy, dispatch, and responsibility to the office."[37] While there was some opposition, the issue was soon settled on the side of unity and the Convention went on to the other executive provisions. In *Federalist* 70 Alexander Hamilton elaborates the framers' reasons for choosing a single executive and a numerous legislature. It is worth quoting at length:

> Those politicians and statesmen who have been the most celebrated for the soundness of their principles and for the justness of their views have declared in favor of a single executive and a numerous legislature. They have, with great propriety, considered *energy* as the most necessary qualification of the former, and have regarded this as most applicable to power in a single hand; while they have, with equal propriety, considered the latter as best adapted to *deliberation* and *wisdom*, and best calculated to conciliate the confidence of the people and to secure their privileges and interests.
>
> That unity is conducive to energy will not be disputed. *Decision, activity, secrecy,* and *dispatch* will generally characterize the proceedings of one man in a much more eminent degree than the proceedings of any greater number; and in proportion as the number is increased, these qualities will be diminished.[38] [Emphasis added.]

In short, deliberation and wisdom are promoted by plurality, decision making and activity by unity. Competent government must have a capacity for both deliberation *and* decision, for wisdom *and* action.

The acid test of a government's capacity for swift, decisive action is armed conflict with a foreign nation; this "most peculiarly demands those qualities which distinguish the exercise of power by a single hand."[39] Decision, activity, and dispatch are the qualities needed for military success, and they are qualities that only an energetic executive possesses. "The direction of war," Hamilton continued, "implies the direction of the common strength; and the power of directing and employing the common strength forms a usual and essential part in the definition of the executive authority."[40] This "essential part" of the executive function reaches, however, beyond military conflicts to international relations more generally; for foreign policy is the direction of the common strength to secure national advantages. It is thus especially, though not wholly, the province of the executive department. It was implicit in the framers' design, then, that the executive's importance would grow as the United States came to play a central role on the international stage.

The political advantages of a unified, energetic executive branch are not restricted to the foreign policy sphere, for Hamilton shows that the qualities of an energetic executive are indispensable to the whole administration of government:

> Energy in the executive is a leading character in the definition of good government. . . . A feeble executive implies a feeble execution of the government. A feeble execution is but another phrase for a bad execution; and a government ill executed, whatever it may be in theory, must be, in practice, a bad government.[41]

Insofar as the administration of government falls within the domain of the executive department, it includes "[t]he actual conduct of foreign negotiations, the preparatory plans of finance, the application and disbursement of the public moneys in conformity to the general appropriations of the legislature, the arrangement of the army and navy, the direction of the operations of war . . . and other matters of a like nature. . . ."[42] Foreign affairs, economic and financial policy, national defense, and like matters—these are the great governmental concerns for which executive energy is essential and over which the executive is to exercise primary responsibility, subject where appropriate to legislative action. Hamilton's performance as Secretary of the Treasury under Washington, formulating the new nation's economic and financial programs and guiding them through Congress, is evidence of the scope of the executive's administrative responsibility.

It may be asked why it is essential that the executive assume primary responsibility over the formulation of domestic policy in areas like economics and finance, why this cannot be left to the legislature—to which Hamilton's implied response is that the legislature's proper business is deliberation; that it is institutionally incapable of formulating coherent and complex packages of legislation designed to meet the nation's general interests; that only an energetic executive branch responsible to the whole nation has the capacity to act with the unity of mind and will essential for such purposes. (The President's proposals, of course, have no legal force unless they can pass the scrutiny of Congress.) If Hamilton's understanding of the respective institutional capacities of Congress and the presidency is broadly accurate, then it is to be expected that as national legislation grew more extensive and complex, as the national government expanded its role in the regulation of the nation's domestic concerns, Congress would become increasingly dependent on presidential initiative in domestic policy making. This is precisely what has happened in the twentieth century, and explains why the President has become our "chief legislator." The causes that led to, and the purposes that were to be served by, the Budget and Accounting Act of 1921, often considered a landmark in executive-legislative relations, are instructive in understanding the modern movement toward presidential policy leadership.[43]

Prior to the budgetary reform of 1921 appropriation requests were transmitted by executive department heads to the Secretary of the Treasury who did little more than compile the independent requests and transmit them to Congress. In the House and Senate the proposals were parceled out to half a dozen or more committees whose recommendations were acted on independently by the full bodies. With an increase in the complexity and expense of the government's administrative operations from the Civil War through the beginning of the twentieth century, budgetary decision making grew increasingly chaotic, irresponsible, and wasteful, becoming something of a national scandal. In the second decade of this century there began a sustained movement to provide for a more rational and responsible budget system. In 1919 a select committee of the House reported on the evils of the existing system:

> Expenditures are not considered with revenues. . . . Congress does not require of the President any carefully thought-out financial and work program representing what provision in his opinion should be made for meeting the financial needs of the Government; . . . the estimates of expenditure needs now submitted to Congress represent only the desires of the individual departments, establishments, and bureaus; and . . . these requests have been subjected to no superior revision with a view to bringing them into harmony with each other, . . . or of making them, as a whole, conform to the needs of the Nation as represented by the condition of the Treasury and prospective revenues. . . .[44]

The legislation that finally emerged in 1921 gave the President, through the agency of a Bureau of the Budget serving directly under him, responsibility for coordinating a coherent national budget. Congress would be assisted in examining the proposed budget by the newly established General Accounting Office. Though not required by the legislation, it was expected that each house would consolidate budget review under a single appropriations committee. Shortly after the new law took effect this reform was made.

By 1920 Congress had come to recognize that the President, as head of the executive establishment, was in the best position to bring the various budget requests into "harmony" so that the budget "as a whole [would] conform to the needs of the Nation." Congress, however, was in no way abrogating its legislative responsibilities; on the contrary, it was providing for a more intelligent exercise of its own powers. In the spirit of Hamilton's understanding of the chief executive's administrative role, the President's control over the executive establishment was consolidated and he was given the initiative in formulating coherent national policy. In this respect the budget reform is the pattern for subsequent concessions by Congress of presidential initiative in policy formulation. Especially important is the Full Employment Act of 1946 which, in making it the official policy of the national government to foster and maintain a healthy economy, gave the President the responsibility to construct a coherent economic program and to keep Congress informed of the nation's economic well-being.

Modern political conditions have, then, added new form and scope to the chief executive's intended role as the energizer of the governmental system. The framers' original design continues to shape the way the institutions of government act to meet the national needs. There is, however, one historical development in the nature of the executive office that appears to run counter to the original plan; for the democratization of the presidency seems neither to have been intended nor desired by the framers. By the terms of the Constitution the President was not even to be elected by the people but by a select group of men chosen as the state legislatures saw fit. It was the transformation of this original scheme into one of de facto popular election that made possible, indeed likely, the democratization of the presidential office.

Although Andrew Jackson demonstrated in the early nineteenth century that the executive office had a capacity for popular leadership, it is especially in the twentieth century that the President has become the spokesman and leader of the American people. We have come to expect such leadership from our Presidents and they have not been reluctant to assume the role. This increased democratization of the presidency in the public mind is reflected in the steady movement throughout this century toward an ever more democratic means of presidential election. The nominating system has become more democratic both through the extension of presidential primary elections, which register the people's preference before the nomination, and through changes in the rules governing delegate apportionment and voting in the national party conventions. Moreover, the electoral college system, which controls the final outcome, has been subject in recent years to a renewed effort to replace it with direct popular election. Should this effort be successful, it could well be followed by the establishment of a national presidential primary, thereby making the election of the President as democratic as the election of representatives and senators. "The time has come," argues one of the principal proponents of direct popular election, reflecting a widespread sentiment, "to amend our Constitution to implement the direct vote, so that in fact as well as in theory, in constitutional guarantee as well as by happenstance in the electoral college, the man we choose may truly be the people's President."[45]

The notion that the chief executive should be the *People's President* was not unknown to the framers, for one can find a forceful defense of a popular presidency in the speeches of James Wilson and Gouverneur Morris at the Constitutional Convention. Although Wilson and Morris agreed with their colleagues that the legislative branch would be the primary source of danger to the success of the new government, they attributed that danger to a different cause and consequently proposed a different remedy. This is most clearly seen in the case of Morris:

> The Legislature [he maintained,] will continually seek to aggrandize and perpetuate themselves. . . . It is necessary then that the Executive Magistrate should be the guardian of the people, even of the lower classes, agst. Legislative tyranny, against the Great and the wealthy who in the course of things will necessarily compose—the Legislative body. . . . The Executive therefore ought to be so constituted as to be the great protector of the Mass of the people.[46]

The President would be a democratic safeguard against the abuses of an oligarchic legislature. In this, however, Morris' presidency is not the presidency constructed by the Convention. Though the body of the delegates agreed with Morris on the need for an independent, unified, and vigorous executive, they intended their energetic President to counteract in the main a different kind of danger.

"[T]he general object [of the new scheme of government]," argued Edmund Randolph, in expounding the more widespread view, "was to provide a cure for the evils under which the U.S. laboured; . . . in tracing these evils to their origin every man had found it in the turbulence and follies of democracy; . . . some check therefore was to be sought for agst. this tendency of our Governments. . . ."[47] More generally stated: republican government, like other forms, has its peculiar virtues and vices; its peculiar vice, manifested in the states under the Articles of Confederation, is its susceptibility to democratic excesses. The multiplicity, mutability, and injustice of the state laws, Madison argued, had "forfeited the respect and confidence essential to order and good Govt., involving a general decay of confidence and credit between man and man. . . . [T]hose most devoted to the principles and forms of Republics were alarmed for the cause of liberty itself. . . ."[48] The state experience had thus called into question "the fundamental principle of republican government": that the majority should rule.[49] Though doubts had been raised, the delegates at Philadelphia never wavered in their firm conviction that a just and competent government could be constructed on a popular foundation, that "a republican remedy [could be devised] for the diseases most incident to republican government."[50] Their whole effort, it can be said, was directed to this one great end.

The institution of the presidency was to be a major part of the republican remedy. With an indirect mode of election and a four-year term of office, the President would be insulated somewhat from the momentary passions that might grip the people and be communicated to their representatives in Congress, especially in the House of Representatives. The veto power enables the executive to check popular but pernicious measures in the hope that the people will return to a more temperate state. The President's check on Congress thus serves a more fundamental purpose than preventing legislative encroachments; for it serves to restrain the people themselves from giving immediate effect to every passing inclination. It restrains them, however, in the name of their true interests. It restrains them from doing what their own good sense would resist if it were in control. By preventing immediate action and by holding up to the people and their representatives an alternative view of what is really in the public interest, this partial check fosters cooler deliberation on national policy issues. It is the "deliberative sense of the community"[51] that should prevail in a republic, and a wise use of the presidential veto will help to prevent something less from controlling the government.

One should note that the President's veto is a very modest one indeed, requiring to be overriden that only one-sixth of the House and Senate above the original majority support the vetoed bill. Such a check will not long prevent a determined people from realizing their demands. It was not, however, the framers' design to place unbreachable barriers in the way of popular control. Instead they hoped to channel, moderate, and improve the popular influence so as to make self-government truly sound and effective. In this they considered themselves to be the true friends of popular government. Though the veto power is a modest contribution to governmental competence, the principle on which it is based extends more generally to the whole functioning and character of the presidential office. In the wise conduct of foreign affairs, the steady administration of government, and the faithful execution of the laws the President was to take his cues not from popular inclinations but from the duties and responsibilities imposed on him by the people speaking in their most authoritative voice, that is, through the United States Constitution. He serves the people best when he fulfills the high purposes of the executive office implicit in the fundamental law.

Given this understanding of the vices to which republican governments are especially prone and of the need for institutional mechanisms to moderate the democratic impulse, one may surmise that the framers would have been troubled with the notion of a *people's President,* of a President who was particularly close to the people, who reflected their attitudes and desires, and who served as their "tribune" in the national government. It is characteristic of contemporary commentators to accept the democratization of the presidential office as wholly good, as a kind of historical fulfillment of the true principles of the American polity. A serious examination of the framers' understanding, however, leads us to think less uncritically about this historical development; for it leads us to wonder whether this *people's President* will have the inclination and capacity to pursue the common good with independence and fortitude, to resist popular desires when unsound, and to guide and inform the public mind as to the nation's true interests. This presumes, of course, what we all know from our common experience, that there are times when inclinations and interests do not coincide. On this the framers were very clear, and that clarity can be the basis of a fuller and deeper understanding of the principles of the American constitutional order.

In view of our history, however, one may wonder whether the vision of the architects of our governmental system was somewhat deficient in not appreciating the propensity, perhaps the inevitability, of the executive office to become the focal point of national issues and national aspirations. Although unintended by the framers, who designed the Presidency to check and moderate the democratic impulse but not to provide positive, active leadership of the American people, the office has become, as Franklin Roosevelt described it, "preeminently a place of moral leadership."[52] Recent Presidents have concurred, though they have understood moral leadership in different ways. For Eisenhower it meant fundamentally standing as a moral example:

> I believe deeply that every occupant of the White House, whether he be conservative, liberal or middle-of-the-road, has one profound duty to the nation: to exert moral leadership. The President of the United States should stand, visible and uncompromising, for what is right and decent—in government, in the business community, in the private lives of the citizens. For decency is one of the main pillars of a sound civilization. An immoral nation invites its own ruin.[53]

For Truman it meant the President's responsibility "to rally the people to a sustained effort of will . . . [and] to lead and inspire public opinion."[54] For Kennedy it meant both this inspirational leadership—"[the President must be] willing and able to summon his national constituency to its finest hour . . . [and] to demand of them the sacrifices that will be necessary"—and also fighting for "great ideals."[55] For Franklin Delano Roosevelt it seems even to have included a restoration of traditional political and moral values:

"The money changers have fled from their high seats in the temple of our civilization. We may now restore that temple to the ancient truths."[56]

Standing as an example of moral rectitude, inspiring national enterprises, fighting for great ideals, and restoring traditional values—these were not leadership capacities provided for by the framers; indeed, they seem to have believed that moral leadership of this kind would be unnecessary in a nation governed by their carefully contrived institutions. It remains one of the great unanswered questions of the American experiment in self-government whether a purely institutional solution can ultimately be successful; or whether every republican regime must at its base rest on a firm popular foundation of sound moral character, steady devotion to the public good, and a clear appreciation of the duties, as well as the rights, of citizenship. If, in fact, the ability of our institutions to provide for just and competent republican government depends finally on the character of the American citizenry, then it is a kind of happy accident that one of the framers' institutions, the presidency, has a special capacity for inspiring, guiding, and instructing the American people.

Notes

1. Data on the executive provisions of the state constitutions can be conveniently found in Charles C. Thach, Jr., *The Creation of the Presidency, 1775-1789* (Baltimore: Johns Hopkins Press, 1969), pp. 25-54.
2. Thomas Jefferson, "Notes on Virginia," in *The Life and Selected Writings of Thomas Jefferson,* ed. Adrienne Koch and William Peden (New York: Random House, Modern Library, 1944), pp. 237-238.
3. Quoted in Thach, *Creation of the Presidency,* pp. 32-33.
4. Max Farrand, ed., *The Records of the Federal Convention of 1787,* 4 vols. (New Haven: Yale University Press, 1966), 2:35 (July 17).
5. Alexander Hamilton, James Madison, and John Jay, *The Federalist Papers,* ed. Clinton Rossiter (New York: New American Library, 1961), nos. 47-51.
6. The following account is taken from Thach, *Creation of the Presidency,* pp. 55-75.
7. Farrand, *Records,* 1:65 (June 1).
8. "Helvidius no. 1" in Robert S. Hirschfield, ed., *The Power of the Presidency,* 2d ed. (Chicago: Aldine Publishing Co., 1973), p. 59.

9. Quoted in Leonard D. White, *The Republican Era* (New York: Macmillan Co., 1958), p. 21.
10. U.S., Congress, Senate, Judiciary Committee, *Congressional Oversight of Executive Agreements: Hearings*, 92d Cong., 1st sess., 1972, p. 6.
11. Farrand, *Records*, 2:52 (July 19).
12. *Federalist* 71, p. 433.
13. James D. Richardson, *A Compilation of the Messages and Papers of the Presidents, 1789-1897*, 10 vols. (Washington: U.S. Government Printing Office, 1896-1899), 4:669.
14. Quoted in Hirschfield, *Power of the Presidency*, p. 83.
15. Farrand, *Records*, 1:65 (June 1).
16. Ibid., p. 85 (June 2).
17. Ibid., p. 80 (June 2).
18. Ibid., 2:114 (July 25).
19. Ibid., 1:80 (June 2).
20. George Mason, ibid., p. 86 (June 2).
21. Ibid., 2:33 (July 17).
22. Ibid., p. 501 (Sept. 4).
23. *Federalist* 51, pp. 321-322.
24. Leonard D. White, *The Jacksonians* (New York: Macmillan Co., 1954), p. 47.
25. Wilfred E. Binkley, *President and Congress*, 3d ed. rev. (New York: Random House, Vintage Books, 1962), pp. 115-116.
26. Ibid., pp. 118-119.
27. Ibid., pp. 125-130.
28. Richardson, *Papers of the Presidents*, 5:615.
29. White, *Republican Era*, p. 25.
30. Ralph Volney Harlow, *The History of Legislative Methods in the Period Before 1825* (New Haven: Yale University Press, 1917), p. 194.
31. Joseph Story, *Life and Letters of Joseph Story*, ed. William W. Story, 2 vols. (Boston: Charles C. Little and James Brown, 1851), 1:311.
32. Edward S. Corwin, *The President: Office and Powers* (New York: New York University Press, 1957), p. 21.
33. Richardson, *Papers of the Presidents*, 3:7.
34. *Federalist* 73, p. 443.
35. Richardson, *Papers of the Presidents*, 4:669.
36. Quoted in Binkley, *President and Congress*, p. 166.
37. Farrand, *Records*, 1:65 (June 1).
38. *Federalist* 70, p. 424.
39. Ibid., 74, p. 447.
40. Ibid.
41. Ibid. 70, p. 423.
42. Ibid. 72, pp. 435-436.
43. The following account is taken from Joseph P. Harris, *Congressional Control of Administration* (Washington: Brookings Institution, 1964),

pp. 46-67, and Fritz Morstein Marx, "The Bureau of the Budget: Its Evolution and Present Role," *American Political Science Review* 39 (Aug. 1945): 653-684.

44. Quoted in Marx, "Bureau of the Budget," p. 657.
45. Neal R. Peirce, *The People's President* (New York: Simon and Schuster, 1968), p. 26. Peirce, himself, is opposed to the establishment of a national presidential primary, ibid., 267-269; yet, the majoritarian principles on which he defends direct popular election seem to demand nothing less.
46. Farrand, *Records*, 2:52 (July 19).
47. Ibid., 1:51 (May 31).
48. Ibid., 3:548.
49. Marvin Meyers, ed., *The Mind of the Founder* (Indianapolis: Bobbs-Merrill, 1973), "Vices of the Political System of the United States," p. 88.
50. *Federalist* 10, p. 84.
51. Ibid., no. 71, p. 432.
52. Hirschfield, *Power of the Presidency*, p. 101.
53. Ibid., p. 123.
54. Ibid., p. 117.
55. Ibid., p. 133.
56. Ibid., p. 105.

The author wishes to thank Professor Herbert J. Storing of the University of Chicago for guiding this project throughout and for his valuable comments on a first draft of this chapter. Errors of fact or interpretation are solely the responsibility of the author.

[8]

CONGRESS

—MURRAY DRY

This chapter examines both the original and the current application of American founding principles to Congress, concentrating on the framing of the Constitution, the establishment of the government under the First Congress, and the reclaiming of constitutional power on the part of the 93d Congress, which met from 1973 to 1974. Inquiry will be directed primarily to two questions: What, on the basis of their understanding of republican government and their construction of the Constitution, did the Founders expect from Congress? In the light of the current requirements of a large bureaucracy and the capacity of the executive to respond immediately to emergencies throughout the world, what may we expect today?

Congress and Republican Government

Congress's distinctiveness as a legislative body is related to the unique character of both the American separation of powers and American federalism, which Tocqueville described in *Democracy in America* (1835). While emphasizing the importance of local institutions in fostering in the people a spirit of liberty, he commended the framers for resisting the tendency to concentrate all power in the legislative branch. He also lauded the federal system for its capacity to combine the security of monarchy with the internal well-being of a republic. He distinguished the American republic from previous confederations as the framers did: the new federal government not only passed laws, but also saw to their execution. This change reversed the traditional tendency toward discord and weakness in federal governments, without sacrificing the benefits of local institutions. The states still governed internal affairs, although they left the actual administration to local governments.[1] Noting that there was not yet a new word for America's new form, Tocqueville called it an "incomplete national government." Still, he suggested that the requirements of security would force this national government to consolidate its power, and that would necessitate an increase in executive control.[2] Consequently, if the American federal system permits a large nation to remain a republic, as Tocqueville implied, then state governments will need the assistance of Congress to maintain freedom in America.

America's first Congress, the Continental Congress, met from 1774 to 1789. At that time, the term *congress* referred to an assembly of delegates, just as *federal system*, or *confederation*, referred to an assembly of states. Congress under the Articles of Confederation was even weaker politically than it was legally; for example, according to Article II: "Each state retains its sovereignty, freedom, and independence, and every Power, Jurisdiction and right which is not by this confederation expressly delegated to the United States, in Congress assembled."[3] In Articles VI and IX, however, the states expressly delegated to Congress power to conduct foreign affairs and to make war. These authorizations were recognized in the Declaration of Independence as features of sovereignty. Each state delegation had an equal vote in Congress, and the state legislatures controlled the delegations with the power of recall. Nine states had to agree before Congress could exercise its major powers, such as war, raising military forces, treaty-making, and appropriating money. Congress had no power to regulate commerce; and the raising of men and money was left to requisitions from the state governments. Moreover, requisitions passed by nine states were ignored by other states.

The ineffectiveness of requisitions, the need for uniform commercial regulation, and concern over the rights of creditors led James Madison and other nationalists to urge the states to call for a Federal Convention in 1787. While Congress authorized the delegates to meet "for the sole and express purpose of revising the Articles of

Confederation,"[4] the Convention determined, almost from the outset, that "a Union of the States merely federal will not accomplish the objects proposed by the articles of Confederation" and therefore a "*national* government ought to be established." Gouverneur Morris explained the difference between a federal and a national government in a clear and generally accepted manner:

> The former being a mere compact resting on the good faith of the parties, the latter having a compleat and *compulsive* operation.[5]

The difference between the old Congress and the new Congress follows from this distinction: the former was an assembly of delegates, the latter was a branch of government in which the legislative powers granted by the Constitution were vested.

The original Virginia Plan had proposed a general grant of legislative power to Congress, a national negative on state laws, and the power to coerce, with the force of the union, any state failing to meet expectations laid upon it.[6] Madison soon reconsidered the collective force provision, but he was reluctant to give up the national negative. He proposed that the grant of power be of general character, because he doubted the feasibility of an enumeration of particular powers. He suggested the following principle for the scope of the general government's authority:

> As far as its operation would be practicable, it could not in this view be improper; as far as it would be impracticable, the conveniency of the general government itself would concur with that of the people in the maintenance of subordinate governments.[7]

The general grant was later changed to an enumeration of powers, including the *necessary and proper* clause; but Madison did not support a narrow interpretation of control over commerce, taxing and spending, and war and foreign relations. In *Federalist* 44 he wrote of the necessary and proper clause:

> Had the Constitution been silent on this head, there can be no doubt that all the particular powers requisite as means of executing the general powers would have resulted to the government by unavoidable implication. No axiom is more clearly established in law or in reason, than that wherever a general power to do a thing is given, every particular power necessary for doing it is included.[8]

In the congressional debates on the Tenth Amendment, Thomas

Tucker of South Carolina moved that "expressly" be added to the phrase "the powers not delegated by this Constitution."

> Mr. Madison objected to this amendment, because it is impossible to confine a government to the exercise of express powers; there must necessarily be powers by implication, unless the Constitution descended to recount every minutiae.[9]

The Convention had to decide to form a genuine government before any debate could take place on the sphere of that government's power. The decision to form a national government required a national apportionment of representation, either by population or quota of contribution, in the lower house. What about the upper house, however? "We are partly national, partly federal," Oliver Ellsworth of Connecticut argued,[10] and many supporters of national government agreed with him, from principle as well as interest. That argument led to equal representation of the states in the upper house and senatorial election by the state legislatures.

Madison, James Wilson, and other strong nationalists regarded the Great Compromise, which established equal suffrage in the Senate, as their greatest defeat. They feared that this influence of the state governments on the national legislature would subordinate the entire government to the states. Fortunately, the partly national, partly federal advocates were not insistent on giving the state governments control of the Senate. They approved a motion to change the voting in the Senate from a vote by state delegations (which would often split) to one vote for each senator, since, as Elbridge Gerry said, "it would give a national aspect and spirit to the management of business."[11] Nor did they insist on rotation and recall by state legislatures, although this point was pressed by Anti-Federalist critics.[12]

In arguing against equal state representation Madison contested the partly national, partly federal designation. He defined a federal government as one which affected citizens only through the agency of their state governments. Since the proposed government would act directly on the people in all cases, Madison argued that it was totally national. Later in the ratification debate he used the compromise on representation to respond to the charge that the government was wholly national, inconsistent with federalism, and dangerous to the states. Under Madison's new definition, in *Federalist* 39, and recognition of the states was a federal feature.[13]

Madison's fear of state usurpation of federal authority was based on his opinion that majority faction was the critical problem for republican government in America. Madison argued in the Convention and in the *Federalist* that individual rights would be more secure in a larger and more diversified republic, such as the Union at large. Factions would have to moderate their claims in order to gather enough votes to form a majority coalition. In the first session of Congress Madison reiterated this point, claiming that majority faction was a greater source of danger in America than any possible abuse of power by the executive or the legislative branch.[14]

The establishment of a national government required a separate executive department. Debate on the proposal for a unitary executive, and on the mode of election, revealed a genuine concern about monarchy. Roger Sherman, the strongest proponent of legislative supremacy, argued that "the Executive magistracy [was] nothing more than an institution for carrying the will of the Legislature into effect, that the person or persons ought to be appointed by and accountable to the Legislature only, which was the depository of the supreme will of society."[15] Advocates of this position viewed unity in the executive as the "foetus of monarchy."[16] Hamilton, on the other hand, acknowledged the problems inherent in a republican executive, but he went on to argue that there could be no good government without an energetic executive.[17] In establishing unity and also an electoral schema that permitted re-election, the strong executive proponents won a substantial victory, but that did not clarify the scope of executive power; for example, James Wilson, who advocated a strong, popularly elected executive, disclaimed the prerogatives of the British monarch as the proper model for executive power. Madison, even less certain than Wilson on this point, requested a definition of executive power before deciding whether there should be a unitary executive.[18]

The Convention's limited treatment of specific powers sheds little light on legislative-executive relations. An enumerated power to appoint a treasurer by joint legislative ballot was dropped, leaving this appointment to the President.[19] The enumerated power to "make war" was changed, after brief debate, to "declare war." The best explanation for this change was given by Madison and Gerry: it would leave the executive with the power to "repel sudden attacks." Rufus King approved of the change because it removed any suggestion that the legislature would conduct war, which was a function of the President as "commander in chief."[20] The President was also given the apparently ministerial task of receiving foreign ambassadors, while Congress was given additional powers to raise and support armies, make rules for the regulation of military forces, as well as all other powers necessary and proper for carrying out the enumerated ones.

The Convention thus constructed a wholly new federalism, and a separation of powers on the republican mode. A fuller expounding of Congress's powers, vis-à-vis the states and the executive, would have to await the First Congress.

The First Congress

The First Congress is justly considered "almost an adjourned session of the Federal Convention."[21] Eighteen members of the Federal Convention sat in its first session.[22] Meeting in three sessions, from March 4, 1789 to March 3, 1791, the First Congress established the branches of government, funded the national and state debts, incorporated a national bank, proposed a bill of rights, and established the permanent seat of government and a full federal judicial system. Since we are interested in the character of the government that Congress established, we shall consider the House debates on the removal of department heads and on Treasury Secretary Hamilton's proposals for funding the debt and establishing a national bank.[23] Finally, we shall examine the Pacificus-Helvidius debate over the Neutrality Declaration of 1793, since it involves the protagonists of the First Congress, Madison and Hamilton, and is the most famous founding debate on the powers to make war and to attend to foreign relations.

On May 20, 1789, Madison moved "that there shall be established an Executive Department, to be denominated by the Department of Foreign Affairs", with a Secretary to head it appointed by the President by and with the advice and consent of the Senate "and . . . removable by the President."[24]

Four different positions were stated in the House debate on the removal of department heads: 1. That the Constitution, by delegating the appointive power to the President, with the advice and consent of the Senate, gave those branches, by implication, the removal power; 2. That removal was an executive power and was therefore vested in the President alone; 3. That since removal was not mentioned, Congress could vest it where it pleased; and 4. That since it was not mentioned, removal could take place only by impeachment of the officeholder.

Madison's original position was that wherever the Constitution was silent the legislature could set the tenure of offices by virtue of its power to establish them. He acknowledged the force of Richard Bland's argument that "the same power that appointed had, or ought to have, the power of removal," but he found this inexpedient. Since "it is one of the most prominent features of the Constitution . . . that there should be the highest possible degree of responsibility in all the executive officers thereof," Madison opposed anything contrary to the Constitution's "spirit and intention" unless "it is saddled upon us expressly by the letter of that work."[25] The inexpediency of joining Senate and President in the power of removal (bolstered no doubt by the general confidence in the first President) understandably overcame the constitutional argument for Senate participation in removal and also the political argument that too much power was thereby given to the President.

A few days later Madison indicated that he now read the Constitution as implying presidential removal. Therefore, Congress was "absolutely tied down to the construction declared in the bill." The argument depends on identifying the "power of appointing, displacing, and controlling those who execute the laws" as executive.[26] Since the Constitution "affirms that the executive power shall be vested in the President," any exceptions, such as Senate participation in appointment, are to be strictly construed. Therefore, the Constitution's silence on removal means that the power is vested in the President.

In response to Madison, William Smith of South Carolina raised the key question about executive power and its relation to republican government:

> What powers are Executive, or incidental to the Executive Department, will depend upon the nature of the Government; because some powers are vested in the Executive of a monarchy that are not in an

> aristocracy, and in the Executive of an aristocracy that are unknown in a democracy. The Legislatures of republics appoint to office; this power is exercised by the executive of monarchies.[27]

The state constitutions confirmed Smith's point. Most of the executives were chosen by the legislatures and only Maryland's governor possessed the power of appointment. The Virginia Constitution explicitly prohibited the executive's exercise of any prerogative powers.[28] Smith referred to several prerogatives, such as the power to confer titles of nobility and to establish corporations, which are "exercised as executive powers by the King of Great Britain."[29]

Madison did not respond directly to Smith's point about the dependence of executive power on the form of government. He did draw the following distinction between legislative and executive power in the field of administration:

> The Legislature creates the office, defines the powers, limits its duration, and annexes a compensation. This done, the Legislative power ceases. They ought to have nothing to do with designating the man to fill the office. That I conceive to be an Executive nature.[30]

Madison's reference to the tenure of office being fixed by the legislature apparently does not include setting fixed tenure for the President's subordinates. By complex parliamentary maneuvering Congress established the President's constitutional power to remove executive officials.[31] This strengthening of the executive reflects a new form of republican government.

Four years later Madison had a chance to reconsider the relation between executive power and republican government. On April 22, 1793, President Washington issued a proclamation noting a state of war between France and the rest of Europe and declaring that "the duty and interest of the United States require that they should with sincerity and good faith adopt and pursue a conduct friendly and impartial toward the belligerent powers."[32] In so doing Washington annulled the eleventh article of the Treaty of Alliance between the United States and France, ratified in 1778.[33]

Writing in defense of this presidential action under the pseudonym "Pacificus," Hamilton argued that the executive department was the organ of intercourse between the nation and foreign nations; that it was the interpreter of treaties in cases where the judiciary was incompetent; "that it was the *power* charged with the execution of the laws, of which treaties form a part"; and that it was "charged with the command and disposition of the public force." Hamilton's constitutional argument started where Madison's left off in the removal debate. The vesting of executive power in a President is a grant of power; the subsequent enumeration is "intended merely to specify the principal articles implied in the definition of executive power."[34]

For Hamilton, however, not only is Senate participation in appointment and treaty-making an exception from the executive power, but so is Congress's power to declare war and to grant letters of marque and reprisal. Hamilton could cite the legislation establishing the Foreign Affairs and War Departments, which recognized them explicitly as executive departments (as opposed to the Treasury Department).[35] At this point, however, the exceptions appear to overwhelm the rule. Leaving the war power aside, one could argue that the decision regarding removal implied an intention to reduce the senatorial participation in treaty-making as well as in making appointments.[36] A two-thirds vote, however, is required in the Senate to ratify treaties, as opposed to a simple majority to confirm appointments. Furthermore, nomination is distinctively given to the President, with Senate approval necessary for appointment; but, with treaties, no distinction is made between negotiation and ratification. From the Convention debate it appears that three considerations governed the placement of the treaty-making power: the need for secrecy, the desire for state equality in representation in the Senate, and the view that since treaties could have the force of law they should also have the sanction of law.[37]

The event which practically decided this matter occurred in connection with the Jay Treaty with England in 1796. The Senate rebuffed Washington when he appeared in person to consult with them on the Treaty. After supporting a successful motion to table Washington's request, Senator Maclay recorded in his Journal: "As I sat down, the President of the United States started up in a violent fret. '*This defeats every purpose of my coming here*' were the first words he said."[38]

In order to defend the presidential neutrality declaration, Hamilton actually did not need to prove that making war was an executive power. He simply had to argue that the Constitution created a "concurrent authority" in foreign affairs:

> While, therefore, the legislature can alone declare war, can alone actually transfer the nation from a state of peace to a state of hostility, it belongs to the "executive power" to do whatever else the law of nations, co-operating with the treaties of the country, enjoin in the intercourse of the United States with foreign powers.[39]

This position drew on the natural advantages of a unitary executive while remaining consistent with the constitutional division of powers.

Responding under the pseudonym "Helvidius," Madison cited Hamilton's general argument on executive power, attributing it, as Smith had done with the argument on removal, to conceptions of executive power appropriate to England's monarchy, not to America's republic. Madison even said that Locke and Montesquieu were "warped by a regard to the particular government, to which one of them owed allegiance, and the other professed an admiration bordering on idolatry."[40] The source of the theoretical confusion regarding executive power lay in Locke's distinguishing it from federative power, while placing both in the monarchical executive, and also in Montesquieu's dropping altogether the distinction between executive and federative powers.[41] Perhaps intentionally, neither Locke nor Montesquieu clarifies the distinction between executive powers and monarchical prerogatives.

Madison claimed that Hamilton's thesis on concurrent authority would be "as awkward in practice as it is unnatural in theory." As for the theory, Madison seems to consider the powers capable of being precisely identified. The Constitution distributes powers among different branches. In the absence of a clear delineation of legislative and executive powers, a demarcation especially difficult in the field of foreign affairs, joint participation by Congress and the President cannot be called unnatural in theory. As for practice, Madison argued that it would be both embarrassing and confusing if the executive decided that the United States was not going to war one day and Congress declared war the next.[42] Hamilton conceded that the presidential decision, coming first, would influence the legislature, but the executive's actions were limited to conducting foreign policy short of taking the nation to war. If we judge Hamilton's theory here by the expediency test that Madison used in connection with removal, it stands up tolerably well. Energy and dispatch are frequently useful in foreign affairs, and those characteristics are to be found in the unitary executive.

The immediate sequel to this controversy confirms that interpretation. Although Congress passed the first neutrality act in 1794, establishing its power over the subject, Edward S. Corwin notes that Hamilton's argument gave rise to the following tendencies in constitutional interpretation:

> (1) That of regarding the "executive power" clause as an always available peg on which to hang any and all unassigned powers in respect to foreign intercourse; and (2) that of treating these and all other presidential powers in the diplomatic field as potential *policy-forming powers*, and constitutionally independent of direction by Congress, though capable of being checked by it. [Emphasis in original.][43]

In conclusion, the decision of 1789 on presidential removal, and its immediate sequel regarding neutrality, involved political and constitutional issues the resolution of which revealed a flexible approach to legislative-executive relations. Ultimate legal control may reside in the Congress, but practical considerations support constitutional interpretations that expand presidential power; the constitutional articulation of legislative-executive relations seems general enough, or incomplete enough, to permit these constitutional controversies to be resolved in the light of practical problems without doing violence to the letter or the spirit of the Constitution.

The second major controversy in the First Congress involved economic policy and the extent of the national legislature's powers. Pursuant to a House resolution of September 21, 1789, Secretary Hamilton submitted his *Report Relative to a Provision for the Support of Public Credit* on January 9, 1790. Hamilton argued that public credit is maintained by good faith, which is established by a punctual performance of contracts. This in turn required funding the national debt: converting floating liabilities into interest-bearing bonds having a definite time to run before maturity, and establishing permanent funding for liquidating the entire debt.[44] Hamilton computed this debt, both foreign and domestic, and including principal and unpaid interest, at, roughly, fifty-four million dollars. In addition, he estimated the states' debts at twenty-five million. Hamilton proposed various schemes for funding which included partial deferment of interest payments in exchange for a guaranteed high interest rate and partial payment in western lands.[45]

Congress, on August 4, 1790, passed an act which adopted one of Hamilton's schemes: every hundred dollars in subscriptions of old securities was to be exchanged for new securities paying 6 percent interest, with interest on two-thirds of the principal to be paid immediately and the remainder commencing in 1800.[46] Congress assumed the state debts and funded them in the same manner.

In his *Second Report on Public Credit,* dated December 13, 1790, Hamilton proposed the incorporation of a national bank. The principal advantages of such a bank he considered to be: an increase in the money supply, greater facility in obtaining emergency loans for the government and also in arranging the payment of taxes (due to the bank's ability to lend money).[47] On March 2, 1791, Congress passed an act to incorporate subscribers to the Bank of the United States. The corporation was authorized to sell stock not to exceed ten million dollars. As Hamilton had proposed, individual subscribers could purchase shares with their newly-funded government securities, provided that one-quarter of the amount subscribed was paid for in gold or silver. The government could purchase up to two million dollars in stock, paying for half with money borrowed under the acts providing for the public debt and half with a bank loan.[48] The Government would thus have a major interest in the welfare of the bank, without running it, and the bank would have a major interest in the government's well-being.

The implications of Hamilton's Reports for the character of our federal and commercial republic were not lost on members of the House. James Madison thought public justice, public faith, and public opinion necessitated a discrimination between the original creditors and subsequent holders of the securities of the United States.[49] He opposed assumption of the state debts, since it would concentrate the money supply in a particular part of the Union, thus increasing "the evil of discordant interests and local jealousies." Most of the debt would "go into the hands of foreigners" causing a burden in interest payments. This would increase and perpetuate public debt, which he apparently considered a public evil; and, finally, Virginia had discharged a significant portion of its debt, and might fare better on a separate accounting of state and federal debts.[50] Madison also opposed the proposal to incorporate a bank because it would exchange gold and silver for "articles of no permanent use" to the country in its "present habits"; and it would expose "the public and individuals to all the evils of a run on the bank," which he considered "particularly calamitous in so great a country as this."[51]

Hamilton was surprised by Madison's opposition to his economic plan. Writing a lengthy and confidential letter to Edward Carrington in 1792, he said:

> This kind of conduct has appeared to me the more extraordinary on the part of Mr. Madison as I know for certainty it was a primary article in his creed that the real danger in our system was, the subversion of the National authority by the preponderency of the state governments. All his measures have proceeded on an opposite supposition.[52]

Apparently the concentration of wealth in the political center of the Union, or the increase in paper debt (which also increased speculation in government paper), caused Madison to change his opinion regarding the fundamental source of danger to the new republic. This division between Hamilton and Madison, the latter of whom was joined by Jefferson, makes it difficult to speak with precision about the Founders' view of the place of Congress in American government.

On February 2, 1791, Madison presented the House with his fullest constitutional argument against the incorporation of a national bank. Noting that the federal government is limited in its powers, he articulated rules for interpreting their enumeration. The most interesting was:

> In admitting or rejecting a constructive authority, not only the degree of its incidentality to an express authority, is to be regarded, but the degree of its importance also; since on this will depend the probability or improbability of its being left to construction.[53]

Madison considered two of the enumerated powers and also the necessary and proper clause as the basis for incorporating a bank. The power to lay and collect taxes to pay the debts and provide for the general welfare was restricted to purposes "limited and explained by the particular enumeration subjoined." Otherwise, the clause would give Congress an unlimited power and "render nugatory the enumeration of particular powers." The clause empowering Congress to borrow money could not be stretched to include "a power of creating the ability, where there may be the will, to lend." Finally, the necessary and proper clause was "limited to means necessary to the end, incident to the nature of the specified powers."[54]

Madison also argued that a broad interpretation of the necessary and proper clause would convert the enumeration into a general grant, while the power of incorporation depended on a broad interpretation.

> Mark the reasoning on which the validity of the bill depends. To borrow money is made the end, and the accumulation of capitals implied as the means. The accumulation of capitals is then the end, and a Bank implied as the means. The Bank is then the end, and a charter of incorporation, a monopoly, capital punishments, &c., implied as the means.
>
> If implications, thus remote and thus multiplied, can be linked together, a chain may be formed that will reach every object of legislation, every object within the whole compass of political economy.[55]

Madison's response in terms of the Constitution to those who might welcome this result examined some of the lesser enumerated powers;[56] for example, Congress has the power to regulate the value of money; yet, the enumeration also mentions the power to punish counterfeiters. Congress has the power to raise and support armies and also to make rules and regulations for their government.[57] It must be admitted that not all the enumerated powers are "great and substantial" powers; some are incidental to the others enumerated. Does that, by itself, however, rule out a construction of the enumerated powers that would permit the establishment of a national bank? As Hamilton, and later Justice Marshall, note, the power of incorporation does seem dependent on the purpose of the corporation. Hence one cannot generalize about corporations from an argument for incorporating a national bank.

In conclusion, the debates in the First Congress and between Madison, the Father of the Constitution and leading member of the House of Representatives, and Hamilton, the most influential member of Washington's cabinet, covered two major constitutional issues: the scope of Congress's power, and the legislature's relation to the administration of government. The constitutional issues were thoroughly examined in the political branches and this examination combined strictly legal and broadly political considerations. The original decisions favored a liberal construction of the powers of Congress and of the President, although there were strong advocates for the alternative positions. Finally, while Congress was active and powerful, the economic plans came from Hamilton and the removal decision deferred to the President for administrative responsibility.

Congress in Evolution

It is not clear to what extent our Founders expected Congress to take the lead in government. We have seen how, soon after their famous collaboration regarding the Constitution, Madison and Hamilton disagreed sharply over the scope of Congress's powers. Madison argued that in America, unlike other countries, "the term Administration" applied equally to "both the Executive and the Legislative branches."[58] The failure of that usage to become accepted reflected the reality of administration in the executive branch. If Hamilton was right in connecting good government to good administration, then good government in America would have to be presidential government.

Congressional government flourished after the Jeffersonian "revolution" of 1800. The Congressional Caucus picked the next three Presidents, either by nomination (Madison, Monroe) or by vote in the House after an indecisive vote in the electoral college (John Quincy Adams). John Marshall foresaw this congressional control of the executive beginning with Jefferson's election. He predicted that Jefferson "will embody himself with the House of Representatives. By weakening the office of President he will increase his personal power. He will diminish his responsibility, sap the fundamental principles of government, and become the leader of that party which is about to constitute the majority of the legislature."[59] Marshall's foresight failed to see that Jefferson was laying the foundation for a President whose strength directly depended on his national popularity. Republican leadership in Congress controlled government until Andrew Jackson organized the first national nominating convention and won the first popular presidential election, in 1828. In his debate with the Senate over the national bank and control of the treasury department, Jackson firmly established himself as the true representative of the American people. Senator Daniel Webster unsuccessfully opposed Jackson with arguments about the separation of powers and complex government which the *Federalist* had made to weaken the legislature and strengthen the executive.[60] Since that time, Congress has been the branch of consent-giving or withholding, not the branch of constructive leadership.

American government differs from parliamentary government by its fixed terms of office for members of Congress and the President; the complete separation of personnel; and the absence of an executive power to dissolve the legislature, as well as a legislative power to retire an executive with a vote of no confidence. Congress cannot govern, due to the President's fixed term and his veto. Congress, however, can assert its independence by way of obstruction, because of its own fixed terms and the absence of a power to dissolve the legislature. The tenure of two powerful House Speakers, Thomas B. Reed and Joseph G. Cannon, from 1890 to 1910, illustrates the first point. Presidents William McKinley and Theodore Roosevelt worked with the Speakers while establishing their legislative leadership. The most famous example of congressional independence, which illustrates the second point, occurred during Reconstruction.

By one senate vote, the radicals failed to convert impeachment into a vote of no confidence. Disagreement over reconstruction policy led Congress to pass the Tenure of Office Act of 1867 over President Johnson's veto. The Act required Senate approval for the removal of cabinet officers. Johnson's firing of Secretary of War Edwin Stanton, who had been appointed by President Lincoln, led to the impeachment vote in the House and to the Senate trial. Representative Benjamin Butler, leader of the prosecution, responded as follows to the argument that the Constitution vested the removal power solely in the President: "The momentous question here and now is raised whether the Presidential office (if it bears the prerogatives and power claimed for it) ought, in fact, to exist as a part of the constitutional government of a free people."[61] Apparently nothing short of a constitutional revolution was necessary to establish congressional government, and it failed by one vote.

Another indication of the decline of Congress as governmental leader is the decline in its initiation of important legislation. In his essay, "Congressional Responses to the Twentieth Century," Samuel P. Huntington cites a study demonstrating that Congress had a major influence on 55 percent of the major legislation from 1882 to 1910, on 46 percent from 1910 to 1932, and on only 8 percent from 1933 to 1940.[62]

Noting the trend toward presidential leadership in 1927, George Galloway argued that Congress had kept pace with the expanding powers of the President through its investigative and standing committees, which he described as " 'the *buckle* that binds, the *hyphen* that joins' the legislature and the executive."[63] This shift from legislative leadership to control of administration has led Stephen K.

Bailey to describe Congress's two main functions as "watch dog" of the purse and "hound dog" of administration. Huntington also approves of the change, asking rhetorically: "How can national institutions be represented in a locally-elected legislature?"[64]

Congress's decentralized geographic constituencies ordinarily produce a decentralized legislature, since it is not easy for a popular congressman or senator to control elections in districts or states other than his own; hence, while the size of Congress requires specialization for efficiency, the decentralized mode of election makes centralization of authority difficult by assuring the independence of individual members of Congress. The revolt against House Speaker Cannon, for example, in 1910, took the form of a majority vote depriving him of membership on the Rules Committee, where he had directed committee assignments.

With no single person in charge of those appointments, the seniority system produces an oligarchy of committee chairmen. Huntington pointed out that the Legislative Reorganization Act of 1946, which reduced the number of standing committees from 81 to 34, ended up strengthening that oligarchy by clarifying jurisdictions which formerly gave the leadership some discretion in assigning bills to committees.[65] What little discretion remains depends on the skill with which the draftsmen can direct a bill to a friendly committee.[66] An act which strengthens congressional control of administration thus decentralizes power in the Congress, making it less capable of legislative leadership.

Huntington concluded that, since legislation is "too complex politically to be handled by a representative assembly," Congress should accept its fate and expand its functions of constituent service and administrative oversight. He even suggested that Congress bind itself to act on urgent presidential proposals within a short but fixed period. It is not clear, however, how Congress can vigorously assert its investigative function and its control over administration if it completely abdicates responsibility for legislation. At the same time, Congress may be organized to act more effectively as critic than as governor. Studying the major accomplishments of the Ninety-Third Congress lets us see how far our national legislature can do both.

The Ninety-Third Congress

If a constitutional revolution is taking place as a result of the Ninety-Third Congress, it is due to a congressional attempt to reclaim its right to a substantial share in legislative leadership, as well as a vigorous reassertion of its power to control the executive branch. Our study of this reclamation begins with Watergate and then turns to the Budget and Impoundment Act of 1974 and the War Powers Act of 1973. In the latter case, we will look at the subsequent application of the legislation during the Mayaguez incident.

WATERGATE

The constitutional crisis known as "Watergate" reached its climax during the week of August 5 to 9, 1974, when Richard Nixon became the first American President to resign from office.This resignation terminated an impeachment inquiry in which the House Judiciary Committee voted articles of impeachment for the obstruction of justice in the Watergate cover-up, the misuse of executive power, and contempt of Congress.

Watergate presented Congress with three constitutional questions: the meaning of an impeachable offense, the extent and mode of enforcing a congressional subpoena, and the status of a special prosecutor.

The Constitution vests the power of impeachment solely in the House. For the meaning of *an impeachable offense,* the Judiciary Committee went to the framers, who took the phrase *high crimes and misdemeanors* from English constitutional law.[67] The Committee divided over whether this meant a serious violation of the criminal code. The constitutional language is the source of some confusion on this point, since different clauses imply that impeachment is and is not a criminal offense;[68] however, the framers' intention, as interpreted from the Convention debates and the *Federalist,* was to make impeachment an extraordinary remedy for dealing with political offenses "done immediately to the society itself."[69] Congress therefore could reasonably conclude that the Constitution does not restrict its impeachment power to statutory crimes. A minority of the Committee was ready to vote impeachment on Madison's principle of presidential responsibility for the actions of his subordinates.[70] While these issues might have been crucial in a Senate trial where a vote of two-thirds of the members present is needed to convict, the transcript of the March 21, 1973 tape confirmed the Committee's 27 to 11 decision to impeach the President for the serious criminal offense of an obstruction of justice.

The second constitutional issue of Watergate involves Congress's subpoena power. The Judiciary Committee's deliberations on whether to impeach President Nixon for his refusal to honor its subpoenas were affected by the Supreme Court's opinion in the Nixon tapes case. As Gerald Gunther said, the Court used *Marbury* v. *Madison* to suggest "that every constitutional issue required final adjudication on the merits by the judiciary."[71] Partly in reaction to the Court's sweeping application of Marbury, the vote on impeachment for failure to comply with the Committee's subpoena was only 21 to 17 in favor; while 27 and 28 members had voted, respectively, for impeachment on the grounds of obstruction of justice and abuse of power. To Gunther this meant that:

> Somehow it was incongruous in the American scheme that Congress should decide that constitutional issue on its own; somehow it was inappropriate to have the legislature rather than the judiciary resolve this dispute between the legislative and executive branches.[72]

Gunther's position is similar to the one Madison took in the First Congress, when he asserted the right of all departments "to declare their sentiments" on the scope of their powers.[73] Without denying judicial review, Madison thought—and Gunther agrees—that each department may assert itself in adjusting contested powers. On the other hand, Raoul Berger and some members of the Judiciary Committee seem to view all constitutional disputes as judicial. According to Berger, "One branch cannot finally decide the reach of its own power when the result is to curtail that claimed by another."[74] Gunther claims that resorting to the courts to enforce subpoenas in support of impeachment inquiries would have required determining the relevance of the material sought; and that, in turn, "would have required at least a tentative judicial position in the controversy regarding the scope of impeachable offenses."[75] A court's tentative judgment, however, to decide whether a bona fide impeachment inquiry was in progress, need not assume congressional responsibility for the precise definition; and if the House ever did have to consider impeachment for presidential failure to respond to a subpoena, it would be on stronger grounds if that President found himself in contempt of both the Court and Congress. The extended process might also give the public more time to become acquainted with the serious issues and give both parties a chance to reconsider their positions.

The final issue raised by Watergate concerns a special prosecutor.

Does Congress need the assistance of the courts to require a legally independent prosecution when a member of the executive branch is a suspect for indictment? If so, the President would no longer be in control of the prosecutorial function, which requires discretion in its exercise. One proposal called for Congress to authorize district court judges to appoint special prosecutors in certain cases. Unlike the judges, the President is *politically* responsible for the exercise of this function; for example, President Nixon succeeded in firing Special Prosecutor Archibald Cox, but only after losing the two senior members of the Department of Justice. Public and congressional reaction subsequent to the "Saturday Night Massacre" led to the reinstatement of the office and the appointment of a new special prosecutor, as well as to the impeachment inquiry. Vigorous assertion of the power of congressional investigation can succeed in uncovering and checking an abuse of power without turning control of prosecution over to the judiciary.

In conclusion, Watergate revived not only the constitutional power of impeachment, but also respect for Congress's ability to inform itself and the public of abuses of power in the executive branch. Some persons would have preferred to see the impeachment process played out to its conclusion. Gunther even criticized the Supreme Court for taking the *Nixon* case before the Court of Appeals decided it, and, thereby, predictably, affecting the impeachment process. As it turned out, however, Congress asserted its emergency power without dismantling the presidency, and the Nixon resignation avoided what might have been a protracted Senate trial. We appear to have experienced the benefits of impeachment without having had to suffer through the entire proceedings.

IMPOUNDMENT

Both Vietnam and Watergate may have provided necessary votes for the Budget and Impoundment Act of 1974 and the War Powers Resolution of 1973, but the impetus for such legislation actually arose out of a long train of events which substantially reduced congressional participation in public policy decisions.

In the struggle for governmental leadership it is frequently difficult to tell whether the President has gained victories through usurpation or through legislative abdication. The case for usurpation is strongest in connection with the presidential war power in Southeast Asia and presidential impoundments under the Nixon administration; but, in the former case, Congress had passed the Tonkin Gulf Resolution authorizing the President to "take all necessary measures to repel any armed attack against the forces of the United States and to prevent further aggression." In the latter case, the Anti-deficiency Act of 1950 authorized the President to establish reserves or effect savings wherever possible "by or through changes in requirements, greater efficiency of operations, or other developments," which might include fighting inflation.[76]

Prior to the legislation in these two fields, the courts found it easier to intervene on the side of Congress in defense of its spending powers than in support of its war powers. This is understandable, although individual congressmen were more concerned about constitutional usurpation in connection with war powers than with presidential impoundment. Many of them felt that, since they had not yet assumed responsibility for planning and following a budget, the President was justified in impounding funds. In one of the five lower court decisions in 1973 which found presidential impoundment illegal, the court said the Anti-deficiency Act meant that the savings "must not be accomplished at the expense of the program. The President can trim the fat but he must not disturb the meat." The court continued:

> If it is conceded that the President has the power to impound congressionally appropriated funds to promote sound fiscal policy, who is to determine whether the impoundment was purposed upon the achievement of sound fiscal policy or upon presidential disapproval of the congressional program for which the funds were appropriated? . . . Should the power be conceded to the President, the very nucleus of congressional power would pass to the executive sphere. The system of checks and balances would be emasculated.[77]

To the extent that usurpation is a valid description, it was largely uncontested until the Ninety-Third Congress.

Until the Budget and Impoundment Act of 1974, the executive branch determined budgets.[78] Congress, mainly through its appropriations committees, scrutinized the estimates, with the help of testimony by the various agencies and departments as well as the Office of Management and Budget (formerly the Bureau of the Budget). This Office also provided estimates of tax revenues, and separate congressional committees—Ways and Means in the House, and Finance in the Senate—were responsible for reporting out tax bills to their respective Houses.

The first part of the 1974 Act established a Congressional Budget Office and House and Senate Budget Committees. Starting in 1976 the fiscal year will begin in October. From the middle of January until April 15 the Congressional Budget Office and the Budget Committees are to scrutinize the presidential budget, hear from the congressional committees, and then report spending levels for every major category, the amount of surplus or deficit which is expected, the recommended level of federal revenues, and the corresponding level for the public debt.[79] From May 15 to October 1, Congress, in the appropriations subcommittees and in the two Houses, will make final appropriation decisions. Floor debate will be limited in each House to insure passage of a comprehensive bill before the fiscal year begins.

The impoundment provisions authorize the President to reduce government spending by means of recision and deferral. To rescind any budget authority, the President must submit a message to Congress, explaining what he proposes to rescind and why; the proposal fails, however, unless Congress passes a recision bill within forty-five days. To defer budget authority, the President must submit a similar message, and the budget authority "*shall be made available* for obligation if either House of Congress passes an impoundment resolution disapproving such proposed deferral."[80] [Emphasis added.]

Less than a week after the Nixon resignation, the Senate Budget Committee held its first hearings. Calling it an historic occasion, Senator Muskie, the Committee chairman, said that the Committee's purpose was "to help provide a steadier aim for the Congress in putting its fiscal house in order."[81] Testimony revealed that the discretionary part of the $305 billion federal budget for the fiscal year 1975 was only $23 billion. Roy Ash, Director of the Office of Management and Budget, argued that small budget cuts, totaling approximately $5 billion, would have significant long-term effects, even if the short-term effects were negligible, because $53 billion of the mandatory spending for fiscal year 1975 came from prior year obligations; but, as Gardner Ackley has said, people do not believe that an administration would stick to spending reductions in the face of growing unemployment. Also, the experts disagree on which budget figures to consider, the actual expenditures and receipts or what these figures would be in a full-employment economy.[82] In the face of these restrictions on government action, and the disagreement over whether cutting federal spending would ease inflationary pressures, unity in the executive branch gives it a decisive advantage over Congress in setting budget priorities. The President and his director of the Office of Management and Budget can control non-elected agency heads more easily than any congressional leadership can control its popularly elected membership. The constituency demands of congressmen are particular and immediate, while controlling government spending is a long-term and dubious project.

At least Congress has established machinery for a comprehensive budget review; it has set a schedule for itself, and it has established procedures for reviewing any executive deferral or recision of budget authority.

WAR POWERS

Before the War Powers Act of 1973 was passed, one could have concluded that "the struggle for the privilege of directing American foreign policy" had been won by the President.[83] His constitutional means were delegated plus inherent powers, each supported by popular approval of the supposition that the President was the man of the people. The war in Vietnam caused a reconsideration of this development. Testifying before the Senate Foreign Relations Committee in 1973, Alexander Bickel said:

> If Congress is ever again to take meaningful specific measures in matters of war and peace, it is apparent to me that it must first perform some quasi-constitutive act, an act of standing forth before the people as responsible, or declaring its responsibilities to itself and to the country with some clarity.[84]

The bill that passed was not as comprehensive as what Bickel proposed, but it still fits his characterization. In its deliberations on the war powers bill, which began in 1970, and included public hearings in 1971, 1972, and 1973, Congress attempted, for the first time, to define and regulate presidential war powers.

On January 18, 1973 Senator Javits, with 57 cosponsors, introduced his War Powers bill, S 440.[85] On June 14, it was favorably reported out of the Foreign Relations Committee and on July 20 it passed in the Senate. Section three of the bill enumerated the President's war powers in the absence of a declaration of war. The list covered four broad categories: 1. The power "to repel armed attack upon the United States, its territories and possessions," or to retaliate in case of such an attack, and to "forestall the direct and imminent threat of such an attack"; 2. The power to repel an armed attack against the armed forces of the United States and "to forestall the direct and imminent threat of such an attack"; 3. The power to act to protect citizens and nationals of the United States against any threat to their lives on the high seas or in countries where they are present by the express or tacit consent of the government; and 4. The power to act pursuant to any specific statutory authorization, which, however, cannot be inferred from any appropriations act, unless the authorization is specific, or from any treaty, unless implemented by legislation specifically authorizing it. There was no reference to prior consultation, nor was there a provision for the termination of hostilities by concurrent resolution. The President was obligated to report promptly to Congress the circumstances that led to his action and the details of that action. It had to cease in thirty days unless Congress passed a specific authorization for it to continue; the only exceptions to these deadlines concerned the safety of American forces and Congress's physical inability to meet in session.

The House version of the War Powers bill,[86] introduced May 3, 1973, and reported with amendments by the Committee on Foreign Affairs on June 15, declined to enumerate the circumstances permitting presidential commencement of armed hostilities; instead, it required consultation in every possible instance where American forces might be committed to armed hostilities, and a subsequent reporting to Congress in every case (in the absence of a declaration of war) where the President had committed forces to hostilities or substantially enlarged the number of forces equipped for combat. The presidential report would be considered in both the Senate and the House in an expeditious manner, and, without specific congressional authorization after one hundred and twenty days, the President would have to terminate the commitment or the enlargement of combat troops. In addition, Congress could, by a concurrent resolution, order the immediate disengagement of forces.

The bill which came out of a Joint Conference Committee was closer to the House version. The time period was compromised to be an initial sixty-day period, with a maximum presidential extension of thirty days; the immediate termination of hostilities by concurrent resolution was retained. The Senate enumeration of the circumstances under which a President may be permitted to initiate hostilities was put in a purpose and policy section of the act. When congressman Zablocki, the House sponsor of the bill, reported it out of the Conference Committee, he said of that section:

> Section 2(c) is a statement of the authority of the Commander-in-chief respecting the introduction of United States Armed Forces into hostilities or into situations where imminent involvement in hostilities is clearly indicated by the circumstances. Subsequent sections of the joint resolution are not dependent upon the language of this subsection, as was the case with a similar provision of the Senate bill (section 3).[87]

Aside from an occasion following a declaration of war, or specific statutory authorization otherwise, the President's commander in chief powers were to be exercised "only pursuant to . . . a national emergency created by attack upon the United States, its territories or possessions, or its armed forces."[88] If this part of the act were more than merely declaratory it would be a far more restrictive statute than the Senate version. Omitted are the responses to imminent threat of attack and the power to protect American lives.

On October 24 of that year President Nixon sent his veto message to Congress. Citing the Founders' wisdom in not drawing a precise and detailed line of demarcation between the two branches with reference to foreign policy powers, he argued that the time limits and the concurrent resolution, neither of which was subject to presidential veto, were both also unconstitutional. In debate on the floor of the House on November 7, the opponents of the bill argued that it would tempt aggression, and that, besides, limitation by appropriations cutoffs had proven sufficiently effective. Others opposed the bill for allegedly expanding presidential power by putting a "stamp of approval" on presidentially initiated hostilities for sixty to ninety days.[89] The House finally voted to override the veto, 284 to 135.

In the Senate, a dramatic and instructive debate took place between senators Javits and Eagleton, two advocates of war powers legislation since 1971. Senator Eagleton argued that a vote to override the presidential veto would be a pyrrhic victory:

> Some of my colleagues will celebrate. The President has beaten us 8 to 0 so far in the veto league, so some of us are eager for our first victory. And so there will be some handshakes and some jubilation. But what a mistake we are about to make. If we want to defeat Richard Nixon by

> overriding his veto, we are going to give him more authority, and legalize it, than he ever dreamed he had.[90]

That contention depends on how one interprets the clauses regarding the commander-in-chief and executive power; President Nixon viewed the act as restricting his power, and previous Presidents, back to Franklin Roosevelt, would have agreed. Eagleton's argument nonetheless clarified the differences between the House and Senate versions; the congressional enumeration of the presidential war power was no longer operative and the President could therefore deploy troops to the Middle East without prior authority.[91] Senator Javits responded to Senator Eagleton that before the President commits forces to the Middle East, "he should come to Congress for authority, by resolution":

> Mr. EAGLETON. Where does it say that in the bill?
>
> Mr. JAVITS. It does not have to. It says so by virtue of the fact that the constitutional authority of the President and of Congress remain completely unimpaired. And also by virtue of the fact that that has been the historical practice during times when the President worked closely and successfully with the Congress in this area.
>
> We have taken the precaution of reciting in section 2(c), which was hotly debated in conference, what we consider to be a declaration. We could not go the distance that the Senate bill went. If we had tried to do that, we would not be here today; we probably would have no bill. It is far more important in terms of the future of our Nation than to be sticklers on that point.
>
> In section 2(c) we have declared what we understand to be the constitutional authority of the Commander in Chief, and it means in this respect putting our forces in imminent danger of hostilities or in the hostilities, only exercised pursuant to a declaration of war, specific statutory authorization, or a national emergency created by attack upon the United States, its territories, its possessions, or its Armed Forces.
>
> One of the closely considered questions before the conference was over the omission of the rescue of individual American citizens. Our decision was that we felt that the recital of it was undesirable and unnecessary, in that it was so much a question of degree as to when an incident such as that could be converted into a conflagration that we would rather not state it. If a President felt, under given circumstances, that it was his constitutional authority under the terms of this bill, we could contest it or not in the particular circumstances. Other than that, we did declare our finding. It is not as strong in this respect as the Senate bill, which actually specified those as the President's emergency powers and no more.[92]

This is the fullest explanation of the reasons for the shift to the House version. The final enumeration of the President's power to act in advance of specific authorization is more restrictive than the Senate version was, but it is nonoperative. The conference committee preferred to leave it nonrestrictive on presidential initiative as long as the commander in chief was required to give a full report within forty-eight hours after the introduction of troops into hostilities, and as long as Congress could either terminate the operation immediately by concurrent resolution or cause its termination after ninety days by not enacting supportive legislation. The Senate passed the bill, 75 to 19.

A SEQUEL

On May 12, 1975, Cambodian vessels seized the American merchant ship Mayaguez and its crew of thirty-nine in the Gulf of Siam. After diplomatic efforts to secure the release of the crew and the ship failed, President Ford ordered an attack on Cambodian patrol boats in order to prevent the movement of the Mayaguez into a mainland port. House and Senate leaders were "informed"—not seriously consulted—three hours before the attack. President Ford's report to Congress, which was delivered to the homes of aides to the Speaker of the House and the President pro tempore of the Senate at 2:30 A.M. on May 15, was made within the forty-eight hour count-down period and approximately three hours after the ship and its entire crew were rescued.[93]

Congressional reaction was generally favorable, with the most serious reservations being expressed about the "consultation." Two other constitutional questions were raised: the absence of any explicit reference to presidential power to rescue American citizens in the War Powers Resolution; and the apparent conflict between the action and the August 15, 1973 cutoff date for any funds to be used to finance combat activities in Southeast Asia.[94]

The 1973 cutoff of funds was generally understood not to prevent rescue operations of this sort. Furthermore, if the President, as commander in chief, has power to act to rescue Americans, regardless of this power not being enumerated in the purpose and policy section of the War Powers Resolution, then the August 15 cutoff of funds could not be considered to permit Congress to restrict that power.

As for the absence of the rescue clause in the War Powers Resolution, while it may have puzzled citizens unfamiliar with the Senate floor debate, no congressman criticized the President's action for that reason. Senator Javits, in a report before the Zablocki subcommittee of the House Foreign Affairs Committee, recommended that some language regarding the rescue of American citizens be added to the bill by amendment. He did not, however, recommend that Congress reconsider the Senate's operative enumeration.[95]

When George Ball testified in opposition to the Javits Bill in 1973, he warned Congress not to attempt to do "what the Founding Fathers felt they were not wise enough to do: to give precision and automatic operation" to legislative-executive collaboration regarding the use of armed forces. The Mayaguez experience suggests that the War Powers Resolution is not being interpreted so strictly as to deprive the President of "sufficient flexibility to defend the country against any threats that might suddenly appear."[96]

Conclusion

A crisis of confidence in our presidential government, brought on by Vietnam and Watergate, gave the Ninety-Third Congress an opportunity matched only by the Reconstruction Congress and the First Congress. Congress not only exercised its powers of inquiry and impeachment in a remarkable manner, but reclaimed substantial constitutional power in matters of money and war. It is doubtful, however, that a trend toward congressional government will develop from this.

The American people still do not look to Congress for leadership in government; for example, a Harris poll of public ratings of Congress from 1963 through February 1974 showed a majority approving of Congress only during 1964 and 1965. That preference seems to reflect satisfaction with President Johnson's Great Society legislation more than with Congress. Even one week after the forced resignation of President Nixon, which was itself preceded by the televised hearings of the House Judiciary Committee's impeachment resolutions, only 48 percent approved of Congress.[97] Furthermore, it is difficult for Congress to lead a President who is himself determined to lead. During the five months that he dealt with the Ninety-Third Congress, President Ford vetoed 27 bills, only three of which were overridden.[98]

While Congress is not well-organized to govern, it is well-organized to respond to presidential initiatives, to state and local government interests, and to individual constituent requests. Since the geographic bases of representation follow state lines in both Houses, the members of Congress are encouraged to work with state and local governments; and, since single member districts encourage compromises among factions, Congress not only reflects diversity, but also is capable of building majority coalitions to pass legislation. The leadership normally comes from the President, but the diversified national consent comes from Congress.

Our reliance on presidential government is compatible with our founding principles for two reasons. First, the advent of democracy and the development of a complete national government increased the demands on government. This necessitated presidential leadership in legislation and administration. If Congress tried to lead, it could not do as well as the unitary executive, and meanwhile it would cease to represent various local interests. Consent of the governed would take the form of a national plebiscite. Second, today foreign affairs and war require constant attention and a capacity to act with energy and dispatch that only the President can provide.

As Congress is our rule of law branch of government, the Presidency is the branch of prerogative. Prerogative, according to Locke,[99] is the power to act for the public good in the absence of law and, sometimes, in opposition to a given law; but the purpose is always to maintain the rule of law and, in American government, the people ultimately judge the wisdom of a given act of asserting a prerogative. Reporting the War Powers bill from the Foreign Relations Committee, Senator Fulbright said, "The point the Committee wishes to stress is not that the President—the one now in office or any other—is an untrustworthy person but that all men wielding power must, in the interest of freedom, be treated with a certain mistrust."[100] It was closer to the truth to say that the Ninety-Third Congress no longer trusted President Nixon; he kept information from them, lied to them, terminated congressionally approved programs by impoundment, and generally treated the nation's legislators as if they had no responsibility for governing.

The particular case of Nixon may have reminded some Congressmen of the general principle that power corrupts, but their major legislation reflects a concern, stated by Gouverneur Morris in the Federal Convention, for the twin dangers of unqualified resistance of authority and abuse of authority.[101] Congress must do more than simply oppose presidential power. It must be informed so that it can assess the prudence of a given President's exercise of power; it must then be prepared to resist or support a President, as circumstances dictate.

The Ninety-Third Congress deserves praise for reclaiming its constitutional powers and for reviving constitutional debate in the legislative branch. Perhaps events thrust the task on them, but the lawmakers proved themselves capable of serious deliberation and action. They also demonstrated that the evolution toward Presidential government has not essentially transformed our founding principles. The constitutional structure of government still gives "to those who administer each department the necessary constitutional means and personal motives to resist encroachments of the others."[102]

Notes

1. Alexis de Tocqueville, *Democracy in America*, ed. J. P. Mayer, trans. George Lawrence (Garden City, N.J.: Doubleday & Company, Inc., Anchor Books, 1969), pp. 114-120, 151-163.
2. Ibid., pp. 157, 159-161, 125-126.
3. In Winston U. Solberg, ed., *The Federal Convention and the Formation of the Union of the American States* (Indianapolis: Bobbs-Merrill Company, Inc., American Heritage Series, 1958), pp. 42, 44-50.
4. Ibid., p. 64.
5. Max Farrand, ed., *The Records of the Federal Convention of 1787*, 4 vols. (New Haven and London: Yale University Press, 1966), 1:33-34. Hereinafter cited as Farrand.
6. Ibid., 1:20-23.
7. Ibid., 1:53, 54, 357.
8. Alexander Hamilton, James Madison, John Jay, *The Federalist Papers*, ed. Clinton Rossiter (New York and Toronto: New American Library, Mentor Books, 1961), p. 285. Hereinafter cited as *Federalist*.
9. *The Debates and Proceedings in the Congress of the United States; with an Appendix, Containing Important State Papers and Public Documents and All the Laws of a Public Nature; with a copious Index* (Washington: Printed and published by Gales and Seaton, 1834), 1:761. The citations are to the edition entitled *History of Congress*. Since two printings were made in 1834, with different paginations, a date will be given in the note if not in the text. Hereinafter cited as *Annals*.
10. Farrand, 1:468.
11. Ibid., 2:5, 246.
12. Richard Henry Lee, *An Additional Number of Letters From the Federal Farmer to the Republican* (Chicago: Quadrangle Books, Americana Classics, 1962), 11:92-96.
13. Compare his July 14 speech to the Convention, in Farrand, 2:8-9, with *Federalist* 39, pp. 243-246.
14. Farrand, p. 65.
15. *Annals*, 1:437.
16. Ibid., pp. 66, 101-102.
17. See Ibid., p. 289, and *Federalist* 70, p. 423.
18. Farrand, 1:65-66, 66-67.
19. Ibid.,2:614.
20. Ibid., 2:318-319.
21. Charles Warren is responsible for the phrase, which he attributes to an unnamed source. *Congress, the Constitution, and the Supreme Court* (Boston: Little, Brown and Company, 1925), p. 99. Raoul Berger drew it to my attention in *Executive Privilege*, pp. 38, 263.
22. From Charles Thach, *The Creation of the Presidency, 1775-1789.* New edition with an introduction by Herbert J. Storing (Baltimore: Johns Hopkins Press, 1969), p. 142.

23. Until 1795 the Senate met in closed session. *See Annals*, 1:15-16. This examination, consequently, is limited to the House debates.
24. *Annals*, 1:370-371.
25. Ibid., 1:374, 379.
26. Ibid., 1:463 (June 16).
27. Ibid., 1:545 (June 18).
28. Thach, *Creation*, pp. 29, 35.
29. Ibid.
30. *Annals*, 1:582 (June 22).
31. *Annals*, 1:578, 585, 591; for the subsequent judicial interpretation, see *Myers v. United States*, 272 US 52 (1926) and *Humphrey's Executor (Rathbun) v. United States*, 295 US 602 (1935).
32. In James D. Richardson, ed., *A Compilation of the Messages and Papers of the Presidents, 1789-1908*. 11 vols. (Bureau of National Literature and Art, 1909), 1:156.
33. See the statement of Eugene V. Rostow before a subcommittee on National Security, Policy, and Scientific Developments, U.S., Congress, House, Committee on Foreign Affairs, *War Powers Hearings*, 93d Cong., 1st sess., 1973, p. 401. The treaty is printed on pp. 409-412. Hereinafter cited as *House War Powers Hearings*.
34. J. C. Hamilton, ed., *The Works of Alexander Hamilton*. 7 vols. (New York: Joint Library Committee of Congress, 1850-51), 7:79-81. Hereinafter cited as *Works*.
35. *Annals*, 2:2132, 2158, 2174-2176.
36. See Thach, *Creation*, pp. 159-162.
37. Farrand, 2:538-541, 547-549.
38. Quoted in Leonard D. White, *The Federalists: A Study in Administrative History* (New York: Macmillan Company, 1961), p. 60.
39. Hamilton, *Works*, 7:84.
40. *Helvidius* 1, in *Letters and Other Writings of James Madison* (Philadelphia: J. B. Lippincott & Co., 1865), 1:614.
41. See John Locke, *Two Treatises on Government*, ed. Peter Laslett (Cambridge: Cambridge University Press, 1960), Second Treatise, secs. 147-148; and Baron de Montesquieu, *The Spirit of the Laws*, ed. Franz Neumann, trans. Thomas Nugent (New York: Hafner Publishing Company, 1949), bk. 11, chap. 6, p. 51.
42. *Helvidius* 2, in *Letters and Other Writings of James Madison*, p. 625.
43. *The President: Office and Powers*, 4th ed. (New York: New York University Press, 1957), p. 181. Hereinafter cited as *President*.
44. Jacob E. Cooke, ed., *The Reports of Alexander Hamilton* (New York: Harper and Row, Harper Torchbooks, 1964), p. 51.
45. Ibid., pp. 19-23.
46. *Annals*, 2:2243-2251.
47. Cooke, pp. 48-51.
48. *Annals*, 2:2312-2318.
49. Ibid., 2:1191-1195 (11 February 1790).

50. Ibid., 2:1537-40 (22 April 1790).
51. Ibid., 2:1895 (2 February 1791).
52. Letter to Edward Carrington, 26 May 1792, in Harold C. Styrett, ed., *The Papers of Alexander Hamilton* (New York and London: Columbia University Press, 1966), 11:438.
53. *Annals*, 2:1869.
54. Ibid., 2:1846-1848.
55. Ibid., 2:1899.
56. Hamilton advocated such a program in his *Report on Manufactures*, in Cooke, pp. 115-205. Smith of South Carolina was not disturbed by this consequence either, since he said that "matters of fiscal nature necessarily devolve on the General Government." *Annals*, 2:1929 (5 February 1791).
57. *Annals*, 2:1899.
58. *The Writings of James Madison*, 9 vols. (New York: G. P. Putnam's Sons, 1900-1910), 5:423.
59. Quoted in Wilfred E. Binkley, *President and Congress*, 3d ed. rev. (New York: Random House, Vintage, 1962), p. 63.
60. Cf. *Federalist*, 47, 48, 51, 71.
61. Binkley, pp. 175, 173.
62. Samuel P. Huntington, in David B. Truman, *The Congress and America's Future* (Englewood Cliffs, N.J.: Prentice-Hall, Inc., 1965), p. 24. The study is that of Lawrence H. Chamberlain, *The President, Congress and Legislation* (New York: Columbia University Press, 1946), pp. 450-452.
63. "The Investigative Function of Congress," in *American Political Science Review*, 21 (1927):70. Binkley cited it on p. 207. He neglected to note that Galloway put the phrase in quotation marks, thus acknowledging his debt to Walter Bagehot. In his study, *The English Constitution*, Bagehot described the cabinet as "a *hyphen* which joins, a *buckle* which fastens, the legislative part of the state to the Executive part of the state."
64. *Congress in the Seventies* (New York: St. Martin's Press, 1976), chap. 7. See Huntington, p. 17.
65. Huntington, p. 20.
66. See Nelson W. Polsby, *Congress and the Presidency*, 2d ed. (Englewood Cliffs, N.J.: Prentice-Hall, 1971), pp. 91-92.
67. See Raoul Berger, *Impeachment: The Constitutional Problems* (Cambridge, Mass.: Harvard University Press, 1973), chap. 2.
68. United States Constitution, Art. I, sec. 3, cl. 7; Art. II, sec. 2, cl. 1; Art. III, sec. 2, cl. 3; Amend. VI.
69. See Farrand, 2:550, and *Federalist* 65, p. 396.
70. *Annals*, 1:372-373 (19 May 1789). This speech was included in U.S., Congress, House, Committee on the Judiciary, *Impeachment: Selected Materials*, House Documents Nos. 93-97, 93d Cong., 1st sess., pp. 10-11.

71. "Judicial Hegemony and Legislative Autonomy: The Nixon Case and the Impeachment Process," *UCLA Law Review*, 22, no. 1 (October 1974):34.
72. Ibid., p. 35. For the tally of votes and the minority report on the third impeachment article, see U. S., Congress, House, *Impeachment of Richard M. Nixon, President of the United States*, Reports no. 93-1309, 93d Cong., 2d sess., pp. 335-339, 503-505. Hereinafter cited as *Impeachment Report*.
73. *Annals*, 2:500-501.
74. *Executive Privilege*, p. 330. The minority report on the third impeachment article cited this passage, as well as *United States v. Nixon*. See *Impeachment Report*, p. 505.
75. Gunther, p. 38. Berger willingly accepts this consequence. See *Impeachment: The Constitutional Problems*, chap. 3.
76. Pl 188-408, 78 Stat 384;Pl 81-759, 64 Stat 765. *See also* 31 U.S. sec. 665 (C) (2) (1970).
77. *Sioux Valley Electric Assn*. v. *Butz*, US District Court, South Dakota, 11/29/73, in *United States Law Week*, 42:2322-3.
78. Public Law 93-344, 88 Stat 297, enacted 12 July 1974.
79. See ibid., sec. 300 for the congressional budget timetable.
80. See ibid., secs. 1011-13.
81. U. S., Congress, Senate, Committee on the Budget, *The Federal Budget and Inflation: Hearings*, 93d Cong., 2d. sess., 1974, pp. 1-2.
82. Ibid., pp. 19, 83, 117-122.
83. Corwin, *President*, p. 171.
84. U. S., Congress, Senate, Committee on Foreign Relations, *War Powers Legislation*, 1973, 93d Cong., 1st sess., pp. 20-21. Hereinafter cited as *Senate War Powers Hearings, 1973*.
85. The text is in *Senate War Powers Hearings, 1973*, pp. 333-341.
86. House Joint Resolution 542, Report 93-287, in *House War Powers Hearings*, pp. 531-532.
87. Conference Report on War Powers, no. 93-547, 93d Cong., 1st sess., p. 8.
88. War Powers Resolution, 93-148, sec. 2(c) (3).
89. *Congressional Record*, daily edition, 7 November 1973, pp. H 9653, 9644, 9643-44.
90. Ibid., p. S 20095.
91. Ibid.
92. Ibid., p. S 20106.
93. See text of President Ford's statement, *New York Times*, 16 May 1975, p. 15. The account of events and of the congressional response relies on the *Times* of May 15 and 16.
94. See Anthony Lewis's column, "The Laws Under Which Mr. Ford Took Action," *New York Times*, 18 May 1975, sec. 4, p. 2.
95. Senator Javits's statement reviewing the workings of the War Powers Resolution, which was given before the Zablocki subcommittee of the House Foreign Affairs (now International Affairs) Committee on June 4,

1971, was printed in the *Congressional Record*, June 11, daily edition, pp. S 10338-10340.

96. *Senate War Powers Hearings*, 1971, p. 625.
97. *Congressional Quarterly Weekly Reports*, 32, no. 10 (9 March 1974): 602.
98. The number of vetoes was arrived at by checking the *Weekly Compilation of Presidential Documents*. Checking the congressional number on each bill in the *Congressional Information Service* revealed that only three became laws (the Railroad Retirement Act Amendments, Pl 93-445; Freedom of Information Act Amendments, Pl 93-502; and the Veterans' Education Bill, Pl 93-508).
99. *Second Treatise on Government*, chap. 14.
100. *Senate Report*, pp. 20-21.
101. Farrand, 1:512.
102. *Federalist* 51.

[9]

THE SUPREME COURT

—GEORGE J. GRAHAM, Jr.

Rule by law, popularly consented to, and the protection of the rights of the individual from an arbitrary authority by way of constitutional guarantees were two presuppositions held by those who drafted the Constitution of the United States in 1787. Although these presuppositions had developed out of the experience of the American colonials with an English political tradition, they contain a serious logical dilemma. Rule by law according to a written constitution lays a limitation on the authority of a government, but somewhere within that government itself some institution must be given the authority to articulate and to enforce those limitations. A presumption of legislative supremacy is embedded in the republican solution of a mixed representative democracy, in the tradition of law as generated by the great legal theorist Sir William Blackstone, and in the American heritage as influenced by the 1688 revolution in England that established parliamentary supremacy.[1] On the other hand, the right of a lawmaking body to judge its own constitutional limits was insufficient to create successfully a mechanism to enforce these "higher law" limits to the exercise of political power. Both in the natural and moral law as interpreted by Sir Edward Coke and James Otis and in a simple faith in written covenants to provide binding limits to governmental authority, one finds a conflicting principle of constitutional supremacy that lies beyond simple legislative determination.[2] Aspiring to both a constitutionally limited government and popular control of government thus requires a pragmatic settlement of this theoretical paradox.

There have been more debates over how the pragmatic settlement emerged than discussion of the appropriate mode of constitutional review at the Constitutional Convention in 1787; indeed, the Constitution itself remains silent on where final arbitration ought to lie. Though most persons today accept—in fact they assume—that the Supreme Court of the United States should be the final arbiter in disputes over the meaning and the application of the Constitution, the route to the Court's gaining this power is less clear. Simply tracing this fact back to either John Marshall's famous assertion of the power of judicial review over the acts of Congress in *Marbury* v. *Madison* (1803) or Alexander Hamilton's careful exposition of judicial authority in *Federalist* 78—although both acts represent important points in the history of the emerging Supreme Court—fails to take fully into consideration the difficulties in the way of the Court's development. Its originally weak position as a lesser partner in a tripartite government—perhaps most dramatically illustrated by John Jay's resigning as the first Chief Justice to become Governor of New York—was less the result of an intentional design than an accident due to indecision and serious doubt that any effective solution could be obtained to the problem of how to secure a final interpretation of the Constitution.

The position of the Supreme Court as the final arbiter of relations among the states and between the states and the national authority, and involving conflicts between state and national statutes and the Constitution, now appears only to reflect a part of the logic of a separation of powers. Charles A. Beard saw judicial control to have been built into the system of 1787, indeed as the "most unique contribution" of American political genius.[3] This implicit certainty, however, expressed strongly in Louis Hartz's belief that law had replaced philosophy in America in order to enhance the Court's prominence, can be appropriately counterbalanced by careful attention to the history of judicial review;[4] for example, the constitutional convention did not find convincing James Madison's argument for an executive-judicial board of review; instead, it reflected a breadth of options that extended beyond any assumption that the Supreme Court should possess final powers of constitutional review.[5] The complexity of this dilemma concerning review suggests that the Supreme Court may best be understood by way of its cloudy prehistory in colonial relations with England and in early statehood, as well as in the Federalist era which preceded and set the stage for the establishment, under John Marshall, of its authority as an essential partner in the American constitutional republic.

English Power of Review over Colonial Laws

The relation of colonial legislatures to the "higher" or natural law is rather complex, since it involves issues of charter (local constitutional) limits on legislatures, and special colonial positions vis-à-vis the superiority of England's law and authority. The former issue invites consideration of the power relations within colonies; and this will be considered in the discussion of American colonial and state precedents for judicial review. The latter deals with relations between each colony and England. In both cases the issues turn on the rights and powers of the people's representatives to pass laws and the "higher" rights and powers that are used as criteria for setting laws aside.

English review of colonial laws was one of the irritants preceding the Revolution, resulting as it did in delays when applying legislation and settling legal cases. Whether the colony was organized under a company or proprietary charter, or direct royal sanction, the legal power had been granted by the English government. After the Glorious Revolution of 1688, the English government became based largely on legislative authority; and the source of that authority in practice, if not in theory, had now become centered in Parliament rather than in the Crown. The weakened position of the latter was apparent in the fact that the royal veto over Parliament disappeared a few years after the beginning of the eighteenth century. Though the Crown remained important in parliamentary politics through the revolutionary period, English government had found its base in legislative authority. The English right of legislative self-government was seen by some colonists to be the proper model for the relation of their own legislatures to the Crown.[6]

In addition to control over the colonies through legislative acts, Parliament had even more direct control over the colonial legislatures through the Privy Council—or, more exactly, its extension, the Board of Trade. The latter was established in 1696 to unify the colonies administratively with Great Britain. As the coordinator of colonial affairs, the Board of Trade, speaking for the king in council, examined colonial laws in order to determine whether they were in conflict with British policy. All colonies, except Rhode Island, Maryland, and Connecticut, were required to submit their laws to the Board within time limits established in their charters, which varied from six months for Pennsylvania to three years for Massachusetts.[7] The Board's power to *disallow* laws, as controlled by Parliament, made them an integral part of ten of the colonial governments. This act of royal approval or disapproval had to occur *before* a colonial act could become law. The fewer than four hundred acts disallowed included mostly encroachments on the mother country's prerogative by way of the legislature's control of the purse.[8] The Board also acted against Rhode Island's establishing an admiralty court without a chartered right to do so; against Massachusetts' passing a judicial act that challenged the English use of non-jury admiralty courts; and against several private acts of an extra-judicial nature that did not conform to the Board's attempt to standardize these acts and give due warning to all parties to private acts.[9]

The three "free" colonies (Connecticut, Maryland, and Rhode Island) were not overlooked by the Board. The Rhode Island example has been noted above. The Board of Trade also called in all the laws from Maryland and the two corporate colonies in the 1730s.[10] In addition, the Privy Council itself heard and reviewed, in 1730, the case of *Winthrop* v. *Lechmere,* in which it was ruled that, although Connecticut was not required by her charter to submit her laws for review, the charter did require that her laws be consistent with those of England. The Privy Council then ruled that the law in question was void, because it was in conflict with the common law of England.[11]

Embedded in the powers of the Board of Trade is a distinction between two types of acts referred to above. The disallowance of colonial acts within the time-limits granted in the charters was actually a part of the *lawmaking* process. Colonial legislation became law only after it had received the sanction of the Board of Trade. The Connecticut incident involved the *constitutional review* of a law in conflict with English law. The first of these two types is legislative action by the Board; the second is one of the infrequent examples of the Privy Council exercising the power of judicial review over colonial legislation.[12] Judicial action was used only when legislative powers were not relevant. In general the colonial experience during the eighteenth century was one of external control by an external legislature.

These external controls over the colonies were not so restrictive that they seriously hindered internal political development. The action of the Board of Trade varied with the interests of Parliament and the appointees. Even when the Board disallowed legislation, the colonies often rewrote the act to satisfy both English and colonial interests.[13] Even when England actively advanced her interests in the American colonies, the colonial legislatures thus were still relatively free internally. While keeping in mind this external review of the acts of colonial legislatures before 1776, let us now examine the development of a division of powers between the legislature and the judiciary in the provincial governments up to and through the establishment of the first state constitutions.

Judicial Review under Colonial and Early State Governments

The differences among colonial governments make it difficult to summarize the general characteristics shared by them on many issues, but not on the question of judicial review. Charters (whether proprietary, company, or royal) divided authority in such a way that legislatures served as the dynamic voice of popular interests. Issues of judicial independence were generally issues over colonial or English control of the judiciary. Though a limited interpretation of the statutes is involved whenever a law is applied in judicial cases, examples of colonial courts claiming any form of final constitutional review of legislation are, at best, only marginal cases. For the most part, this lack is explained by legislative, executive or executive-legislative bodies having served as the highest courts of appeal in the colonies.

South Carolina provides two colonial examples relevant to our consideration of judicial review. Once, in 1693, the lower house of the colonial legislature complained "that inferior courts take upon themselves to try, and judge and determine the power of assemblies, or the validity of acts by them."[14] Little has been discovered about the reason for this complaint. The other example was the case of *Dymes* v. *Ness* (1724), in which the Charles Town judges declared a statute unconstitutional, again not without protest from the lower house;[15] but legislative power seems not to have been seriously challenged, since a 1776 legislative act was all that was needed to establish a new constitution, an assertion of power which was repeated in 1778 by another "legislative constitution." The courts, in *Thomas* v. *Daniel,* interpreted these assertions of power as evidence that *neither* constitution served as a limit on the legislature.[16]

Rhode Island provides one of the few specific examples of a successful assertion of legislative review of judicial decisions. In 1752, the General Assembly overruled a Superior Court decision. In this case, *Mawney* v. *Pierce,* the defendant had appealed to the Assembly as the appellate judicial authority in the colony.[17] In no case before the Revolution was this power doubted in practice; yet, in 1729 and reaffirmed in 1765, the legislature had established a Superior Court, modeled after the King's Bench, which, according to statute, could be reviewed only in England.[18] Here the legislature delegated legal powers but ignored its own limits. Since Rhode Island's stormy politics, in which the Ward and Hopkins factions played a dominant role, involved the courts in political events—annual appointments to the Superior and Inferior courts were based on factional victories in the General Assembly—it is not surprising that the Assembly, in 1763, reversed a Superior Court decision when the Hopkins faction took legislative power.[19] The reason this continuous legislative battle was allowed to proceed and a movement to revoke the charter repelled lies in the only alternative available, namely, recourse to the English Admiralty Courts, certainly a distasteful option in a colony concerned about the Stamp Act.

This survey of cases of judicial review fails to demonstrate any clear precedents, especially in the light of a growing hesitation to give up "local" legislative authority. The issue of independent judicial powers of review was of limited interest because of the peculiar character of this contest between one of the colonies and England, and also because the overlap of legislative and judicial functions continued to remain a formal part of the judicial system.

The rise of executive control over the judiciary reflected the assurance of English power as outlined in the charter or the proprietor's strength in Delaware, Georgia, New Hampshire, Maryland, New Jersey, New York, North Carolina, Pennsylvania, and South Carolina; but often these judicial powers were shared or affected by the legislatures. In Maryland, where the legislature had lost some control over the courts in 1694, it could reverse decisions by private bills.[20] The legislature, composed of so many county court justices that court sessions and meetings of the House of Delegates could not overlap, attempted to gain legislative control. By 1732 the legislature instructed the courts to use Maryland laws and English law "as used and practiced in Maryland."[21] Delaware and New York legislatures held equity jurisdiction, while South Carolina asserted executive control in 1769 by fixing judicial salaries.[22] In all the colonies, private legislation afforded an effective response to adversely-viewed judicial decisions.

In Connecticut, Rhode Island, and Virginia, and gradually also in Massachusetts, there were increasingly direct legislative controls over judicial functions. Connecticut's legislatively centered republican government was assured by the Fundamental Orders (1638)—which became the Charter of Connecticut in 1662—and by England's lack of interest in the colony. In 1711 a Superior Court was established to lighten the heavy docket of the General Assembly; but this delegated authority did not prevent the Assembly from reversing a Superior Court decision.[23] Rhode Island, as we have seen, possessed legislative control over the courts. In Massachusetts the judicial power moved from complete dominance on the part of the executive toward increasing legislative influence, although an act in 1696 established a Superior and an Inferior court.[24] Virginia affords an extreme case of legislative dominance over judicial functions. From 1619 through 1683 the House of Burgesses was the highest court in civil and criminal cases, it indeed being required in 1647 that all cases without precedent go *directly* to the House of Burgesses.[25] Though the Governor and Council were made by legislation the supreme appellate power in 1683, private legislation remained a legal remedy.

The lack of firm precedents for judicial review in the colonial period was followed by no less Delphic a response under the early state constitutions. The removal of English sovereignty resulted in varying constitutional changes that provided little assurance of much beyond an increased power to legislative bodies. Connecticut and Rhode Island maintained their charters as constitutions until 1818 and 1842, after England no longer had any control. A provision for a separation of powers was clearly made in the new state constitutions of Delaware (1792), Georgia (1776 and 1798, but not 1789), Maryland (1776), Massachusetts (1780), New Hampshire (1784), North Carolina (1776), Pennsylvania (1790), South Carolina (1790), and Virginia (1776)—but the place of constitutional review was not settled.[26] Georgia, for example, gave the General Assembly these powers in a 1789 constitution, and established no high court until 1835. New Jersey's solution in its 1776 constitution was to make the governor and his council the high court. Though the New York constitution of 1777 provided a Council of Revision, the legislature could override its decision by a two-thirds majority. Though the importance of solidifying a requirement for a separation of powers in these documents should not be underestimated when considering the logic of judicial review, the explicit rights of the courts to have such powers did not get established in the early state constitutions.

Because most of these state documents, like the federal Constitution of 1787, are silent on the constitutional review issue, the court precedents before *Marbury* v. *Madison* (1803) are important. The Rhode Island case of *Trevett* v. *Weedon* (1786) is a specific example of a state's Supreme Court refusing to enforce an act of the legislature regarding paper money. The Court had told the lower courts not to apply the act in decisions. The Assembly's response was to attack "ungranted powers" that are "unprecedented in this state and may tend to abolish legislative authority thereof."[27] The Court based its decision on such factors as the absence of a jury—a protected English right that the Board of Trade earlier would not permit any legislature to ignore—but that was not the issue. In the view of the legislature the attitude of the Court was an usurpation of power; and, by joint resolution, it demanded that the Court show reason for its action.[28] On the advice of the Attorney General, the legislature did not discharge the members of the Court on the spot but waited until the time for annual appointments before letting go all but the Chief Justice.[29] The legislature continued to overrule the decisions of Rhode Island courts by private legislation until 1856, when, in *Taylor* v. *Place*, the Supreme Court refused to give effect to this action.

Other examples exist of an assertion of judicial power to decide the constitutional authority of a statute. In Maryland, Chief Justice Chase asserted this power in *Wittington* v. *Polk* (1802), only to rule that the statute in question was valid.[30] One historian tells of a New

Hampshire case which established a precedent being heard in 1785, but adds that "details regarding it are not available."[31] He does offer evidence of a dismissal in 1791 of a lower court case in New Hampshire when an appeal to the General Assembly resulted in a new trial. In *Mayo* v. *Wilson* (1817), the courts of New Hampshire upheld a statute that deprived an individual of rights guaranteed in the state constitution, because that document "was not intended to abridge the power of the legislature"; only to decide the same year, in *Merrill* v. *Sherbrome,* that the legislature could not grant new trials after a three-year period.[32] Both cases came fourteen years after *Marbury* v. *Madison.* A New Jersey precedent, *Holmes* v. *Walton* (1780), questioned the constitutionality of a law setting up a jury of only six men with no appeal rights, but the court waited a year to decide the case in the hope that the legislature would change the law—which the legislature did.[33] Similar assertions of authority on the part of courts can be found in Pennsylvania, but either a revision of the law in question or support of legislation by the courts avoided any showdown.

The Carolinas provide several cases of note. In South Carolina the courts once excepted a case from a law, and on another occasion voided an eighty-year-old statute because it conflicted with the Magna Carta (though the jury ignored the court), thus providing a precedent for judicial review strong enough for Governor Charles Pinckney to challenge this alleged power in 1792, saying that if it existed it should be constitutionally removed.[34] A reorganization of the Court in 1798 removed the six-year-old assertion of a right to review by the South Carolina courts. North Carolina, however, provided the most important case to serve as a precedent for judicial review, namely, *Bayard* v. *Singleton* (1787). This case, heard before the Supreme Court of Law and Equity, involved the confirming, without a trial by jury, of Tory-confiscated titles to the purchasers of such land. The case was first heard in 1786, but the decision was postponed for a year while the Court attempted to get the law rewritten by the legislature.[35] Two of the justices appeared before a committee of the legislature, but were released because no charges of malpractice could be approved against them.[36] A decision was finally rendered against the constitutionality of the law. Even though the legislature knew what the decision was to be, the court was permitted to act without any serious attempt at legislative intervention. In *State* v. —— (1794), the question of judicial review was again raised, but the law in question was accepted because the Bill of Rights of North Carolina was held to be a limitation on British, and not on North Carolinian, legislative power.[37] In a third case, *Trustees of the University of North Carolina* v. *Foy* (1805), a statute of 1800 was overruled that had repealed a land grant to the University of North Carolina, but it of course followed *Marbury* v. *Madison* by two years.[38]

The precedents from colonial experience certainly provided no complete answer in favor of judicial review, as the delegates gathered to construct a new Constitution in 1787, nor even before the 1803 judicial assertion. Indeed, in the New York Constitution of 1777, a special Council of Revision had been created. This council consisted of the governor, the chancellor, and the justices of the Supreme Court.[39] Its function was to investigate the acts of the legislature and decide whether they were constitutional. This judicial review could be overridden by a two-thirds vote of the legislature. In fact, of sixty-one laws that were not accepted by this council, one was amended in order to meet the complaints and thirty were passed over the veto;[40] thus we have further evidence that constitutional review could be (and was) handled by other institutional arrangements and also that legislative supremacy, though "checked," was not always denied.

Constitutional Review at Philadelphia

The weight of support for a popularly elected legislative branch had diminished as deliberations began at Philadelphia in the summer of 1787.[41] Important structures of government were considered and seriously debated, but a direct confrontation with the issue of final constitutional review did not occur. Some delegates, including such major figures in the debates as James Madison and Luther Martin, either demonstrated their belief that the Supreme Court should possess review powers in applying the laws or offered arguments that seemed to assume that belief. In discussing the nature of the federal compact, Madison argued: "A law violating a constitution established by the people themselves, would be considered by the Judges as null and void."[42] Martin, in arguing against one of Madison's efforts to link the executive and the judiciary in a legislative review panel that had veto powers, asserted:

> As to the Constitutionality of laws, that point will come before the Judges in their proper official character. In this character they have a negative on the laws. Join them with the Executive in the Revision and they will have a double negative.[43]

The arguments for review, however, neither limited such action to the Supreme Court nor went unanswered. (Later, Madison's efforts in support of the Kentucky Resolutions were to establish him as a spokesman for constitutional review as a right of the states.)

Arguments that assumed judicial review to be a part of a separate issue under debate, such as Martin's, sometimes went unanswered as the issue at hand was pursued. John Francis Mercer, who supported the justification of a separate and independent judiciary, disapproved of "the Doctrine that the judges as expositors of the Constitution should have authority to declare a law void."[44] Impressed by Mercer, John Dickinson observed that to have the power to set aside a law was wrong, that "no such power ought to exist;" but he added, according to Madison's notes, what may have provided the crux of the later solution:

> He was at the same time at a loss what expedient to substitute. The Justiciary of Aragon he observed became by decrees the law-giver.[45]

The inconclusiveness of the debates over the executive veto—which was, in part, a constitutional review—emphasized the diversity of opinions regarding the best way to check a headstrong legislature. Madison and James Wilson repeatedly presented the mechanism of constitutional review by an executive-judiciary revision council, but they always lost by rather lopsided votes. Oliver Ellsworth's urgency to decide the issue reflects the pragmatic aspect of debates which involved checks on the legislature by the other departments: "We grow more and more skeptical as we proceed. If we do not decide soon, we shall be unable to come to any decision."[46]

The fact that in Philadelphia no constitutional provision emerged to resolve the issue, added to the lack of a general tradition of judicial review in the colonies or states, can lead, and has led, to debates over its legitimacy. But a consideration of these questions is not as important as understanding that no decision was made. The contradiction between constitutional review and the principle of popular sovereignty, as expressed in the legislature and checked by the presidential veto, remained at the end of the Constitutional Convention of 1787. An independent theory was needed to resolve (or offset) the contradiction.

The Federalist Response

The lack of a decision in Philadelphia opened the way for a decisive interpretation of judicial authority, a way taken in the Federalist response to the problem. The public resolution of issues on the "intent" of the Convention very often turns on the interpretation of this intent by James Madison, Alexander Hamilton, and John Jay in the *Federalist Papers*. In an introduction to an edition of these papers, Willmoore Kendall and George W. Carey make a case for recognizing them as key documents for interpreting the American system—along with the Declaration of Independence, the Constitution, and the Bill of Rights; and also for identifying this Federalist overview as the one that most affected the *applied* meaning of these other basic documents in a form that limited legislative supremacy, even as outlined at the Philadelphia Convention.[47] Though argument may arise over how supreme the Convention wished the legislature to be, one cannot dispute the fact that the *Federalist Papers* did, and do, provide one of the most significant interpretations of what the Constitution actually *means*. It was in the *Federalist,* and not at Philadelphia, that Alexander Hamilton's discussion of judicial authority adumbrated the future role of the Supreme Court.

The special focus of *Federalist* 78 through 83 is on the Supreme Court and the rest of the judiciary, with the first in this series providing the classic defense of an independent judiciary empowered with a constitutional review of the laws and other acts of government. Though in *Federalist* 81 Hamilton admits of other possible institutions which might discharge this obligation—for instance, the Senate—thus opening up some ground for controversy, the facts that an independent judiciary was built into the system and a Supreme Court also was constitutionally defined, led him to put confidence in a constitutional limitation on legislation requiring an independent Court. Were we unfamiliar with the historical precedents, *Federalist* 78 alone would set forth so straightforward a case for judicial review that no one could doubt its necessity.

The case is simple: In considering the character of the judicial branch under an assumption of a separation of powers, the appropriate questions that emerge are over how judges are to be appointed and for how long, and how to apportion judicial authority. The first question was referred back to a discussion of appointments made by the President and ratified by the Senate (*Federalist* 76 and 77), which focused on the natural checks which might be expected to lead to the appointment of quality individuals. The "good behavior" criterion is to be judged in terms of a need for a non-political administration of the laws, and also as a guarantee against despotic acts on the part of the legislative body. Some constitutional constraints on legislative action therefore are necessary, or the Constitution would not have limited the branches of government. As the weakest branch, without the power to give honors or to wield the sword, as has the executive, and also without the powers of the purse and of prescribing rules affecting the rights and duties of citizens, as has the legislature, the Court cannot itself, alone, force the public to conform to its mandates. The decisions of the Court "must ultimately depend upon the aid of the executive arm even for the efficacy of its judgments."[48] The judiciary is too weak to challenge the other branches and must be protected from their fiscal (*Federalist* 79) or other control. Since liberty depends on an independent judiciary, the judicial system must be independent. Terms during "good behavior" and nonreducible salaries are necessary safeguards for the justices involved.

These arguments develop around the important insertion of the idea of a *limited* constitution. If legislative authority is to be limited—e.g., if there are to be no bills of attainder—then the courts must declare infractions void. If no institution can pronounce legislative action void, the entire notion of a limited constitutional government, and of its protection of human rights, "would amount to nothing." This power does not place the courts above the legislative power, according to Hamilton, but rather makes them serve as the only guarantee that the Constitution is itself superior to a legislative act. Otherwise the representatives of the people would be superior to the will of their constituents as expressed in the Constitution. The Constitution is fundamental law, and if a conflict develops, it is superior in application to any statute. Review becomes the same judicial act as that to be exercised when contradictory laws apply to a given case. The facts that federal judges will have no purse or sword, and that the other branches of government are parties to passing laws which are limited by the Constitution, put the judiciary in the most eligible position for determining constitutional limits.

Hamilton's arguments beyond the logic of review emphasized the need for permanence in office in order to attract men of technical and legal competence and other high qualities to the difficult task of sitting on the bench. The technical skills that are required limit the number of men competent to be judges; and Hamilton saw those who could fulfill the requirements as moderating, nonpolitical men of character. In arguing that "good behavior" is the appropriate criterion for the length of a term in judicial office Hamilton dealt with the power of judicial review *as if it had been assumed* in Philadelphia, and as if it also were one of the reasons for accepting terms during "good behavior." His arguments were, in effect, repeated when the Supreme Court first articulated the logic of judicial review of acts of Congress.

The first—and indeed the only—case of judicial review in which congressional legislation was rejected previous to the famous Dred Scott decision (*Scott* v. *Sanford*, 1857) was *Marbury* v. *Madison* (1803). This case was politically complex, since it involved competing political parties when Thomas Jefferson replaced the last Federalist President, John Adams. The outgoing Secretary of State, John Marshall, had failed to deliver several last minute appointments to the courts made by the departing Federalists. The so-called midnight justices involved had been appointed in keeping with congressional legislation permitting Adams to name justices of the peace for the District of Columbia. William Marbury, one of these appointees, did not receive his commission from Marshall before the new Secretary of State, James Madison, had refused to deliver the late commissions that Jefferson had chosen to ignore. Marshall thus had a part in a political event that produced the important assertion of the right of constitutional review on the part of the Supreme Court—a fact which resulted from Marshall's having been appointed to the Supreme Court while still holding the position of acting Secretary of State as a "lame duck."

Since the Supreme Court's rulings are confined to issues brought to it by individuals, the request by Marbury that the Court issue a *writ of mandamus* requiring Madison to deliver this commission, as prescribed in the Judiciary Act of 1789, Section 13, gave the Court its opportunity. Marbury's fate would have remained dubious, since Jefferson's conception of constitutional review permitted the *executive* to refuse to do what *it* considered unconstitutional.[49] Madison could thus greet a court order with inaction. Because of the masterful argument of John Marshall, however, the Supreme Court unanimously laid down a path between the political dimensions of the case and the problem of enforcement, by declaring Madison to be in error but also suggesting a self-enforcing remedy by saying that the Court constitutionally did *not* have the power to exercise congressionally granted powers. In the process the Court asserted the much more permanent power of a judicial review of national legislation without having to concern itself with enforcing its decision. Its own inaction in this respect made impossible any countermove by the executive branch.

The route to this conclusion was by way of Hamilton's reasoning in *Federalist* 78. To get to the argument, Marshall was able to criticize his political opponents by noting that justice was on Marbury's side. Marbury's appointment had been made in conformity with the Congressional Act of February 1801. Since it was a judicial appointment, the commission was not revocable. Consequently, even though the commission itself had not been delivered, Marbury had rightly been commissioned and his rights violated. Since every injury has a remedy in a government of laws, there should be a remedy in this case. The Secretary of State had the duty of following the 1801 legislation. Marbury's application for the directive writ to deliver his commission required that the act fit the case; but such a writ of mandamus requires that no remedy exist and also the legal capacity to demand an action. Mandamus, indeed, applies; but can the Supreme Court grant the writ under Section 13 of the Judiciary Act of 1789? *Original* jurisdiction on writs of mandamus is granted by the Act, but this grant is contrary to the constitutional description of cases of original jurisdiction. This grant of power is unconstitutional. Marbury won only a moral victory, since Marshall's argument went on to the question of judicial review.

The constitutional principles are established by the people, according to Marshall, and cannot often be repeated. These fundamental principles derive their authority from the people; and they are designed to be permanent, with certain limitations laid on each branch of government. These written commitments of the Constitution cannot be altered by ordinary legislation without denying the meaning of a limited government. Those who apply laws must interpret them; and, if two laws conflict, they must decide which should apply in a given case. If the Constitution and a law conflict, the Court must decide which governs the case. This, Marshall saw as the "essence of judicial duty." Otherwise, the legislature would be superior to the Constitution. Using examples like the restriction on bills of attainder, Marshall showed that without review the Constitution would not be a limit. He asked how a judge sworn to uphold the Constitution could keep from giving it precedence over an ordinary act in conflict with it.

The opinion of Marshall reflects the reasoning in *Federalist* 78. Independent of the history of judicial review and the counterargument that legislative power represents the popular will, the decision turns on whether to have a constitutionally limited government, plus a healthy Lockean distrust of any institution—including the legislature—judging its own case. To be sure: congressmen and Presidents swear to uphold the Constitution, but only the courts are in a position to judge whether they have overstretched their constitutional powers. The written Constitution was a fundamental expression of popular opinion, and therefore served as a permanent limit on the people's representatives. The power of judicial review, in Marshall's and Hamilton's reasoning, is a logical consequence of limited government.

In a sense, *Marbury* v. *Madison* settled the question by articulating a compromise between a limited constitution and legislative authority; but, shortly thereafter, on September 11, 1804, Thomas Jefferson wrote Mrs. John Adams to suggest that each branch be given rights of review in order to avoid the possibly arbitrary or unrestrained exercise of power on the part of the courts over the other branches.[50] The Virginia and Kentucky Resolutions, instigated earlier by Jefferson and Madison, asserted and defended the rights of the states to review the constitutionality of national legislation.[51] In a dissenting opinion in the case of *Eakin* v. *Raub* (1825) before the Pennsylvania Supreme Court, Justice John Bannister Gibson directly challenged Marshall.[52] He felt that federal limitations laid on the states had to be taken into account by state legislatures, but that the limits set by state constitutions could not be used to overturn legislation because this would place the courts in a position of political supremacy.

Perhaps the most significant debates over the merits of Marshall's doctrine were those heard earlier in Congress. As early as June 18, 1789, Madison took up the question of the propriety of the "Legislature to expound the Constitution so far as it relates to the division of power between the President and Senate."[53] He begged "to know upon what principle it can be contended that any one department draws from the Constitution greater powers than another, in making out the limits of the powers of the several departments?" In the debate in the House of Representatives, Alexander White reflected on the advisability of leaving the issue open, and of responding to it only by way of the actions of the departments themselves in providing constitutional comment. In 1802, in a debate over the repeal of the Judiciary Act of 1801 that generated *Marbury* v. *Madison,* John Breckinridge questioned the power of the courts to annul congressional legislation, wondering "who checks the courts when they violate the Constitution?"[54] The idea of coordinate branches means that the departments are "responsible for their own motion, and are not to direct or control the course of others." For Breckinridge, therefore, "the Legislature have the exclusive right to interpret the Constitution in what regards the lawmaking power, and the judges are bound to execute the laws they make."

Such views were reinforced by John Bacon's extended remarks in the House on February 17, 1802; but, they were opposed three days later by James A. Bayard: "The Constitution is absolutely the law of the land. Not so the acts of the Legislature. Such only are the law of the land as are made in pursuance of the Constitution."[55] He notes that in 1789 the legislature itself, in Section 25 of the Judiciary Act, gave to the Supreme Court the final decision on the constitutional validity of a treaty or a statute, or any action in relation to them. The views on the issue evident in the many references made to it and points of view expressed in Congress mirror the earlier divisions. The principle of judicial review was really a pragmatic settlement of two vital but conflicting principles of American democracy: 1. the people ought to rule through their representatives; but, 2. the Constitution also ought to limit all the departments of government by providing a superior expression of the popular will. In practice, support for the decisions of the Court obviously depends on the capacity of the Court to have them obeyed. This remains today the key to the legitimacy of the Federalist response.

Maintaining the Federalist Response

The early impact of the Supreme Court's authority depended more on its application of federal legislation and consequent support for congressional action than on its power to overturn laws. Early cases, such as *Ware* v. *Hilton* (1796), established the supremacy of national treaties over state laws. This case is all the more interesting because the great legal spokesman for Virginia's side, Patrick Henry, was accompanied in his defeat by a younger lawyer—John Marshall. The expansion of national powers has been dealt with in earlier chapters; but, one should note that the Supreme Court under Marshall established national supremacy over the states; and it also used support of the Contract Clause to set economic enterprise on the trajectory of growth that has led to our present economic strengths. A second great Chief Justice, Roger B. Taney, extended the Court's support of the economy through the Commerce Clause. The Court favored industrial growth, but at the same time it encouraged the efforts of the states to control the economy by legislative action. The serious economic collapse of the Great Depression did lead to the most intense political debates over the Court's role, and this resulted in major revisions of Court interpretations after 1937; but these were generally accepted by the public. A key element in the Court's history has been the relation between public demands and judicial interpretation, a relation that at times has been stretched almost beyond normal limits; but it has always been close enough for the Court to interpret the law and have its interpretations enforced without the control of either "purse" or "sword."

The Court's powers have nonetheless been almost constantly debated; and well they should be if they are to preserve the delicate balance between popular control and constitutional limits. The delay between the termination of "appointments for life" and the appearance of shifting winds of popular opinion provides a natural check on government. A justice may attempt to live through the next election in hopes of determining the political background of his replacement; but judges cannot outlive the public. The public eventually is the direct judge of the Court; and it has demonstrated that even when controversial settlements are pronounced by the Court, its long-term support remains. To be sure: Alexander Bickel's apt observation that the Court has "no earth to draw strength from" holds as true today as it was important to Hamilton in settling on the Court as the institution to carry out constitutional review;[56] but tradition draws public strength enough for the Court's decisions to offset a threat from a President to "pack" it, even a President as popular as Franklin D. Roosevelt. This new strength is somewhat offset, however, by the institutional checks that have always been there. Congress and/or the President must accept the Court's decisions if they are to be enforced.

The Supreme Court has recently developed areas of positive intervention in enforcing its views of the Constitution, asserting criteria government *must* meet rather than merely overturning laws in conflict with the Constitution. The Court has, according to Graham Hughes, "hoisted itself with some boldness" into the "legislative preserve."[57] He is concerned not with specific decisions like those which set criteria for reapportionment statutes per se, or for school districting; rather, he is worried about maintaining the delicate balance of public support. This public support is essential to keeping the present settlement; and it must be strong enough to provide the Court sufficient legitimacy to withstand institutional checks on the part of the executive and legislative branches. As a vivid example of American democracy successfully on trial, however, the Federalist response continues to enjoy support today. To those who challenge Hamilton's and Marshall's position, we may repeat the response of another who challenged it—John Dickinson—who was "at a loss what expedient to substitute." By a continual discussion of the constitutional settlement we can be assured that a substitution will remain unnecessary.

Notes

1. Edward S. Corwin, "The Progress of Constitutional Theory between the Declaration of Independence and the Meeting of the Philadelphia Convention," *American Historical Review,* 30, no. 3 (April 1925): 517. See also his earlier work, *The Doctrine of Judicial Review* (Princeton: Princeton University Press, 1914).
2. See Alexis de Tocqueville, *Democracy in America,* 2 vols. (New York:

Vintage Book Edition, 1954), 1: 102-109, for a classic justification of the American solution. Gordon S. Wood, *The Creation of the American Republic, 1776-1787* (Chapel Hill: University of North Carolina Press, 1969), is the best survey of the growing hesitancy toward unlimited support of legislative power.

3. Charles A. Beard, *An Economic Interpretation of the Constitution of the United States* (New York: Macmillan, 1962), p. 162. See also, for Beard's views of the Court, *The Supreme Court and the Constitution* (New York: Macmillan, 1912).
4. Louis Hartz, *The Liberal Tradition in America: An Interpretation of American Political Thought Since the Revolution* (New York: Harcourt, Brace, and World, 1955), pp. 9-10.
5. For examples of Madison's arguments and the responses, *see* Max Farrand, ed., *The Records of the Federal Convention*, 4 vols. (New Haven, Conn.: Yale University Press, 1937), 1: 104-110, 131, 144; and 2: 73-83. On the "intentions" of the Philadelphia convention, compare the contrasts in L. B. Boudin, *Government by Judiciary* (New York: William Godwin, 1932), 1, chaps. 3-10; Edward S. Corwin, "The Constitution as Instrument and Symbol," *American Political Science Review* 30 (December 1936): 1071-1078; Beard, *The Supreme Court*, chap. 1; and Robert H. Birkby, "Politics of Accommodation: The Origin of the Supremacy Clause," *Western Political Quarterly*, 19, no. 1 (March 1966): 135.
6. On this issue, see Carl Lotus Becker, *The Declaration of Independence* (New York: Harcourt, Brace and Co., 1922), passim, but especially pp. 80-134.
7. Oliver Morton Dickerson, *American Colonial Government, 1695-1765: A Study of the British Board of Trade in Its Relation to the American Colonies, Political, Industrial, Administrative* (Cleveland: Arthur H. Clark Co., 1912), p. 225.
8. Ibid., pp. 227, 230.
9. *See* ibid., pp. 235, 236, 258, 259, 260, for examples.
10. Charles Albro Barker, *The Background of the Revolution in Maryland* (New Haven, Conn.: Yale University Press, 1940), pp. 192-193.
11. Dickerson, pp. 102, 274-275.
12. Ibid., p. 274.
13. Ibid., p. 274n.
14. Quoted in David Duncan Wallace, *South Carolina* (Chapel Hill: University of North Carolina Press, 1951), p. 116.
15. Wallace, pp. 116-117.
16. Walter Fairleigh Dodd, *The Revision and Amendment of State Constitutions* (Baltimore, 1910), p. 18.
17. F. L. Riley, "Colonial Origins of New England Senates," *Johns Hopkins Studies in Historical and Political Science*, 14 (March 1896): 63.
18. Roscoe Pound, *Organization of Courts* (Boston: 1940), p. 67.
19. David S. Lovejoy, *Rhode Island Politics and the American Revolution* (Providence, 1958), pp. 94-96.

20. Roscoe Pound, *Appellate Procedure in Civil Cases* (Boston, 1941), p. 74.
21. Barker, pp. 161-179, 216-217.
22. Pound, *Organization*, pp. 65, 68-69, 77; Pound, *Appellate Procedure*, p. 74.
23. Forrest Morgan, *Connecticut as a Colony and a State, or One of the Original Thirteen*, 4 vols. (Hartford, Conn., 1904), I, 494; and for the reversal see Charles J. Hoadley, ed., *The Public Records of the Colony of Connecticut, May, 1768, to May, 1777* (Hartford, 1865), 13:27.
24. Riley, pp. 10, 16; Thomas Hutchinson, *The History of the Colony and Province of Massachusetts-Bay*, ed. Lawrence Shaw Mayo, 3 vols. (Cambridge, Mass.: Harvard University Press, 1936), p. 379; Pound, *Organization*, pp. 29-33; Pound, *Appellate Procedure*, p. 74; Robert Luce, *Legislative Principles: The History of Lawmaking by Representative Government* (New York: Houghton Mifflin Co., 1930), p. 105.
25. Richard L. Morton, *Colonial Virginia*, 2 vols. (Chapel Hill: University of North Carolina Press, 1960), 2:763; Pound, *Appellate Procedure*, p. 74; Pound, *Organization*, pp. 54-55; and, for private legislation examples, *see* William Waller Henning, ed., *The Statutes at Large, being a Collection of All of the Laws of Virginia* (Richmond, 1823), 8:230, 627.
26. The source for the constitutions is Francis N. Thorpe, ed., *The Federal and State Constitutions, Colonial Charters, and other Organic Laws of the United States of America*, 7 vols. (Washington, D.C.: Government Printing Office, 1907). An earlier version is also available in Ben Perley Poore, ed., *The Federal and State Constitutions, Colonial Charters, and Other Organic Laws of the United States*, 2 vols. (Washington, D.C.: United States Government Printing Office, 1878).
27. Charles Grove Haines, *The American Doctrine of Judicial Supremacy* (Berkeley: University of California Press, 1932), p. 109.
28. John Russell Bartlett, ed., *Records of the State of Rhode Island and Providence Plantations in New England (1784-1792)* (Providence, 1863), 10:220.
29. Edward Channing, *A History of the United States, 1761-1789*, 6 vols. (New York: Macmillan, 1912), 3:506.
30. Haines, p. 161.
31. Ibid., p. 149-150.
32. *See* the discussion of *Mayo* v. *Wilson* in Oliver P. Sikes, et al., *Bates and Field's State Government* (New York, 1949), p. 214; and *Merrill* v. *Sherbrome* in Pound, *Organization*, p. 110.
33. Channing, p. 503; and Haines, p. 93. No case records have survived.
34. The cases were *Ham* v. *McClaws* (1789) and *Bowman* v. *Middleton* (1792). *See* Haines, pp. 148-149; Pound, *Organization*, p. 64; and Wallace, p. 409.
35. Channing, 3:506.
36. Haines, p. 113.
37. Sikes, p. 214.
38. Haines, pp. 164-165.

39. Poore, 2:1332.
40. Alexander C. Flick, *The American Revolution in New York* (Albany, 1926), p. 85.
41. Wood, pp. 430-463; and this present book, chaps. 2, 3, and 6.
42. Farrand, 1:93.
43. Farrand, 2:76.
44. Farrand, 2:298.
45. Farrand, 2:299.
46. Farrand, 2:301.
47. "Introduction: How to Read the Federalist Papers," in *Federalist Papers* (New Rochelle, N.Y.: Arlington House, n.d.), pp. v-xx.
48. Ibid., p. 465. It should be noted that the most recent interpretation of the state ratifying conventions—to be found in Raoul Berger, *Congress* v. *Supreme Court* (Cambridge, Mass.: Harvard University Press, 1969), chap. 4—does not remove the uncertainty regarding the acceptance of judicial review in the light of the post-Convention debates.
49. There is little doubt that this was the response to be expected from Jefferson. The following summary of the decision is from 1 Cranch 137, 2 L. Ed. 60 (1803), reprinted in Paul A. Freund, et al., *Constitutional Law: Cases and Other Problems* (Boston, Mass.: Little, Brown and Co., 1961), pp. 3-11.
50. Ibid., pp. 15-16.
51. The materials are brought together in *The Kentucky-Virginia Resolutions and Mr. Madison's Report of 1799* (Richmond: Virginia Commission on Constitutional Government, 1960).
52. 12 *Serge and Rawle* (Penna) 330.
53. Quotes are from the useful selection of the *Annals of Congress* in Charles S. Hyneman and George W. Carey, eds., *A Second Federalist: Congress Creates a Government* (New York: Appleton-Century-Crofts, 1967), p. 64.
54. Ibid., pp. 85-86.
55. Ibid., quote on p. 91, but also see pp. 87-92.
56. Alexander Bickel, *The Least Dangerous Branch: The Supreme Court at the Bar of Politics* (Indianapolis: Bobbs-Merrill, 1962), p. 184.
57. Graham Hughes, "Social Justice and the Courts," *The Limits of Law: Nomos XV*, eds., J. Roland Pennock and John W. Chapman (New York: Lieber-Atherton, 1974), p. 121. *See* the earlier and more comprehensive treatment in Charles S. Hyneman, *The Supreme Court on Trial* (New York: Atherton, 1963).

[10]

POLITICAL PARTIES AND POPULAR GOVERNMENT

—CHARLES H. McCALL

At first glance it seems incongruous to include an examination of the institutions we know as the political party and the party system in a book devoted to a scrutiny of the founding principles of the American republic. Parties were not established by the state constitutions which emerged following the act of separation from England, in the Articles of Confederation, or in the Constitution of the United States. Had parties been mentioned in those documents, it would probably have been in order to prohibit them or to so fetter them about as to render them innocuous; for, one of the judgments most widely shared by the Founding Fathers was that such institutions were an anathema to good government. Furthermore, if we follow Charles Hyneman's lead and identify the founding period as the quarter century ending in 1800, this attitude among the architects and builders of the republic remained almost completely unshaken at the time of the Constitutional Convention, even though they divided into groups with mutually irreconcilable views on many other concerns.

The groups into which the Founders of American government divided, the Federalists and the Republicans, were usually called parties; and by the end of the founding period they had developed many of the characteristics we associate with political parties today. If we explore the reasons why these early leaders so earnestly dreaded and condemned parties while at the same time they devoted considerable energy to party organization and development, we will begin both to appreciate the ambivalent views which Americans continue to hold toward parties and to understand their place in our political system.

The Evils of Political Parties

In his letter to the Galatians, the apostle Paul included party spirit as one of the desires of the flesh which those concerned with their immortal souls should forswear.[1] The authors and orators of the founding period, while principally concerned with other goals, tendered the same advice. An election address given in Delaware quoted in a Philadelphia newspaper in 1776 warned the people to "be on your guard against a party-spirit, or you will be misled."[2] Less than three years later the editor of a Trenton newspaper editorialized that parties are one of the most "dangerous diseases of civil freedom; they are only the first stages of anarchy. . . ."[3]

The Founders also advanced these judgments; and they sought to create a system in which parties would either not arise or, failing that, would only minimally trouble the new nation. Alexander Hamilton, in an address to New York's ratifying convention in 1788, announced that "we are attempting by this Constitution to abolish factions, and to unite all parties for the general welfare."[4] Washington concurred in that view; and, perhaps more than any of the others who guided the country through this period, he was energetic in his efforts to prevent the development of parties, even devoting much of his Farewell Address to warning of their evils. While Madison and Jefferson denied that parties could be avoided, finding their causes in the nature of man, both were convinced that they had malign consequences. In accord with Paul's epistle, Jefferson wrote in 1789, "If I could not go to heaven but with a party, I would not go there at all";[5] and Madison, in that elegant essay, *Federalist* 10, applied his thought to methods of controlling the pernicious effects of parties which he labelled a "dangerous vice."[6]

Whereas almost all the early leaders concluded that parties were evil, it would be incorrect to infer that none saw merit in them. Hamilton, in *Federalist* 70, admitted that party conflict in a legislature often has the salutary effect of promoting careful reflection on proposals and thus restraining hasty, ill-considered actions by the majority.[7] Washington acknowledged in his valedictory that "parties in free countries are useful checks upon the administration of the government and serve to keep alive the spirit of liberty."[8] Sagacious Ben Franklin agreed; and he also felt that "sparks of truth are struck" in the clash of differing opinions resulting from party opposition.[9] Jefferson, focusing on the need for an informed electorate, as was his custom, suggested that parties were useful in scrutinizing the behavior of each other and reporting disturbing findings to the public—a function which we have come increasingly to esteem during the past four years.[10] Given these avowed contributions, why were parties so feared and so frequently denounced?

To understand what seems to be the most important of the four principal reasons these men advanced to account for their antipathy toward political parties, we must first realize that when they mentioned parties, their conception was quite different from our own. They were not thinking of broad groupings, linking private citizens, party functionaires, and public officials together in organizations trying to gain or hold control of the government in the midst of a widely shared consensus regarding the appropriate limits to governmental action and the proper procedures for reaching governmental decisions. The source of their fear of parties is perhaps best captured in Madison's definition in *Federalist* 10: "a number of citizens. . . united and actuated by some common impulse of passion, or of interest, adverse to the rights of other citizens, or to the permanent and aggregate interests of the community."[11]

Given their view of parties, it is hardly surprising that the Founders feared them. America was a new nation, and one born of revolution. Now they were attempting to found and nurture a new governmental system, and they were certain of the need for unity if that system was to survive. At best then, they were convinced that parties would weaken devotion to the national interest. As a group of legislators came to discover that they shared common concerns and common goals, and as they began to act in concert to pursue them, it would be natural for the group to take on special meaning for its members, for each member to consider first how a proposed policy would be judged by the group, and to begin to repay those who had voted as he had wished them to vote by voting in his turn as they desired. Concern for the interests of the whole society thus might come to be ignored in favor of the interests of a part. Add rivalry among parties, and that tendency would become even more pronounced. On such behavior, John Adams blamed the sluggishness with which the science of government makes progress. Writing to Jefferson late in life, our second President raised the question and answered it:

> What is the reason? I say, parties and factions will not suffer improvement to be made. As soon as one man hints at an improvement, his rival opposes it. No sooner has one party discovered or invented any amelioration of the condition of men, or the order of society than the opposite party belies it, misconstrues it, misrepresents it, ridicules it, insults it, and persecutes it.[12]

This then is the first pernicious consequence: "The public good is disregarded in the conflicts of rival parties. . . ."[13] The second, widely feared consequence was worse. The disunity spawned by parties might lead to instability and disorder. As revolutionaries, the Founders had opposed not only a government's policies, but that government itself. Moreover, the founding period was not without armed uprisings in opposition to governmental acts. Shays's Rebellion in 1786-87 and the Whiskey Insurrection of 1794 are the most obvious examples. Their apprehension of disorder was thus not baseless, although fear led them sometimes to equate public criticism with sedition.[14] President Washington used the involvement of a few of the Democratic Societies in the Whiskey Rebellion to attack all of them.[15] When a state legislature passed resolutions critical of his policies, Hamilton complained that such action was a "symptom of a spirit which must either be killed, or it will kill the Constitution."[16] One member of Congress, William Vans Murray of Maryland, even went so far as to assert that attempts to organize opposition to the Jay Treaty in the House of Representatives were "subversive of the Constitution and . . . poisonous to our national faith."[17]

A third and related charge against parties was that they distorted what would otherwise be democratic outcomes. Clever men, by combining resources, would be able to accomplish more than the same number of individuals with the same resources could achieve in the absence of cooperation. A party, by magnifying the influence of a small group of men, could thus lead to minority tyranny. This is the danger which concerned Washington when he asserted that a party has "an artificial and extraordinary force; [it puts]. . . in the place of the delegated will of the Nation, the will of a party; often a small but artful and enterprising minority of the community."[18]

The fourth major criticism may have been less important, but it was the most widespread. Party allegiances, these men believed, led to uncivil, brutish behavior. William Wyche, a New York jurist, observed that party spirit often led to "bespattering the character of a man" who was of different persuasion.[19] Jefferson felt that party conflict, particularly where both antagonists are nearly matched in strength, produced "paroxysms of bitterness."[20] Washington spoke of "jealousies and heart burnings" and "the spirit of revenge" occasioned by party attachment.[21] Madison, too, regretted this result of party spirit and tied it to the earlier criticisms when he concluded that parties roused in men "mutual animosity, and rendered them much more disposed to vex and oppress each other than to cooperate for their common good."[22]

In sum: the early leaders of our nation saw parties as organizations which arouse base emotions in individuals so that they are often incapable of harmonious effort in behalf of the national interest. In addition, many of them believed that parties would hinder popular control of government by rewarding cunning, and by giving the power to determine policy to a small part of the population. Finally, some persons were convinced that by organizing opposition to governmental policies in an attempt to modify them, the parties would sow disorder and perhaps endanger the government itself. Given these views, it would not be difficult to conclude that a "party is a monster who devours the common good."[23]

These men, however, created parties, for they needed them. It is to an examination of how that need emerged and how they met it that we now turn.

The Emergence of Parties

THE EARLY EXPERIENCE

Prior to the Revolution, experience with a political organization which might develop into something akin to a party was factional experience; that is, voting blocs appeared in some colonial legislatures, but they tended to be organized around particular families or outstanding personalities rather than ongoing issues. Moreover, even this experience varied from colony to colony. Rhode Island typified bifactional politics with relatively stable organizations centering around leading figures. In contrast, New Jersey legislative politics was multifactional during the decade before the Revolution. At the opposite pole, Connecticut's legislature showed little evidence of enduring factions. Perhaps because these loose organizations were more concerned with obtaining power than with taking positions on issues, or because the alignments shifted often and sometimes abruptly, there is little evidence of a sense of identification with factions among the people in the colonies; however, this was also true in Pennsylvania, a state which was exceptional in that its two legislative blocs were quite stable, tied to political issues, and even engaged in some organized electioneering. Still, in that colony, as in others, the blocs were loosely aligned collections of individuals rather than formal organizations.[24]

The pattern changed rather quickly following the Revolution. The stakes of legislative politics had also changed, for no longer was there a royal governor with an absolute veto. Equally important: the players in the political game changed as well. During the colonial period, most legislatures contained few small farmers, craftsmen, or men of similar status. During the Revolutionary War, however, such men became active participants and gained valuable experience as army officers, members of important committees, and of state assemblies. Moreover, their opportunities increased following the war, as political reform made its way unevenly from state to state. The voting membership of the lower houses grew, and representation of the backcountry was enlarged. The right to hold office and the right to vote were extended in some cases to a wider range of residents. As a result, a more diverse segment of the population made its way into legislative bodies.[25]

The historian, Jackson Turner Main, in an important study of roll call votes and biographical data regarding the members of the lower houses in seven state legislatures during the years before the Constitutional Convention of 1787, discovered that two opposed voting blocs developed rather quickly in each state. Not only were they stable, but they also differed from most of the alignments in the colonial legislatures by focusing their attention on alternative policies regarding issues of continuing importance. Furthermore, these nascent parties took substantially the same positions on issues in each state.

The issues were primarily economic but also political, social, and cultural. The cosmopolitan bloc in each state favored both higher taxes and greater government expenditures, opposed laws favoring debtors over creditors, and favored more lenient treatment of loyalists. Its adherents tended to cluster along the coast, to have experiences and acquaintances which provided them with perspectives extending beyond the borders of their states, and to have occupations which were not agricultural. The other bloc was agrarian-localist, and stood in opposition to the cosmopolitan one on these issues.

Generally, these blocs made no attempt to organize outside the legislature; however, there was some campaigning by groups of candidates in Pennsylvania, New York, and Rhode Island, and also in Massachusetts as the Constitutional Convention drew nearer. Such campaigning attracted considerable criticism wherever it occurred.[26]

With the experience in the states to serve as models, it may seem peculiar that the seeds of party did not appear at a national level in the legislature established by the Articles of Confederation. That they did not is due to the limited authority enjoyed by that body. Unable to legislate at all without the agreement of nine of the thirteen states, the Congress established under the Articles could regulate commerce by neither statute nor taxation. It had the right to regulate coinage, but the states could and did issue paper money as they pleased. Congress could make treaties, but it had no way to compel the observance of them. The national legislature even had to depend on contributions from the states to support its budget. Perhaps most importantly, it had no direct contact with the people. Elected by the state legislatures, Congress could make no laws that directly regulated the behavior of the citizens of the states. In such circumstances the appearance of blocs could only be interpreted as evidence that certain individuals were bent on personal aggrandizement. The development of intragovernmental party organization would have to await the creation of a national political body with sufficient authority to offer a strong incentive for organization.

That body was the national government devised by the Constitutional Convention of 1787 and established following ratification by the ninth state, New Hampshire, in 1788. The new government came to rest on four principles which Charles Hyneman has explicated in his chapter in this volume. It was to be a republican government and one of law, sharing power with state governments, and characterized by a separation of powers, coupled with checks and balances. Those who supported the adoption of the Constitution would have agreed that these four tenets were characteristics of the plan. Some adherents might have included one or another as a major principle. One point on which they all would have agreed is that the national government was not to be the enfeebled dependent with which they had become familiar under the Articles.

Alexander Hamilton, who was Secretary of the Treasury in the new government and the principal innovator of policy in Washington's Cabinet, was one of the chief proponents of a strong central government. Furthermore, he resolved to use bold strokes of public policy to insure that the new government be a strong and lasting one. To be so, he believed it had to involve men of property and wealth in such a way that it was to their economic advantage that the government grow vigorous and remain healthy. To this end he devised the financial plan presented to Congress in 1790 and 1791.

The plan had four elements. First, the securities issued by the national government under the Articles would be funded; that is, even though they had depreciated considerably in the market, they would be replaced at face value by new interest bearing securities guaranteed by the new government. Second, the national government would assume the debts which the states had contracted during the Revolutionary War, these also to be met at face value. Third, the funds to pay the interest and retire the principal on these new debts were to be raised by a protective tariff on manufactured goods and an internal excise tax on liquor (the eventual cause of the Whiskey Rebellion). Fourth, the government's financial transactions would be handled by a congressionally chartered bank which would involve a mixture of public and private elements doing private as well as public business.

The plan was audacious. It offered large and immediate profits to stock speculators; and it gained support from bankers, merchants, small manufacturers, and their employees. Furthermore, it was designed to stimulate the movement of goods and to encourage national economic growth. Such a program would have been impossible under the Articles of Confederation. Moreover, its immediate implications in terms of the interests it advantaged and disadvantaged, and its longer range implications for the shape and direction of American government, offered exactly the kinds of incentives which make party organization attractive.

INTRAGOVERNMENTAL PARTY DEVELOPMENT

In order to promote the adoption of his financial plan, Hamilton began to organize support in Congress, meeting individually with members friendly to it, arranging gatherings of his supporters, and urging those strongly committed to keep the vacillating ones in line. He also began marshalling support outside Congress, carrying on an extensive correspondence with an ever-widening circle of acquaintances and raising money to found a newspaper which would advance his policies; thus was born what was to become the first national political party, the Federalist.

Opposition to Hamilton's financial plan in Congress was led by James Madison. That opposition was not organized, nor was it directed against every facet of Hamilton's program. Madison did not oppose funding; but he did want the government to distinguish between the original holders of the securities (ex-soldiers, their families, and those who had lent support when the outlook was bleak) and speculators who later had purchased the notes, often at a fraction of their worth. That it did not so discriminate angered many, and set the South and Pennsylvania, where most original holders had sold their securities, in opposition to the remainder of the nation. Madison also objected to details in the plan to assume state debts, but the proposal to establish the Bank of the United States was the first one to which he objected totally. In this, he had the support of Washington's Secretary of State, Thomas Jefferson, who viewed the proposal as unconstitutional; yet, even after this break with Hamilton, they both supported him on the revenue measures needed to execute the adopted program.

Nonetheless, in 1790 to 1791, Madison, other congressmen, Jefferson, and some other notable leaders in the states were becoming increasingly suspicious regarding the motives and actions of Hamilton and his organization. They correctly viewed Hamilton's programs as being designed to produce a central government considerably stronger than those of the states, to encourage close ties between the new nation and her former colonial ruler, and to advance the fortunes of the privileged classes. While there is no doubt that

Hamilton believed these goals to be inextricably tied to the national interest, Madison and those who shared his concern saw them as objectives "adverse to the rights of other citizens, or to the permanent and aggregate interests of the community."

Counter organization began. Late in 1791 Madison was instrumental in the establishment of an anti-Hamilton newspaper in Philadelphia, and frequently spoke against Federalist policies in House debates during the following year. At the same time, John Beckley of Virginia, who, with Madison's help, had become Clerk of the House, took up the task of marshaling the anti-Federalist forces in that body.

Washington's proclamation of neutrality in the war which broke out between England and France in 1793, and his censure of the pro-French, anti-Federalist Democratic Societies provided further incentive for party organization. Jefferson urged Madison to attack Hamilton's arguments regarding executive prerogatives, and Madison did so. At the same time, Jefferson's position in the cabinet was becoming so intolerable that he resigned at the end of the year. Attempts at intragovernmental organization by both parties were meeting with success. While 42 percent of the members of the House of Representatives were aligned with neither the Federalist bloc nor its fledgling opposition of 1790 to 1791, that figure had fallen to 19 percent by the Third Congress (December 1793 to March 1795).[27]

EXTRAGOVERNMENTAL PARTY DEVELOPMENT

By the mid-1790s both parties were beginning to gain support outside the government. Those in Pennsylvania and New York were moving to conform with the pattern developing in the United States Congress. The anti-Hamilton organization, which would soon grow into the Republican party, by correspondence among its leaders and by trips and visits for consultation had managed to arrive at a nomination of its candidate for the vice-presidency in 1792. These efforts at communication and coordination continued, though not at a constant pace. The impetus to accelerate them and to begin serious efforts at extragovernmental organization for the purpose of recruiting support from the bulk of the citizens came with the Jay Treaty and the debate which raged following the Senate's consent to it.

The Jay Treaty, with which Washington himself was unhappy,

gave considerable advantage to England and little in return to the United States. In particular, it failed to settle the issue of British impressment of American seamen or of British seizure of slaves during the Revolutionary War. The Senate considered the treaty in secret and passed it after lengthy debate by the barest possible margin; but, in spite of attempts to keep its terms confidential, the treaty was published in the Republican press almost immediately after ratification.

The results were remarkable. Mass meetings to protest the terms of the treaty were held throughout the country. Effigies of Jay were burned, north and south. The Republican organizer, Beckley, busied himself with correspondence with local leaders, urging them to exert their influence to stir up opposition to the treaty among members of Congress. His efforts, in combination with those of state and local leaders, were responsible for a series of public meetings in major cities which resulted in petitions and resolutions addressed to the President and condemning the treaty. In this way serious attention to mass organization began.

Madison and the other Republican leaders determined to oppose appropriations needed to put the treaty into effect. That struggle occupied the House of Representatives in 1796. Both parties exerted themselves to hold their own votes and to win others. As a part of that effort, the Republicans organized the first full congressional party caucus. Both parties achieved some success. While nineteen percent of the members of the House had remained unaligned with either party during the Third Congress, that figure dropped to only seven percent in the First Session of the Fourth Congress which met from December 1795 until June 1796.[28] The Republicans managed to hold the majority throughout much of that session. Nonetheless, they lost narrowly to the Federalists on the crucial vote regarding appropriations. The handful of Republican defections on that vote could be attributed in large part to intense constituency pressures; indeed, the use of constituency influence to guide the behavior of Representatives now became a common practice in both parties.

The Federalist victory in connection with the Jay Treaty had three immediate effects on party politics. First, the issue became the crucial one in election campaigns at all levels of public office in 1796, thus climaxing the process of bringing state and local parties into alignment with those at the national level. Second, it provided an incentive for local organizations to attempt to discipline those who had deserted the Republican banner on the key vote, namely, by defeating them at the polls. Third, the vote on appropriations was instrumental in convincing Jefferson to become the Republican candidate for President in 1796.

Writing to William Branch Giles, a Representative from a Virginia constituency, early in the session which revolved around the treaty, Jefferson demonstrated how he dealt with the conflict between his distaste for parties and his inclination to take a more active role in one:

> Were parties here divided merely by a greediness for office, as in England, to take a part with either would be unworthy of a reasonable or moral man, but where the principle of difference is as substantial and as strongly pronounced as between the Republicans and the Monocrats of our country, I hold it as honorable to take a firm and decided part, and as immoral to pursue a middle line, as between the parties of honest men, and rogues, into which every country is divided.[29]

The party which Madison had nurtured was about to become Jefferson's. Revered by average farmers, artisans, and workers as the principal author of the Declaration of Independence, with its stress on equalitarian principles and self-government, he was the natural candidate.

Thus far we have treated the opposition party as just that. We have stressed the sources of its resistance to Federalist theory and Federalist programs. What did the Jeffersonian Republicans have to offer in contrast? First, there was a commitment to simplicity and frugality. The government, they believed, should pay its debts and as a general matter live within its means—and limited means at that, so as not to place burdensome taxes on the citizens. Second, they promised an open government, one which would actively reveal its workings to the people rather than attempting to conceal them. Third, there was attachment to the idea that the people, when informed, would make wise decisions, and faith that they were most likely to be informed in a context of freedom of speech, of press, and of religion. Like the Federalists, the Republicans were thus committed to a picture of the national interest rich in implications for public policy.

The election of 1796 did little to alter the party balance. John Adams won a narrow victory over Jefferson in the Electoral College, and the Federalist and Republican strength in the House was nearly identical. Perhaps the most significant change was that Jefferson, as Vice-President, was now back in the capital and actively involved after an absence of four years.

Adams's term as President was marked by continuing party conflict favorable first to the Federalists and then to the Republicans. The threat of war with France, plus a diplomatic scandal which revealed some of her high officials as scoundrels, aided the Federalist cause. The response included the creation of rather large military forces, acts directed against resident aliens, and the nation's first sedition law which, by loose interpretation, made almost any criticism of the government or its officers a crime. The elections of 1798 were, for the most part, held early enough so that the effects of these acts were not yet felt. On the other hand, the tide of anti-French opinion did have its impact. The Republicans suffered a net loss of at least five seats in the House of Representatives.

The same issues and policies soon redounded to Republican advantage. The opposition press made considerable capital of the partisan nature of prosecutions under the Sedition Act; indeed, the attempts to stifle the minority party press led to a great increase in the number of papers supporting Jefferson.[30] In addition, the Federalists were forced to impose a series of new and broad based taxes to cover the new military expenditures. As these taxes became due, the angry responses increased in fervor. In addition, Adams moved to establish better relations with France, thus dashing the hopes of many of the leading Federalists—and splitting the party. These three factors, coupled with what was by now a typically well-organized Republican campaign, with active partisans in villages and neighborhoods throughout much of the nation, brought sweeping Republican victories in 1800.

It is well that the founding period ends in 1800, not only because this description of party development is already overlong, but, more importantly, because the interval closes with a peaceful transition of governmental power from one party to another as a result of the expression of popular will. It was the first such event in modern history. While the Federalists plotted a bit and grumbled a lot, they accepted the verdict. It was an auspicious bit of evidence that the principles of the young nation would serve it well.

Party Development and Popular Government

In introductory courses in American government, the question: "Why does the United States have a two-party system?" most frequently evokes answers which illustrate two kinds of mistaken notions about the origins of political parties. The more common of the two mistakes dwells on the supposed advantages which a two-party system entails. It is as though, having been drilled in high school about the careful deliberation which the framers of the Constitution devoted to working out the principal aspects of our government, students cannot believe that a major institutional pattern of our political system could have arisen without careful advance planning. Some are even convinced that our party system is ordained in the Constitution. More knowledgeable students gleefully respond with the second kind of mistake. As they see it, the national party system and our parties "just happened." Aware that they were not produced as a result of some constitutional or legislative act, these students believe that the institutions resulted from some fortuitous combination of accidental circumstances.

Though both notions are mistaken, they contain elements of truth. Circumstances did have much to do with the development of our parties. As the sketch of early party history given above illustrates, parties, as distinct from factions, develop only after some popularly chosen body with real decision making authority comes into existence. Even then, party organization waits for the appearance of the kind of fundamental issue which has implications for a wide range of public policies;[31] thus the first signs of party did not appear in Congress until the second year of congressional experience, when debate and action centered on the elements of Hamilton's financial plan. Furthermore, while they did not spring full grown from the minds of their creators, considerable thought *was* devoted to the process of building these new devices; and it was *political* thought—thought aimed at practical answers to the question: "How can I so manage events and influence others that my own persuasions regarding the national interest will guide the course of public policy?"

The fact that Hamilton was motivated by such a sweeping vision of the common good to be achieved through governmental action indeed is one of the two principal factors which accounted for a need to develop parties. The other was the pluralist character of American society during the founding period.

The situation confronting Hamilton was not simple. His design required the immediate cooperation of a majority of the members of the House of Representatives and the Senate, as well as that of the President of the new United States. As the years passed, he would find that he needed the assistance of additional public officials, especially state legislators and other cabinet members; thus he was faced with an institutional pluralism which had been designed to prevent the government from tyrannizing, but which might also make it difficult for the government to act with energy in pursuit of any goal.

Had opposition in Congress been unlikely, Hamilton would have had little to fear from institutional pluralism; however, he could be certain that his plan would encounter some hostility and more skepticism in that body and in the wider society. Even at that time, Americans were a diverse people with many occupations, religious identifications, ethnic backgrounds, economic accumulations, social standings, and life experiences. The range of human diversity present in Congress was not as great as that in the population, but the national legislature was far from a homogeneous body. Many of its members and more of their constituents would have opposing conceptions of the national interest; and these opposing conceptions also would differ in what they included, sometimes being wholly contradictory. Hamilton thus also confronted social pluralism, which Madison in *Federalist* 10 had extolled as a natural characteristic which would go far to prevent the tyranny of a majority by making it more difficult to form and maintain a majority for such purpose.[32] Here again, however, the device which prevents iniquity may also prevent commonweal.

To overcome institutional and social pluralism, Hamilton had to cause other officials to act as though his picture of the national interest was their own. He proved to be quite effective. Some he convinced of the attractiveness of his view. Others were persuaded that the bills which would implement his vision would also serve their vision. Still others were induced to act as he wished because they were grateful to whoever was instrumental in providing them with posts of honor. Others exchanged support of Hamilton for his backing of their projects. Still others were moved to vote as he wished by pressure brought to bear by leading constituents. In these and other ways, Hamilton brought together and maintained the Federalist party in Congress. Identical means were used when it was necessary to add officials from other branches and other levels to the coalition.

A coalition, however, is not often a party; and a party would have been superfluous to Hamilton had it not been for the scope of his ideas. Had he been committed to establishing a single program, the same techniques which he used would have been effective, and at a cost trifling in comparison. Hamilton's vision, however, was bold, with implications for many areas of public policy. He began his efforts with a legislative package of a number of interconnected proposals each of which appeared essential to the others. Furthermore, while some would have the desired impact immediately, others would be effective only if maintained for several years. In fact, not only was the financial plan tied clearly to his conception of the national interest, but that also is true of almost all of the other programs he supported as Secretary of the Treasury, and thereafter.

A fragmented government and a fragmented society required coalition for effective action. That coalition could serve Hamilton's purposes capably only if it was institutionalized so that its patterns of behavior became regular and dependable; thus a party was necessary. Being extralegal, it could avoid the fragmenting tendencies of a separation of powers and the federal structure. It did so by embracing officials, whatever their position in an organization in which the incentives rewarded cooperation. Furthermore, as the party became natural to its members, they would very likely develop loyalties to it which would be useful additional incentives to continued cooperation. For Madison and Jefferson, in opposition and in power, the case was very much the same.

We would not be concerned with parties in this volume were they only associations of congressmen and a few administrative officials. Nor would such organizations have served the Founders' purposes. Both parties quickly realized that the press, as a molder and reflector of public opinion, could be of value in influencing the behavior of congressmen; thus the public was soon learning of the issues about which the parties disagreed and also some of the reasoning which they used to support their positions. Local notables were sometimes recruited to communicate with their Representatives either to keep them in line with a position or to try to persuade them to shift their stances.

Popular involvement might have remained at this level for a longer time had it not been for the fact that as the party battles in the House became more intense, one congressman after another became attached to the Federalist or the Republican bloc. As the number of unaligned congressmen decreased, both parties—but particularly the Republicans, who were still the challengers—had to devise new strategies to augment their strength. The solution was to go to the people at elections. Local activists were asked to nominate and support a candidate to stand against an incumbent opponent (by early in the nineteenth century nominations for Congress and for state and local offices were most often made by party caucuses or local party conventions). Press support was provided. Ticketing developed as public opinion focused on the overriding national issues and as the national parties realized the importance of organizing the state legislatures in order to have more impact on the selection of United States senators and presidential electors, particularly in those states where they were not popularly chosen. Finally, by the election of 1800, campaigning was generally coordinated, the party affiliation of candidates was commonly known, and the positions and performance of the two parties relating to the major issues was a matter of much discussion in the press and among the voters.

The election of 1800 was a popular one. The people were faced with choices among candidates many of whom had been chosen by groups of activists rather than by notables or incumbent officials. The people were faced with choices made easier because the candidates were identified with political parties, and made meaningful by the opposed positions regarding the national interest which the parties had developed.

Two important principles relating to parties emerged from the experience of our founding period. The first is that, in a pluralist society with separate governing institutions, broad, coherent public policy is party policy. The second is that popular control of the general direction which the government is to take is furnished most effectively by providing for a choice among parties.

The continued validity of these principles is seriously questioned today. Current criticism suggests that the parties have failed and that, in consequence, elections no longer serve to provide popular control of public policy. It is to these challenges that we now turn.

The Principles Today

Criticism of parties during the founding period was quite unlike that which we find most often today. The early critics believed that parties would destroy the natural harmony which should exist in society and, in consequence, distract men from the national interest. They feared that the parties would be too strong, too committed to their own goals to see the value in others, and hence too violent. In contrast, critics today are convinced that the parties offer no clear-cut choices to the electorate. They argue that each party embraces such a wide range of views along the political spectrum and such a diversity of principal concerns that the platforms to which the nominees are bound, if only loosely, appear to be attempts to promise something to every powerful interest. As a result, the programs are both alike and incoherent. They certainly do not offer the kinds of choices which the Federalists and Republicans presented to the people in the last decade of the eighteenth century. In such a situation, elections may serve a number of useful functions—but not that of popular control of policy direction.

Today's critics speak to a receptive audience. Our own observations and the results of nearly every survey of attitude and opinion, regardless of its technical procedures, confirm that Americans have undergone a massive loss of confidence in their government's ability to cope with the issues confronting the nation. Those who blame parties call for two kinds of reform. Some insist on change which would make the parties more responsive to groups which, it is asserted, have been too long neglected—the young and the old, the poor, women, Blacks, ethnic minorities, consumers, and so on. Others call for changes which will increase the mechanisms through which party discipline can be exercised. The parties have adopted some of the proposed changes, the most significant being the quota system of delegate selection for the 1972 Democratic National Convention and perhaps their midterm conference of 1974; indeed , the last decade has seen more reform in the procedures used by the two major parties than at any time since the development of national nominating conventions in the 1820s and 1830s.[33] Nonetheless, the public malaise continues. There is an increasing sense of powerlessness, a belief that we are adrift and can no longer take control.

The criticisms offered in the last quarter of the eighteenth century and the third quarter of the twentieth are contradictory at least in part because of the different stages of the party process during which they were advanced. To clarify that claim, we must shift our attention briefly to some notions about elections which were initially advanced by V. O. Key and which have been tested and developed by many others.[34]

The Jeffersonian Republicans appear to have been more successful than the Federalists because they extended their organization into the grass-roots and built a large following among the people. As we have already noted, institutions tend to develop a character of their own, and members frequently form lasting attachments to an organization and its symbols. Many ordinary farmers and laborers identified themselves in this way with Jefferson's party. Many more identify themselves with its heir, today's Democratic party, and with its opposition, the present-day Republican party. The system of classifying elections which we shall be summarizing is based on the premise that these identifications which people make with political parties shape their perceptions of events in their political environment; that is, someone who formed a strong attachment to the Democratic party during the campaign which led to John Kennedy's election in 1960, is likely to find more to admire in the Democratic presidential candidate than in his Republican opponent in 1976 and to favor the Democratic issue positions more than those taken by the G.O.P.

Usually, the distribution of such loyalties favors one party; and its supporters can be described in general terms which will identify the components of the party's coalition. In most national elections, that dominant party will emerge victorious. Such elections are called *maintaining* ones because they keep the coalition fairly well intact. Sometimes, however, the larger party will lose an election because many of its supporters are so drawn to the personality of the opposition candidate, or so repelled by their own, or so attracted by a particular issue of importance to them that they switch their vote without abandoning party loyalty. These elections which are less frequent are called *deviating* ones. They supposedly mark an aberration in the normal voting pattern, and, like maintaining elections, they are supposed to cause no substantial damage to the dominant party's coalition. The third, and least frequent kind of election, is the *realigning* one. In such contests, large numbers of voters gain fresh perceptions of their political environment, their partisan loyalties are shattered, and new ones are formed. As a result new coalitions come into being; and the party which emerges with the largest following will move government policy into different channels serving markedly different goals.

Using these categories to classify presidential elections, one might say that 1932 was the most recent realigning election. Maintaining ones followed through the remainder of the 1930s and during the 1940s. The Eisenhower victories were deviating elections resulting principally from concern about government corruption in the late 1940s and early 1950s, opposition to the Korean War, and, most importantly, attraction to "Ike's" personality. The 1960 and 1964 elections were again maintaining ones, giving the dominant party control of the White House once more. Finally, the two elections which made Nixon president were deviating ones again.

Realigning elections have generally captured the attention of those who have examined voting outcomes in this way. Other realignments appear to have occurred in 1800, 1836, 1860 or 1864, and 1896. They were watershed elections; but, we will be misled if we think of the realignments they reflect as being discrete events which happened on particular election days or even in particular years. The conversion of Republicans into Democrats as a result of the Great Depression, the life changes it produced, and the controversies it engendered are likely to have begun in the late 1920s and continued into the mid-1930s; thus it will be more useful for our purposes to refer to realignment periods, and similarly to maintenance ones. How can these concepts help us understand and evaluate realistically the parties as devices to facilitate popular control?

Consider the situation during the maintenance period when each party's platform consists of a set of program commitments arrived at via processes of negotiation and compromise involving each of the important social and economic interests thought to provide major support to the party's election efforts. Then the platforms are likely to show opposed positions on few issues. Much of the document will be devoted to promises regarding proposals on which the other party is silent from ignorance, strategic considerations, or lack of interest. It is even likely that some planks will be shared. The differences between the parties may be clearly visible only with reference to the distribution of support for major groupings; thus today's Republican party is considerably more committed to business interests while the Democratic party remains aligned with organized labor. One party will probably be more liberal or more conservative than the other, but they will not be clearly distinguishable by their positions regarding a set of related issues on which their stands are guided by broad common conceptions of the national interest.

In providing choices like these, parties may be demonstrating their responsiveness during times of widespread agreement regarding the fundamental questions perceived by the electorate. Voters whose party choices are victorious may be rewarded by seeing their candidates in office and their myths predominate. They may punish officials whose choices they do not approve by refusing to reelect them. Furthermore, if they choose carefully, they may be rewarded by seeing a favored policy implemented in the issue area of greatest concern to them, for the parties, by exercising the arts of brokerage and compromise which they have so carefully nurtured, are able to redeem most of their platform pledges.[35] In such a situation, individual voters and interest groups with no substantial party loyalties may shift their votes from party to party on the basis of campaign promises; therefore, in such circumstances these symbolic rewards, and opportunities to replace officials found wanting and to make marginal policy changes may be all that a friend of popular government could expect or desire.

Contrast the preceding image with one offered by the Federalists and the Jeffersonian Republicans or, alternatively, by the Democrats and the Republicans during the New Deal period of the 1930s and early 1940s. Party programs were unified by clear conceptions of the national welfare which reflected economic interests but also social commitments and profound philosophic ones as well. In such periods, the alternatives available at elections were not only real but probably also more accurately perceived by the voters than the proposals advanced by the parties in the 1950s and 1960s. More important still, the policy choices offered by the parties at the turn of the eighteenth century and during the New Deal period dealt with those sets of issues which most vexed the entire society.

Many of those who call for responsible and responsive parties are really seeking a system in which elections always offer the voters choices of the sort just described; but that appears unrealistic. In a rather fragmented system such as ours, it may take several elections for the dominant party to build the kind of support necessary to implement its program, and it will surely take some time to evaluate the program's success. These elections will have the characteristics the critics seek. As accomplishments become visible, however, and as less successful parts of the program are modified or abandoned, the proposals which were so controversial at the outset become objects of a growing consensus. The opposition party is then faced with a choice: it can continue its opposition while ever decreasing in terms of political strength until it atrophies as did the Federalist party during the second decade of the nineteenth century, or it can move to support substantial elements of the majority party's program and begin raising other issues and designing planks for particular minority interests in the hope of improving its electoral fortunes as did the current Republican party, beginning in the 1940s; thus, while the public choices which were so momentous remain basically secure, the party which was responsible for them faces increasing challenge.

In such a manner pluralism has its effects. The wide diversity of minorities, such that every citizen is included in many of them, a fact which Madison relied upon as the chief deterrant to the development of a majority faction bent on tyranny, is a hindrance to the development of any majority. Madison discovered that as he attempted to organize the first Republican party. Writing for a Philadelphia newspaper in 1792, he noted that it was the Federalists' "true policy to weaken their opponents by reviving exploded parties, and taking advantage of all prejudices, local, political, and occupational, that may prevent or disturb a general coalition of sentiments."[36] Pluralism, however, not only impedes the growth of a party to majority status, but also helps insure that once achieved, the dominant party cannot rest secure; thus the *acids of pluralism* guarantee the stubborn recurrence of opposition in American party politics.[37]

Parties thus facilitate the production of public policy and also the opportunities for popular control of that policy in both realigning periods and in those of maintenance; yet, the types of policies and choices they offer differ in the two cases. In realigning periods, those who are convinced that they have too much to lose if the wrong choice is made are likely to fear the choice. To the extent that what they perceive to be the proper course is abandoned, they are likely to condemn parties for their excessive strength and for their tendency to draw us away from the national interest. On the other hand, during a maintenance period minorities most interested in issues not perceived as important by the electorate, or who cling to a favored policy position which is opposed by the general consensus, will probably see little difference between the parties and are likely to judge elections to be meaningless rituals.

What we have christened *maintenance periods* are periods of both growth and decay. Major growth ceases when the choice responsible for the alignment appears to be secure. Decay begins when the opposition party turns away from that issue and begins using others to chip away at the dominant party's coalition. When decay is far advanced, new issues will have arisen, but party and government responses will be for the most part piecemeal and inconsistent. At such a time, those nurtured on populist notions of democracy are likely to feel adrift without controls. That feeling swirls through America today. It is not the mechanism, however, which has failed us. What we lack is the vision to determine our destination. Whatever else party reform may accomplish, it will not provide us with that sweeping image of our national interest so rich in policy implications that it can lead to a realignment in, and a revitalization of, electoral politics and the halls of government. Those who develop so bold a vision can still gain control of a political party and use it to present their course to the people for a verdict. Should that course achieve public favor, a party remains the mechanism which can guide the conversion of the proposals into public policy.

Notes

1. Gal. 5:16-21.
2. *Pennsylvania Packet* (Philadelphia), Oct. 15, 1776, quoted in Jackson Turner Main, *Political Parties before the Constitution* (Chapel Hill: University of North Carolina Press, 1973), p. 399.
3. *New Jersey Gazette* (Trenton), Jan. 13, 1779, quoted in Main, p. 398.

4. *The Debates in the Several State Conventions on the Adoption of the Federal Constitution*, ed. Jonathan Elliot, 5 vols. (1888), 2:320.
5. Quoted in Richard Hofstadter, *The Idea of a Party System* (Berkeley and Los Angeles: University of California Press, 1969), p. 123.
6. *The Federalist Papers*, ed. Clinton Rossiter (New York: New American Library, Inc., 1961), p. 77.
7. Ibid., pp. 426-427.
8 George Washington, "Farewell Address," excerpted in *The Making of the American Party System, 1789-1809*, ed. Noble E. Cunningham, Jr. (Englewood Cliffs, N.J.: Prentice-Hall, Inc., 1965), p. 16.
9. Quoted in Hofstadter, p. 3, n. 1.
10. Thomas Jefferson to John Taylor, June 4, 1798, excerpted in *The Making of the American Party System, 1789-1809*, p. 18.
11. *The Federalist Papers*, p. 78. Madison offered this as a definition of the term *faction*, but he uses that label and *party* interchangeably throughout the essay. A common distinction at the time, however, was between groups concerned simply with capturing office and groups which possessed some unifying interest which they hoped to advance through government. The former were called factions, and the latter, parties. *See* Main, p. xviii.
12. John Adams to Thomas Jefferson, *The Life and Works of John Adams*, ed. Charles Francis Adams, 10 vols. (Boston, 1850-56), 10:50; quoted in Hofstadter, p. 28.
13. James Madison, *Federalist Papers* 10:77.
14. In this, the founders fit into a pattern which seems to be characteristic of new nations. *See* Seymour Martin Lipset, *The First New Nation* (New York: Basic Books, Inc., 1963), pp. 36-45. We have learned that it may characterize older nations as well.
15. The debate in the House of Representatives regarding appropriate limits of free expression which Washington's message aroused remains worthy of careful reading. *See* Charles S. Hyneman and George W. Carey, eds., *A Second Federalist* (New York: Appleton-Century-Crofts, 1967), pp. 223-231.
16. Quoted in William Nisbet Chambers, *Political Parties in a New Nation* (New York: Oxford University Press, 1963), p. 61.
17. Quoted in Alexander DeConde, *Entangling Alliance* (Durham, N.C.: Duke University Press, 1958), p.133.
18. Washington, "Farewell Address," p. 15.
19. William Wyche, "Party Spirit," excerpted in *The Making of the American Party System, 1789-1809*, p. 13.
20. Thomas Jefferson to William Short, Nov. 10, 1804, excerpted in *The Making of the American Party System, 1789-1809*, p. 19.
21. Washington, "Farewell Address," pp. 15-16.
22. *Federalist Papers* 10:79.
23. Wyche, p. 14.
24. Main, pp. 3-13.

25. Ibid., pp. xix-xx.
26. Ibid., *passim*.
27. Joseph Charles, *The Origins of the American Party System* (New York: Harper and Brothers, 1961), p. 94.
28. Ibid.
29. Thomas Jefferson to William B. Giles, December 31, 1795, excerpted in *The Making of the American Party System, 1789-1809*, p. 17.
30. Chambers, pp. 150-151.
31. The pattern of circumstances which characterizes the development of political parties in Western democracies is well described in Austin Ranney and Willmoore Kendall, *Democracy and the American Party System* (New York: Harcourt, Brace & World, Inc., 1956), pp. 88-107.
32. *The Federalist Papers*, pp. 77-84.
33. Austin Ranney, *Curing the Mischiefs of Faction* (Berkeley and Los Angeles: University of California Press, 1975), p. 3. Ranney provides a good examination of both sorts of criticism mentioned here and of the parties' responses.
34. V.O. Key, Jr., "A Theory of Critical Elections," *Journal of Politics*, 17 (February 1955): 3-18. For some further developments, see Angus Campbell, et al., *Elections and the Political Order* (New York: John Wiley and Sons, Inc., 1966), pp. 63-77; Gerald M. Pomper, *Elections in America* (New York: Dodd, Mead & Company, 1968), pp. 99-125; and Walter D. Burnham, *Critical Elections and the Mainsprings of Political Life* (New York: W.W. Norton & Co., Inc., 1970), *passim*.
35. For an excellent discussion of party platforms since 1944 and the degree to which their pledges have been fulfilled, *see* Pomper, pp. 149-203.
36. James Madison, "A Candid State of Parties," *National Gazette* (Philadelphia), September 26, 1792, excerpted in Cunningham, p. 11.
37. The suggestive phrase *acids of pluralism* is to be found in Chambers, p. 15.

[II]

GOVERNMENT AND THE ECONOMY

—SCARLETT G. GRAHAM

Combining the words *government* and *economy* in a single phrase is a comfortable and familiar practice of our time. The close association of these two areas of human endeavor is reflected in the most commonplace activities of day-to-day life, as well as in our most serious and expert considerations of the dimensions of politics and of economics. Debate continues, in both politics and scholarship, over what constitutes the proper relationship between the government and the economy; but the reality and the inevitability of such a relationship are seldom seriously questioned.

A relationship between economic life and political life is not a development new to our time. It seems always to have been characteristic of human society; and it was clearly appreciated by those who most directly influenced the setting up of the American system of government. Although it is fair to claim universality for the interface of governments and economies, the historical and contemporary meanings of this relationship for a particular society can be seen only in the concrete structures, processes, actions, and beliefs which give life to the relationship.

The phrase *government and the economy* evokes two quite distinguishable but ultimately inseparable varieties of questions. To what extent do particular economic arrangements and the differentials in economic resources and power among the various groups in the society affect the institutions, the processes, and the potential benefits to be derived from government? On the other hand, how do governmental structures and processes influence economic arrangements and the potential benefits to be derived from the economy?

It is not at all clear whether these questions existed in the minds of the Founders in precisely the form in which a citizen of the twentieth century would raise them. Nonetheless, it is an unavoidable conclusion that many of the fundamental issues and attendant problems of the relationship of government to the economy bore heavily upon the minds of those who participated in the founding act. Analytical and historical distances almost surely distinguish the political from the economic more than they were in the thoughts of those busied with the practical task of forging a nation. Furthermore, the tendency to treat human activities and institutions according to distinguishable categories such as the political, the economic, or the social is probably much closer to the twentieth- than to the eighteenth-century understanding of the nature of human affairs.

The following treatment of the relationship of the government to the economy at the time of the founding of the American nation, and during its development thereafter, will incorporate as a major premise that the Founders were involved first and foremost in a *political* act, and, additionally, that they understood themselves to be so engaged.[1] Their task was the formation of an improved polity, and their considerations of economic matters are best understood in the context of that larger enterprise. The evidence that such was the case is persuasive. To advocate this premise is in no way to seek to diminish the importance of the economic concerns which came heavily to bear upon the formation of our government, but instead to seek to emphasize a point of view which is easily overlooked in the midst of the pressing and ever-present economic preoccupations of our time.

Economic Forces and the Constitution

In 1913 Charles A. Beard advanced the argument that the Constitution of the United States is to be understood primarily as an economic document forcefully shaped by a few powerful economic interests prevalent at the time.[2] He further argued that the men of the

Constitutional Convention conscientiously and deliberately designed a government which would secure and perpetuate the predominance of these interests in American society. Beard understood both the determinants and the intended consequences of the design of our government to be economic.

As primary support for his argument, Beard surveyed the social backgrounds and economic holdings of each of the participants in the Convention, and, upon the basis of these biographical sketches, maintained with a note of confidence that:

> It cannot be said, therefore, that the members of the Convention were "disinterested." On the contrary, we are forced to accept the profoundly significant conclusion that they knew through their personal experiences in economic affairs the precise results which the new government that they were setting up was designed to attain. . . . [A]s practical men they were able to build the new government upon the only foundations which could be stable: fundamental economic interests.[3]

Beard was entirely correct in his argument that the drafters of the Constitution were men of vast experience. That experience, however, spanned the sphere of politics as well as that of economics, and so too did their concerns throughout the deliberations of the Convention.

Alexander Hamilton addressed himself briefly in *Federalist* 1 to the essence of what was to become Beard's argument a century and a quarter later. Hamilton first discussed those who opposed the adoption of the Constitution, allowing for the possibility that there are men who resist change because it threatens to reduce their power, and that there are other men who hope to improve their positions through the confusions of their country. He refused, however, to dwell upon "observations of this nature." He rightly declared that:

> It would be disingenuous to resolve indiscriminately the opposition of any set of men (merely because their situations might subject them to suspicion) into interested or ambitious views. Candor will oblige us to admit that even such men may be actuated by upright intentions. . . .[4]

Hamilton did not rest the case with the opposition. He recognized that "[a]mbition, avarice, personal animosity, party opposition, and many other motives not more laudable than these, are apt to operate as well upon those who support as those who oppose the right side of a question."[5] The potential influence of an individual's immediate self-interests upon his attitudes and opinions was thoroughly understood by Hamilton. The possibility of rising above those immediate interests in order to take a larger view was equally understood.

In *Federalist* 37 James Madison analyzed the work of the Constitutional Convention and the document which it produced. He drew the conclusion that it could only be explained as having occurred on one of those extremely rare occasions when a group of men did indeed take the larger view. For Madison, history demonstrated that "almost all the great councils and consultations held among mankind for reconciling their discordant opinions, assuaging their mutual jealousies, and adjusting their respective interests, is a history of factions, contentions, and disappointments . . . which display the infirmities and depravities of the human character;"[6] but the Convention was a departure from this historical tendency in Madison's view.

Into the framework of government established by the Constitution there were incorporated a number of principles, such as energy *and* stability in government, which were potentially contradictory if not blended together in the proper proportions. In this framework authority was distributed between the states and the federal government, and the subtle and perplexing problem of the separation of powers in the different branches of government was resolved. All of this was accomplished, according to Madison, in the midst of the natural rivalries of the large and the small states and of other potential divisions of interest. Alluding to *Federalist* 10 he declared that, while this "variety of interests . . . may have a salutary influence on the administration of the government when formed, yet every one must be sensible of the contrary influence which must have been experienced in the task of forming it."[7]

Madison's analysis of the successes of the Constitutional Convention led him to two conclusions regarding the extraordinary nature of the undertaking:

> The first is, that the convention must have enjoyed, in a very singular degree, an exemption from the pestilential influence of party animosities—the disease most apt to contaminate their proceeding. The second conclusion is that all the deputations composing the convention were satisfactorily accommodated by the final act, or were

> induced to accede to it by a deep conviction of the necessity of sacrificing private opinions and partial interests to the public good. . . .[8]

Madison acknowledged the compromises which came to be incorporated into the Constitution, but his characterization of the framing suggests that those compromises were structured by principles of government which were more comprehensive than any simple conflict of economic interest.

The question of the "purity or the contamination" of the Founders' motives is probably, in and of itself, of little consequence. Beard's arguments have been ably addressed on his own grounds and convincingly undermined by a number of students of the founding period.[9] Beard's case is worthy of consideration, however, regardless of how its ultimate merits are judged, because it raised in a most forceful way the question of how best to understand the events, words, and actions which surrounded the drafting of the Constitution, and their influence on the final document.

An awareness among the Founders of the existence of substantial and competing economic interests is clearly manifest in the Convention debates. To argue that the drafters of the Constitution were able to rise above a simple economic perspective in order to take a larger view of the meaning of their project is not to say that the economic perspective was not an integral part of the larger view. Nor is it to argue that the men of Philadelphia believed that, in the ordinary course of human affairs, politics is more important to a society's well-being than is economics. Their project, however, fell outside the ordinary course of human affairs and therefore required a kind of understanding qualitatively different from that which is applied to the routine affairs of an established and ongoing social system.

The Economic Situation and Its Political Implications before 1787

Political times are economic times as well, and questions of extreme political importance often surround economic issues. During ordinary times in a nation's history, the distinction between matters political and those economic tends to be, on the whole, unpronounced and often difficult to make. But there are extraordinary periods when one or the other seems to prevail; and, at the time of the American founding, matters political dominated the thought of the members of a society to an extent perhaps then unprecedented and subsequently unmatched. The questions demanding answers covered the broad expanse from the commonplace concerns of everyday political life to the fundamental and ultimate considerations of the nature of a good polity. An important stimulus to develop such a comprehensive political inquiry, and to construct a system of government as a result, were the economic disturbances of the time.

Compelling economic concerns contributed significantly to the atmosphere of urgency which surrounded the initial meetings of the Constitutional Convention in May 1787. On May 29 Edmund Randolph of Virginia opened the main business of the Convention with an address which was shortly to become known as the Randolph or Virginia Plan.[10] He cited five serious defects of the Articles of Confederation and of the government thereby instituted. The first and most elaborately detailed flaw was the inability of the confederation to provide security against foreign invasion. The second one was the powerlessness of the federal government to "check the quarrals between the states, nor a rebellion in any." The first two defects which Randolph pointed out were stated in negative terms, as were the fourth (that the federal government could not defend itself against encroachments from the states) and the fifth (that the Articles were not even paramount to the state constitutions).

The third, and most purely economic deficiency which Randolph suggested was stated in more positive language:

> That there were many advantages, which the U.S. might acquire, which were not attainable under the confederation—such as a productive impost—counteraction of the commercial regulations of other nations—pushing of commerce *ad libitum*—etc.[11]

In the instance of the third point, Randolph seems to have deplored the inability of the government to realize a positive objective rather than, as is the case with the remaining points, to exercise negative powers.

The defects which Randolph enumerated were not merely imagined, but clearly to be seen in the events arising out of the troublesome experiences of the post–Revolutionary, pre-1787 American states. Economic discontent was widespread and created a degree of economic chaos, in addition to all the other obstacles to genuine national autonomy for the former British colonies. The problems of the domestic economy were seriously aggravated by the confederation's highly disadvantageous position in the international economic order. Events emerging out of the economic situation quickly and vividly revealed a number of serious inadequacies in the prevailing political arrangements.

Economic disarray had been a prominent feature of the Revolutionary period. At the outbreak of the Revolutionary War, committees of citizens, with the blessings of the Congress and the states, had met to deal with problems of regulating the economy. By the late 1770s, official sanction of such meetings began to be withdrawn, but the committees continued to meet outside the governmental structure. They had sprung up "without legislative authorization to take action against monetary depreciation, engrossing, and profiteering, often relying on crude force and intimidation for enforcement." [12] The possible economic justifications for these private actions were not sufficient to offset their incompatibility with the political convictions of a nation which was soon to become openly dedicated to the rule of law and equal protection for individuals under that law.

There is a basis for arguing that the political situation created by economic discontent during the 1780s under the Articles was more serious than, in fact, was the economic situation. Gordon Wood maintains that "the complaints were far from imaginary. They were real, intensely real, rooted, however, not in poverty or in real deprivation but rather in prosperity and in the very unintended promises the Revolution seemed to be offering large numbers of Americans."[13] Shays's Rebellion of 1786 has become the symbol of the potentially grave political implications of economic dissatisfactions in America prior to the Constitution.

Shays's Rebellion was prompted by one of the most enduring and seemingly intractable economic controversies of the period before the Constitution, namely, the increased issue of paper currency. Debtors, including farmers, artisans, and laborers, saw that they had much to gain, at least in the short run, from an inflated currency which offered the promise of reducing the pressures of their existing debts. The Massachusetts legislature, controlled by the creditor coastal towns, refused to yield to demands for an increased issue of paper money. Instead, heavy taxes were levied to pay the war debt.

In the summer of 1786, Daniel Shays, accompanied by an army of two thousand men, forced the adjournment of the court at Springfield. Shays and his companions believed themselves to be acting in the service of liberty, but the notion of liberty which they purported to serve was every bit as economically self-interested as that which, according to Beard's argument, was the guiding force of the drafters of the Constitution. One of the participants in the rebellion is reported to have said to his fellow insurgents:

> My boys, you are going to fight for liberty. If you wish to know what liberty is, I will tell you. It is for every man to do what he pleases, to make other people do as you please to have them, and to keep folks from serving the devil.[14]

This statement of conviction goes far beyond the confines of any conflict between economic interests, between debtors and creditors, or between haves and have nots. Its political implications are vast. The concept of liberty which it expresses is considerably more compatible with Thomas Hobbes's state of nature than with even the most primitive and minimally organized civil society. Wherever one's social sympathies might lie with regard to the economic issue, there is no denying that the political issue was not confined to the clash of this or that economic interest, but instead involved the interest and welfare of the entire society.

Hamilton, during the period preceding the drafting of the Constitution, was one of the most vocal and vigorous advocates of an economic perspective on the issues of the time. Nonetheless, he saw the logical priority of settling those political problems which were aggravated by America's energetic economic pursuits. In his post–Convention efforts in behalf of the adoption of the newly drafted Constitution of 1787, Hamilton, in *Federalist* 6, discoursed at length on the fallacies which reside in the proposition that commercial republics are predisposed toward peace abroad and at home. He argued that the commercial nature of a society is insufficient to guarantee tranquility and stability. Rather, it merely substitutes the passion of a love of wealth for that of power or glory. The economic character of a society, in the absence of reliable and effective political arrangements, guarantees nothing. A society cannot rely upon its economic arrangements to promote its general welfare until it has first put its political house in order. It was Hamilton's support of an increased union among the states through enhanced federal authority that prompted his observations.

Hamilton continued in *Federalist* 7 through *Federalist* 9 to discuss the possible causes of internal war, and its high social costs. He cited "the competitions of commerce" as a "fruitful source of contention."[15] Commercially disadvantaged states would seek to share "in the advantages of their more fortunate neighbors," and each state "would pursue a system of commercial policy peculiar to itself."[16] Hamilton argued that the vigorous pursuit of commerce already typical of America virtually guaranteed economically produced disorder under existing political arrangements:

> The spirit of enterprise, which characterizes the commercial part of America, has left no occasion of displaying itself unimproved. It is not at all probable that this unbridled spirit would pay much respect to those regulations of trade by which particular States might endeavor to secure exclusive benefits to their own citizens. The infractions of these regulations, on one side, the efforts to prevent and repel them, on the other, would naturally lead to outrages, and these to reprisals and wars.[17]

Hamilton was soon to become the great promoter of commerce as the first Secretary of the Treasury under the Constitution of 1787. However, his arguments in the *Federalist Papers* suggest a belief that without the appropriate political framework, commerce was as much a potential threat to society as it was a potential benefit.

Economic difficulties of the period before the Constitution raised serious political difficulties as well. To insist that the members of the Constitutional Convention went to Philadelphia to deal with one set of problems to the exclusion of the other would be erroneous. To insist that the members of the Convention believed that politics were more important than economics probably would be equally unwise. To insist, however, that the men of the Convention believed that the settlement of political issues and the establishment of political arrangements took logical priority over shaping the economy is consistent with the evidence produced by the events of the Convention.

Government and the Economy at the Convention

It is often argued that the delegates who convened in Philadelphia to construct a plan of government brought with them an array of disaffections over the existing political arrangements but no real theory of government by which to redress those disaffections.[18] Since the question of what does or does not constitute a theory of government carries with it the potential for infinite dispute, the issue may never be satisfactorily resolved. However, even with the greatest possible deference to both sides of the argument, it is difficult to avoid the observation that the framers of the Constitution were endowed with a set of assumptions about the nature of man, of society, and of government, and that their conclusions about where the Articles of Confederation went wrong guided their deliberations much as a "theory of government" might have done. This assortment of intellectual paraphernalia left a great deal of latitude for dispute over the final nature of the documents they were producing, but the range of options they were willing to consider was clearly shaped by those assumptions, conclusions, and convictions.

The argument that the Founders had no real theory of economics is considerably more persuasive. While experience played no small part in their political understanding, it seems to have been at the very core of their economic understanding. The Convention debates failed to produce much in the way of economic theory; however, economic matters were on the agenda, and the debates surrounding them provide some insight into the notions about the relationship of government to the economy at the time of the founding.

By the time of the Constitutional Convention, economic thought worldwide was in a state of transition. Mercantilism, with its emphasis on the priority of the whole national economy over its components, and its passion for the accumulation of national wealth above all other considerations, was being vigorously assaulted by the steadily growing laissez faire school of economic thought, with its emphasis on the well-being of the individual economic actor as the key to the well-being of a national economy, and on the very minimal role of government in providing for that well-being. The publication in 1776 of *An Inquiry into the Nature and Causes of the Wealth of Nations* is traditionally considered to be the major battle in the assault on mercantilism.

This competition among economic theories was somewhat reinforced by the variety of economic experiences which Americans had undergone by 1787. Having begun their history in the role of subservient partners in a colonial economy, they soon came to experience the heavy strains of a war economy during the Revolution, followed by the attempt to settle into an independent national economy under the Articles of Confederation. The newly independent American states clearly had vast economic potentials, as well as a variety of already established economic strengths. The range and diversity of economic activity in the former colonies provided the basic ingredients for economic viability. The economy which began to take shape following the Revolution, however, appeared to lack an essential ingredient, namely, predictability.

The lack of economic stability and predictability was seen to stem from political factors, the most prominent being the ease with which temporary majorities could hold sway in the state legislatures. An excess of democracy under no obligation to exercise self-control was considered to be the source of majority excesses.[19] In the Constitutional Convention on June 6, during a consideration of the question of the basis of representation in the first branch of the legislature, Madison discoursed on the problems of temporary majorities and factions, and the instability resulting from a system of government which does not take into account the natural and inevitable rivalries in society. Madison cited the examples of Greece and Rome, in which "the rich and poor, the creditors and debtors, as well as the patricians and plebians alternately oppressed each other with equal unmercifulness."[20] It was not just class-based majorities which Madison feared, but majorities which can form around all the many potential divisions in society—economic, religious, social, and political. Economic majorities, however, had been particularly prominent in the years preceding the Convention. "Debtors have defrauded their creditors," Madison reminded his peers. "The landed interest has borne hard on the mercantile interest. The Holders of one species of property have thrown a disproportion of taxes on the holders of another species."[21] All this had been accomplished, according to Madison, through the power of law.

effects, was examined at some length in *Federalist* 62, which was addressed to a discussion of the composition of the Senate and the role it was to play in the overall scheme of the new government. Stability of policy was deemed to be an important consequence which could be expected to flow from the provisions for the second branch of the legislature; and stability of policy was argued to be a necessary requirement for the functioning of any economy. Without it, normal economic activity was impossible. "Law is defined to be a rule of action; but how can that be a rule, which is little known and less fixed?"[22]

The only beneficiaries of unstable policy are "the sagacious, the enterprising, and the moneyed few" who are given an immense advantage over the "industrious and uninformed mass of the people."

> Every new regulation concerning commerce or revenue, or in any manner affecting the value of the different species of property, presents a new harvest to those who watch the change, and can trace its consequences; a harvest, reared not by themselves, but by the toils and cares of the great body of their fellow-citizens. This is a state of things in which it may be said with some truth that laws are made for the *few*, not for the *many*.[23]

The argument proceeds to point out that actors in the economy become afraid to take risks, which are dramatically increased by the uncertainty of policy. Under such legal fluctuations, "no great improvement or laudable enterprise can go forward which requires the auspices of a steady system of national policy."[24]

In spite of the many arguments to the contrary, there is evidence that class conflict, in the contemporary sense of the term, was no more problematic for the drafters of the Constitution than other sources of conflict in society. A statement by Charles Pinckney of South Carolina during a debate in late June over the composition of the Senate portrays America, not as a rigidly stratified, class-oriented society, but rather as one with an unprecedented lack of class distinction:[25]

> The people of the U. States are perhaps the most singular of any we are acquainted with. Among them there are fewer distinctions of fortune & less of rank, than among the inhabitants of any other nation. Every freeman has a right to the same protection & security; and a very moderate share of property entitles them to the possession of all the honors and privileges the public can bestow: hence arises a greater equality, than is to be found among the people of any other country, and an equality which is likely to continue, because in a new Country, possessing immense tracts of uncultivated lands. . . there will be few poor, and few dependent.[26]

Later in the same address to the Convention, Pinckney suggested that the United States could be divided into three classes—professional men, commercial men, and those with landed interest. His use of the term *class* was not in the modern socio-economic sense, but rather more equivalent to our current notion of economic sectors or interests.

Hamilton, in a discussion of taxation in *Federalist* 35, uses the term *class* with similar intent: "The idea of an actual representation of all classes of the people by persons of each class is altogether visionary. . . [u]nless. . . each occupation should send one or more members."[27] Representation of all classes (that is, occupations) would indeed occur through the "natural representatives" of the various economic sectors—commerce, agriculture, and the professions.

It is perhaps difficult for the twentieth-century mind to think of diversity in society without immediately thinking of class conflict. However, there is reason to believe that class may have been a less complicated concept for the Founders than it is for our own time. They were certainly aware of class distinctions, and, indeed, they relied upon the existence of such distinctions as an important basis for the system of balanced government they were constructing. To have elements of the aristocracy in government was seen as a natural check on the excesses of democracy. This view, however, reached well beyond the simple confines of class interest; it derived from their understanding of the nature of society and the requirements of polity, as well as from their interpretation of the American experience under the Articles of Confederation.

Increased governmental stability was an important objective for the drafters of the Constitution, and increased economic stability was an important element of that objective. There seemed to be general agreement that the new federal government required enhanced powers in economic matters, but what was to be the extent of those powers and the ends to which they were to be exercised was not always clear, in either the wording of the Constitution or the debates which settled what that wording was to be. The potentially divisive nature of the issue of the relationship of the government to the economy very likely accounts for the difficulty of assessing intent.

One of the most visible and persistent controversies over the national government's economic powers centered on the debate over the magnitude of the vote required to pass commercial and navigation laws in Congress. The southern states, convinced that most such legislation would benefit the commercial northern states at their expense, argued vigorously in favor of requiring a two-thirds vote on all questions relating to commerce. The South particularly feared legislation requiring that American ships be employed for export trade. Since shipping was almost entirely a northern enterprise, the South would be left powerless to influence shipping rates.

Pinckney argued that "states pursue their own interests with less scruple than individuals. The power of regulating commerce was a pure concession on the part of the S[outhern] States. They did not need the protection of the N[orthern] States at present."[28] He went on to assert that it was the "true interest of the S[outhern] States to have no regulation of commerce." But given the losses which the eastern states had incurred from the Revolution, and their willingness to make concessions regarding the question of importing slaves, as well as the interest of the southern states in uniting with the strong eastern states, Pinckney thought it proper "that no fetters should be imposed on the power of making commercial regulations."

Pierce Butler, also of South Carolina, chose to vote against requiring a two-thirds vote, but, in so doing, he pointed out that permitting a majority to act on commercial matters was indeed a major concession on the part of the southern states, whose interests were as different from those of the eastern states "as the interests of Russia and Turkey."[29]

James Wilson of Pennsylvania, who also was opposed to the measure to require a two-thirds vote, observed that "if every peculiar interest was to be secured, *unanimity* ought to be required."[30] He maintained that a majority is no more likely to be motivated by interest than is a minority, and that surely it was better to frustrate a minority than to frustrate a majority. Furthermore, an important part of the deficiency of the Articles of Confederation had stemmed from the requirement of a two-thirds vote in certain cases.

Madison used a variation of his by now familiar multiple interests argument, in opposition to the measure. He first pointed to the institutional arrangements, including the independence of the Senate and the executive veto, to curb abuses of the commerce power. He then elaborated the complex pattern of interests which would help to offset the southern disadvantage. Connecticut and New

Jersey were agricultural. Furthermore, the increase in coastal trade and in the number of seamen would increase consumption of southern products. Any disadvantages to the South would be temporary, because migration of northern seamen to the South and increased southern shipping would quickly begin to equalize the disparity between the two sections of the country.

John Rutledge of South Carolina insisted that the Convention not focus on immediate interests, but instead on the future well-being of the nation:

> At the worst a navigation act could bear hard a little while only on the S[outhern] States. As we are laying the foundation for a great empire, we ought to take a permanent view of the subject and not look at the present moment only.[31]

Rutledge then reminded the delegates of the necessity of securing the West Indies trade, which would require a navigation act.

The two-thirds vote provision was not incorporated into the Constitution, but the issue did not die. Two weeks after the lengthy debate and the decision of the Convention to require only a majority vote on matters of commerce, George Mason of Virginia proposed a compromise which would have required a two-thirds vote until the year 1808;[32] but the compromise was also rejected.

Debate over the magnitude of the vote required to pass commercial legislation vividly illustrates the strong regional forces which vastly complicated the problem of drawing up guidelines for the relationship between the government and the economy, but it offered very little insight into the possible dimensions of that relationship. The debate over the taxing of exports also reflected local considerations, but at the same time it produced some indications of differing notions about the extent of governmental power over the economy.

Oliver Ellsworth of Connecticut argued that there were solid reasons why Congess should not be given the power to tax exports. First, he maintained, it would discourage industry just as taxes on imports discourage luxury. Secondly, such a tax could never be uniform because the products of the states were so various. In addition, the taxing of exports would engender incurable jealousies.[33]

Gouverneur Morris of Pennsylvania disagreed that the power should be withheld. He argued that local considerations should not impede the general interest. "The State of the Country also, will change," he added, "and render duties on exports, as skins, beaver & other peculiar raw materials, politic in the view of encouraging American Manufactures."[34]

Madison concurred with Morris's argument that "we ought to be governed by national and permanent views."[35] Although such a tax might not be expedient now, it might become so in the future: "A proper regulation of exports may & probably will be necessary hereafter, and for the same purposes as the regulation of imports; viz, for revenue—domestic manufactures—and procuring equitable regulations from other nations."[36]

Wilson also supported the power of the national government to tax exports, and he did so, according to his own estimation, against the interest of his state. To do otherwise would be to deny the national government half the power to regulate trade, and it was his opinion that it might be the more important half for obtaining beneficial treaties.[37] Wilson's colleague from Pennsylvania, Thomas FitzSimons, was opposed to taxing exports immediately, but in favor of granting the power when the proper time arrived. The power would be justified if America became a manufacturing country; and he pointed to the duties in Great Britain on wool.

Mason and Elbridge Gerry of Massachusetts opposed the power as vigorously as Morris, Madison, and Wilson had supported it. Gerry maintained that the power might be used by the national government to force the states to grant any new powers it might demand. "We have given it more power already than we know how will be exercised,"[38] he said. In a similar vein, Mason said that he could only support the power to tax exports "[i]f he were for reducing the States to mere corporations as seemed to be the tendency of some arguments."[39]

When Madison saw that Congress was about to be denied the power to tax exports, he proposed that a two-thirds vote in each house of Congress be required to lay such taxes. He considered this arrangement to be a lesser evil than to have no power to tax exports at all; but his attempted compromise failed, and Congress was denied this power by the Constitution.

Several notions about the potential relationship of the government to the economy emerged in this debate. Morris and Madison both emphasized the importance of future changes in the economic characteristics of the country and the need to provide Congress with adequate powers to accommodate to those changes. They both gave priority to the national or general interest over local economic interests; and both were willing to grant the government at least limited power to promote that interest. Gerry opposed this grant because it would further enhance the power of a government which he believed probably already possessed too much power and would therefore be an even greater danger to the states. Mason's similar argument was more firmly grounded in the immediate economic interests of the southern states.

When the Constitution was finished, Congress had been given the power "to regulate commerce with foreign nations, and among the several States, and with the Indian tribes;" but the meaning and extent of that power was far from being clear, and may not be fully so even today. A complex system of government had been established and many important political issues at least temporarily resolved. A degree of regularity and predictability for the economy had been achieved through congressional control over currency and the protection of contract, as well as through the increased prospect of governmental stability. But substantive statements on the question of the proper relationship of the government to the economy, and the development of American economic theories, were still to come.

Government and the Economy in the New Nation

With the Constitution ratified, the new government was put into operation in the spring of 1789. Its immediate task was to establish routine mechanisms and procedures for the conduct of day-to-day governing. The priority which had only two years earlier been given to questions of political principles and institutional safeguards quickly began to shift to substantive issues. During the early months of the new republic, the development of the economic infrastructure of the government received concentrated attention under the guidance of its treasurer, Alexander Hamilton.

Issues revolving around the substance of governmental action and the appropriate direction of particular policies activate special interests and arouse economic opponents to an extent that more general considerations of government do not. In questions of policy, as opposed to those of structure and procedure, it is easier to detect the potential benefits and costs which may accrue to one or another interest. What serves the general public interest, on the other hand, often becomes more obscure.

The economic policies promulgated by Hamilton quickly brought opposing interests into open conflict, and the vigorous style with which Hamilton pursued his program no doubt contributed to the intensity of the conflict. The fragile truce among competing economic interests, which facilitated the drafting of the Constitution and permitted the resolution of important political issues, was now abandoned. Men who earlier had appeared to be like-minded on the important issues of the day suddenly became visible antagonists. The important divisions which came to characterize the relationship between Hamilton and Madison were a particularly vivid illustration of the larger phenomenon. Although Madison and Hamilton had pronounced differences of opinion even as they stood on the same side of the issue of the Constitution, mutual adjustment and reciprocal tolerance, rather than conflict, had characterized their early relationship.

Hamilton's mercantilist economic program, as set forth in his Report on Public Credit in 1790 and his Report on Manufactures in 1791, drew a hard and fast line between the commercial interests of the North and the agricultural interests of the South, stimulating into open rivalry the divisions which had lurked beneath the surface of the debates on the Constitution:

> At the time the Constitution was made, Southern planters and Northern merchants were setting their differences aside in order to meet common dangers—from radicals within and more powerful nations without. After the Constitution was adopted, conflict between the ruling classes broke out anew, especially after powerful planters were offended by the favoritism of Hamilton's policies to Northern commercial interests.[40]

Hamilton's proposals for funding the national debt, for assuming the state debts, and for establishing a national bank combined to form an integrated economic program with a decisive direction. The clarity of Hamilton's plans, with their easily detected intent, forced a preoccupation with economic thought on the part of interested factions which had not seemed so urgent before.

Hamilton's justification of his program provided the basis for one body of thought on the appropriate relationship of the government to the economy, and the opposition to his program supplied another. These opposing views had been reflected in the Convention debates, but now they were being carefully articulated. The issue of the establishment of the Bank of the United States quickly became the rallying point for both sides, and it was to remain so for some time to come.

Hamilton and his Federalist cohorts envisioned a positive state, acting decisively to stimulate the economy by encouraging manufactures and promoting the well-being of commercial interests. He argued that this was the most direct route for achieving the economic well-being of the whole society. "He would employ the government to dispense favors to men of industry and commerce, and the resultant economic benefits, he supposed, would percolate down to the other groups in society."[41] The Bank was to become the key instrument to effect this plan.

Questions as to the practical meaning of the principle of limited government were now raised in a forceful and concrete way. This principle had been carefully and caringly built into the framework of the Constitution; but now its bearing on the actions of an operating government were brought into active consideration.

Opponents of the Hamiltonian economic program used the principle of limited government as an important basis of their opposition. Thomas Jefferson was to become the standardbearer of the economic counterresponse to the Hamiltonian design; and the principal arguments of this opposition regarding the scope of governmental action were to be gathered together under the label of *Jeffersonian democracy*.

The Jeffersonians believed government to be a necessary but altogether negative and—desirably—a minimal force in society. Governmental power was to be limited and restrained at every possible juncture. The people of the American democracy were capable of much self-reliance and should be encouraged in that direction. What was required in the way of governmental intrusion into society should originate at the level of state government to the maximum extent possible, because its proximity to the people made it more subject to control.[42]

Social and economic laissez faire were guiding precepts for the Jeffersonians. They believed that the economic prospects of the nation could only suffer from governmental involvement in the economy. Manufacturing, commerce, navigation, and agriculture would thrive if left to unhampered individual enterprise. Contrary to Hamilton's view, the Jeffersonians insisted that the well-being of the parts of the economy assured the well-being of the whole.[43]

Out of this early period of the new republic emerged two clear and distinct bodies of opinion on the question of the appropriate relationship of government to the economy. While the perspectives were taking shape the national government continued to operate and to gain in strength. Hamilton's programs succeeded in putting it on a sound financial footing and enabling it to direct the financial and economic concerns of the country.[44] In spite of the divergent interpretations of the meaning of limited government which arose during this period, a student of the twelve years of the Federalist era has observed that:

> At no time in his career did Hamilton attempt to violate the Constitution, nor has his interpretation of the powers granted the Federal government under that document been nullified by subsequent decisions of the Supreme Court of the United States.[45]

Those early years established a precedent for federal governmental involvement in the economy, at least as a promoter of economic development, if not yet as a serious regulator of that development. The several decades following the era of Federalist supremacy witnessed the strengthening of this precedent from still another quarter in the newly formed government—the Supreme Court.[46]

The Court, under the leadership of Chief Justice John Marshall from 1801 to 1835, expanded the scope of national power (*McCulloch* v. *Maryland*, 1819),[47] and laid the foundation for future economic regulation by government through a broad interpretation of the commerce clause (*Gibbons* v. *Ogden*, 1824);[48] however, national policy during this period did not appreciably exceed the level of involvement in the economy established earlier by Hamilton. While this level was low by contemporary standards, that of economic controversy during the period was not.

The body of economic thought which had characterized Jeffersonian democracy was largely shared by the advocates of Jacksonian democracy in the third and fourth decades of the new government's operation. The Jacksonians' disdain for monopoly and their willingness to have the government act to remove monopoly were not really incompatible with the notion of limited government. "It was a negative rather than a positive approach to the problem of the relationship of the state to business."[49]

The presidency of Andrew Jackson was confronted with serious economic problems and conflicts.[50] The agricultural South had become increasingly disturbed over the disadvantages which it suffered from a pro-commercial tariff policy. The arguments over the tariff issue were very similar to those which accompanied the debate in the Constitutional Convention over the requirement of a two-thirds vote on all commercial legislation. Furthermore, the existence of a national bank was again at issue.[51] The era of Jacksonian democracy witnessed major political realignments, but basic economic views on the relationship of the government to the economy were not substantially altered.

In the period from 1836 to the Civil War, the Supreme Court continued in the same basic vein as the Marshall Court. The Taney Court, however, was less inclined to restrict state actions in matters on which Congress failed to act, and state regulatory activity increased during this period.[52] By the time of the Civil War the federal government was displaying a tendency to intervene less, rather than more, in the economic sector.[53]

In the years immediately following the Civil War, the government was preoccupied with problems of reconstruction, which consumed most of the political energies of the time. While these years produced little economic activity on the part of the national government, major developments bearing upon the relationship of government to the economy were taking place in the economy itself. The important and rapid transformation of the United States into an industrial society was decisively under way, and the implications of this transformation for future views of the proper relationship of government to the economy were vast. The economic traditions descending from Hamilton and Jefferson would require a general revamping before they would be adequate to the tasks raised by the rapidly changing American society.

During the post–Civil War period, the states began to deal with a number of the problems which rapid industrialization was producing at an ever-increasing pace. Until the mid-1880s, the Supreme Court displayed a largely tolerant attitude toward the state police powers and the right of the states to regulate in behalf of the public good.[54] By the middle of the 1880s, however, the Court began to shift its now long-standing views on the government's authority to intervene in the economy, using a due process of law argument as its major restraining device.[55] The Court was supporting a view of limited government reminiscent of the earlier Jeffersonian economic view, but radically different in its foundations. Jeffersonianism had advanced its arguments in the interest of protecting social rights and liberties. The late nineteenth-century Court based its arguments on the rights of property and economic liberty. Both were doctrines of laissez faire, but they were undergirded by two very different rationales.

During this same period, the national government became involved in efforts at economic regulation, but with opposition from the Court. The Interstate Commerce Act of 1887, and the Interstate Commerce Commission thereby established, marked an important turning point in the relationship of the government to the economy. A new mechanism for exercising the power "to regulate commerce" had been developed, and, in spite of immediate opposition from the Court, it was a type of mechanism which was to become increasingly representative of the relationship of the government to the economy.

As industrialization continued, with both its economic and social repercussions being increasingly felt, questions of whether the national government had the power to intervene in the economy began to give way to questions of whether the national government *had the obligation* to intervene in the economy. The Progressives of the early twentieth century began to talk of the government's responsibilities toward the economy and against its evils. The Supreme Court continued to hold its stand against governmental intervention. World War I brought a halt to the momentum the Progressive point of view had gained, but it was soon to be revived, and increased several fold, following the crash of 1929.

President Franklin D. Roosevelt, with his plans for the New Deal, was willing to accept responsibility for intervention in the now debilitated economy; but the Court continued to resist until 1937. After that point, the welfare state, armed with an extensive array of economic regulations, was clearly under way. Following World War II, the Court became a less prominent actor in the relationship of the government to the economy—in some ways less prominent than it had ever been in its entire history—and began to concern itself more with problems of civil liberties; however, the virtual disappearance of the Court from involvement in this relationship in no way diminished the amount of government involvement in the economy. It continued to grow with the new social changes domestically and alterations in the international situation which followed the war.

The transition from concern regarding governmental power over the economy to concern over governmental responsibility toward the economy spans most of American history since the initiation of the new nation in 1789. Government is now held responsible for the level of employment, the rate of inflation, the increase in the gross national product, among other economic responsiblities; and it willingly accepts that role. Groups who wish to distinguish themselves as more "liberal" or more "conservative" than others, debate whether the government's responsibility for these matters implies that the government should directly intervene in the economy or should not intervene and just allow natural economic forces to correct a given situation; but neither group really challenges the government's responsibility in these matters.

The political system which the founders constructed remains essentially intact, having been only temporarily disrupted by the Civil War. The economic system, which they avoided constructing at the Constitutional Convention, has undergone manifold changes within the context of that political system.

In *Federalist* 34 Hamilton had emphasized that:

> We must bear in mind that we are not to confine our view to the present period, but to look forward to remote futurity. Constitutions of civil government are not to be framed upon a calculation of existing exigencies, but upon a combination of these with the probable exigencies of ages, according to the natural and tried course of human affairs. Nothing, therefore, can be more fallacious than to infer the extent of any power, proper to be lodged in the national government, from an estimate of its immediate necessities. There ought to be a capacity to provide for future contingencies as they may happen; and as these are illimitable in their nature, it is impossible safely to limit that capacity.[56]

To the extent that other drafters of the Constitution might have agreed with Hamilton that a government ought to be able to adapt its actions to changes in circumstance, they very well might have accepted the intimate relationship which has now developed between the government and the economy as being compatible with their intentions to construct an energetic, but stable and durable, system of government. If their consideration of the question had been conducted at the same high level as their deliberations at the Convention, they would probably wish to determine whether, with all the changes, the safeguards to liberty, personal and political, which they built into the system are still intact, or have at least evolved sufficiently to keep pace with these changes. While that is an interesting question as posed from the standpoint of the Founders, it is no less engaging from a contemporary standpoint.

Notes

1. An interesting argument on the political nature of the Constitutional Convention has been presented by John P. Roche in "The Founding Fathers: A Reform Caucus in Action," *American Political Science Review*, 55, no. 4 (Dec. 1961): 799-816. Roche vividly captures the political quality of the founding enterprise, but understates the importance of theoretical concerns in guiding the actions of the Convention. The concern of the Founders with practical political problems was clearly constrained by the set of assumptions they held about the nature of a democratic republic and the principles beyond the merely practical considerations required to build such a system.
2. *An Economic Interpretation of the Constitution of the United States* (New York: Macmillan, 1913).
3. Ibid, p. 151.
4. *The Federalist*, ed. Edward Mead Earle (New York: Random House, 1937), p. 4.
5. Ibid, p. 5.
6. Ibid, p. 232.
7. Ibid, p. 231.
8. Ibid, p. 232.
9. There have been several serious studies challenging the findings of Beard. Cf., for example, Robert Brown, *Charles Beard and the Constitution* (Princeton, N.J.: Princeton University Press, 1956), and Forrest McDonald, *We the People: The Economic Origins of the Constitution* (Chicago, 1963).
10. Max Farrand, ed., *The Records of the Federal Convention of 1787*, 4 vols. (New Haven, Conn.: Yale University Press, 1966), 1:18.
11. Ibid, 1:19.
12. Gordon S. Wood, *The Creation of the American Republic 1776-1787* (Chapel Hill: University of North Carolina, 1969), p. 324.
13. Ibid, p. 395.
14. Quoted in John D. Hicks, *The Federal Union*, 2d ed. (Cambridge:

Riverside Press, 1952), p. 179.
15. *The Federalist*, p. 37.
16. Ibid.
17. Ibid.
18. See Roche. The same argument is presented also by Vernon L. Parrington in *The Colonial Mind, 1620-1800* (New York: Harcourt, Brace and Company, 1954), pp. 283 ff. Something of a counter interpretation can be found in Wood, p. 615.
19. Wood, pp. 409-425.
20. Farrand, 1:135.
21. Ibid, 1:135-136.
22. *The Federalist*, p. 406.
23. Ibid.
24. Ibid, pp. 406-407.
25. For a provocative analysis indicating the lack of serious class distinction in America and assessing its implications for the development of American society, *see* Louis Hartz, *The Liberal Tradition in America* (New York: Harcourt, Brace and Company, 1955).
26. Farrand, 1:398.
27. *The Federalist*, p. 213.
28. Farrand, 2:449.
29. Ibid, 2:451.
30. Ibid.
31. Ibid, 2:452
32. Ibid, 2:631.
33. Ibid, 2:359-360.
34. Ibid, 2:360.
35. Ibid, 2:361.
36. Ibid.
37. Ibid, 2:362.
38. Ibid.
39. Ibid.
40. Richard Hofstadter, *The American Political Tradition* (New York: Vintage Books, 1948), p. 14.
41. Sidney Fine, *Laissez Faire and the General Welfare State* (Ann Arbor: University of Michigan Press, 1966), p. 15.
42. Hofstadter, pp. 18-44.
43. Fine, p. 13.
44. John C. Miller, *The Federalist Era, 1789-1801* (New York: Harper and Row, 1960), pp. 70-82.
45. Ibid, p. 82.
46. Merle Fainsod and Lincoln Gordon, *Government and the American Economy* (New York: W.W. Norton, 1941), p. 57.
47. 4 Wheaton 316 (1819).
48. 9 Wheaton 1 (1824).
49. Fine, p. 14.

50. Glyndon G. Van Deusen, *The Jacksonian Era, 1828-1848* (New York: Harper and Brothers, 1959), pp. 70-80.
51. Ibid, pp. 80-91.
52. Fainsod and Gordon, p. 58.
53. Fine, p. 19.
54. Fainsod and Gordon, p. 58.
55. Ibid, p. 59.
56. *The Federalist*, pp. 204-205.

[12]

A CALL FOR POLITICAL THEORY

—CHARLES S. HYNEMAN

I

The first essay in the series now known as *The Federalist* opened with the observation:

> It has been frequently remarked that it seems to have been reserved for the people of this country, by their conduct and example, to decide the important question, whether societies of men are really capable or not of establishing good government from reflection and choice, or whether they are forever destined to depend for their political constitutions on accident and force.

The answer to the question is now in. The Founding Fathers did establish governments, their creative acts were guided by reflection and choice, and two hundred years later the governments they created stand essentially in their original form.

A transition from colonial rule to statehood could have been accomplished without an act of establishment or other ambitious construction. Existing governments could have been fitted to the new political status by a succession of incremental changes unaccompanied by a range and a quality of thought worthy of the label comprehensive political theory. In opting to retain and retitle their colonial charters the people of Connecticut and Rhode Island proved that the continuance of existing forms, with occasional modifications of small import, was feasible. In choosing this course of action political leaders in these two states passed up a chance to be remembered for great feats of statescraft, but they did not remove themselves from involvement in the analytic and projective thought characteristic of the American scene in the last quarter of the eighteenth century. In Connecticut especially, political leaders, ministers, and other persons with active minds contributed importantly to the vigorous intellectual effort which brought to maturity, nationwide, a conception of the essential character and goals of republican government.

Dependence on incremental change was, of course, not confined to Connecticut and Rhode Island. In every one of the colonies then declaring itself to be a state certain aspects of political institutions or political processes that cried out for attention were ignored and let stand without change. That which could not be put off until later was given a "for-the-time-being" treatment, altered just enough to satisfy pressing demands; but, also, in eleven of the thirteen new states—plus Vermont, whose constitution of 1777 anticipated membership in the Union by fourteen years—imagination, far reaching vision, and boldness characterized the response to a need for change. Conventions, appointed by one means or another, drew up constitutions. In every case a new frame of government put officials formally under the control of the people; and in several cases a Declaration of Rights set forth a vision, a "theory," of the conditions of just government, the sovereignty of the people, the trusteeship of public officials, the rights of individuals, and the ends to be secured by government.

Reviewing the documents which they put into effect and the writings which argued what ought to be done or explained what had been done, one is struck by three lessons in the founding experience. Three things which the Founders believed, or which distinguish their method, challenge us to a profound reconsideration of these matters today. The men—and women, since Abigail Adams, Mercy Warren, and some others also may have had the audience their ability and good sense deserved—who dominated the constitution making process in 1776 and the years immediately following, believed that a constitution ought to be, and that theirs was, an act of the people. They also believed that the Constitution was a set of instructions addressed to all officials and instruments of government, binding on them when instructions are clear, and not subject to revision or restatement by any official or branch of the government. These were cardinal beliefs that gave character to the fundamental documents and the governments they established. A third lesson for us is to be found in a model which the Founders provided for all subsequent generations of Americans: their acts of creation were guided by an intellectual exploration; every important forward step in governmental design was preceded or accompanied by an incisive and comprehensive examination of the ends which government ought to secure, and of the dispositions of authority which offer most promise of realizing those ends.

I question whether any sizable or influential part of the American citizenry today believes that the Constitution of the United States, or the constitution of any state, is, in any effective sense, an act of the people; a document in which the people instruct their officials as to what they may and may not do, and describe procedures which must be adhered to in doing what government is permitted or required to do. That decisions and nondecisions, acts and failures to act, on the part of Congress, President, and judges have altered the relation of the United States Constitution to ongoing government is not likely to be disputed by anyone reasonably acquainted with our history. The point is proven by comparing today's view of certain constitutional provisions with the applications given to them a century ago—the division between the national and the state governments of the power to regulate commerce; the meaning to be read into the phrase *due process of law*; the applications given to the guarantees of the First Amendment; and the lifting of the *equal protection of the laws* clause from practical irrelevance to preeminence in fixing the bounds within which critical areas of public policy must be confined. It is not necessary to join in the marathon controversy as to whether the Constitution has lately been subverted by politicians and judges or whether the opposite is true: i.e., explicit constitutional language has too long been ignored or misread and only lately given its proper effect. It is sufficient to say that, if it is appropriate to put in a constitution the provision that Congress shall make no law prohibiting the free exercise of religion, a court announces a rule of constitutional magnitude when it holds that all state legislatures are subject to that same prohibition, even though the Constitution contains no express statement to that effect.

Evidence regarding judgments about "Whose Constitution Is It?"

and about the tendency and ability of politicians and judges to get out from under the Constitution and on top of it, runs in more than one direction. Even more slippery is the evidence which, properly evaluated, would put a measure on our response to the third lesson of the founding experience, namely, the need to challenge their assiduous inquiry and their wisdom in dealing with problems of constitutional gravity.

If, as I believe to be the case, constitutions have ceased to be regarded as emanating from the people, the road traveled in reaching that conclusion has not been paved by reasoning fit to stand beside the analysis and the argument that came out of unsophisticated communities in 1776. Said a petition drawn up in Pittsfield, Massachusetts a month before the Declaration of Independence was signed:

> We beg leave therefore to represent that we have always been persuaded that the people are the fountain of power.
>
> That since the dissolution of the power of Great Britain over these Colonies they have fallen into a state of Nature.
>
> That the first step to be taken by a people in such a state for the Enjoyment or Restoration of Civil Government amongst them, is the formation of a fundamental Constitution as the basis and ground work of Legislation.
>
> That the Approbation of the Majority of the people of this Constitution is absolutely necessary to give Life and being to it. That then and not 'till then is the foundation laid for Legislation. . . .
>
> That a Representative Body may form, but cannot impose said fundamental Constitution upon a people. They being but servants of the people cannot be greater than their Masters, and must be responsible to them. If this fundamental Constitution is above the whole Legislature, the Legislature cannot certainly make it, it must be the Approbation of the Majority which gives Life and being to it. [Oscar and Mary Handlin, eds., *The Popular Sources of Political Authority: Documents on the Massachusetts Constitution of 1780* (Cambridge: Harvard University Press, 1966), pp. 90-91.]

If I had seen a statement put into print since the year 1800 which rejected with equal force the conclusion of the Berkshire petitioners, I would cite it.

Serious efforts to evaluate the thought that has gone into changes of constitutional magnitude since the present Constitution went into effect are bound to end in sharp disagreement. In my judgment, the wide-ranging debate over states rights, nullification, and secession generated impressive reasoning to support each of the opposing conclusions that stood no chance of being reconciled. Some of the women who made the case for their enfranchisement must have brought to their cause a marriage of evidence and reasoning that John Adams or James Madison would have applauded. Certainly, rigor and subtlety went into some of the opinions in which judges sought to account for a decision which had turned a constitutional requirement in a new direction; but just as certainly many judicial and legislative acts of admitted constitutional importance have been severely attacked on the ground that they failed either to make irrelevant or to reduce the force of contentions which stubbornly resisted the change in question. I have not explored the subject myself or encountered a report by another person who has surveyed the thought mobilized either to support or to oppose the many changes of constitutional magnitude brought about by the several methods utilized. I will, however, venture some comments about intellectual preparation for a constitutional crisis which engulfs the American people right now.

II

Not since Congress completed the construction of the new government described in outline by the Constitution—the year 1800 is a convenient date— have the American people witnessed deliberate changes in government and in ways of governing as fundamental as the reassessment and revision now in full swing. The Civil War settled a question of transcendent importance—whether Americans would continue to be one nation with one government, or become two nations with two separate governments. That question being settled, the constitutional amendments and the legislation of the Reconstruction period did not alter the location of authority, the structure of government, and the provisions for control of government as significantly as do the changes we have undergone in the past twenty-five years and are all but certain to undergo in the quarter century immediately ahead.

The remarkable changes in basic provisions for government since World War II were brought about by constitutional amendments, acts of Congress, and decisions of the judiciary. Four amendments to the Constitution have lowered the minimum voting age to 18; put an end to the use of the poll tax (and any other type of tax, for that matter) as an instrument for keeping individuals and classes of people out of the voting booth; extended the right to vote for President and Vice-President to citizens living in the District of Columbia; limited the number of terms any person may hold the office of President; and made new rules for succession to office whenever a President or a Vice-President vacates his office or is found unable to discharge his duties. Changes of like significance have been made by legislation, the most notable being a series of statutes that enable Blacks and other ill-used elements of the population to enjoy the rights which the Constitution promises them. Less disturbing to the constitutional order which preceded it than the civil rights legislation but bound nevertheless to have profound consequences for effective popular control of government, is the recent legislation which opens the federal treasury to the campaign expenses of candidates for President and Congress. Judges have been in the business of making changes of constitutional significance with respect also to the allocation of seats in legislative bodies, the acceleration of racial integration, and the imposition on governmental authorities of standards for equal treatment of individuals, all of which are certain to have consequences far beyond the horizons of present foresight. Right now the federal judiciary appears to be bent on removing from state constitutions and state laws regarding suffrage all residence requirements designed to guarantee some familiarity with local political conditions, letting stand only the short-time requirement considered necessary for getting the newcomer registered.

The swirl of events in which we are caught up today makes it impossible to doubt that we are in the midst of a period of profound constitutional change—and not at the end of it. The electoral college arrangement for choosing presidents is under attack and bound either to be altered or replaced by direct popular election of the President and the Vice-President. Nominating conventions are in the course of being made more representative, and further steps to that end will be taken in both parties if an impulse for more immediate popular participation does not terminate their existence. There also is sentiment in favor of giving the people power to name the party candidates in the summer of an election year and then make a choice between them in the fall. If we go over to nomination by direct primary, the vote might be taken under any of several different arrangments now being discussed. Regardless, however, of whether we have one nationwide primary election or several regional ones, whether all adherents of a party vote on the same day or on different days, no matter how we manage the voting, the popular selection of candidates for the presidency is bound to alter the circumstances under which men and women conclude they can make their way to the nation's highest offices. It is bound to have an effect upon the emergence and survival of new political parties, and to alter the needs for political leadership, the structure of leadership within and outside of political parties, and the prospects that the gifts of leadership will be accepted when offered.

These illustrations of major reforms likely to be realized in the very near future are aspects of a campaign on a broad front to improve the democratic character of our political system. Changes fundamental enough to be called constitutional revision may be pending in other sectors. It is not necessary to speculate about the prospects. The drive for a comprehensive revision of the electoral-representative apparatus, however, is enough to support several observations about the intellectual address accompanying the campaigns for reform.

III

The model which challenges those who seek to revise constitutions today—and, if it be not rejected for sufficient reason, ought to discipline their behavior—lies in the preparation which the first generation of constitution makers brought to their task. They had made a thorough study of their condition, their needs, and the choices open to them. Included were more than a few men who had an impressive knowledge of Europe's experience with different forms of government. The values which ought to be secured and advanced by government for free men had been identified and put in orderly relation to one another. They had thought deeply about alternative instruments for achieving the goals they were determined to attain. Wherever there was theory that could guide them, they had found it and studied it. All this we can deduce from the meagre records of their debates, the sermons of politically-minded ministers, the speeches of political leaders, and the books or lesser essays put into print during the founding period.

The Founding Fathers left a rich legacy of literature which not only reveals how they perceived and analyzed their problems but also is highly educative for us when we contemplate the problems of our day. It would be an error to say that more than a small part of the most interesting writing of that period deserves to be called political theory—if the term theory is reserved for statements combining a number of propositions which, collectively, are thought to have predictive value. Theory becomes a guide for action to those who assume that the propositions involved rest on warranted interpretations of reality and who also are convinced by the reasoning which seeks to project actual experience into areas not yet traversed. John Adams published much analysis and argument that met this test for theory; and the scope of his attention, the keenness of his observations, and his penetrating analysis make it theory of very high quality. *The Federalist* is better known. Without question some of those essays deserve their reputation as political theory of lasting value.

The Federalist and much of John Adams's most valuable writing appeared after the critical steps in constructing republican government had been taken. These masterworks of reasoning were designed principally to explain and to justify decisions which had already been made rather than to influence decisions that must be made in the future. An explanation of opinions held and a justification of positions previously taken appear to be the main purposes back of most of the writing of the early period which impresses one as being interesting today.

The occasion for presenting masterpieces of political theory in the formative period is not central to the argument of this chapter. Critical to the argument, however, is the contention that theory is a necessary guide to action, and that a want of theory forces a resort to guesswork in designing institutions to cope with complicated social problems. The Founders of republican government did not write much political theory, but there were abundant amounts of it in their heads. No doubt there is comprehensive and "hard-bitten" theory in the minds of many of the men and women who are engaged in the fundamental reforms now in process. There are enormous gains to be realized if the theory is precisely stated and made available to others before they are required to act, being subjected meanwhile to the criticism which refines any elaborate thought. The raison d'etre of this chapter is a conviction that an impressive body of theory has not been brought to fruition in America, despite the admirable first strides of the Founders and the occasional appearance of a public address, a speech in Congress, a judicial opinion, or an academic essay of great force. Acknowledging that a citation of things undone affords no measure of work already accomplished, I will note certain problems which recently were disposed of in cursory fashion or are now the subject of debate that shows little promise of being illuminated by hard-reasoned theory. Three examples will be drawn from the comprehensive revision of the electoral-representative apparatus that is now in full swing.

The first example of a theoretic wasteland is exposed by our cursory decision making with reference to the domicile of college students for purposes of voting. In several states, college students, provided they are citizens of the United States and eighteen years old, may vote in a college community, even though for all other purposes they retain a domicile where their parents live, go home in the summers, and have no intention of remaining where they go to school after graduation, or less celebrated exit. This is a new rule of practice, in most places inaugurated not more than fifteen years ago and accomplished principally, it seems, by new interpretations of long-existing voting laws. The innovation appears to have been embraced without public evidence that anyone had made a serious effort to find out what disabilities the students were suffering from and to figure out what remedy would most justly fit their needs. Of a certainty it was incorporated into the suffrage regulations without considering the precept of the Founding Fathers that a right to vote ought to rest upon "sufficient evidence of a permanent common interest with and attachment to the community."

Where a student casts his or her vote for President does not matter very much; and, while a question of principle is involved, it probably does not make much practical difference if young persons who are temporarily in a given electoral jurisdiction vote for the local governor, other state officials, and members of the two houses of Congress. It does, however, make a very great difference in many places if college students participate in the selection of city and county officials.

The young person who spends only nine months out of twelve in a college town and expects to terminate that intermittent residence after four years does have a vital interest in many aspects of local government—traffic rules, police protection, health and sanitary regulations, and so on. On most of these matters there may be no serious conflict between the interests of students and those of permanent residents. Where there is a serious conflict, however, the interests of four-year, part-time residents ought to be weighed carefully against the interests of those residents who expect to remain indefinitely in the community. Many student voters will have departed before the officials they helped elect can convert their campaign promises into effective policies. Government that suits the fancy of young persons has then to be paid for; and even if we devise taxes that require four-year, part-time youthful residents to pay their fair share of the costs, few of them will be around to help pay off the indebtedness incurred by the officials they helped put into office.

Everything so far said about the hazards of student voting is applicable also to the highly mobile population that moves into and out of our cities, their periods of residence limited to a few months or a few years; but the conditions and considerations cited apply to these two situations with greatly different consequences. In the ordinary city transient voters are not bunched together in one age class; they do not live in close association with one another; they cannot easily convene, caucus, and organize for the adoption of a platform and the support of a slate of candidates; and their numbers with relation to the total population are not comparable to those of a student body in relation to college and university communities. There is no prospect that transient residents will dominate the election of local officials in any of our large and middle-sized cities; on the other hand, there is genuine apprehension that part-time and short-term residents will dominate local elections in many communities where large universities are located.

The Founding Fathers reiterated again and again that the right to vote should be restricted to persons having a clearly evident common interest with, and attachment to, the community. They were less explicit about a rule of equality in conferring the right to vote on citizens; but later generations of Americans gave the aphorism "one-man, one-vote" all but universal application. Since no one questioned the right of the college student to vote somewhere, since the only question was how much choice he might have as to where to vote, there could be no argument that an equality principle overruled the "common-interest, community-attachment" principle. We simply ignored the principle which the Founders thought was of first level importance. No student leader, no political science professor, no constitutional lawyer identified the relevant considerations, put them side by side and balanced them out. The extension of an option to students was merely a response to a slogan, a cliché. It was not a response to the force of reason.

The pertinence and the gravity of this experience increase when it is observed that, so far, no more eager reach for theory has marked the crusade to reduce residence requirements for all voters to the minimum necessary for registration.

A second example of inattention to guiding principles involves the right of any citizen to intervene in the election of officials for whom he has no right to vote. In the elections of federal officials every qualified voter is entitled to cast a vote for a President (and a Vice-President), two United States senators, and one member of the lower house of Congress. He is allowed to enlarge his influence upon the outcome of any such election by working for a candidate, contributing money for use in the campaign, and so on. The rightfulness of increasing one's influence by monetary gifts is at the bottom of the current debate about how to regulate campaign contributions and campaign expenditures. There may be ample support for a contention that systematic political theory has not made a noticeable impact on any aspect of that debate, but the claim of the citizen to augment his vote by putting other resources behind the candidate he voted for is not at issue in this second example. The new campaign legislation allows any citizen to contribute $25,000 to candidates standing for federal offices, provided that not more than $1,000 be given to any one candidate. The statute thus, by clear implication, acknowledges a citizen's right to distribute $22,000 among candidates he cannot vote for (more than that if the office of senator is not being filled).

The long prevailing rule has been that political boundary lines impose no restraint on the investment of resources in political campaigns. If money from New York saves a candidate in Nebraska from a defeat he was about to concede, must we not conclude that certain residents of New York are "quasi-voters" in Nebraska? Quasi-voting in this fashion is not confined to rich men. Money collected through labor organizations is spent not where it is raised but where it is needed to assure the selection of candidates friendly to labor. Some of it goes to aid candidates in congressional districts where the resident workers are sharply divided in their estimates of the contending candidates. Aid in the form of personal services has the same consequences as gifts of money. The movie star or other celebrity who goes outside his own political jurisdiction to attract voters to a political speech they otherwise would not listen to, is trying to secure the election of a candidate he has no right to vote for. If his presence, his personality, his remarks produce some votes for the favored candidate, may we not say that the celebrity is a voter at home, a quasi-voter abroad, and a defector from the one-man, one-vote rule to which we universally pay tribute? If this is a necessary conclusion for the crowd-drawing celebrity, it is a necessary conclusion also for all other persons who successfully aid a candidate for whom they are not permitted to vote.

An extraordinary attachment to equality in the voting act has been thoroughly demonstrated by the judges of the Supreme Court in their insistence that the districts where a member of a legislative assembly is selected shall be as near equal in population as can be arranged. There is no reason to doubt that the same devotion to equal voting power marks many members of the present and recent Congresses. A commitment to principle which makes the shattering of communities a fair price for equality in the voting booth ought to generate considerable concern when citizens who have been carefully excluded from an electorate inject themselves into a contest by a strategic placement of resources. The debates in Congress do not indicate that the relation of campaign gifts to the rule of equal numbers excited even an elevation of eyebrows when the most recent revisions of campaign legislation were under consideration.

My third example is drawn from events still fresh in mind, where the nation suffered shameful embarrassment if not crippling injury because conflicts of values were not recognized and the consequences of acts outside the ordinary bounds of behavior were miscalculated. I shall confine my remarks to a part of that complex of events and label it *organized protest and resistance.* Though the unpleasantness spread over a longer period of time, it will, for convenience, be referred to as a phenomenon of the 1960s.

Public thinking was confused by the extortions of the sixties because there was a natural desire on the part of discontented persons to win legitimacy for novel demands by associating them with other demands already recognized as just, and to paste on disputed causes labels that called to mind other causes which enjoyed widespread sympathy. Thus the term *conscientious objection*, referring to what early in our history excused from military service a man whose religion forbade him to bear arms, came to cover also the case of philosophic pacifism and, later, to include refusal to serve in the Vietnam war on such grounds as the assumed unjustness of that particular war, its apparent futility, the lack of an official declaration of war, or the fact that the objector's sympathy was with the population he was asked to fight. In similar fashion public approval of extraordinary activities resorted to by Blacks invited fraudulent claims that the grievances of other parts of the population arose out of injustices no different than those suffered by Blacks.

The nature of rule by law requires exceptions to the rules which are announced. Those who are authorized to make the exceptions will not always recognize that the time for making an exception has come, and some prompting by the citizen is thus appropriate. In the government of a large population, laws of which a majority approve may seem intolerable to some element of the population. The majority ought not to have its way simply because this is what it decided to do. Delay, bargaining, and compromise are intrinsic elements of the legislative process. The resolution of a dispute agreed to in legislative chambers may prove totally inadequate when the views of all the people are made clear by their reactions to a law. Complaint, "foot dragging," and refusal to comply are seen as essential to the legislative process when one includes in his view the original enactment, the amendment of statutes, discretion in the enforcement of law, and the expiration of a law by nonenforcement. The question is: Under what circumstances, for what reasons, by what means, and in what degree may individuals and groups refuse to obey a law and seek to keep it from being enforced upon them and others?

Any path one pursues into this tangle of unresolved questions runs into fine distinctions and narrow margins between good and evil. Blacks went to the streets to induce whites to admit them to the electoral process. It was a just demand; and the exaction of a considerable price in irritation, inconvenience, and economic loss could be defended on the ground that a man who is not allowed to put his hand on the ballot cannot use the ballot to obtain the right to have it put in his hand. When, however, is a citizen admitted to the electoral process? If it proves to be the case that whites will not listen to Blacks in party councils, and will not vote for them if they run for nomination in primary elections, but will consistently outvote them when a few Blacks do make their way into legislative bodies; if all these ifs are resolved against the Blacks, have they been admitted to the electoral process or are they still outside trying to get in? If one holds that he is not admitted until he can win a fair share of victories, then is the farmer excluded from the electoral process if he lives in a state where urban dwellers vastly outnumber farmers and no one is forming coalitions for which he thinks the votes of farmers will be helpful? If, also, you conclude that all consistent losers are thus proven to be excluded from the processes of decision making, what prices are you going to allow them to exact in order to force the rest of the population to treat them as equals?

In the first angry months of opposition to the Vietnam war the attacks on American military intervention were buttressed by the charge that the President and other high officials withheld information essential for debate and persuasion; that they distorted the information which they did disclose; and that they stifled complaint with false references to national security. These allegations lent credence to an assertion that if the American people knew what was going on they would repudiate the policy of the government and pull the troops out of Asia. These allegations also won recruits for a campaign of protest and resistance which sought to hinder and weaken the military operations of the government. In the course of time, and not a long time at that, the Senate conducted hearings, the press published fact and opinion unfavorable to the war, congressmen got into the debate, and the pollsters reported the impact of the new flow of information on the mind of the public. It appeared that there was no solid majority against the war at all; indeed that there was good ground for conceding that a majority of the people actually favored getting on with the war and getting it over with.

The rationale for demanding an end to the war changed accordingly. It became sufficient at first to assert that the war was grossly immoral; that it was futile; and that it was not in the interest of the United States even if it could have been won; and then it was contended that those who recognized the evil character of the war had a duty to refuse to serve in it and also a right to obstruct its conduct, regardless of the authority of the United States Government and the wishes of a majority of the American people. The position taken by a number of persons recognized as leaders of the antiwar movement was summed up in an assertion which I offer in language more restrained than was sometimes heard: "Those members of the society who maintain the highest moral standards must be permitted to decide for the nation whether and when it shall go to war."

If objection to a war on moral grounds is proof that one has the highest of moral standards, then it follows that those who oppose the war (even if they be few in number) always will make the decision and always decide unanimously that there will be no war. If possession of the highest morality is to be determined by other proofs, then we face the task of establishing tests which define a special electorate. Then come the questions of how the decision will be made. If members of the special electorate differ in their preview of a war proposed or in their evaluation of a war in progress, will they vote as equals, and will a majority carry the decision? If a majority of this moral elite approves a war, believing it to be just, must those who voted that the war was immoral respect the judgment of the majority? Or does the logic of an argument for decision by the "most moral" tell us that the special electorate was not correctly defined and that the rightness of the war will go undetermined until it is proven that those who have "the most morals" have also got the most votes?

Displays of force dominated the American political scene in the 1960s, and cerebral activity didn't get much of a chance. Back of the demonstrations, the studied insults, and the flights of missiles, nevertheless, were questions of enduring importance. When dispassionate debate was able to make itself heard in those days it did not bring much illumination to the age-old questions: What courses of action ought to be available to a passionate minority bent on convincing a majority that one of its policies is not acceptable? And, after what amount of delay and disturbance of the peace may the majority say: "The decision is final; from now on obstruction is not protest, but defiance?"

The intellectual address which political leaders brought to the establishment of republican government two hundred years ago provides a standard against which we may measure the statesmanship of a later day. The worth of that model will not be disputed. Is it not possible that the Founders provided us with another model of comparable value, namely, the breadth and the boldness that controlled their construction of a new style of government? Their readiness to combine distant vision with penetrating inquiry may have been quickened by a realization that they were building anew, not merely fixing up a bit of machinery that, if necessary, could continue to operate without benefit of repair.

Revision of fundamental law by an incremental process does not encourage diligent search for the interrelationships of values which set limits to the pursuit of any end. Congressmen who keep an ear tuned to constituents seeking advice on how to do business in Washington and who respond to legitimate demands for friendly intervention when bureaucrats do not move, stand little chance of making the intellectual inquiry that ought to precede decisions of constitutional significance. The judicial process operates under rules which restrict the parties to a debate, cramp the flow of relevant evidence and prudential judgment, and focus the attention of judges on particular aspects of a problem at the risk of diverting attention from interconnected and equally important matters that are not under scrutiny. It is timely to consider whether the revision of the electoral-representative process which congressmen, state legislators, and judges have brought about in the past few decades would have been better accomplished by a constitutional convention charged solely with obtaining a more equitable and more effective popular control of government. It is also timely for students of political history to consider whether a more ample body of theory might not be available to guide constitutional revision today if conventions had been assembled to deal with problems that "rattled the teeth" of the nation at certain previous stages of our history.

[13]

THE FUTURE OF AMERICAN DEMOCRACY

—SCARLETT G. GRAHAM
AND GEORGE J. GRAHAM, Jr.

It is altogether too easy to assume a favorable attitude toward a polity that has operated as successfully as the American one. The Constitution has withstood tremendous strains for two centuries without the prospect of major revision unless contemporary social, economic, and political forces combine differently in the immediate future than they have in the past; but this strongest of laissez-faire nations entered its bicentennial years under a dark economic shadow that covered as well the bicentennial of Adam Smith's publication of *An Inquiry into the Nature and Causes of the Wealth of Nations*. The general malaise of the economy makes a favorable prognosis more difficult when the potential for a political revision generated by social and economic conditions and public disaffection are considered. Competing social and economic theories have emerged, some of which are incompatible with and even challenge the founding principles of American democracy; and there is a less widespread response to these challenges in thought and argument. In this context the real trial of American democracy is occurring. Add to these the postmaterialist movements of the 1960s, the distrust of government generated by public reaction to Watergate, the difficulties of controlling inflation coupled with increasing concern for "full employment," talk of an inevitable crisis in the social security system, and the ordeal of adjustment may seem as critical today as it must have seemed in the 1776-89 period.

The Search for Political Discourse

The greatest impediment to the realization of our high hopes for maintaining the long-standing agreements of the founding era is the fact that political discussion has fallen prey to expediency and political pressure. News comes often, almost instantly, through contemporary media, but it is seldom complete enough to permit even a cursory evaluation of public issues. Where are these issues debated? In Congress, with its nearly 30,000 measures introduced in the 1969 and 1970 sessions?[1] In congressional committees, where testimony is often balanced between opposing factional interests, each of which has a stake in the outcome? In presidential budget policies or veto messages concise enough for the evening news? In federal agencies filled with representatives of the industries to be controlled? In a Congress that cannot come to sufficient agreement to pass the nation's budget? These are clearly not promising arenas for serious political discussion as they now function.

In earlier times it was not unusual for political discourse within Congress to provide printed materials for discussion in remote congressional districts across the nation. Rhetoric, one of the great medieval liberal arts, provided the keystone of early American political education, and political discourse was the arch it supported. As John Quincy Adams said from his position as the first Boylston Professor of Rhetoric at Harvard University:

> Under governments purely Republican where every citizen has a deep interest in the affairs of the nation, and, in some form of public assembly or other, has the means and opportunity of delivering his opinions, and of communicating his sentiments by speech; where government itself has no arms but those of persuasion; where prejudice has not acquired an uncontrolled ascendence, and faction is yet confined within the barrier of peace; the voice of eloquence will not be heard in vain.[2]

The role of leadership was seen as the mechanism for continuous public deliberation over, and education in, the major issues facing society.

The relation between the public and political leaders was originally based on representatives viewed as responsible; the public expected leaders to lead, limited only by the internal norms and values that carried public support. Though democratic control served as a popular check on the actions of leaders, the electorate did not see the vote merely as a weapon of accountability to be used against any representative who felt that the general interest required the responsible act of sacrificing selfish constituency interest. Much as Edmund Burke informed his Bristol constituency that the public good held precedence over their particular interest, the representative was expected to act responsibly and to inform his constituency.

James Madison argued the point in *Federalist* 63:

> As the cool and deliberate sense of the community ought, in all government, and actually will, in all free government, ultimately prevail over the view of its rulers; so there are particular moments in public affairs when the people, stimulated by some irregular passion, or some illicit advantage, or misled by the artful misrepresentations of interested men, may call for the measures which they themselves will afterwards be the most ready to lament and condemn. In these critical moments, how salutary will be the interference of some temperate and respectable body of citizens, in order to check the misguided career, and to suspend the blow mediated by the people against their authority over the public mind.[3]

The roles of political leaders and institutions—here Madison speaks of the Senate—include publicly recognizing the limits in responding to public concerns by weighing the general interest against private wants. But the language employed by Madison is seemingly archaic: "sense of community," "temperate," "justice," "truth," and "public mind" are ideas that have become empty or alien in current political discourse. Abstract rights and individual entitlements, the language of special-interest requests to government, are no longer balanced in political discussions against shared conceptions of community, justice, and temperance. If deliberation is the proper contrast with interest-group liberalism, common conceptions of purpose and meaning must be developed in the discussions of candidates and elected officials in order to balance the universal claims to entitlement.

Deliberation, or political discussion in general, is possible only where there are *or can be* found common values, shared assumptions, and common interests—the foundation for a notion of public. To move privatized interest claims on government toward political deliberation on proper actions of government, someone must appeal to or, in some cases, develop common grounds for discourse. Once these grounds are attended to by articulate leaders, it is possible to imagine public policy evaluation based on ethical concerns and serious pursuit of the best policy through deliberative rhetoric. But someone must first lead toward this shore, someone must take on the obligation of responsible leadership and thereby redirect our institutional discourse toward public rather than private interests.

If the arena for the deliberation of public issues is difficult to isolate, it is even more difficult to find a meaningful theoretical foundation for modern democracy. Contemporary theories seem to be of two varieties. One arises out of ideological discourse based on unquestioned—and usually abstract—presuppositions that lead to specific policies; the other emerges in the search for objective, scientific explanations of how democracies function. Each variety possesses an ethereal quality when contrasted with the political understanding to be found in the works so central to the backgrounds of the Founders and their deliberations.

Locke, Montesquieu, the more influential historians, and even such legal theorists as Coke and Blackstone brought to their work a perspective of human frailty and human potential as reflected in the experiences of the great nations (and in those of the states ruled by tyrants), as well as in other historical tendencies also well known to those who were forging a new nation. Political and social philosophy can be treated abstractly without any need to consider human participants, as can be seen in the works of two widely read contemporaries—John Rawls and Robert Nozick.[4] A consideration of individualism or of equality, viewed as a linguistic or logical problem, can help to create political demands and keep them before the public, but not to develop and maintain policies for a real world in which individuals with differing conceptions of freedom and dignity live together and work side by side. Democratic theory can also be treated at the behavioral level, *democracy* being explained by way of social and economic prerequisites, without a need to consider the humanly significant reasons for wishing it to survive.

Although American universities have assumed an ever-increasing role in articulating appropriate public policies, and although they have moved more and more toward a new focus on action, it would be difficult to say where in the universities serious thought about political institutions and arrangements and about the justification of appropriate political and social goals takes place. Indeed, many social scientists and historians not only do not attempt any justifications of this sort but argue that such analysis is not legitimate or even possible. The movements of the 1960s stimulated groups of serious scholars to question the value-free stance of social scientists and historians, but the evidence today indicates that few groups have gone beyond the ideological assumptions that guided their challenges to scholarly neutrality.

To be sure, political magazines and journals flourish; but each tends to attract contributors and readers so closely related to a *specific* political philosophy or point of view that one can characterize the individuals involved by the subscriptions they take or the periodicals they write for. Valuable as such publications are as an indication of serious political discourse, they constitute little more than private voices, since they do not "speak" to each other.

This admittedly overdrawn picture should give everyone pause and force him or her to ponder the problem of political discourse in a contemporary democracy. Though the value of freedom of speech commands near unanimity of support among Americans, the mechanisms for its practice—indeed, even knowing how to consider the options involved—are so difficult to identify in a twentieth-century context that one wonders how a constitutional debate could be pursued if needed. Political discourse has become linked so much to the immediacies of social and economic pressures that most references to political rights and duties have less to do with the public interest than with the symbols of specific social and economic interests. Do Americans speak the same political language today? Do they share a commitment to the principles upon which American democracy was founded? We began this assessment of the founding principles of American government by recognizing the importance of the Founders' having undertaken the responsibilities of their enterprise. Now we must ask: What possibility is there for Americans to "refound" their political institutions, should that become necessary?

Is "Refounding" Possible?

Though serious discourse on basic political principles and on the character of American political institutions is seldom heard today, there certainly is evidence that many serious-minded individuals concern themselves publicly with important problems. Recently, there has been evidence that an individual or group can generate considerable attention to such broad public issues as auto safety, pollution, and the environment and exert a not inconsequential influence on and within public institutions regarding them. Though economic realities have clearly influenced the success or failure of such movements, the evidence clearly indicates that the public *can* become concerned with public issues. Moreover, Ronald Reagan has demonstrated during his Presidency that the media can be used to bring public pressure to bear as a counterbalance to interest-group influence in Congress.

Independent of the breadth of public debate over reapportionment, most of which occurred ex post facto, the Supreme Court decision in *Baker* v. *Carr* (1964) did permit the adjudication of the issue in question; however, the young lawyers who instigated, developed, and presented the case had to have sufficient energy to withstand long years of work in the courts. Though not able to debate reapportionment openly in the Tennessee legislature, they mustered the legal expertise and political arguments necessary to win; yet public political discussion meanwhile faltered, since even the "interested" parties were willing to ignore the issue for reasons of expediency.[5] They won a battle, stimulated by political principles, but the battle was forced into the courts because political leaders refused to face the problem of representation. If state legislatures believe that the one-man, one-vote criterion for determining representation is too narrow to take into account the representation of regional and other limited interests within a state—as many legislators argued after the decision—one must meditate over their failure to discharge the obligations prescribed for representatives in the state constitution that forced the question into the judiciary. In any case, though the appropriate forums did not develop and the debate was forced into the nonpolitical arena, the action of the young lawyers gives evidence of the survival of a serious commitment to political principles. Though languishing in party and university debates, this commitment is alive elsewhere.

Frequently, the paucity of political discussion in the media, and the results of surveys indicating that many citizens do not even know the names of their representatives in various levels of government, lead one to the conclusion that the public is uninformed about politics, that it is politically ignorant. In some ways we are confronted with an impossible dilemma: The public ought to rule, but its members are incompetent to rule. Social scientists have been known to debate whether the impact of these findings constitutes evidence that the full participation of a public is dangerous because it would lead to governmental instability or that the American system has been designed to maintain an elitist control over the public. Independent of these suppositions, neither of which reflects a serious attention to the principles and intentions of the Founders or to the political history of the nation, the facts do not answer to the questions entailed in the dilemma. Even Thomas Paine, whose commitment to democracy and to the right of a revolution for each generation was unrivaled as a theorist, believed that democracy should involve representatives. What was important to democratic control was the commitment of these representatives to their constituents. Statesmen who would devote their energies to politics were to be selected as leaders, with the double task of following public wishes and generating just resolutions to problems. The public need not know all the facts being brought out in a debate in order to weigh the deliberations; indeed, Montesquieu once argued that the strength of a republic is greatest when the names of its leaders are unknown. Estimates of the possibility of a public consideration of political principles and institutions cannot be based merely on the level of public information.

A survey of Americans recently indicated that the public's confidence in its leaders, including political ones, had fallen far below 50 percent.[6] The only organization or institution able to muster a majority in confidence ratings were those of citizens' groups.

Given the nature of public opinion, the figures from polls can be expected to fluctuate; but the point here is the relative trust of fellow citizens, in spite of serious doubts about the government and about specific leaders. What is more, interest in the discussion of basic notions of democracy is not alien to the average American. Though political information is limited, it is not hard to imagine that if the present long-range adjustment of the American economy and the financial crises of our urban governments continue, serious public discussion of the basic purposes of government will be stimulated. Given at least this possibility of an interested public if the American system turns out to require fundamental revision, the necessity of a "refounding" becomes an issue to consider.

Out of the difficult constitutional crisis during which serious impeachment proceedings against President Nixon were begun comes additional evidence that "refounding" is possible. National attention was focused on reasoned debate in the House Judiciary Committee as it assessed and voted Articles of Impeachment against a President. The gravity of the situation tested the depth of thought on government on the part of these members of the House of Representatives and found these congressmen capable of overcoming immediacies in their thought. After reflecting on their realization of the importance of the moment, and on the seriousness with which the event was treated in the media, we are convinced that Americans can muster the resources necessary to consider carefully the most profound principles of government.

Is "Refounding" Necessary?

The growth of government has greatly "stretched" the founding principles. An advanced economy and the corresponding involvement in international trade are among the many sources of pressure on the government to respond to the heavy demands laid upon its regulatory functions. The rising expectations generated by the government's promising more than it can deliver have produced economic strains in larger urban areas. The dramatic increase in the number of issues qualitatively different from the bulk of items on the political agenda of the American past has produced still other strains. Social bonds are being tested by the politicization of questions involving abortion, women's rights, and greater public awareness of the abuse of human rights in regimes endorsed by U.S. foreign policy. The enormously complex but deeply felt problems of environmental quality seem at times to demand more of a response from our political institutions than they are capable of producing. And the rise of consumerism and the widespread popular referenda on nuclear arms limitation have introduced not only new issues but also new voices demanding governmental recognition. The practice of employing incremental adjustments to demands on government tends to obviate any thought that major political adjustments might be necessary, and the development of political analysis—even of the recent policy studies research variety—has generally failed to evaluate political institutions to any serious extent.[7]

Over the past several years, many of the specific principles of government addressed in this volume have been called directly into question or have been subjected to interpretation and reinterpretation. A "new" federalism in the form of revenue sharing under Nixon or a "return" to federalism in the form of national programs to be adopted and eventually financed solely by the states under Reagan have both been touted as the needed remedy for most of the ills of the American polity. These various "federalisms" in many important respects bear only the vaguest resemblance to that structure intended by the Founders and carefully described earlier in this volume.

A lengthening series of one-term Presidents and the low popular esteem accorded to those who leave the office have combined to generate concern over the adequacy of our electoral process, including many of our postconstitutional nominating practices. Questions of how to assure that the most able candidates for office are presented to the American public and are subsequently chosen at the ballot box have taken on a certain urgency of late, emphasized by a growing awareness of the formidable powers of the modern Presidency. These perceived electoral ills are posed against a backdrop of what some observers describe as a decline in the strength of political parties that has left the electorate fragmented and disoriented.

The increasing volume of bureaucratically imposed administrative rules and regulations carrying with them the force of law seems to some observers to be threateningly close to a breach of the notions of separation of powers and checks and balances as understood by the drafters of the Constitution. Others would suggest that the Supreme Court has sat as a legislature on more than one occasion and in more than one area of social policy. While these and other situations constitute gray areas of government that are difficult to clarify on the basis of pure principle, they do call into question the serviceability of some of our institutional articles of faith in an increasingly complex age.

While there is reason to be concerned about our failure to carry on continuous debate over constitutional principles, this failure also makes it difficult to know whether the principles, or our patterns of thought about them, need revision. Political discourse requires that language beyond that generated by special interests be developed; this requires the focusing of attention of both theorists and political leaders on the need for revision. Incremental political settlements by government that fail to consider such basic questions as these can result in government attending to "politics as usual" so long that it no longer enjoys public support. It may well be that a serious reflection on principles will demonstrate that those held by the Founders need no revision. It may be that new problems will force Americans to rethink their institutions and alter them where needed. Perhaps what is necessary may be merely the bringing into consciousness of our own fundamental beliefs so that we can measure them against contemporary practices. It is to be hoped that the exposition of the founding principles and their history presented here will be a solid first step in that direction and that it will stimulate a serious evaluation of the future of American democracy and promote a new understanding of America as a nation.

Notes

1. John Bibby and Roger H. Davidson, *On Capitol Hill: Studies in the Legislative Process*, 2nd ed. (Hinsdale, Ill.: Dryden, 1972), p. 19.
2. *Lectures on Rhetoric and Oratory Delivered to the Class of Senior and Junior Sophisters in Harvard University* (Cambridge, Mass., 1810), 1:22.
3. *The Federalist*, 1787 (New York: Modern Library, 1937), pp. 409-10.
4. John Rawls, *A Theory of Justice* (Cambridge, Mass.: Harvard University Press, 1971); and Robert Nozick, *Anarchy, State, and Utopia* (New York: Basic Books, 1974).
5. Gene Graham, *One-Man, One-Vote: Baker v. Carr and the American Levellers* (Boston: Atlantic Monthly Press, 1972), traces the events leading to the 1964 decision.
6. Harris poll, August 1975.
7. One prominent exception to this statement is the work of Theodore J. Lowi, which pointedly raises questions about the aberrant effects of American institutional developments over the last several decades. However, it is usually other aspects of Lowi's work and not his efforts to encourage a debate on American institutions that are seized upon and pursued by scholars.

BIBLIOGRAPHY

Adams, John. *The Political Writings of John Adams: Representative Selections*. Edited by George A. Peck, Jr. Indianapolis: Bobbs-Merrill, 1954.

Adams, Randolph G. *Political Ideas of The American Revolution*. New York: Barnes & Noble, Inc., 1959.

Alden, John Richard. *The American Revolution, 1775-1783*. New York: Harper & Brothers, 1954.

Ames, E., and Goodell, A. Cheney, eds. *The Acts and Resolves, Public and Private, of the Province of Massachusetts Bay*. 21 vols. Boston: Wright and Potter, 1869-1922.

Aptheker, Herbert. *The American Revolution, 1763-1783*. New York: International Publishers, 1960.

Bailyn, Bernard. *The Ideological Origins of the American Revolution*. Cambridge, Mass.: Harvard University Press, 1967.

______. *The Origins of American Politics*. New York: Knopf, 1968.

Bancroft, George. *History of the United States*. 10 vols. Boston: Little, Brown & Co., 1860.

______. *History of the Formation of the Constitution of the United States of America*. 3d ed. New York: D. Appleton and Company, 1883.

Barker, Charles Albro.*The Background of the Revolution in Maryland*. New Haven, Conn.: Yale University Press, 1940.

Bartlett, John Russell, ed. *Records of the State of Rhode Island and Providence Plantations in New England (1784-1792)*. Providence, 1863.

Basler, Roy P., ed. *The Collected Works of Abraham Lincoln*. 2 vols. New Brunswick, N. J.: Rutgers University Press, 1953.

Beard, Charles A. *The Supreme Court and the Constitution*. New York: Macmillan, 1912.

______. *An Economic Interpretation of the Constitution*. New York: Macmillan, 1913.

Becker, Carl L. *The Declaration of Independence: A Study in the History of an Idea*. New York: Harcourt, Brace and Co., 1922.

______. *The History of Political Parties in the Province of New York, 1760-1776*. Madison: University of Wisconsin Press, 1960.

Benson, George C. S., ed. *Essays in Federalism*. Claremont, California: Institute for Studies in Federalism, 1961.

Benson, Lee. *Turner and Beard: American Historical Writing Reconsidered*. Glencoe, Ill.: Free Press, 1960.

Berger, Raoul. *Congress v. The Supreme Court*. Cambridge, Mass.: Harvard University Press, 1969.

______. *Impeachment: The Constitutional Problems*. Cambridge, Mass.: Harvard University Press, 1973.

______. *Executive Privilege: A Constitutional Myth*. Cambridge, Mass.:

Harvard University Press, 1974.

Bibby, John F., and Davidson, Roger H. *On Capitol Hill: Studies in the Legislative Process*. 2nd ed. Hinsdale, Ill.: Dryden Press, 1972.

Bickel, Alexander M. *The Least Dangerous Branch: The Supreme Court at the Bar of Politics*. Indianapolis: Bobbs-Merrill, 1962.

Binkley, Wilfred E. *American Political Parties: Their Natural History*. New York: Alfred A. Knopf, 1958.

———. *President and Congress*. 3d rev. ed. New York: Random House, Vintage Books, 1962.

Birkby, Robert H. "Politics of Accommodation: The Origin of the Supremacy Clause," *Western Political Quarterly* 19 (March 1966).

Blackstone, Sir William. *Commentaries on the Laws of England, 1765-1769*. 18th ed., 2 vols. New York, 1836.

Boorstin, Daniel J. *The Genius of American Politics*. Chicago: The University of Chicago Press, 1953.

———. *The Americans: The Democratic Experience*. New York: Random House, 1973.

Boudin, L. B. *Government by Judiciary*. New York: William Godwin, 1932.

Bowen, Catherine Drinker. *John Adams and the American Revolution*. New York: Grosset & Dunlap, 1949.

———. *Miracle at Philadelphia: The Story of the Constitutional Convention, May to September 1787*. Boston: Little, Brown, 1966.

Boyd, Julian P. *The Declaration of Independence: The Evolution of the Text as Shown in Facsimiles of Various Drafts by Its Author, Thomas Jefferson*. Princeton, N.J.: Princeton University Press, 1945.

Broder, David S. *The Party's Over: The Failure of Parties in America*. New York: Harper and Row, 1972.

Brown, Robert E. *Charles Beard and the Constitution*. Princeton, N.J.: Princeton University Press, 1956.

———. *Middle Class Democracy and the Revolution in Massachusetts*. New York: Russell, 1968.

Brown, Samuel Gilman, ed. *Works of Rufus Choate*. 2 vols. Boston: Little, Brown, & Co., 1862.

Burgh, James. *Political Disquisitions*. 3 vols. London: Printed and sold by Robert Bell and William Woodhouse, 1774.

Burnham, James. *The Coming Caesars*. New York: Coward-McCann, Inc., 1957.

———. *Congress and the American Tradition*. Chicago: Henry Regnery Co., 1959.

Burnham, Walter Dean. *Critical Elections and the Mainsprings of American Politics*. New York: W. W. Norton and Co., 1970.

Burns, James McGregor. *Deadlock of Democracy*. Englewood Cliffs, N.J.: Prentice-Hall, 1963.

———. *Presidential Government*. New York: Houghton Mifflin Co., 1965.

Campbell, Angus, et al. *Elections and the Political Order*. New York: John Wiley and Sons, Inc., 1966.

Carr, Robert K. *The Supreme Court and Judicial Review*. New York: Rinehart and Co., 1942.

——— et al. *Essentials of American Democracy*. 7th ed. Hinsdale, Ill.: Dryden Press, 1974.

Chafee, Zechariah. *Free Speech in the United States*. Cambridge, Mass.: Harvard University Press, 1941.

Chambers, William N. *Political Parties in a New Nation*. New York: Oxford University Press, 1963.

Channing, Edward. *A History of the United States, 1761-1789*. 6 vols. New York: Macmillan, 1912.

Charles, Joseph. *The Origins of the American Party System*. New York: Harper and Brothers, 1956.

Chute, Marchette. *The First Liberty: A History of the Right to Vote in America, 1619-1850*. New York: E. P. Dutton, 1971.

Colbourn, H. Trevor. *The Lamp of Experience*. Chapel Hill: University of North Carolina Press, 1965.

Conkin, Paul K. *Self-Evident Truths*. Bloomington: Indiana University Press, 1974.

Constitutions of the United States: National and State. Legislative Drafting and Research Fund, Columbia University. Dobbs Ferry, New York: Oceana, 1962.

Cooke, Jacob E., ed. *The Federalist*. Cleveland: Meridian Books, 1967.

———, ed. *The Reports of Alexander Hamilton*. New York: Harper and Row, 1964.

Corwin, Edward S. "The Progress of Constitutional Theory Between the Declaration of Independence and the Meeting of the Philadelphia Convention," *American Historical Review* 30 (April 1925).

———. "The 'Higher Law' Background of American Constitutional Law," *Harvard Law Review* 42 (1928).

———. "The Constitution as Instrument and Symbol," *American Political Science Review* 30 (December 1936).

———. *The President, Office and Powers, 1787-1957*. New York: New York University Press, 1957.

Cunningham, Noble E., Jr. *The Jeffersonian Republicans: The Formation of Party Organization, 1789-1801*. Chapel Hill: University of North Carolina Press, 1957.

———, ed. *The Making of the American Party System, 1789 to 1809*. Englewood Cliffs, N.J.: Prentice-Hall, 1965.

Curti, Merle. *The Roots of American Loyalty*. New York: Columbia University Press, 1946.

———. *An American Paradox: The Conflict of Thought and Action*. New Brunswick, N.J.: Rutgers University Press, 1956.

———. *The Growth of American Thought*, 3d ed. New York: Harper and Row, 1964.

Dahl, Robert A. *A Preface to Democratic Theory*. Chicago: University of Chicago Press, 1956.

DeConde, Alexander. *Entangling Alliance*. Durham, N.C.: Duke University Press, 1958.

Demophilus. *Genuine Principles of the Ancient Saxon, or English Constitution*. Philadelphia, 1776.

Diamond, Martin. "Democracy and the Federalist," *American Political Science Review* 53 (March, 1959).

______. "The Federalist's View of Federalism." In *Essays in Federalism*, edited by George C. S. Benson. Claremont, Calif.: Institute for Studies in Federalism, 1961.

Dickerson, Oliver Morton. *American Colonial Government, 1695-1765: A Study of the British Board of Trade in Its Relation to the American Colonies, Political, Industrial, Administrative*. Cleveland, Ohio: Arthur H. Clark Co., 1912.

Dishman, Robert B. *State Constitutions: The Shape of the Document*. New York: National Municipal League, 1968.

Documents Illustrative of the Formation of the Union of the American States. Washington, D.C.: U. S. Government Printing Office, 1927.

Dodd, Walter Fairleigh. *The Revision and Amendment of State Constitutions*. Baltimore, 1910.

Dorfman, Joseph. *The Economic Mind in American Civilization*. 2 vols. New York: Augustus M. Kelley, 1966.

Douglass, Elisha P. *Rebels and Democrats: The Struggle for Equal Political Rights and Majority Rule During the American Revolution*. Chapel Hill: University of North Carolina Press, 1955.

Dumbauld, Edward, ed. *The Political Writings of Thomas Jefferson*. New York: Liberal Arts Press, 1956.

______. *The Declaration of Independence and What it Means Today*. Norman: University of Oklahoma Press, 1960.

Eidelberg, Paul. *The Philosophy of the American Constitution*. New York: Free Press, 1968.

Elliot, Jonathan, ed. *The Debates in the Several State Constitutions on the Adoption of the Federal Constitution*. Philadelphia: J. B. Lippincott, 1836-1845.

Fainsod, Merle, and Gordon, Lincoln. *Government and the American Economy*. New York: W. W. Norton & Co., 1941.

Farrand, Max, ed. *The Records of the Federal Convention of 1787* rev. ed., 4 vols. New Haven, Conn.: Yale University Press, 1937.

Fenno, Richard F., Jr. *The President's Cabinet*. Cambridge, Mass.: Harvard University Press, 1959.

______. *The Power of the Purse: Appropriation Politics in Congress*. Boston: Little, Brown, 1966.

Ferguson, E. James. *The Power of the Purse: A History of American Public Finance, 1776-1790*. Chapel Hill: University of North Carolina Press, 1961.

Fine, Sidney. *Laissez Faire and the General Welfare State*. Ann Arbor: University of Michigan Press, 1966.

Fisher, Louis. *President and Congress: Power and Policy.* New York: Free Press, 1972.

Fisher, Sydney George. "The Twenty-Eight Charges Against the King in the Declaration of Independence," *Pennsylvania Magazine of History and Biography*, 31 (3d quar., 1907).

———. *The Struggle for American Independence.* 2 vols. Philadelphia: J. B. Lippincott Co., 1908.

Fletcher, John. *A Vindication.* Dublin: Printed for W. Whitestone, 1776.

Flick, Alexander C., ed. *The American Revolution in New York.* Albany, N.Y.: Empire State Historical Publications, 1926.

Ford, Paul Leicester. *Pamphlets on the Constitution of the United States, 1787-88.* Brooklyn, New York, 1888.

Ford, Worthington Chauncey, ed. *Journals of the Continental Congress, 1774-1789.* 34 vols. Washington, D.C.: U.S. Government Printing Office, 1904-1937.

Frankfurter, Felix. *The Commerce Clause Under Marshall, Taney, and Waite.* Chicago: Quadrangle Books, 1964.

Freund, Paul A., et al. *Constitutional Law: Cases and Other Problems.* Boston, Mass.: Little, Brown, 1961.

Friendenwald, Herbert. *The Declaration of Independence: An Interpretation and an Analysis.* New York: Macmillan Company, 1904.

Froman, Lewis. *The Congressional Process: Strategies, Rules and Procedures.* Boston: Little, Brown, 1967.

Frothingham, Richard. *The Rise of the Republic of the United States.* Boston: Little, Brown & Co., 1872.

Gay, Peter. *A Loss of Mastery: Puritan Historians in Colonial America.* Berkeley and Los Angeles: University of California Press, 1966.

Ginsberg, Robert, ed. *A Casebook on the Declaration of Independence.* New York: Crowell, 1967.

Gipson, Lawrence Henry. *The Coming of the Revolution, 1763-1775.* New York: Harper & Brothers, 1954.

Goodricke, Henry. *Observations on Dr. Price's Theory.* York, England: Printed by A. Ward, 1776.

Gordon, William. *The History of the Rise, Progress, and Establishment of the Independence of the United States of America.* 3d Amer. ed., 3 vols. New York: Samuel Campbell, 1801.

Graham, Gene. *One-Man, One-Vote: Baker v. Carr and the American Levellers.* New York: Atlantic Monthly Press, 1972.

Gwyn, W. B. *The Meaning of Separation of Powers.* Tulane Studies in Political Science, vol. IX. New Orleans, La.: Tulane University Press, 1965.

Haines, Charles G. *The Revival of Natural Law Concepts.* Cambridge, Mass.: Harvard University Press, 1930.

———. "The Law of Nature in State and Federal Judicial Decisions," *Yale Law Journal* 25 (1916).

———. *The American Doctrine of Judicial Supremacy.* Berkeley: University of California Press, 1932.

Hall, Van Beck. *Politics Without Parties: Massachusetts, 1780-1791.* Pittsburgh, Pa.: University of Pittsburgh Press, 1972.

Hamilton, J. C., ed. *The Works of Alexander Hamilton.* 7 vols. New York: Joint Library Committee of Congress, 1850-51.

Handlin, Oscar, and Handlin, Mary, eds. *The Popular Sources of Political Authority: Documents on the Massachusetts Constitution of 1780.* Cambridge, Mass.: Harvard University Press, 1966.

Harlow, Ralph Volney. *The History of Legislative Methods in the Period Before 1825.* New Haven: Yale University Press, 1917.

Harris, Joseph P. *Congressional Control of Administration.* Washington, D.C.: The Brookings Institution, 1964.

Hartz, Louis. *The Liberal Tradition in America.* New York: Harcourt, Brace and Company, 1955.

Hazelton, John H. *The Declaration of Independence: Its History.* New York: Dodd, Mead & Company, Inc., 1906.

Henkin, Louis. *Foreign Affairs and the Constitution.* Mineola, N.Y.: Foundation Press, 1972.

Henning, William Waller, ed. *The Statutes at Large, being a Collection of All of the Laws of Virginia.* Richmond, 1823.

Hicks, John D. *The Federal Union.* 2d ed. Cambridge: The Riverside Press, 1952.

Hirschfield, Robert S., ed. *The Power of the Presidency,* 2d. ed. Chicago: Aldine Publishing Co., 1973.

Hoadley, Charles J., ed. *The Public Records of the Colony of Connecticut, May, 1768, to May, 1777.* Hartford, 1865.

Hofstadter, Richard. *The Idea of a Party System: The Rise of Legitimate Opposition in the United States, 1780-1840.* Berkeley: University of California Press, 1969.

______. *American Political Tradition.* New York: A. A. Knopf, 1973.

Hooker, Richard. *The Works of Mr. Richard Hooker in Eight Books.* 3 vols. London, 1821.

Hughes, Graham. "Social Justice and the Courts," *The Limits of Law: Nomos XV,* eds. J. Roland Pennock and John W. Chapman. New York: Lieber-Atherton, 1974.

Hutcheson, Francis. *A System of Moral Philosophy.* 2 vols. London: Sold by A. Millar and J. Longman, 1775.

Hutchinson, Thomas. *The History of the Colony and Province of Massachusetts-Bay.* Edited by Lawrence Shaw Mayo. 3 vols. Cambridge, Mass.: Harvard University Press, 1936.

Hyman, Harold. *To Try Men's Souls: Loyalty Tests in American History.* Berkeley and Los Angeles: University of California Press, 1959.

Hyneman, Charles S. "Conflict, Toleration and Agreement: Persisting Challenge for Democratic Government," *University of Illinois Bulletin,* no. 75 (1965).

______. *The Supreme Court on Trial.* New York: Atherton, 1963.

———, and Carey, George W., eds. *A Second Federalist: Congress Creates a Government*. New York: Appleton-Century-Crofts, 1967.

Ingersoll, Robert G. *The Ghosts and Other Lectures*. Washington, D.C.: C. P. Farrell, 1882.

James, Judson L. *American Political Parties in Transition*. New York: Harper and Row, 1974.

Jameson, J. Franklin. *The American Revolution Considered As a Social Movement*. Princeton, N.J.: Princeton University Press, 1926.

Jensen, Merrill. "The Idea of a National Government during the American Revolution," *Political Science Quarterly* 58 (1943).

———. *The Articles of Confederation: An Interpretation of the Social-Constitutional History of the American Revolution, 1774-1781*. Madison: University of Wisconsin Press, 1962.

Kallenbach, Joseph E. *The American Chief Executive*. New York: Harper & Row, 1966.

Kendall, Willmoore, and Carey, George W., eds. *Liberalism v. Conservatism*. Princeton, N.J.: D. Van Nostrand and Co., 1966.

Kendall, Willmoore, and Carey, George W. *The Basic Symbols of the American Political Tradition*. Baton Rouge: Louisiana State Press, 1970.

Kenyon, Cecelia M. "Men of Little Faith: The Anti-Federalists on the Nature of Representative Government," *William and Mary Quarterly* 12, (1955).

———, ed. *The Antifederalists*. Indianapolis: Bobbs-Merrill Co., 1966.

Key, V. O., Jr. *Politics, Parties and Pressure Groups*. 5th ed. rev. New York: Thomas Y. Crowell Co., 1964.

———. "A Theory of Critical Elections." *Journal of Politics* 17 (February 1975).

Kirkland, Edward C. *A History of American Economic Life*. New York: Appleton-Century-Crofts, Inc., 1951.

Koch, Adrienne. *Power, Morals and the Founding Fathers: Essays in the Interpretation of the American Enlightment*. Ithaca, N.Y.: Great Seal Books, 1961.

Koch, Adrienne, and Peden, William, eds. *The Life and Selected Writings of Thomas Jefferson*. New York: Random House, The Modern Library, 1944.

Kurtz, Stephen G. *The Presidency of John Adams: The Collapse of Federalism, 1795-1800*. Philadelphia: University of Pennsylvania Press, 1957.

———, ed. *The Federalists: Creators and Critics of the Union, 1780-1801*. New York: John Wiley and Sons, 1972.

Lee, Richard Henry. *Letters of the Federalist Farmer* in *Pamphlets on the Constitution of the United States, 1787-88*. Edited by Paul Leicester Ford. Brooklyn, New York, 1888.

Levy, Leonard W. *Legacy of Suppression: Freedom of Speech and Press in Early American History*. Cambridge, Mass.: Harvard University Press, 1960.

Lewis, John D., ed. *Federalists vs. Anti-Federalists.* San Francisco: Chandler, 1967.

Lipset, Seymour Martin. *The First New Nation.* New York: Basic Books, Inc., 1963.

Locke, John. *A Second Treatise of Government.* Edited by Peter Laslett. New York: New American Library, 1965.

Lovejoy, David S. *Rhode Island Politics and the American Revolution, 1760-1776.* Providence, R. I.: Brown University Press, 1958.

Lowi, Theodore J., ed. *Private Life and Public Order.* New York: W. W. Norton & Co., 1968.

______. *The End of Liberalism.* New York: W. W. Norton & Company, 1969.

______ and Ripley, Randall B., eds. *Legislative Politics U.S.A.* 3d ed. Boston: Little, Brown, 1973.

______. *American Government: Incomplete Conquest.* Hinsdale, Ill.: Dryden Press, 1976.

Luce, Robert. *Legislative Principles: The History of Lawmaking by Representative Government.* New York: Houghton Mifflin Co., 1930.

Lynd, Staughton. *Class Conflict, Slavery, and the United States Constitution.* Indianapolis: Bobbs-Merrill, 1968.

McDonald, Forrest. *We the People: The Economic Origins of the Constitution.* Chicago: University of Chicago Press, 1958.

McWilliams, Wilson Carey. *The Idea of Fraternity in America.* Berkeley: University of California Press, 1973.

Madison, James. *Journal of the Federal Convention.* Chicago: Albert, Scott and Company, 1893.

Main, Jackson Turner. *The Antifederalists: Critics of the Constitution, 1781-1788.* Chicago: Quadrangle Books, 1961.

______. *The Social Structure of Revolutionary America.* Madison: The University of Wisconsin Press, 1965.

______. *The Upper House in Revolutionary America.* Madison: The University of Wisconsin Press, 1967.

______. *Political Parties before the Constitution.* Chapel Hill: University of North Carolina Press, 1973.

Mason, Alpheus T. *The States Rights Debate: Antifederalism and the Constitution.* Englewood Cliffs, N.J.: Prentice-Hall, 1964.

______, and Garvey, Gerald, eds. *American Constitutional History.* New York: Harper & Row, 1964.

Meiklejohn, Alexander. *Political Freedom: The Constitutional Powers of the People.* New York: Harper, 1960.

Meyers, Marvin, ed. *The Mind of the Founder.* Indianapolis: Bobbs-Merrill, 1973.

Montesquieu, Baron de. *The Spirit of the Laws.* Translated by Thomas Nugent. New York: Hafner Publishing Co., 1949.

Morgan, Donald G. *Congress and the Constitution: A Study of Responsibility.* Cambridge, Mass.: Harvard University Press, 1966.

Morgan, Edmund S. *The Birth of the Republic, 1763-89.* Chicago: University of Chicago Press, 1956.

Morgan, Forrest. *Connecticut as a Colony and a State, or One of the Original Thirteen.* 4 vols. Hartford, Conn., 1904.

Morison, Samuel Eliot. *The Oxford History of the American People.* New York: Oxford University Press, 1965.

Morton, Richard L. *Colonial Virginia.* 2 vols. Chapel Hill: University of North Carolina Press, 1960.

Neustadt, Richard E. *Presidential Power.* New York: John Wiley & Sons, 1960.

Nevins, Allan. *The American States During and After the Revolution.* New York: Augustus M. Kelley, 1969.

Niles, Hezekian, ed. *Principles and Acts of the Revolution in America.* Baltimore: Printed and published by W. O. Niles, 1822.

Nozick, Robert. *Anarchy, State, and Utopia.* New York: Basic Books, 1974.

Paine, Thomas. *Common Sense and Other Political Writings.* Edited by Nelson F. Adkins. Indianapolis: Bobbs-Merrill, 1953.

Palmer, R. R. *The Age of the Democratic Revolution, Vol. I.: The Challenge.* Princeton, N.J.: Princeton University Press, 1959.

Parrington, Vernon L. *The Colonial Mind, 1620-1800.* New York: Harcourt, Brace and Company, 1927.

______. *Main Currents in American Thought: An Interpretation of American Literature from the Beginnings to 1920.* 2 vols. New York: Harcourt, Brace, and Co., 1927, 1930.

Patterson, Stephen E. *Political Parties in Revolutionary Massachusetts.* Madison: University of Wisconsin Press, 1973.

Peck, George A., ed. *The Political Writings of John Adams.* New York: Liberal Arts Press, 1954.

Peirce, Neal R. *The People's President.* New York: Simon and Schuster, 1968.

Plamenatz, John P. *Consent, Freedom, and Political Obligation.* 2d. ed. London: Oxford University Press, 1968.

Pole, J. R. *Political Representation in England and the Origins of the American Republic.* New York: St. Martin, 1966.

Pomper, Gerald M. *Elections in America.* New York: Dodd, Mead and Company, 1968.

Poore, Ben Perley, ed. *The Federal and State Constitutions, Colonial Charters, and Other Organic Laws of the United States.* 2 vols. Washington, D.C.,1878.

Pound, Roscoe. *Organization of Courts.* Boston: Little, Brown, 1940.

______. *Appellate Procedure in Civil Cases.* Boston: Little, Brown, 1941.

Ranney, Austin. *The Doctrine of Responsible Party Government.* Urbana: University of Illinois Press, 1962.

______. *Curing the Mischiefs of Faction: Party Reform in America.* Berkeley: University of California Press, 1975.

______, and Kendall, Willmoore. *Democracy and the American Party System.* New York: Harcourt, Brace and World, 1956.

Rawls, John. *A Theory of Justice.* Cambridge, Massachusetts: Harvard University Press, 1971.

Reincourt, Amaury de. *Congress and the American Tradition.* Chicago: Henry Regnery and Co., 1957.

Richardson, James D., ed. *A Compilation of the Messages and Papers of the Presidents, 1789-1897.* 10 vols. Washington, D.C.: U.S. Government Printing Office, 1896-1899.

Rieselbach, Leroy N. *Congressional Politics.* New York: McGraw-Hill, 1973.

Riley, F. L. "Colonial Origins of New England Senates," *Johns Hopkins Studies in Historical and Political Science* 14 (March, 1896).

Roche, John P "The Founding Fathers: A Reform Caucus in Action," *American Political Science Review* 55 (December 1961).

Rossiter, Clinton L. *Documents in American Government.* New York: William Sloane Associates, Inc., 1949.

———. *The First American Revolution.* New York: Harcourt, Brace and Company, 1953.

———. *Seedtime of the Republic.* New York: Harcourt, Brace, and Co., 1955.

———. *The American Presidency.* 2d ed. New York: Harcourt, Brace and Co., 1960.

———. *1787: The Grand Convention.* New York: Harcourt, Brace and Co., 1966.

Rutland, Robert A. *The Ordeal of the Constitution: The Anti-federalists and the Ratification Struggle of 1787-1788.* Norman: University of Oklahoma Press, 1966.

Sanderson, John. *Biography of the Signers to the Declaration of Independence.* Philadelphia: William Brotherhood, 1865.

Schachner, Nathan. *Alexander Hamilton.* New York: A. S. Barnes & Company, Inc. 1946.

Sikes, Pressly S., and Stoner, John E. *Bates' and Field's State Government.* New York: Harper and Row, 1949.

Smith, David G. *The Convention and the Constitution.* New York: St. Martin's Press, 1965.

Smith, James Allen. *The Spirit of American Government.* New York: Macmillan and Co., 1908.

Snow, Alpheus Henry. *The American Philosophy of Government.* New York: G. P. Putnam's Sons, 1921.

Stewart, Donald H. *The Opposition Press of the Federalist Period.* Albany: State University of New York Press, 1969.

Story, William W., ed. *Life and Letters of Joseph Story.* 2 vols. Boston: Charles C. Little and James Brown, 1851.

Sturm, Albert L. *Thirty Years of State Consitution-Making: 1938-1968.* New York: National Municipal League, 1970.

Sundquist, James. *Making Federalism Work.* Washington, D.C.: The Brookings Institution, 1969.

Swindler, William F. *Sources and Documents of the United States Constitutions.* Dobbs Ferry, N.Y.: Oceana, 1973.

Swisher, Carl Brent. *American Constitutional Development.* 2d. ed. Cambridge, Mass.: Houghton Mifflin Co., 1954.

Sydnor, Charles S. *American Revolutionaries in the Making: Political Practices in Washington's Virginia.* New York: Free Press, 1952.

Tansill, Charles C., ed. *Documents Illustrative of the Union of the American States.* Washington, D.C.: U.S. Government Printing Office, 1927.

Taylor, John. *An Inquiry into the Principles and Policy of the Government of the United States.* Fredericksburg, Va., 1814.

Thach, Charles C., Jr. *The Creation of the Presidency, 1775-1789.* Baltimore: Johns Hopkins Press, 1969.

Thorpe, Francis N., ed. *The Federal and State Constitutions, Colonial Charters, and other Organic Laws of the United States of America.* 7 vols. Washington, D. C.: U.S. Government Printing Office, 1907.

Tocqueville, Alexis de. *Democracy in America.* Edited by J.P. Mayer. Translated by George Lawrence. Garden City, N.J.: Doubleday & Co., 1969.

Tyler, Moses Coit. *The Literary History of the American Revolution, 1763-1783.* New York: G.P. Putnam's Sons, 1897.

U.S., Congress, Senate, Judiciary Committee, *Congressional Oversight of Executive Agreements: Hearings,* 92d Congress, 1st sess., 1972.

Van Deusen, Glydon G. *The Jacksonian Era, 1828-1848.* New York: Harper and Brothers, 1959.

Van Osdol, James A. *Sketches from Our Constitutional History.* Rev. ed. Anderson, Ind.: Herald Publishing Co., 1935.

Van Schaack, Henry C. *The Life of Peter Van Schaack.* New York: D. Appleton & Co., 1842.

Van Tyne, C. H. *The War of Independence.* Boston: Houghton Mifflin, 1929.

Vile, M.J.C. *Constitutionalism and the Separation of Powers.* Oxford: Oxford University Press, 1967.

Wallace, David Duncan. *South Carolina.* Chapel Hill: University of North Carolina Press, 1951.

Warren, Charles. *Congress, the Constitution and the Supreme Court.* Boston: Little, Brown, 1925.

______. *The Making of the Constitution.* Boston: Little, Brown, 1937.

Wells, Richard. *The Middle Line.* Philadelphia: Printed and Sold by Joseph Crukshank, 1775.

West, Samuel. *A Sermon.* Boston: Printed by John Gill, 1776.

Wheeler, John P., ed. *Salient Issues of Constitutional Revision.* New York: National Municipal League, 1961.

White, Leonard D. *The Federalists: A Study in Administrative History.* New York: Macmillan Co., 1948.

______. *The Jeffersonians.* New York: Free Press, 1951.

______. *The Jacksonians.* New York: Macmillan Co., 1954.

______. *The Republican Era.* New York: Macmillan Co.. 1958.

Whiting, William. *Address to the Inhabitants.* Hartford, Conn.: Printed by Watson and Goodwin, 1778.

Williamson, Chilton. *American Suffrage: From Property to Democracy, 1776-1860.* Princeton, N.J.: Princeton University Press, 1960.

Wilson, Woodrow. *Congressional Government.* New York: Meridian Books, 1956.

Wood, Gordon S. *The Creation of the American Republic, 1776-1787.* Chapel Hill: University of North Carolina Press, 1969.

CONSTITUTION
OF THE UNITED STATES

Proposed by Convention September 17, 1787
Effective March 4, 1789

WE the people of the United States, in order to form a more perfect union, establish justice, insure domestic tranquillity, provide for the common defense, promote the general welfare, and secure the blessings of liberty to ourselves and our posterity, do ordain and establish this Constitution for the United States of America.

ARTICLE I

SECTION 1. All legislative powers herein granted shall be vested in a Congress of the United States, which shall consist of a Senate and House of Representatives.

SECTION 2. 1. The House of Representatives shall be composed of members chosen every second year by the people of the several States, and the electors in each State shall have the qualifications requisite for electors of the most numerous branch of the State legislature.

2. No person shall be a representative who shall not have attained to the age of twenty-five years, and been seven years a citizen of the United States, and who shall not, when elected, be an inhabitant of that State in which he shall be chosen.

3. Representatives [and direct taxes]* shall be apportioned among the several States which may be included within this Union, according to their respective numbers, [which shall be determined by adding to the whole number of free persons, including those bound to service for a term of years, and excluding Indians not taxed, three fifths of all other persons.]† The actual enumeration shall be made within three

* See the 16th Amendment.
† See the 14th Amendment.

years after the first meeting of the Congress of the United States, and within every subsequent term of ten years, in such manner as they shall by law direct. The number of representatives shall not exceed one for every thirty thousand, but each State shall have at least one representative; and until such enumeration shall be made, the State of New Hampshire shall be entitled to choose three, Massachusetts eight, Rhode Island and Providence Plantations one, Connecticut five, New York six, New Jersey four, Pennsylvania eight, Delaware one, Maryland six, Virginia ten, North Carolina five, South Carolina five, and Georgia three.

4. When vacancies happen in the representation from any State, the executive authority thereof shall issue writs of election to fill such vacancies.

5. The House of Representatives shall choose their speaker and other officers; and shall have the sole power of impeachment.

SECTION 3. 1. The Senate of the United States shall be composed of two senators from each State, [chosen by the legislature thereof,]* for six years; and each senator shall have one vote.

2. Immediately after they shall be assembled in consequence of the first election, they shall be divided as equally as may be into three classes. The seats of the senators of the first class shall be vacated at the expiration of the second year, of the second class at the expiration of the fourth year, and of the third class at the expiration of the sixth year, so that one third may be chosen every second year; and if vacancies happen by resignation, or otherwise, during the recess of the legislature of any State, the executive thereof may make temporary appointments until the next meeting of the legislature, which shall then fill such vacancies.*

3. No person shall be a senator who shall not have attained to the age of thirty years, and been nine years a citizen of the United States, and who shall not, when elected, be an inhabitant of that State for which he shall be chosen.

4. The Vice President of the United States shall be President of the Senate, but shall have no vote, unless they be equally divided.

5. The Senate shall choose their other officers, and also a president *pro tempore,* in the absence of the Vice President, or when he shall exercise the office of the President of the United States.

6. The Senate shall have the sole power to try all impeachments. When sitting for that purpose, they shall be on oath or affirmation.

* See the 17th Amendment.

When the President of the United States is tried, the chief justice shall preside: and no person shall be convicted without the concurrence of two thirds of the members present.

7. Judgment in cases of impeachment shall not extend further than to removal from office, and disqualifications to hold and enjoy any office of honor, trust or profit under the United States: but the party convicted shall nevertheless be liable and subject to indictment, trial, judgment and punishment, according to law.

SECTION 4. 1. The times, places, and manner of holding elections for senators and representatives, shall be prescribed in each State by the legislature thereof; but the Congress may at any time by law make or alter such regulations, except as to the places of choosing senators.

2. The Congress shall assemble at least once in every year, and such meeting shall be on the first Monday in December,* unless they shall by law appoint a different day.

SECTION 5. 1. Each House shall be the judge of the elections, returns and qualifications of its own members, and a majority of each shall constitute a quorum to do business; but a smaller number may adjourn from day to day, and may be authorized to compel the attendance of absent members, in such manner, and under such penalties as each House may provide.

2. Each House may determine the rules of its proceedings, punish its members for disorderly behavior, and, with the concurrence of two thirds, expel a member.

3. Each House shall keep a journal of its proceedings, and from time to time publish the same, excepting such parts as may in their judgment require secrecy; and the yeas and nays of the members of either House on any question shall, at the desire of one fifth of those present, be entered on the journal.

4. Neither House, during the session of Congress, shall, without the consent of the other, adjourn for more than three days, nor to any other place than that in which the two Houses shall be sitting.

SECTION 6. 1. The senators and representatives shall receive a compensation for their services, to be ascertained by law, and paid out of the Treasury of the United States. They shall in all cases, except treason, felony, and breach of the peace, be privileged from arrest during their attendance at the session of their respective Houses, and in going to and returning from the same; and for any speech or debate in either House, they shall not be questioned in any other place.

* Modified by the 20th Amendment.

2. No senator or representative shall, during the time for which he was elected, be appointed to any civil office under the authority of the United States, which shall have been created, or the emoluments whereof shall have been increased during such time; and no person holding any office under the United States shall be a member of either House during his continuance in office.

SECTION 7. 1. All bills for raising revenue shall originate in the House of Representatives; but the Senate may propose or concur with amendments as on other bills.

2. Every bill which shall have passed the House of Representatives and the Senate, shall, before it becomes a law, be presented to the President of the United States; if he approves he shall sign it, but if not he shall return it, with his objections to that House in which it shall have originated, who shall enter the objections at large on their journal, and proceed to reconsider it. If after such reconsideration two thirds of that House shall agree to pass the bill, it shall be sent, together with the objections, to the other House, by which it shall likewise be reconsidered, and if approved by two thirds of that House, it shall become a law. But in all such cases the votes of both Houses shall be determined by yeas and nays, and the names of the persons voting for and against the bill shall be entered on the journal of each House respectively. If any bill shall not be returned by the President within ten days (Sundays excepted) after it shall have been presented to him, the same shall be a law, in like manner as if he had signed it, unless the Congress by their adjournment prevent its return, in which case it shall not be a law.

3. Every order, resolution, or vote to which the concurrence of the Senate and the House of Representatives may be necessary (except on a question of adjournment) shall be presented to the President of the United States; and before the same shall take effect, shall be approved by him, or being disapproved by him, shall be repassed by two thirds of the Senate and House of Representatives, according to the rules and limitations prescribed in the case of a bill.

SECTION 8. The Congress shall have the power

1. To lay and collect taxes, duties, imposts, and excises, to pay the debts and provide for the common defense and general welfare of the United States; but all duties, imposts, and excises shall be uniform throughout the United States;

2. To borrow money on the credit of the United States;

3. To regulate commerce with foreign nations, and among the several States, and with the Indian tribes;

4. To establish a uniform rule of naturalization, and uniform laws on the subject of bankruptcies throughout the United States;

5. To coin money, regulate the value thereof, and of foreign coin, and fix the standard of weights and measures;

6. To provide for the punishment of counterfeiting the securities and current coin of the United States;

7. To establish post offices and post roads;

8. To promote the progress of science and useful arts, by securing for limited times to authors and inventors the exclusive right to their respective writings and discoveries;

9. To constitute tribunals inferior to the Supreme Court;

10. To define and punish piracies and felonies committed on the high seas, and offenses against the law of nations;

11. To declare war, grant letters of marque and reprisal, and make rules concerning captures on land and water;

12. To raise and support armies, but no appropriation of money to that use shall be for a longer term than two years;

13. To provide and maintain a navy;

14. To make rules for the government and regulation of the land and naval forces;

15. To provide for calling forth the militia to execute the laws of the Union, suppress insurrections and repel invasions;

16. To provide for organizing, arming, and disciplining the militia, and for governing such part of them as may be employed in the service of the United States, reserving to the States respectively, the appointment of the officers, and the authority of training the militia according to the discipline prescribed by Congress;

17. To exercise exclusive legislation in all cases whatsoever, over such district (not exceeding ten miles square) as may, by cession of particular States, and the acceptance of Congress, become the seat of the government of the United States, and to exercise like authority over all places purchased by the consent of the legislature of the State in which the same shall be, for the erection of forts, magazines, arsenals, dockyards, and other needful buildings; and

18. To make all laws which shall be necessary and proper for carrying into execution the foregoing powers, and all other powers vested by this Constitution in the government of the United States, or in any department or officer thereof.

SECTION 9. 1. The migration or importation of such persons as any of the States now existing shall think proper to admit, shall not be prohibited by the Congress prior to the year one thousand eight hundred and eight, but a tax or duty may be imposed on such importation, not exceeding ten dollars for each person.

2. The privilege of the writ of *habeas corpus* shall not be suspended, unless when in cases of rebellion or invasion the public safety may require it.

3. No bill of attainder or *ex post facto* law shall be passed.

4. No capitation, or other direct, tax shall be laid unless in proportion to the census or enumeration hereinbefore directed to be taken.*

5. No tax or duty shall be laid on articles exported from any State.

6. No preference shall be given by any regulation of commerce or revenue to the ports of one State over those of another: nor shall vessels bound to, or from, one State be obliged to enter, clear, or pay duties in another.

7. No money shall be drawn from the treasury, but in consequence of appropriations made by law; and a regular statement and account of the receipts and expenditures of all public money shall be published from time to time.

8. No title of nobility shall be granted by the United States: and no person holding any office of profit or trust under them, shall, without the consent of the Congress, accept of any present, emolument, office, or title, of any kind whatever, from any king, prince, or foreign State.

SECTION 10. 1. No State shall enter into any treaty, alliance, or confederation; grant letters of marque and reprisal; coin money; emit bills of credit; make anything but gold and silver coin a tender in payment of debts; pass any bill of attainder, *ex post facto* law, or law impairing the obligation of contracts, or grant any title of nobility.

2. No State shall, without the consent of the Congress, lay any imposts or duties on imports or exports, except what may be absolutely necessary for executing its inspection laws; and the net produce of all duties and imposts laid by any State on imports or exports, shall be for the use of the treasury of the United States; and all such laws shall be subject to the revision and control of the Congress.

3. No State shall, without the consent of the Congress, lay any duty of tonnage, keep troops, or ships of war in time of peace; enter into any agreement or compact with another State, or with a foreign

* See the 16th Amendment.

power, or engage in war, unless actually invaded, or in such imminent danger as will not admit of delay.

ARTICLE II

SECTION 1. 1. The executive power shall be vested in a President of the United States of America. He shall hold his office during the term of four years, and, together with the Vice President, chosen for the same term, be elected as follows:

2. Each State* shall appoint, in such manner as the legislature thereof may direct, a number of electors, equal to the whole number of senators and representatives to which the State may be entitled in the Congress: but no senator or representative, or person holding an office of trust or profit under the United States, shall be appointed an elector.

The electors shall meet in their respective States, and vote by ballot for two persons, of whom one at least shall not be an inhabitant of the same State with themselves. And they shall make a list of all the persons voted for, and of the number of votes for each; which list they shall sign and certify, and transmit sealed to the seat of the government of the United States, directed to the president of the Senate. The president of the Senate shall, in the presence of the Senate and House of Representatives, open all the certificates, and the votes shall then be counted. The person having the greatest number of votes shall be the President, if such number be a majority of the whole number of electors appointed; and if there be more than one who have such majority, and have an equal number of votes, then the House of Representatives shall immediately choose by ballot one of them for President; and if no person have a majority, then from the five highest on the list the said House shall in like manner choose the President. But in choosing the President, the votes shall be taken by States, the representation from each State having one vote; a quorum for this purpose shall consist of a member or members from two thirds of the States, and a majority of all the States shall be necessary to a choice. In every case, after the choice of the President, the person having the greatest number of votes of the electors shall be the Vice President. But if there should remain two or more who have equal votes, the Senate shall choose from them by ballot the Vice President.†

* See 23rd Amendment.

† This paragraph was superseded by the 12th Amendment.

3. The Congress may determine the time of choosing the electors, and the day on which they shall give their votes; which day shall be the same throughout the United States.

4. No person except a natural born citizen, or a citizen of the United States, at the time of the adoption of this Constitution, shall be eligible to the office of President; neither shall any person be eligible to that office who shall not have attained to the age of thirty-five years, and been fourteen years a resident within the United States.

5. In case of the removal of the President from office, or of his death, resignation, or inability to discharge the powers and duties of the said office, the same shall devolve on the Vice President, and the Congress may by law provide for the case of removal, death, resignation, or inability, both of the President and Vice President, declaring what officer shall then act as President, and such officer shall act accordingly, until the disability be removed, or a President shall be elected.*

6. The President shall, at stated times, receive for his services a compensation, which shall neither be increased nor diminished during the period for which he shall have been elected, and he shall not receive within that period any other emolument from the United States, or any of them.

7. Before he enter on the execution of his office, he shall take the following oath or affirmation:—"I do solemnly swear (or affirm) that I will faithfully execute the office of President of the United States, and will to the best of my ability, preserve, protect and defend the Constitution of the United States."

SECTION 2. 1. The President shall be commander in chief of the army and navy of the United States, and of the militia of the several States, when called into the actual service of the United States; he may require the opinion, in writing, of the principal officer in each of the executive departments, upon any subject relating to the duties of their respective offices, and he shall have power to grant reprieves and pardons for offenses against the United States, except in cases of impeachment.

2. He shall have power, by and with the advice and consent of the Senate, to make treaties, provided two thirds of the senators present concur; and he shall nominate, and by and with the advice and consent of the Senate, shall appoint ambassadors, other public ministers and consuls, judges of the Supreme Court, and all other officers of the United States, whose appointments are not herein otherwise provided

* See the 25th Amendment.

for, and which shall be established by law: but the Congress may by law vest the appointment of such inferior officers, as they think proper, in the President alone, in the courts of law, or in the heads of departments.

3. The President shall have power to fill up all vacancies that may happen during the recess of the Senate, by granting commissions which shall expire at the end of their next session.

SECTION 3. He shall from time to time give to the Congress information of the state of the Union, and recommend to their consideration such measures as he shall judge necessary and expedient; he may, on extraordinary occasions, convene both Houses, or either of them, and in case of disagreement between them with respect to the time of adjournment, he may adjourn them to such time as he shall think proper; he shall receive ambassadors and other public ministers; he shall take care that the laws be faithfully executed, and shall commission all the officers of the United States.

SECTION 4. The President, Vice President, and all civil officers of the United States, shall be removed from office on impeachment for and conviction of, treason, bribery, or other high crimes and misdemeanors.

ARTICLE III

SECTION 1. The judicial power of the United States shall be vested in one Supreme Court, and in such inferior courts as the Congress may from time to time ordain and establish. The judges, both of the Supreme and inferior courts, shall hold their offices during good behavior, and shall, at stated times, receive for their services, a compensation, which shall not be diminished during their continuance in office.

SECTION 2. 1. The judicial power shall extend to all cases, in law and equity, arising under this Constitution, the laws of the United States, and treaties made, or which shall be made, under their authority;—to all cases affecting ambassadors, other public ministers and consuls;—to all cases of admiralty and maritime jurisdiction;—to controversies to which the United States shall be a party;—to controversies between two or more States;—between a State and citizens of another State;*—between citizens of different States;—between citizens of the same State claiming lands under grants of different States, and between a State, or the citizens thereof, and foreign States, citizens or subjects.

* See the 11th Amendment.

2. In all cases affecting ambassadors, other public ministers and consuls, and those in which a State shall be party, the Supreme Court shall have original jurisdiction. In all the other cases before mentioned, the Supreme Court shall have appellate jurisdiction, both as to law and to fact, with such exceptions, and under such regulations as the Congress shall make.

3. The trial of all crimes, except in cases of impeachment, shall be by jury; and such trial shall be held in the State where the said crimes shall have been committed; but when not committed within any State, the trial shall be at such place or places as the Congress may by law have directed.

SECTION 3. 1. Treason against the United States shall consist only in levying war against them, or in adhering to their enemies, giving them aid and comfort. No person shall be convicted of treason unless on the testimony of two witnesses to the same overt act, or on confession in open court.

2. The Congress shall have power to declare the punishment of treason, but no attainder of treason shall work corruption of blood, or forfeiture except during the life of the person attained.

ARTICLE IV

SECTION 1. Full faith and credit shall be given in each State to the public acts, records, and judicial proceedings of every other State. And the Congress may by general laws prescribe the manner in which such acts, records and proceedings shall be proved, and the effect thereof.

SECTION 2. 1. The citizens of each State shall be entitled to all privileges and immunities of citizens in the several States.*

2. A person charged in any State with treason, felony, or other crime, who shall flee from justice, and be found in another State, shall on demand of the executive authority of the State from which he fled, be delivered up to be removed to the State having jurisdiction of the crime.

3. No person held to service or labor in one State under the laws thereof, escaping into another, shall, in consequence of any law or regulation therein, be discharged from such service or labor, but shall

* See the 14th Amendment, Sec. 1.

be delivered up on claim of the party to whom such service or labor may be due.*

SECTION 3. 1. New States may be admitted by the Congress into this Union; but no new State shall be formed or erected within the jurisdiction of any other State; nor any State be formed by the junction of two or more States, or parts of States, without the consent of the legislatures of the States concerned as well as of the Congress.

2. The Congress shall have power to dispose of and make all needful rules and regulations respecting the territory or other property belonging to the United States; and nothing in this Constitution shall be so construed as to prejudice any claims of the United States, or of any particular State.

SECTION 4. The United States shall guarantee to every State in this Union a republican form of government, and shall protect each of them against invasion; and on application of the legislature, or of the executive (when the legislature cannot be convened) against domestic violence.

ARTICLE V

The Congress, whenever two thirds of both Houses shall deem it necessary, shall propose amendments to this Constitution, or, on the application of the legislatures of two thirds of the several States, shall call a convention for proposing amendments, which in either case, shall be valid to all intents and purposes, as part of this Constitution when ratified by the legislatures of three fourths of the several States, or by conventions in three fourths thereof, as the one or the other mode of ratification may be proposed by the Congress; Provided that no amendment which may be made prior to the year one thousand eight hundred and eight shall in any manner affect the first and fourth clauses in the ninth section of the first article; and that no State, without its consent, shall be deprived of its equal suffrage in the Senate.

ARTICLE VI

1. All debts contracted and engagements entered into, before the adoption of this Constitution, shall be as valid against the United States under this Constitution, as under the Confederation.

2. This Constitution, and the laws of the United States which shall

* See the 13th Amendment.

be made in pursuance thereof; and all treaties made, or which shall be made, under the authority of the United States, shall be the supreme law of the land; and the Judges in every State shall be bound thereby, anything in the Constitution or laws of any State to the contrary notwithstanding.

3. The senators and representatives before mentioned, and the members of the several State legislatures, and all executive and judicial officers, both of the United States and of the several States, shall be bound by oath or affirmation to support this Constitution; but no religious test shall ever be required as a qualification to any office or public trust under the United States.

ARTICLE VII

The ratification of the conventions of nine States shall be sufficient for the establishment of this Constitution between the States so ratifying the same.

Done in Convention by the unanimous consent of the States present the seventeenth day of September in the year of our Lord one thousand seven hundred and eighty-seven, and of the independence of the United States of America the twelfth. In witness whereof we have hereunto subscribed our names. [Names omitted]

Articles in addition to, and amendment of, the Constitution of the United States of America, proposed by Congress, and ratified by the legislatures of the several States pursuant to the fifth article of the original Constitution.

AMENDMENTS

First Ten Amendments passed by Congress Sept. 25, 1789.
Ratified by three-fourths of the States December 15, 1791.

ARTICLE I

Congress shall make no law respecting an establishment of religion, or prohibiting the free exercise thereof; or abridging the freedom of speech, or of the press; or the right of the people peaceably to assemble, and to petition the government for a redress of grievances.

ARTICLE II

A well regulated militia, being necessary to the security of a free State, the right of the people to keep and bear arms, shall not be infringed.

ARTICLE III

No soldier shall, in time of peace be quartered in any house, without the consent of the owner, nor in time of war, but in a manner to be prescribed by law.

ARTICLE IV

The right of the people to be secure in their persons, houses, papers, and effects, against unreasonable searches and seizures, shall not be violated, and no warrants shall issue, but upon probable cause, supported by oath or affirmation, and particularly describing the place to be searched, and the persons or things to be seized.

ARTICLE V

No person shall be held to answer for a capital, or otherwise infamous crime, unless on a presentment or indictment of a grand jury, except in cases arising in the land or naval forces, or in the militia, when in actual service in time of war or public danger; nor shall any person be subject for the same offense to be twice put in jeopardy of life or limb; nor shall be compelled in any criminal case to be a witness against himself, nor be deprived of life, liberty, or property, without due process of law; nor shall private property be taken for public use without just compensation.

ARTICLE VI

In all criminal prosecutions, the accused shall enjoy the right to a speedy and public trial, by an impartial jury of the State and district wherein the crime shall have been committed, which district shall have been previously ascertained by law, and to be informed of the nature and cause of the accusation; to be confronted with the witnesses against him; to have compulsory process for obtaining witnesses in his favor, and to have the assistance of counsel for his defense.

ARTICLE VII

In suits at common law, where the value in controversy shall exceed twenty dollars, the right of trial by jury shall be preserved, and no fact tried by a jury shall be otherwise reëxamined in any court of the United States, than according to the rules of the common law.

ARTICLE VIII

Excessive bail shall not be required, nor excessive fines imposed, nor cruel and unusual punishments inflicted.

ARTICLE IX

The enumeration in the Constitution of certain rights shall not be construed to deny or disparage others retained by the people.

ARTICLE X

The powers not delegated to the United States by the Constitution, nor prohibited by it to the States, are reserved to the States respectively, or to the people.

ARTICLE XI

Passed by Congress March 4, 1794. Ratified February 7, 1795.

The judicial power of the United States shall not be construed to extend to any suit in law or equity, commenced or prosecuted against one of the United States by citizens of another State, or by citizens or subjects of any foreign State.

ARTICLE XII

Passed by Congress December 9, 1803. Ratified July 27, 1804.

The electors shall meet in their respective States, and vote by ballot for President and Vice President, one of whom, at least, shall not be an inhabitant of the same State with themselves; they shall name in their ballots the person voted for as President, and in distinct ballots, the person voted for as Vice President, and they shall make distinct lists of all persons voted for as President and of all persons voted for as Vice President, and of the number of votes for each, which lists they shall sign and certify, and transmit sealed to the seat of the government of the United States, directed to the President of the Senate;—The President of the Senate shall, in the presence of the Senate and House of Representatives, open all the certificates and the votes shall then be counted;—The person having the greatest number of votes for President, shall be the President, if such number be a majority of the whole number of electors appointed; and if no person have such majority, then from the persons having the highest numbers not exceeding three on the list of those voted for as President, the House of Representatives shall choose immediately, by ballot, the President. But in choosing the President, the votes shall be taken by States, the representation from each State having one vote; a quorum for this purpose shall consist of a member or members from two thirds of the States, and a majority of all the States shall be necessary to a choice. And if the House of Representatives shall not choose a President whenever the right of choice shall devolve upon them, before the fourth day of March* next following, then the Vice President shall act as President, as in the case of the death or other constitutional disability of the President. The person having the greatest number of votes as Vice President shall be the Vice President, if such number be a majority of the whole number of electors appointed, and if no person have a majority, then from the two highest numbers on the list, the Senate shall choose the Vice President; a quorum for the purpose shall consist of two thirds of the whole number of Senators, and a majority of the whole number shall be necessary to a choice. But no person constitutionally ineligible to the office of President shall be eligible to that of Vice President of the United States.

ARTICLE XIII

Passed by Congress January 31, 1865. Ratified December 6, 1865.

SECTION 1. Neither slavery nor involuntary servitude, except as punishment for crime whereof the party shall have been duly convicted,

* See 20th Amendment.

shall exist within the United States, or any place subject to their jurisdiction.

SECTION 2. Congress shall have power to enforce this article by appropriate legislation.

ARTICLE XIV

Passed by Congress June 13, 1866. Ratified July 9, 1868.

SECTION 1. All persons born or naturalized in the United States, and subject to the jurisdiction thereof, are citizens of the United States and of the State wherein they reside. No State shall make or enforce any law which shall abridge the privileges or immunities of citizens of the United States; nor shall any State deprive any person of life, liberty, or property, without due process of law; nor deny to any person within its jurisdiction the equal protection of the laws.

SECTION 2. Representatives shall be apportioned among the several States according to their respective numbers, counting the whole number of persons in each State, excluding Indians not taxed. But when the right to vote at any election for the choice of electors for President and Vice President of the United States, representatives in Congress, the executive and judicial officers of a State, or the members of the legislature thereof, is denied to any of the male inhabitants of such State, being twenty-one years of age, and citizens of the United States, or in any way abridged, except for participation in rebellion, or other crime, the basis of representation therein shall be reduced in the proportion which the number of such male citizens shall bear to the whole number of male citizens twenty-one years of age in such State.

SECTION 3. No person shall be a senator or representative in Congress, or elector of President and Vice President, or hold any office, civil or military, under the United States, or under any State, who having previously taken an oath, as a member of Congress, or as an officer of the United States, or as a member of any State legislature, or as an executive or judicial officer of any State, to support the Constitution of the United States, shall have engaged in insurrection or rebellion against the same, or given aid or comfort to the enemies thereof. But Congress may by a vote of two thirds of each House, remove such disability.

SECTION 4. The validity of the public debt of the United States, authorized by law, including debts incurred for payment of pensions and bounties for services in suppressing insurrection or rebellion, shall not be questioned. But neither the United States nor any State shall assume or pay any debt or obligation incurred in aid of insurrection or rebellion against the United States, or any claim for the loss or emancipation of any slave; but all such debts, obligations, and claims shall be held illegal and void.

SECTION 5. The Congress shall have power to enforce, by appropriate legislation, the provisions of this article.

ARTICLE XV

Passed by Congress February 26, 1869. Ratified February 3, 1870.

SECTION 1. The right of citizens of the United States to vote shall not be denied or abridged by the United States or by any State on account of race, color, or previous condition of servitude.

SECTION 2. The Congress shall have power to enforce this article by appropriate legislation.

ARTICLE XVI

Passed by Congress July 2, 1909. Ratified February 3, 1913.

The Congress shall have power to lay and collect taxes on incomes, from whatever source derived, without apportionment among the several States, and without regard to any census or enumeration.

ARTICLE XVII

Passed by Congress May 13, 1912. Ratified April 8, 1913.

The Senate of the United States shall be composed of two senators from each state, elected by the people thereof, for six years; and each senator shall have one vote. The electors in each State shall have the qualifications requisite for electors of the most numerous branch of the State legislature.

When vacancies happen in the representation of any State in the Senate, the executive authority of such State shall issue writs of election to fill such vacancies: *Provided,* That the legislature of any State may empower the executive thereof to make temporary appointments until the people fill the vacancies by election as the legislature may direct.

This amendment shall not be so construed as to affect the election or term of any senator chosen before it becomes valid as part of the Constitution.

ARTICLE XVIII*

Passed by Congress December 18, 1917. Ratified January 16, 1919.

After one year from the ratification of this article, the manufacture, sale, or transportation of intoxicating liquors within, the importation thereof into, or the exportation thereof from the United States and all territory subject to the jurisdiction thereof for beverage purposes is hereby prohibited.

The Congress and the several States shall have concurrent power to enforce this article by appropriate legislation.

This article shall be inoperative unless it shall have been ratified as an amendment to the Constitution by the legislatures of the several States, as provided in the Constitution, within seven years from the date of the submission hereof to the states by Congress.

ARTICLE XIX

Passed by Congress June 4, 1919. Ratified August 18, 1920.

The right of citizens of the United States to vote shall not be denied or abridged by the United States or by any State on account of sex.

The Congress shall have power by appropriate legislation to enforce the provisions of this article.

ARTICLE XX

Passed by Congress March 2, 1932. Ratified January 23, 1933.

SECTION 1. The terms of the President and Vice President shall end at noon on the 20th day of January, and the terms of Senators and Representatives at noon on the 3d day of January, of the years in which such terms would have ended if this article had not been ratified; and the terms of their successors shall then begin.

* Repealed by the 21st Amendment.

SECTION 2. The Congress shall assemble at least once in every year, and such meeting shall begin at noon on the 3d day of January, unless they shall by law appoint a different day.

SECTION 3. If, at the time fixed for the beginning of the term of the President, the President-elect shall have died, the Vice President-elect shall become President. If a President shall not have been chosen before the time fixed for the beginning of his term, or if the President-elect shall have failed to qualify, then the Vice President-elect shall act as President until a President shall have qualified; and the Congress may by law provide for the case wherein neither a President-elect nor a Vice President-elect shall have qualified, declaring who shall then act as President, or the manner in which one who is to act shall be selected, and such person shall act accordingly until a President or Vice President shall have qualified.

SECTION 4. The Congress may by law provide for the case of the death of any of the persons from whom the House of Representatives may choose a President whenever the right of choice shall have devolved upon them, and for the case of the death of any of the persons from whom the Senate may choose a Vice President whenever the right of choice shall have devolved upon them.

SECTION 5. Sections 1 and 2 shall take effect on the 15th day of October following the ratification of this article.

SECTION 6. This article shall be inoperative unless it shall have been ratified as an amendment to the Constitution by the legislatures of three-fourths of the several States within seven years from the date of its submission.

ARTICLE XXI

Passed by Congress February 20, 1933. Ratified December 5, 1933.

SECTION 1. The Eighteenth Article of amendment to the Constitution of the United States is hereby repealed.

SECTION 2. The transportation or importation into any State, Territory, or possession of the United States for delivery or use therein of intoxicating liquors in violation of the laws thereof, is hereby prohibited.

SECTION 3. This article shall be inoperative unless it shall have been ratified as an amendment to the Constitution by conventions in the several States, as provided in the Constitution, within seven years from the date of the submission thereof to the States by the Congress.

ARTICLE XXII

Passed by Congress March 21, 1947. Ratified February 27, 1951.

No person shall be elected to the office of the President more than twice, and no person who has held the office of President, or acted as President, for more than two years of a term to which some other person was elected President shall be elected to the office of the President more than once.

But this article shall not apply to any person holding the office of President when this article was proposed by the Congress, and shall not prevent any person who may be holding the office of President, or acting as President, during the term within which this article becomes operative from holding the office of President or acting as President during the remainder of such term.

This article shall be inoperative unless it shall have been ratified as an amendment to the Constitution by the legislatures of three-fourths of the several states within seven years from the date of its submission to the states by the Congress.

ARTICLE XXIII

Passed by Congress June 16, 1960. Ratified March 29, 1961.

SECTION 1. The District constituting the seat of Government of the United States shall appoint in such manner as the Congress may direct:

A number of electors of President and Vice President equal to the whole number of Senators and Representatives in Congress to which the District would be entitled if it were a State, but in no event more than the least populous state; they shall be in addition to those appointed by the states, but shall be considered, for the purpose of the election of President and Vice President, to be electors appointed by a state; and they shall meet in the District and perform such duties as provided by the twelfth article of amendment.

SECTION 2. The Congress shall have power to enforce this article by appropriate legislation.

ARTICLE XXIV

Passed by Congress August 27, 1962. Ratified January 23, 1964.

SECTION 1. The right of citizens of the United States to vote in any primary or other election for President or Vice President, for electors for President or Vice President, or for Senator or Repesentative in Congress, shall not be denied or abridged by the United States or any State by reason of failure to pay any poll tax or other tax.

SECTION 2. The Congress shall have the power to enforce this article by appropriate legislation.

ARTICLE XXV

Passed by Congress July 6, 1965. Ratified February 10, 1967.

SECTION 1. In case of the removal of the President from office or his death or resignation, the Vice President shall become President.

SECTION 2. Whenever there is a vacancy in the office of the Vice President, the President shall nominate a Vice President who shall take the office upon confirmation by a majority vote of both houses of Congress.

SECTION 3. Whenever the President transmits to the President pro tempore of the Senate and the Speaker of the House of Representatives his written declaration that he is unable to discharge the powers and duties of his office, and until he transmits to them a written declaration to the contrary, such powers and duties shall be discharged by the Vice President as Acting President.

SECTION 4. Whenever the Vice President and a majority of either the principal officers of the executive departments, or of such other body as Congress may by law provide, transmit to the President pro tempore of the Senate and the Speaker of the House of Representatives their written declaration that the President is unable to discharge the powers and duties of his office, the Vice President shall immediately assume the powers and duties of the office of Acting President.

Thereafter, when the President transmits to the President pro tempore of the Senate and the Speaker of the House of Representatives his written declaration that no inability exists, he shall resume the powers and duties of his office unless the Vice President and a majority of either the principal officers of the executive department, or of such other body as Congress may by law provide, transmit within four days to the President pro tempore of the Senate and the Speaker of the House of Representatives their written declaration that the President is unable to discharge the powers and duties of his office. Thereupon Congress shall decide the issue, assembling within 48 hours for that purpose if not in session. If the Congress, within 21 days after receipt of the latter written declaration, or, if Congress is not in session, within 21 days after Congress is required to assemble, determines by two-thirds vote of both houses that the President is unable to discharge the powers and duties of his office, the Vice President shall continue to discharge the same as Acting President; otherwise, the President shall resume the powers and duties of his office.

ARTICLE XXVI

Passed by Congress March 23, 1971. Ratified June 30, 1971.

SECTION 1. The right of citizens of the United States, who are eighteen years of age or older, to vote shall not be denied or abridged by the United States or any state on account of age.

SECTION 2. The Congress shall have the power to enforce this article by appropriate legislation.

INDEX